THE
SCARECROW
PRESS,
INC.

●

Metuchen,
N.J.,
&
London

●

1983

Women composers, conductors, and musicians of the twentieth century

•

selected biographies

•

volume ii

•

Jane Weiner LePage

Library of Congress Cataloging in Publication Data
[Revised for vol. II]

LePage, Jane Weiner, 1931-
  Women composers, conductors, and musicians of
the twentieth century.

  Includes index.
  1. Women musicians--Biography. I. Title.
ML82. L46   780'. 92'2 [B]   80-12162
ISBN 0-8108-1597-4

Dedicated to my husband,
William E. LePage

CONTENTS

Acknowledgments	vii
Preface	ix
BETH ANDERSON	1
DALIA ATLAS	23
SARAH CALDWELL	39
POZZI ESCOT	58
VIVIAN FINE	71
KAY GARDNER	92
MIRIAM GIDEON	118
PEGGY GLANVILLE-HICKS	142
DORIS HAYS	163
FREDERIQUE PETRIDES	191
MARTA PTASZYNSKA	221
DARIA SEMEGEN	240
SUSAN SMELTZER	261
JULIA SMITH	274
ELINOR REMICK WARREN	305
JUDITH LANG ZAIMONT	322
ELLEN TAAFFE ZWILICH	340
Index	361

ACKNOWLEDGMENTS

It was an inspiring experience to work with the composers, conductors, and musicians presented in this book. Their willingness to share personal experiences as well as to give their attention to detail and authenticity made possible a thoroughly documented publication. To these women I am deeply grateful. At the end of each biography, the selected lists of compositions were chosen by the composer. It is neither desirable nor practical to list every composition written by each artist; music catalogues are readily available for this purpose. Sarah Caldwell was the only artist not personally interviewed.

My research was facilitated by many library staffs, and I am especially grateful to those of North Adams State College, Williams College, Bennington College, and the New York Public Library.

I wish to acknowledge my colleagues, Dr. Kathy Heiligmann and Dr. Ellen Schiff; Suzanne Kemper, research librarian; and the support staff of North Adams State College. Without their help this book could not have been completed.

A special thanks to Dr. Anthony P. Ceddia, President of Shippensburg State College, in Shippensburg, Pennsylvania, for his years of encouragement and support, and to Adele P. Manson for her editing of the manuscript.

My total absorption in my research, writing, and interviewing was thoughtfully supported by my husband and family. Special thanks to my daughters Jane Weiner Sumner and Renay LePage Donelan, and to my sons Bruce Weiner and Buddy Weiner.

PREFACE

Volume II is a sequel to my first book, Women Composers, Conductors, and Musicians of the Twentieth Century, also published by The Scarecrow Press. Biographies included in volume I are: VICTORIA BOND, ANTONIA BRICO, RADIE BRITAIN, RUTH CRAWFORD (SEEGER), EMMA LOU DIEMER, MARGARET HILLIS, JEAN EICHELBERGER IVEY, BETSY JOLAS, BARBARA ANNE KOLB, WANDA LANDOWSKA, THEA MUSGRAVE, PAULINE OLIVEROS, EVE QUELER, MARGA RICHTER, LOUISE TALMA, ROSALYN TURECK, NANCY VAN DE VATE.

Reference books and textbooks generally have dismissed women composers and conductors in a few sentences. My primary focus is to make readily available the contributions and accomplishments of some of the gifted women musicians of the twentieth century. The role of women in the arts has been neglected, and accurate historical information must be collected if we are to preserve their achievements for posterity.

Ideally, there should be no need to separate the sexes; merit should be based solely on artistic ability. Unfortunately, this has not happened, even though recorded history shows that women have been composing since the third century. The societal structure did not provide for public presentation or documentation of their work. A few compositions written by women were performed and published under the names of their brothers or husbands, or under male pseudonyms. The talents of many women have never been preserved or shared with the world. Society has been the loser because of its failure to recognize these talented and creative women. Negativism should not be accepted, but I do not fault society for its past history. The important issue is to swiftly eliminate the inequities.

My research, interviewing, and writing will continue

ix

in hopes of publishing another volume in order to document the contributions of all those women not mentioned in the first two books.

BETH ANDERSON

Avant-Garde Romantic Composer,
Performance Artist, Astrologer

Beth Anderson is an avant-garde romantic composer, performance artist, and astrologer. Her text-sound and performance situation-pieces as well as her artistic activism,
writing, organizing, and performing have made her one of
the major new creative figures in the downtown New York
artistic scene.

Some distortions are unavoidable; thus, when Anderson
built her reputation on the West Coast as a young, wild avant-
garde composer, her image remained solidly established even
though her compositional approach drastically changed over a
period of time. She said, "Today my style is close to Aaron
Copland's, but lots of people are afraid of my reputation.
They think, 'Oh! that's the weirdo from California.'" One
must feel a sympathetic sense of victimization for she has
demonstrated unusual creative ability.

Anderson was born in Lexington, Kentucky in 1950,
the only child of Marjorie and Sidney Anderson. Her mother
studied piano and voice but insists that she has no talent,
just persistence. Her father once took a correspondence
course in piano, using colors for notation, but dropped it because it was too hard. However, her parents did encourage
her in music and her mother has appeared in concert with
Beth and still attends some of her performances.

When Beth was a child studying piano, she began writing compositions with the encouragement of her women piano
teachers. Returning from Mt. Sterling to Lexington when she
was fourteen years old, she studied piano with Helen Lipscomb, a composer who had published many pieces of music.
Lipscomb was contrapuntally oriented and taught Beth all the
rules of form and counterpoint, which enabled her to write
very simple, traditional music. By reading books during the

Gretta Wing Miller

BETH ANDERSON

last two years of high school, she started to write serial
music, finding it a fun game. "You can work the material
backwards, sideways, and so-forth and nobody can tell where
it came from. You don't have to sit at the piano and wait
for an inspiration. "

Following graduation from high school Anderson at-

tended the University of Kentucky for two years. She recalls,

> That was a bizarre experience; apparently the fac-
> ulty was stuck somewhere around the music of the
> 1850's. The University had a very tight approach
> to education and a real conservatory approach to
> music. If you didn't memorize all the Bach pre-
> ludes, take four-part dictation, do a recital, all
> your juries, your partial senior recital, and your
> full senior recital, you would never graduate.
> Many brilliant students failed or transferred; I
> knew that I would never finish because they de-
> pressed the hell out of people. I got the reputa-
> tion at the University of Kentucky of being this wild
> hysterical person, so the more they called me this,
> the more it egged me on, and for my final project
> in music history I organized a Happening. I had
> been influenced by the work of John Cage, and I
> included in this Happening people from all over the
> university, dogs, ladders, strobe-lights and lots of
> confetti--it was the most absurd, unbelievable mess
> possible. I transferred to the University of Cali-
> fornia at Davis.

Anderson's transfer to the University of California at
Davis resulted from her University of Kentucky library job,
which provided her the opportunity to read numerous periodicals and newsprints and to find out where interesting and innovative ideas were being generated on college campuses.
Source Magazine published at Davis was a key factor in helping her to make the decision, and when she arrived at the
University, John Cage was there. Beth said, "I had fallen
in love with Cage through library books when I was in high
school and I thought he was fantastic. It was a time in my
life when I wanted to be in revolt, and there was John Cage;
he was wonderful and it was like a miracle. Some people
thought his music was garbage but I was not one of them."
Richard Swift, a serial composer, headed the department of
music. Anderson completed her undergraduate degree.

Beth Anderson received her Master of Fine Arts Degree in Piano Performance in 1973. Just before she completed the requirements for this degree, her Peachy Keen-O
was programmed (March 3, 1973), at Mills College by Hys-
teresis, a group of women composers and performers to
which she belonged. The name transformation refers to energy and the strange occurrences that result from this energy.

As it happened, Bob Ashley was in town and heard her composition; he encouraged her to stay at Mills College to complete an M. A. in composition, which she did.

Anderson studied with outstanding composition teachers
throughout her training, including John Cage, Robert Ashley,
Larry Austin, Terry Riley, Helen Lipscomb, Richard Swift,
Kenneth Wright, John B. Chance, and Nate Rubin. In the
Bay Area of California she quickly established herself as
one of the new crop of avant-garde feminist composers, critics, and poets. During this time her opera Queen Christina,
produced at Mills College, and an oratorio Joan, commissioned
and staged by the Cabrillo Music Festival at Aptos, California, were performed to raised eyebrows and critical "har-
rumphs. " She also became co-editor of Ear Magazine, which
she also later established in New York. Anderson explains:

> I didn't want to be just a composer, I wanted to
> be a fantastic composer and I wanted to write some-
> thing really great.
>   I always held onto the desire for beautiful mu-
> sicianship that I had acquired from practicing six
> hours a day. So I was never interested in using
> visual artists who could not play; that was never
> my trip.
>   When I did the opera Queen Christina at Mills
> College I had been working on Ear Magazine for a
> number of months and I felt tremendously in-touch
> with the community so I made the work an enormous
> collage of a celebration. The orchestra was made
> up of friends, the singer Jim Shields from the San
> Francisco Opera who was a student at Mills, Peg
> Ahrens, a composer who had a huge voice, played
> the role of Christina. Nobody wanted to play the
> role of Ebba, (the name came from using my ini-
> tials Barbara Elizabeth Anderson) Christina's lover,
> so I did the part myself. I was accompanist for
> the dance classes so I had a group do a ballet.
> Also included were pornographic movies about queens
> and members of Bay Area women's groups marching
> on stage for the coronation.

Reviewed by Charles Shere for the Oakland Tribune on December 3, 1973:

QUEEN CHRISTINA--AN EVOLVING OPERA

What we know as "opera" is evolving away from the

old Italian description "dramma pre-musica"--
drama expressed in musical terms. Quite likely
the greatest musical usefulness of all the new
"media technology" will be found in their contributions of new energies to opera. Certainly the "oldest mixed" media art form still going. Opera can
still be enriched further.

All this comes to mind after seeing Beth Anderson's
opera Queen Christina, in a Mills College production Saturday night. The opera is about the Swedish Queen who abdicated in 1654 in favor of a con-
version to Catholicism and other pleasant calls to
the South. Its loose scenario treats Christina's
coronation, her love life, the crisis her power
made in her life, and her abdication in a manner
which sees pastiche, pageantry, mime, dance and
song, with music ranging from avant-garde sound
poetry to mountain music and "Pale Hands I Loved."

A long introduction established the feminist stance
of the opera, playing a tape recording of an un-
identified feminist lecturing on the Movement su-
perimposed on a half-speed recording of a woman
singing a Schubert song. The small orchestra
gradually infiltrated with a complex, slow montage
of sustained pitches while images of clouds were
projected over the stage.

The Queen was introduced as a child of two, of
three, of four, as seen receiving guests--each
time as a projection of Gainsborough's "Blue Boy."
A Chinese pantomine was followed by a coronation
procession through the audience, completely unlike
yet recalling the similar scene from Boris Godu-
nov, banjo music on stage. A solo aria from Christina, her introduction to René Descartes, a love
duet sung while a film showing the enrobing and
coronation of a male "queen" at the beach is projected.

Descartes sings "Zippety Doo Dah" Christina
sings "The Temple Bells," and then a long abstract
spoken piece begins via tape while the audience is
encouraged to discuss among themselves "relationships with women in their lives."

The Queen's political crisis continues with a
ballet to the waltz from "Gayne," represented traditionally on stage but including a Flit gun playing
afterbeats in the audience. Christina's mistress
appears, seducing her away from Descartes; on
succeeding, Christina sings "Shalimar" and "Dia-

monds Are A Girl's Best Friend" in rapid succession and the opera is over.
This wasn't all 100% successful, of course.
Some of the elements seemed insufficiently theatrical, not considerate of the need to project to the
audience. The introduction was a bit long--one
critic left before it was over. And the entire production was woefully under-rehearsed.
But in spite of these matters, and in spite of
a shockingly rude audience, the opera was absorbing. The three longest "serious" sections were
quite moving: separate pieces well integrated into
the opera, they include the orchestral collage after
the introduction, the "dream-sequence" tape piece
"Supplication," and the abstract sounding poem
"Valid For Life," which puts a touching tribute to
the composer by her mother in crazy juxtaposition
with voiced consonants repeated by another female.
Perhaps the most telling thing to the opera's
credit is its ability to maintain interest and to
further its subject by alternating stage action and
abstract sound. The proportions work in general,
and it would be worth reviving under better conditions. (Reprinted by permission of the Oakland
Tribune.)

Immediately following graduation from Mills College,
Beth Anderson received numerous grants and comissions
which gave her the sensation that it was all going to continue
forever. In 1974 the Cabrillo Music Festival did three of
her pieces. It was an exciting time for her because at that
point everyone in California was looking for a woman composer in the North (Pauline Oliveros was in the South). She
wrote the oratorio Joan, commissioned by Dennis Russell
Davies for the Cabrillo Music Festival through a California
Arts Commission.

Joan was written for orchestra, four singers, dancer,
tape, and live electronics. The world première was presented at the Cabrillo Music Festival on August 22, 1974
with soloists Victoria Bond, soprano; Anna Carol Dudley,
soprano; Philip Kelsey, tenor; Tom Buckner, baritone; and
Margaret Fisher, dancer. Anderson wrote the oratorio because she was inspired by Joan of Arc, a young woman of
the early fifteenth century who did what she felt compelled
to do and died because of it. According to Anderson,

She was judged by the Church of a divided France

in a matter of heresy, while in point of fact she
was simply a prisoner of war whose fate depended
on the English government. In the performance,
the mixed elevations of the performers suggest the
co-existence of the heavenly beings, of supercon-
sciousness and consciousness, of political and religious aspects, of air and earth, of duality and
oneness, and of double dualities--2 x 2 = 4, Joan.
It was written in Anderson's old post-Cage style
and used a modulating coding system.

Although there were some difficulities encountered in
staging the first production, there were many positive aspects, as pointed out by the reviewers present. Anderson
was miffed by a statement made by one of the critics who
commented on the streaker who ran across stage during the
performance. "Joan would not have approved," he wrote.
Anderson's retort, "How foolish that the half-wit critic
thought it could possibly be part of the score."

Excerpts from a review by Mark Lawshe in the Santa
Cruz Sentinel on August 23, 1974:

THURSDAY CONCERT A STUDY IN CONTRASTS

Joan marked the greatest departure from traditional
orchestration yet seen in this admittedly innovative
festival.
Beth Anderson's score, more a map or set of tonal
clues, required relocation of musicians throughout
the theater.
Five principal groups of musicians, each relat-
ing to one of the soloists, including dancer Margaret Fischer, were deployed on stage and in the
aisles to bring the performance closer to the audience. "Each one of the five," Anderson explained,
"is associated with a constellation of people and
ideas involved in Joan's labyrinth."
The visions of Joan of Arc, she said, were subjected to testing by the medieval military authorities before she was given command of her battalion.
Later she would be martyred after an Inquisition
of 70 questions, which with her answers form the
text of the taped background of the work.
Center of the cross formed by orchestral and
soloist sections was a gleaming aluminium platform,
arena for the dance interpretation of Margaret Fisher.
Economy of movement marked her performance,

evocative of the peasants vacillating favor for Joan's
faith and the vagaries of success and failure.
It brought to mind, as well, the politics of this
festival, new and newer music, the struggle for
recognition of women artists, the willingness of
audiences to be educated if imperfect. "Joan" is
Anderson's--and the festival's--vibrant answer to
the tyranny of so-called perfection. (Reprinted
courtesy of the Santa Cruz Sentinel.)

   While on the West Coast Anderson became co-editor
of Ear Magazine with Charles Shere. Ann Kisch, founder of
the publication, had moved to France. This publication was
one of only a few serious new music publications and was
staffed entirely by volunteers, certainly not an easy task.
When Anderson moved to New York she continued her work
with Ear and did not miss an issue from March 1973 to
September 1979. She did find it extremely difficult to find
people in New York who had the energy to devote to the publication on a long-term basis.

   When Anderson received a National Endowment for
the Arts Grant in 1975, it not only provided the necessary
time to continue to write and compose but enabled her to
move from the West Coast to New York City. She said,
"I felt I had accomplished what I could on the West Coast
and it was time to leave." She was in no way prepared for
the shock that was to greet her in New York when she found
out that the cost of two short rehearsals and a crummy performance of her music would cost up to $100 per player.

   It did not take the young artist long to realize that
she would have to create material that was shorter, tighter,
lighter, and without the use of other performers and equipment. Her answer was poetry--she said, "Today they call
it disco rap, jazz rap, but I was really doing avant-garde
rap. Actually it's text-sounds, the use of words in place of
instruments to make music." The result in 1981 was Poetry
Is Music, a series of eighteen eight-minute text-sound programs of the works of contemporary poet/composers, funded
by the Satellite Program Development Fund of National Public
Radio. They were poems that were meant to be heard and
not seen. Music made from words, parts of words, and
other vocal sounds--sometimes combined with musical instruments and electronic sounds. From one voice to 512 voices,
the art form is "text-sound, 'poetry concrete,' poesy sonore,
tone gedichte, sound poetry," said Beth Anderson of her radio
production, Poetry Is Music. The series included not only

Anderson's works but also other artists--Charles Amirkhanian, John Giorno, Tony Gnazzo, Doris Hays, Dick Higgins, Bob Holman, Tom Johnson, Bliem Kern, Richard Kostelanetz, Jackson Mac Low, Charlie Morrow, Norman Pritchard, Steve Reich, Carlos Santos, Arleen Schloss, Carolee Schneemann, and Ellen Zweig. The artists, from all over the country, represented a wide variety of styles and approaches to this new genre. Anderson's 45rpm record, I Can't Stand It and Ocean Motion Mildew Mind, is available from New Music Distribution and is well worth the investment.

As one critic stated, "Anderson's an underground favorite all the way to Long Island City and it's hard to go underground through the East River." She does not take one position and defend it forever and ever; she writes in the style that to her seems appropriate to the time and the situation. She has numerous artistic gifts and composing is but one of them. Robert Palmer wrote for the New York Times on May 16, 1978 (partial):

> EAST AND WEST MEET ON STAGE
>
> Margaret Fisher and Beth Anderson are working at different ends of the country, Miss Fisher in the San Francisco Bay Area and Miss Anderson in New York, but both of them are performing artists whose pieces include elements of music, dance, poetry and theater. They shared a program at the Experimental Intermedia Foundation on Sunday night, and the contrasts were as interesting as the similarities.
> Miss Anderson was more overtly concerned with her identity as a woman, with sound, and with words. One of her pieces, a succession of non-sequitur questions without any answers, exchanged by two housewives in a soap commercial, was pure theater. Her set of text sound pieces was a kind of a poetry, but in the most musical of these works, practically everything that makes music, music--a coherent pitch vocabulary, patterned rhythms--was present. (Copyright © 1978 by The New York Times Company. Reprinted by permission.)

According to Anderson, text-sound as a medium of expression is very practical, for the artist needs only to get his/her body to the place where the performance is being held. There is no need for costly equipment or a high-priced accompanist. She said, "When I first started to perform in

this manner, I had the audience stomping their feet so I
wouldn't feel I was yelling into a well.   Eventually I bought
some drums and accompanied myself. "

Nancy Jones reviewed the January Performance Series
at the Franklin Furnace, titled Words and Music, for Live
(Performing Art #3) in May 1980.   Anderson shared the
series with Walter Abish and Douglas Davis (partial):

> The series' moniker was more direct with Douglas
> Davis's Night Voices and Beth Anderson's Hegemony
> HodgePodge; the pieces may be poles apart in the
> arena of theoretical assumption, but they stand
> side-by-side in their respective concerns for the
> affective powers of verbal and non-verbal sound.
> Davis's urban orientation paid more attention to the
> politics of sound technology, while Anderson's was
> pastoral, focusing on the emotive interplay of the
> structure and content of sound.
>   Beth Anderson's Hedgemony HodgePodge was a
> collection of exercises (sometimes tedious, some-
> times humorous and sweet), poems with sound as
> text, short narratives with or without a brooding
> B-flat accompaniment, and musical pieces for flute,
> piano, and ocarina.
>   The sound poems worked with repetition, which
> can be as boring as it is mesmerizing, but Ander-
> son managed, more or less, to hold off the bore-
> dom with rambunctious delivery.   Her reiterative
> permutations of the phrase/question "If-I-were-a-
> poet-what-would-I-say," came out sounding like a
> half-crazed yodil/hermit breaking out of silence on
> a hilltop under the stars.   That was nice.   The
> light-weight quality of word-play can be good, clean
> fun; a magic-square piece, Poem to Pauline, John
> & Martha, reduced Martha Graham's name to "Art-
> Hag. "   However, not all the text/sound poems were
> as successful, after three minutes of "Can't stand it
> I can't stand can't stand I can't it stand can't" this
> witness couldn't care, and standing was not even a
> possibility.
>   Six Stories in Series was a train of narratives
> of personal catastrophe, rather like summaries of
> magazine stories from True Life or True Romance.
> The readers' voices provided the irony; they were
> naive and cheerful, with that special, depraved,
> "oh-by-the-way" quality of the Southern-Gothic mood.
>   The musical pieces were distillations from medi-

eval and folk traditions--light and soft with a slow
and careful exploration of scale. They were full
of "sweetness and light"--especially the final ocarina solo, Preparation for the Dominant which
cleared one's mind of the occasionally pithy ironies
of the preceding pieces and again filled the evening
with air. (Reprinted by permission of Live.)

At times during her career Anderson associates herself with new music and artistic expression that is far from
the mainstream of contemporary academic sounds; yet she
still relates to the explorations that are familiar with other
new composers. She is a fine example of what younger composers and poets are doing in a non-traditional and avant-
garde medium that is enthusiastically shared by some members of the listening audience, but certainly not by all. Then
again, one must ask, is there any concert that is enthusiastically received by all members of the audience? The
answer would be an emphatic "No!" Beth Anderson represents the younger generation of artists who are dedicated
and committed to the exploration of new sound media as well
as to creating in forms long established and accepted by the
status quo. She's young, exciting and not afraid to reach
out and express her individuality in new and different artistic
endeavors that contribute to a healthy and changing environment.

Anderson describes some of her recent works, as

cut-ups, arrangements of material--some composed,
some found, some generated by a process. Unlike
the collage writing of the past, the intention is to
make the diverse elements into a harmonious whole.
As a professional astrologer, I am always involved
with ideas of harmony, cosmic wholeness, and overall sense-making. These concerns, together with
a fascination with numerology, produce a work of
patterns, secret clues, boxes within boxes. Nevertheless it would be a mistake to assume that these
works are dry or mathematical. Quite the contrary,
the aim is to create and sustain strong emotional/
dramatic states and my work is full of very intense
personal and psychological resonances. As a com-
poser/performer I combine two strands of contemporary artistic endeavor: the formalistic and the
confessional.

The New York Times, May 7, 1979 reviewed by Robert Palmer (partial):

MIXED MEDIA: ANDERSON AND SAHL

Beth Anderson and Michael Sahl called their Saturday evening program at the Kitchen "Romantic Al-
lusions for Instruments, Machines and People."
It included new works in a number of media, from
piano-accompanied songs to text-sound to jazz to
tape, but it was mostly tonal and often positively
rhapsodic.
The scattershot effect of Miss Anderson's extreme eclecticism is somewhat mollified by her
overall concern with the inflections, rhythms and
organizational patterns of verbal expression. Her
text-sound pieces are the most obvious expressions
of this interest, but "Skate Suite," the longest composition on her part of the program, used text as
a basis for instrumental writing.
A violin and cello, joined briefly toward the end
by voice and electric bass, played conversational
modal music in a variety of traditional dance forms,
from gigue to waltz. According to the composer's
notes, the pitches and rhythms were decoded from
dictionary definitions of the word "skate," and a
tape of skating sounds provided a somewhat gratui-
tous backdrop for the music. Some piano-accompanied songs were less ambitious but more satisfying. (Copyright© 1979 by The New York Times
Company. Reprinted by permission.)

Anderson's comments about music critics in general
are loud and clear. She said,

I am hysterical about music critics not talking to
composers. I feel it is important if they are going
to review new pieces. The critics need to have
some way to find out what is supposed to happen,
but as a general rule they don't speak with the
composer. Only once in my career has a critic
talked with me about my music, and it was a wonderful experience. He understood what I was doing
and could intelligently review the work. In New
York I am constantly being harassed by idiotic critics and it has an effect on me.

Anderson publicly states her intense personal feelings in regard to critical reviews. These are shared by other artists
who would not even consider allowing their statements to be
made public for fear of reprisal by the so-called "establish-

ment. " She has the courage of her convictions and deserves
to be heard.

   To dare to be different and write compositions that
stray from the ordinary often means long and frustrating attempts to have the music performed in the setting that the
composer envisioned. Anderson traveled this road too, when
she tried for over two years to find a church that would
allow her to use their bells so that she could hear her piece
the way she had intended it to be heard. The pastor of Our
Savior Lutheran church, the Rev. Paul Winterstein, was
open to the idea of allowing the Festival of Disappearing
Art(s) to use the eighteen bells in the church in the festival
to be held in Baltimore, Maryland in the spring of 1980.
The majority of the church council agreed with the idea and
felt it was important to have the church be more active in
the community and in supporting the arts. Hence, Beth Anderson's dream came true after two years of waiting for the
right performance location. Excerpt from the Baltimore Sun
on May 4, 1980:

   BELLS, BELLS, BELLS TOLL A NEW SONG FOR
   THEE

   "I'm getting conservative in my old age," she quip-
   ped. "The style of my compositions now is mostly,
   melodic, folk music from ... nowhere."
      As with many of Ms. Anderson's pieces the
   May Day Bell Tower Event was inspired by a dream,
   one she had back in 1973. At the center of it was
   a maypole. Using the imagery and the mood born
   of nocturnal fantasy, she went on to create a spring
   rite.
      Perhaps because we were overlooking the sanc-
   tuary of a Christian church, she hastily stressed
   this was no pagan celebration with naked nymphs
   gamboling around the pole.
      But a maypole was part of it, and so before
   leaving from New York, Ms. Anderson packed her
   bags with yards and yards of crepe paper streamers
   in red, yellow, green, purple and turquoise for
   hanging from the crenelated top of the church's
   Tudor tower, transforming it into a giant maypole.
      The event, running an hour, features several
   of Ms. Anderson's compositions. "It's straight
   me," she said. "I don't want to do fifteenth century melodies. They've had their chance."
      "It's nice for a change to be playing for so many

people who don't expect to hear me, and right in
their own neighborhood too." (Reprinted by permission of the Baltimore Sun.)

Of all the many articles written by Beth Anderson in
her young life the most quoted and perhaps the most beautiful
was published in Ear Magazine, New York edition, in April
1981, Vol. 6, #3. It is well worth reprinting and a must
for every reader who cherishes beauty.

BEAUTY IS REVOLUTION

To make something beautiful is revolutionary (not
low class, not easy, not a sign of low intelligence).
Last year I wrote an article about my approach to
music for Heresies. In it, I said that "relationship of feminism to my work and the evolution of
the form of my music are in violent flux." They
still are, but the dust is settling.
The idea that beauty is revolution, is a revela-
tion to me. I once believed that the concept of the
music was far more important than the sound ...
that the politics of the notation was more important
than the time limits of the rehersals and therefore,
more important than the sound of the performance
... that the numerological equivalents for the instruments were the determining factor for the instrumentation ... that pitch must be explicit and
rhythm improvised ... that if the composer says
it is so, two string players and two lighting tech-
nicians can be a string quartet ... that any composition must be consistent throughout and that internal change in the piece showed lack of compositional concentration ... that more than three chords
in one piece meant confusion or commercial music
or both .. and on and on. It is a very liberating
feeling to come back to my childhood definition of
composition, ie. , writing down inspirations. I've
rediscovered the part of my brain that can't decode
anything, that can't add, that can't work from a
verbalized concept, that doesn't know anything about
Zen eternity and gets bored and changes, that isn't
worried about being commercial or avant-garde or
serial or any other little category. Beauty is
enough.
And of course, it's a problem, too. At different
times in my life I have looked out and decided that
Grieg's music was the most beautiful ... that Scho-

enberg's music was the most beautiful ... that
Cage's music was the most beautiful ... that Oliveros' music was the most beautiful. Now, I feel
as if my own music is the most beautiful and the
feeling is one of having jumped off the cliff with
my wings on. I don't know if they are going to
work, but it's too late now. This deciding about
the "most beautiful" is necessary and I think composers make decisions like this all the time. How
else could they choose a style to work in and stick
with it for fifty years?

Beauty means perfect to me, but it also has an
additional meaning having to do with being pleasur-
able, rather than painful. Beauty is hard to make.
The making is painful, and involves a certain amount
of craft, and a relaxation of the part of the brain
that says, "Don't write that. 'X' wrote those four
notes in 1542 or 1979 or 1825 or whatever period
you are worried about being influenced by." You
have to say yes to what comes out. You can scoot
it around a bit, but the basic material that jumps
out of you is you. If you say, "That sounds like
a raisin commercial," you are telling yourself you
are trashy. You are allowing others to tell you
what real art is.

Real music soars above class society. Musical
careers have a lot to do with class and money but
they don't influence society's acceptance of the
music, after the stuff has been broadcast to the
people. Composers are people who create music--
not concepts, not machines, not posters, not parties. It takes just as much (maybe more) intelligence to invent a synthesizer or to make a crowd-
pleasing poster for your concert, as it does to
make beautiful music. But doing those other activities does not make you a composer, though they
may add to your career or savings account. Being
a composer of playable music still does not guar-
antee beauty. That's a problem you have to solve
for yourself.

Beauty got a bad name some time after the first
World War. Musical craft (ear training, orchestration, the real reasons for voice leading, etc.) was
hardly even taught in the 1960's and 70's, probably
because of the revolt against a tradition that could
allow the war in Viet Nam to happen. Beauty seemed
a low value in relation to life itself. But life goes
on and ugliness and lack of skills and nihilism are

no excuse. The destruction of the world would not
improve social conditions, and making painful, ugly
music will not redistribute the wealth.
Beauty is a revolution of the spirit. The euphony
of the animating principle of humanity has the revolutionary power of healing, expanding, and revital-
izing. Life is worth living and beauty is worth
making and, in relation to current attitudes, these
ancient ideas are radical. They are capable of
making certain people swoon. If you think beauty
is counter-revolutionary, ask yourself if you think
mutilation improves the state of mind of the de-
pressed. (Reprinted by permission of Ear, published by the New Wilderness Foundation.)

Anderson's first major concert in New York was in
1975 at the Kitchen. The evening was reviewed for the New
York Times on December 7, 1975 by John Rockwell who
wrote, " ... Miss Anderson concerns herself with the new
music of a decidedly non-academic, experimental, post-Cag-
eian sort. Her earlier works betrayed studentish toyings
with abstract chromaticism and French insouciance, but by
the 1970's she had settled into exploration of idioms familiar
from other new composers." Her composition Skate Suite
scored for violin, bass, cello, and voice was premièred at
the Kitchen at a later date (in 1979). In the summer of
1979, the series "New Music New York" was presented at
the Kitchen and Anderson was omitted even though she had
been in the mainstream of new music in the city for several
years. Understandably her feelings were hurt when she did
not receive an invitation to be part of the series. Undaunted,
she went to the festival every day and reviewed the concerts
and published her findings in a series of nine "Reports from
the Front" that not only included critical reviews of the series
but also offered critical comments on the major conference
held by music critics in the city during the same time period.

"Reports from the Front" is a fine collection of her
reviews of the festival of new music at the Kitchen. Her
reviews are both witty and at times brutal in her interpretation of what actually was heard during the series. There is
some concern as to whether her writings have interfered
with or helped her music. However, she admitted, "I made
some friends, but more enemies." The entire series is
available for $10.00 from 26 Second Avenue, 2B, New York,
N.Y. 10003. The following are excerpts from the series:

#1

After all these years, Mr. Reich is too fucking
loud. Men Hitting Things: I remember hearing this
piece in 1973 in a big church in Berkeley and it
was voluptuous. His music needs a hall with high
ceilings and rugs.

Aside from the sound, the formality is reassur-
ing--rather like having your parents stay together
for your sake. Comforting, but bad for the stomach.
But, it's fun for the players--wearing black shirts
and getting off beating skins.

#2

Many Many Women, by Mr. Peter Kotik was the
most beautiful and musical work on the festival to
date.   An enormous work in many parts and of
vast duration, of which we heard about 45 minutes
in a version performed by 4 pairs of musicians.
Since Mr. Kotik gave the audience permission to
leave if they felt the need, they took advantage of
his offer, especially after seeing the critic for
The Voice leave.   Stein's text related to death,
marriage, and the irregularity of life after children,
the satisfaction of one man, kissing and not kissing
and needing some kissing and so on.   It sounds
like intersecting organum, Gregorian Chant, Virgil
Thomson, real music (I hope he doesn't get kicked
out of experimental music for this), and Satie's
Socrate.   Of course it only really sounds like Mr.
Kotik but that should give you an idea of the sounding quality.   The continuum was aurally decorated
with great care by both the composer and the performers.   This work represents one intelligent persons's way out of the aesthetic convolution and confusion in which we currently swim.   Of course,
everyone's attention comes and goes, but I give it
a 10 (out of 10).

#3

Laurie Speigel's short improv on digital computer
sounded like snowflakes bursting in air with the
raw materials dwindling down from a place high
above, over a deep wobbly volcano-like sound.   At
the end it became calm, streamy, sensual, and

then it stopped. Both of her pieces tonight had an
image-producing effect on this reviewer, as well
as a kind of narrative feel. Voices Within, a tape
composition made on the Electrocomp (a fairly historic model), was new and beautiful. It evoked
the feeling of multitudes crying for help in the
dark, far away, with the wind blowing. Lives were
flashing by. Again there was that quality I call
'streaming.' It faded and surged in again, seethed,
slid out, and came to rest on a second inversion
tonic. Carol Baron, (a musicologist), said: "This
is straight out of the European romantic and its
really nice. It had a real beginning, middle, and
end--with a development. And a coda." It was
a beautiful extension of the idea of the character
piece.

Beth Anderson, in her writings on the music critics
conference, revealed many interesting and perhaps little
known idiosyncrasies of some of the leading New York critics.
For example, Eric Salzman says, "The trouble with critics
is that they are forced to have opinions when in fact most
of the time they really don't." Mr. Palmer felt that people
don't pay attention to reviews anyway (which explains a lot
about what he writes) and that if he gives someone a rave
that it won't increase their audience (at least on the Soho
scene) but it might help with grants/records. Mr. Rockwell
discussed the best background for critics, the possibilities
as to who actually read reviews and for whom are they written, the functions of the critic, the possible ways of writing
(descriptive, evocative, reportive, literal, judgmental ...),
and the effect on the composers' and performers' lives of
the review. Although Anderson's published series may never
make the best-seller list, it does provide interesting reading; it's different.

After Anderson moved to New York her music received more European performances and by 1980 her text-
sound was heard in Brussels, Ghent and Cologne. The International Society for Contemporary Music chose her quartet
The Eighth Ancestor to be performed at the World Music
Days in October 1981 at the Royal Conservatory in Brussels.
She said,

> The piece is about the eighth patriarch (in Zen)
> whose advice is not to be angry, that it doesn't do
> any good and you might as well give up. (I cer-
> tainly spent a great deal of my life being angry.)

It was an attempt to write something that was as
un-angry as possible. Many of my sound-texts
are energetic; people like the high-energy stuff.
I was also influenced by the many years I spent at
the piano as a dance accompanist--people need
music that has a beat--the original version was
performed at the First National Congress on Women
In Music and at the Experimental Intermedia Foundation. I made certain changes including scoring
it for quartet and it was performed by a baroque
ensemble (baroque flute, alto recorder, harpsichord
and cello).

The score is published by Joshua Corp./General Music.
Anderson will be going to Europe for the performance, for
she realizes that there are more opportunities to record in
Europe than in America.

It is more important for a composer to be recorded
than to be published. As far as dissemination is concerned,
recordings open the door to numerous listenings that a live
performance does not offer. Only a few composers can make
a living from their music. The economic situation is extremely poor, so for the most part, a composer must eke
out a living by doing other work. For Anderson this meant
years of necessary piano accompanying. At the present
time she is writing film music and loves teaching at the
Manhattan campus of the College of New Rochelle.

Anderson has received numerous awards and commis-
sions, including: Broadcast Music, Inc., guaranteed for
five years; Special Projects Program at Project Studio One,
made available from the Institute for Art and Urban Resources
New York City; National Federation of Music Clubs, Award
of Merit; Meet The Composer Grants, two years from NYSCA;
Foundation for the Contemporary Performance Arts grant;
ZBS Media Artist-In-Residence funded by the NYSCA; National
Endowment for the Arts grant; Elizabeth Mills Crothers
Award, two years; commissions: Cabrillo Festival, made
possible by the California Arts Commission; San Francisco
Conservatory of Music's New Music Ensemble; Nannie Goat
Hill in San Francisco; and the Staten Island Symphony.

If one values new sounds and experiences, then composers must be free to experiment. Neither old nor new is
necessarily good. How often does an audience applaud its
own liberality and congratulate itself on its unshockability
when it is afforded the opportunity to attend a concert with

no preconceived notions about the music? Beth Anderson's
music speaks for itself. Whether it stands or falls, only
time will answer. It cannot be denied that she demonstrates
unusual creative ability but no defender of tradition would
compose in such a manner.

Yin-yang fits neatly, balancing the stresses, and reflects Beth Anderson's creative endeavors.

Scores Published

1980   Skaters' Suite, (quartet) Joshua Corp.
1980   The Eighth Ancestor, (quartet) Joshua Corp.
1980   Preparation for the Dominant, outrunning the inevitable
          (solo) Joshua Corp.
1980   The Praying Mantis and the Bluebird, (fl./piano),
          Joshua Corp.
1980   Twinkle Tonight, (voice/piano), Joshua Corp.
1980   Womanrite, (voice/piano), Joshua Corp.
1980   Time Stands Still, (voice/piano), Joshua Corp.
1980   Beauty Runs Faster, (voice/piano), Joshua Corp.
1979   He Said, appears in the Mills College Center for Con-
          temporary Music anthology, "Break Glass in Case
          of Emergency."
1974- Valid for Life, appears in the Schirmer Books anthol-
1980   ogy, "Scores," edited by Roger Johnson, 1980,
          and in Intermedia vol. 1, #2 edited by Harley Lond
          in 1975, and in "Women's Work" edited by Anna
          Lockwood and Alison Knowles, 1975, as well as in
          "Assemblings" edited by Richard Kostelanetz, in
          1974.
1974   Tower of Power, appears in "Scores," 1980, Schirmer
          Books. It was also published in Ear #18, August
          1974.
1973   Tulip Clause, appears in Ear #8, October 1973.
1973   Peachy Keen-O, appears in Ear #5, May 1973.

Film Score

1980   World Honeymoon, for Sunrise Films.

Radio Production

1980   Music is Poetry, for National Public Radio, 1980, 20
          programs.

Compositions: Published by Joshua Corp./General Music

1980 Ensemble: Skaters' Suite, (violin, cello, flute, piano;
     or, flute, oboe, cello, and piano; or, flute, clar-
     inet, cello, piano; or, baroque flute, alto recorder,
     cello, harpsichord; or, violin, cello, voice, string
     bass)
1979 Water-Strider Courrente, from Skate Suite (flute, clar-
     inet, piano, organ, string bass, percussion). "The
     Eighth Ancestor" (violin, cello, flute, piano; or,
     flute, oboe, cello, and piano; or, flute, clarinet,
     cello, piano; or, baroque flute, alto recorder, cello,
     harpsichord; or, flute, clarinet, organ, piano,
     string bass, percussion).
1978 Alleluia, two cellos and two tenors, or two trumpets
     and two tenors.
1979 Flute and Piano: The Praying Mantis and the Bluebird
1979 Flute or Violin or Ocarina Solo: Preparation for The
     Dominant: Outrunning The Inevitable

Text-Sound

If I Were a Poet, appears in Richard Kostelanetz' "Text-
    sound Texts," 1980, and in "Assemblings," 1975,
    and in Ear vol. 2, #1, Feb. 1976.
Crackers and Checkers, appears in "Text-sound Texts," 1980
    and in "Break Glass in Case of Emergency" (1979).
He's Not Afraid of Marrying Me, also in "Break Glass in
    Case of Emergency" (1979), and in Dramatika Magazine
    vol. XI, #21, Spring 1978, edited by John Pyros.
Soap Tuning, also appears in Dramatika Spring 1978.
Nongovernmental Process, is in the Dec. 1976 issue of the
    Poetry Mailing List, edited by Steven Paul Miller.
Poem to John and Alison, is in Ear Vol. 1, #3, Summer 1975.
Twelve Bar Blues, appears in Ear vol. 2, #2, April 1976.
Let It, is in Ear 2, #4, summer 1976.
6.76 Kentucky Poem, is in Ear vol. 2, #5/6, Sept. 1976.
The People Rumble Louder, is in "Assemblings," 1975.
various text-sound and scores are published in the Feb. 1976
    issue of Heute Kunst and in the Dec. 1975 issue of
    Flash Art.

Addresses of Publishers

Joshua Corp./General Music Inc., Paul Kapp, 145 Palisade
    St., Dobbs Ferry, NY 10522

Intermedia, P.O. Box 31-464, San Francisco, CA 94131

Break Glass in Case of Emergency, c/o C.C.M. Mills College, Oakland, CA 94613

Sun Rise Films, c/o Paul Rothman, 230 West 13 St., N.Y., NY 10011

Ear, 325 Spring St., N.Y., NY 10013

Poetry Mailing List, c/o Stephen Paul Miller, 18 Cheshire Pl., Staten Island, NY 10301

Discography

"10+2=12 American Text-sound Pieces" anthologizes Torero Piece; it is edited by Charles Amirkhanian on Arch Records #1752, (1974).
"Sugar, Alcohol, & Meat" anthologizes I Can't Stand It--a Dial-A-Poem Poets LP, edited by John Giorno, 1980.
I Can't Stand It and Ocean Motion Mildew Mind was privately produced 1980 and is available from New Music Distribution (45rpm).
"Black Box 15" (cassette) anthologizes If I Were a Poet; it is edited by Mac Wellman (1977) and alternatively called "Breathing Space/77" and is available from Watershed Foundation in Washington, D.C.

Addresses

Dial-a-Poem Poets, LP, c/o John Giorno, 222 Bowery, N.Y., NY 10012

Arch Records, 1750 Arch Street, Berkeley, CA

New Music Distribution, 500 Broadway, N.Y., NY 10012

DALIA ATLAS

Conductor, Professor, Concert Artist

Israeli orchestra conductor, Dalia Atlas, is one of a few
women to receive worldwide recognition in a field almost
completely dominated by men. She has built her reputation
on the podium by successfully entering international conducting
competitions. Her extraordinary effort and imaginative faculties, based on intellectual and musical pursuits, have made
a more lasting contribution to the art of conducting than any
other single woman. She is a first-class orchestral conductor. Audiences who cherish star-quality in a conductor
soon realize that Atlas offers a deep and abiding sense of
beauty, sensitivity, and order in her leadership capacity.
The orchestra unites behind the gifted maestra, who has received plaudits on five continents.

She is the recipient of the following prestigious inter-
national fellowships and awards in conducting, the first woman
so honored: Eugene Ormandy Award, Philadelphia Orchestra;
Leopold Stokowski Prize; Villa-Lobos Vermeil Medals, Villa-
Lobos International Competition for Conductors, Rio de Jan-
eiro; Royal Liverpool Philharmonic Competition, Liverpool,
England; Dimitri Mitropoulos Competition, New York; and
Guido Cantelli Competition, Novara, Italy.

Dalia Atlas is a first generation Sabra born in Haifa,
Israel in 1935, the daughter of Shoshana and Joshua Sternberg. Her mother's family has a long history of rabbinical
service and her father's family were cantors. The Stern-
bergs met in Israel, pioneers constituting the "third aliya"
arriving in Palestine between 1928 and 1930, harbingers of
a new period in the history of the settlement of Israel.

Reflecting on her early childhood, Dalia Atlas said,

I reacted to music since I was a baby. I was told

23

DALIA ATLAS

later that even at the age of two years I responded
to orchestra music, I was able to listen to entire
symphonies and reacted with my body. (I was conducting by natural response.) Later when I began
to understand music I knew that I wanted to be a
conductor. However, I was always discouraged
from pursuing this career by all my teachers because it was hard work for men, and for a woman
there would be no justice; I would not be allowed
to conduct. My teachers believed I should major
in piano, composing, or voice but I wanted only
to conduct.

Dalia Atlas was surrounded by music from all sides;
yet she did not begin the study of piano until she was ten
years old, considered late by many musicians. The serious
formalized study of piano at the age of ten was not a deterrent for the talented young artist. She received her early
musical training as a pianist and studied at Haifa Conservatory, the Tel Aviv Academy of Music, and the Rubin Academy
of Music in Jerusalem. At age fifteen she was performing
in recitals and in concerts with orchestras, including the
Israel Radio Symphony Orchestra. Her college degree was

awarded at the age of seventeen, based on credits allowed
for her previous training and study.

Following graduation she became a teacher of piano
in addition to her many public performances. At eighteen,
Dalia Sternberg married Joseph Atlasowitz, an engineer.
They are parents of a daughter, Hana, and two sons, Ilan
and Rafael.

Conductor Atlas said, "I always separate my private
life from my professional life; I never grant interviews concerning my family life. When I'm a mother I'm home and
when I'm a conductor I'm a conductor. That has always
been my philosophy."

A mother of three children by the age of twenty-two,
she continued as a pianist and a teacher during their forma-
tive years. The dream of conducting, however, never dim-
med. In time, when her family responsibilities lessened,
she pursued her dream with the support of her husband and
family.

No road to the professional conducting podium has
ever been attained without long and arduous hours of demanding personal sacrifice for both men and women. In addition,
the successful conductor must possess a passionate musical
temperament and a first-class mind. Dalia Atlas is most
brilliantly gifted, a clear indication that success comes with
talent not gender. Women conductors are a rarity but an
outstanding woman conductor is even more rare.

The orchestra conductor must have outstanding qualifications in several areas: conducting ability, leadership,
administrative ability, wide knowledge of repertoire, and
wide musical experience outside learning institutions. Dalia
Atlas knew as a young woman that she would have to obtain
the required training if her dream were to come to fruition.

In 1961 the Italian government sponsored an orchestral
conducting competition scholarship for professional conductors
to study under Franco Ferrara. One entered the competition
at a financial risk, since all competitors paid their own way
to Italy and could face possible elimination. Dalia Atlas took
advantage of this competition because it was a summer period
when she could make arrangements for her family's care.

She said, "I entered the competition without professional conducting experience, just musical background know-

ledge. I was one of the eleven finalists, and the only woman accepted for scholarship study with Maestro Ferrara. At the conclusion of the program of study, I was one of the four chosen to conduct the final concerts. This was my first experience conducting a professional orchestra."

Following this period of study Atlas returned to Israel where she conducted student instrumental groups because at that particular time in her country no professional orchestras would permit a woman to conduct.

During the early 1960's, aided by scholarships from the America-Israel Cultural Foundation, she continued her studies in Europe. In the summer of 1962 she returned to Italy to attend two courses, one in Venezia with Franco Ferrara, and the other in Siena with Sergiu Celibidache. Of this experience she relates,

> My time was limited and my conditions were different from the male conductor. I had to take every advantage to study, so I spent two days a week in each city taking the night train as a means of transportation--during which time I always studied my scores for my courses. I learned a tremendous amount of conducting skills from these two maestros with the knowledge that I had to separate the two systems taught because they were very different from each other. Since I was a piano teacher and a music educator, I was able to eliminate the difficulties.

Upon returning to Israel she met Zubin Mehta. He decided that she must study with his teacher, Professor Hans Swarowsky in Vienna, and sent a letter of recommendation for her. She received a cable from Professor Swarowsky that he would accept her for two weeks of study on his vacation time because his regular teaching schedule was completely filled.

Dalia Atlas studied with this master teacher and relates her experience as follows:

> I spent hours and hours with Professor Swarowsky studying a huge repertoire, (perhaps the amount the regular student might study over a period of two years). I had lessons from early morning until late in the evening. Finally he said to me, "Your character does not suit the character of a

conductor because a conductor needs elbows to
fight and be a politician." When I resisted doing
this he said, "Without these traits and being a
woman I can't see how you will make it." Since
I could not change my character, he offered me
a job conducting in Vienna but for private reasons
I could not accept.

Finally Professor Swarowsky suggested that Dalia Atlas go
the route of International Conductors Competition which would
provide the opportunity to conduct professional orchestras.
With the recognition that she would receive, it would open
other doors to professional podiums. It was a brilliant idea
and it provided Mrs. Atlas with the opportunity to conduct
all the symphonies she had studied, but had not had the
chance to conduct with an orchestra.

The competitions often required the participant to be
prepared to conduct as many as thirty different scores.
Elimination occurs on every round with the performance of
ten different pieces. Dalia Atlas reflected on this experience, "Within one and one half years I entered three international competitions in conducting; I won prizes in all of
them. They were the Guido Cantelli Competition in 1963 in
Novara, Italy; the Royal Liverpool Philharmonic Competition
in 1964 in England; and the Dimitri Mitropoulos Competition
in 1964 in New York."

Although a few women did enter International Conducting Competitions, Dalia Atlas was a pioneer and the only
woman to receive recognition every time she entered one.
She won five conducting competitions, paving the road and making
it easier for future women conductors to attain such goals.
Immediately following each competition she received invitations to conduct professional orchestras, including the Royal
Philharmonic in Liverpool. Reviewed in the Liverpool Daily
Post in 1964:

> Dalia Atlas handled the first movement (of Bee-
> thoven's Second Symphony), competently and sen-
> sitively. Her natural style wisely makes no at-
> tempt to emulate masculine forcefulness and pre-
> fers to rely on a very sensitive ear--Her reading
> ... was enchanting and she drew exquisite playing
> from the orchestra. (Reprinted by permission of
> the Liverpool Daily Post.)

On December 13, 1964 Dalia Atlas was one of the

finalists in the Third Dimitri Mitropoulos International Music
Competition for Conductors. She conducted, sharing the
podium with all-male conductors representing the Netherlands,
Guatemala, France, Bulgaria, Japan, Great Britain, Switzer-
land, and the United States. Of the original thirty-seven
competitors there were eighteen countries represented. Each
conductor remained nameless and was assigned a number
which changed each time they tried out before a panel of
judges. The anonymity was to eliminate any prejudice based
on extra-musical considerations. The competition for conductors between the age of twenty to thirty was sponsored
by the Women's Division of the Jewish Philanthropies of New
York. Leonard Bernstein, then conductor of the New York
Philharmonic Orchestra, presented Dalia Atlas with a silver
medal and a special citation at the close of the competition.
Maestro Bernstein commented, "Dalia Atlas is too brilliant
to be passed by."

Following the Dimitri Mitropoulos Competition she
received three invitations to stay in the United States to conduct: one was to be assistant conductor to Leopold Stokowski
and the American Symphony Orchestra of New York, one was
to go to Philadelphia for a year to work with Eugene Ormandy,
and the third was to become assistant to Fausto Cleva at the
Metropolitan Opera in New York. There were several reasons why Atlas could not stay in America to conduct--she
had three children whom she wanted to raise in Israel and
provide with a normal life. A conductorship away from
Israel would have precluded her accepting this important
family responsibility: she considered it unfair to neglect her
children because of her career. She also found in the United
States, like everywhere else, a resistance to a woman conductor at that time and she said,

> I am not of the character to fight for this socially
> [conducting] as my normal right, more than that,
> I believe only in doing constructive things. In
> America I would have started conducting in pres-
> tigious positions and being honest to myself I knew
> that the biggest enemy of the young conductor is to
> start at the top. I decided to take the hard road
> and start from the bottom, and if I was worthwhile
> I would reach the top on my own! This has been
> the principle which I followed all my life.

When she returned to her country Dalia Atlas was invited to conduct the Radio Orchestra of Israel. They recognized her talent and provided some opportunities to conduct.
She said,

With the orchestras I always had wonderful relationships; there were no problems, it was pure
colleague work and they respected me from the
very beginning--my upbeat! I found it was a pleasure to work with orchestras, and the audience also
accepted me as a normal conductor. Normally the
only resistance was from the music directors who
had been conductors, and somehow the greatest
enemy appears to be male conductors who for years
thought being a conductor was something heroic and
Godish and they couldn't accept that a woman is
able to accomplish this role. Today this had been
changed, but in 1964 it was unbearable for the male
conductors to see a woman on the podium. Some
orchestras even had a rule that prohibited women
from playing in the orchestra. For example, when
I was in New York [1964] the Philharmonic Orchestra did not have any woman musicians.

In 1966 Dalia Atlas returned to the United States and
was one of the three conductors-in-residence at Tanglewood.
She was invited by Erich Leinsdorf on the recommendation
of Isaac Stern. On a scholarship from Leonard Bernstein,
she was a member of the Tanglewood faculty with two other
aspiring young conductors, James Foster and Martin Springer.
Their efforts not only inspired the musicians but audiences
as well.

The Berkshire Music Festival at Tanglewood near
Lenox, Massachusetts, was founded in 1940 as the summer
home of the Boston Symphony Orchestra. Tanglewood is one
of the world's most esteemed summer music festivals and
probably has no equal in all of America. Concerts by the
Boston Symphony Orchestra under the baton of the world's best-
known conductors are a special feature. In addition there are
several other aspects: opera workshops, composers-in-resi-
dence, conductors-in-residence, and a contemporary music
series.

Having been born in Israel, Dalia Atlas feels so much
a part of what is happening in that country, surrounded by
the complexities of the ancient and the modern, that it was
part of her instinctive nature in 1964 to contribute to the
building and growth of the culture. She is the founder, musical director, and conductor of the Israel Pro-Musica Soloists
Orchestra and the Symphony Orchestra and Choir of the Technion University. She believes that the establishment of these
groups was important for two reasons:

It was necessary for Israel; I took a wide look at
my country to see what was necessary and what
was necessary at that time was to establish a small
chamber orchestra to travel in the country. There
are many immigrants, from all over the world,
and some of them had never heard music in their
lives. I worked with this orchestra mainly for
educational reasons. The musicians are all professional players with the same idea as mine, and
we performed throughout the country and in other
countries on a volunteer basis in the beginning.
Later on we received a subsidy from the Israeli
Educational Cultural Ministry.

Dalia Atlas was a faculty member at Technion University in Haifa when she established the Technion Orchestra
and Choir for students and faculty members of this science
university. She believed in the strong connection between
music and science. At that time no university in Israel had
an orchestra. Many people believed it could not be accomplished, especially at a science school. Some fifteen years
later she is still music director with the Technion Orchestra
and Chorus performing a regular series of concerts during
the season. Dalia Atlas, always fascinated by the relationship between science and music, wanted to make experiments
to see what a conductor could achieve with an analytical
brain and music. The results were excellent; eventually she
built a beautiful relationship through music with the Technion
University groups and the Massachusetts Institute of Technology in Cambridge, Massachusetts. Conductor Atlas
has visited MIT on three different occasions, including a
sabbatical leave, and has been invited to return. She also
spent time lecturing and conducting in the United States at
universities in Washington, Cleveland, and Boston.

Reviewed as a conductor by Thor Eckert, Jr. for
The Christian Science Monitor on December 9, 1974:

> The MIT Symphony Orchestra played host to a most
> remarkable talent Saturday evening: conductor
> Dalia Atlas. Israeli-born Miss Atlas is one of the
> few women conductors in the world....
> From the opening moments of the Beethoven Eg-
> mont Overture, however, it was obvious that here
> was an exceptionally interesting musician. The
> sweep and power of this work were, under her
> direction, revelatory. Her delineation of the beat
> is crystalline; her ear for the top and bottom of a

phrase, for what musical point needs special emphasis--through dynamic or tempo variation--is exceptionally accurate and effective. With all this meticulous attention to inner detail, however, she never loses sight of the piece as a whole.

Miss Atlas closed the program with Debussy's La Mer. It was a downright exciting performance. She has an exceptional feel for tempo variations as a means of musical emphasis--a slight ritard or a brief accelerando--and her tonal canvas for this popular but tricky Debussy work was superbly vivid. The Atlas approach blends the best of the straightforward style with the best of the romantic-- in which the conductor takes liberties with tempi and dynamics for his own special effect.

Miss Atlas would be welcome in front of any orchestra: The better the group, the better for the listener. (Reprinted by permission from The Christian Science Monitor © 1974 The Christian Science Publishing Society. All rights reserved.)

In the fall of 1977 she returned to the United States on a last moment call for a replacement and again conducted a concert with works by Stravinsky, Schoenberg, and Mahler. Praise of her musicianship included reviews and the following letter from Dr. David Epstein, professor of music and conductor of the MIT Symphony.

Dear Dalia,

What you accomplished last Saturday night was a small miracle and I am not only deeply grateful to you, but enormously impressed as well. I think there are very few conductors at any level of our profession who would have had the musicianship as well as the courage to take such a difficult program--all strange music and none of it of the conductor's choice--to learn it while preparing it with the orchestra, and to bring it off so beautifully. You are really a remarkable musician and I hope that this concert will prove a benefit to you in many ways, perhaps some that we cannot even foresee at this moment. I can certainly tell you that MIT feels that you are one of the family and thinks of you with the greatest warmth and fondness.

I look forward with pleasure to seeing you and your family in Israel. Meanwhile, with great friendship, as always.

On a visit to the United States in 1976 Dalia Atlas
met an old friend, Lawrence Foster, conductor of the Houston Symphony Orchestra. He has long held her conducting
skill in esteem and he invited her to conduct his orchestra
the following season. Dalia Atlas, who appreciates every
orchestra she conducts, likens conducting different orchestras
to the work of a sculptor: "Each orchestra is composed of
different materials and we create together a new piece of
art." Since she enjoys the role of visiting conductor, she
accepted Lawrence Foster's invitation and made two guest
appearances with the Houston Symphony Orchestra in the
summer of 1977.

Charles Ward reviewed the opening concert for the
Houston Chronicle on June 28, 1977. Excerpts from that
review are as follows:

ATLAS DEBUT IS IMPRESSIVE

The Houston Symphony returned to Miller Theater
with an impressive debut of Israel conductor Dalia
Atlas that culminated in a stirring performance of
Sibelius' Symphony No. 2.
Atlas achieved a poise and power that was both
lovely in its aural results and compelling in its
emotional intensity.
This was a convincing debut for Atlas. She set
a high standard that will be a challenge to maintain for the rest of the orchestra's crowded Miller
Theater schedule. She proved to be a forceful conductor who might produce exciting results. (Reprinted by permission of the Houston Chronicle.)

Carl Cunningham reviewed the final performance of
Dalia Atlas' schedule on July 1, 1977 for the Houston Post:

MUSIC: HOUSTON SYMPHONY ORCHESTRA

Israel guest conductor Dalia Atlas concluded her
Houston Symphony engagement with a powerful performance of Brahms' First Symphony Thursday
evening at Miller Theater.
The performance brought together all the best
traits of Atlas' conducting style, as observed in
various works she conducted with the orchestra
during her two concerts here. Her fondness for
big rich tonal effects came to the fore in flattering
fashion time and time again throughout the symphony

and, with minor exceptions, she elicited excellent
playing from the brass section.

While there was an intense emotional drive in
Atlas' conducting, she maintained a tightly disci-
plined control over the total form of the symphony.
Rubato effects were made subservient to generally
straightforward tempos that gave the music the
kind of lean, purposeful excitement that Toscanini
in his prime used to achieve with this work. (Copyright © 1977 by The Houston Post. Reprinted by
permission.)

In the early 1970's as Dalia Atlas' children matured
and her home responsibilities required less of her time, she
again aspired to continued growth and visibility as a professional orchestral conductor.   The distinctive recognition
that she had received was important and the continuance in
international conducting competition still remained the only
positive avenue for women to succeed in an area that remained traditionally dominated by males.   She said, "I needed
visibility outside Israel so I entered another competition in
1978.   I went to Rio de Janeiro in Brazil to the Villa-Lobos
International Competition for Conductors, sponsored by the
Educational Ministry.   At this competition I was awarded both
the Leopold Stokowski Prize for Conductors and the Villa-
Lobos Medal, and of course, many invitations to conduct all
over the world."   It was inevitable with Mrs. Atlas' passion
for music and knowledge of conducting that she would receive
the plaudits of the musical world.

Her many conducting interests are reflected in her
guest conducting schedule in 1979: A. B. C. Orchestras in
Australia, B. B. C. Symphony Orchestra in Rio de Janeiro
and São Paulo Symphony Orchestra, Halle Orchestra, Helsinki, Stockholm Philharmonic, Israel Philharmonic, and
Israel Radio Symphony Orchestra.   Dalia Atlas commented
on her impressive schedule,

> The most fascinating periods in my life are to go
> from one orchestra and country to another, differ-
> ent styles, different cultures, and different pro-
> grams.   I don't like to repeat programs; I choose
> my own repertoire and I am not limited to one
> composer or style.   I select from great classics
> to the avant-garde.   I conduct music that I find
> good and which has a message to bring to the world.

Reviewed in the Evening Echo, Bournemouth, England
on January 19, 1979, by Ken Williams (partial):

MADAM MAESTRO

The perfect escape from impending national doom
and January weather--splendid music, magnificently
played, with a lady as escort and guide.

She was Israel-born Dalia Atlas, and her concert
with the Bournemouth Symphony Orchestra was exciting, enriching.

Miss Atlas' big success was in the Ravel orchestration of Moussorgsky's Pictures From An Exhibition. She has an appropriately elegant, pliable
technique.

She was obviously communicating almost fault-
lessly with the orchestra, and she had much that
was fresh to say about this much-played music.
The music's big gestures were imposingly made,
and there was an overall intensity and vividness
about the performance.

But its smaller scale aspects were commendable,
too. Textures were rich, but never cloying, details were particularly well observed.

The BSO were, as ever, marvellously professional and dedicated servants of their guest conductor. Our lady guest deserved almost unreserved
praise for her accompaniments.

It was good to see Miss Atlas requiring not the
slightest concession to her sex at the exalted level
which the BSO concert nowadays represents. (Reprinted by permission from the Evening Echo.)

Reviewed by Karl Hubert for The Mercury, Australia,
on January 9, 1978:

PRECISE, ELEGANT

Conductor first-rate

Last night it was the turn of Israeli conductor,
Dalia Atlas.

Judging by what one saw and heard, Dalia Atlas
is a first-rate conductor who may have certain pref-
erences for the exquisite, but who, no doubt, can
do Mahler as well as her colleagues.

Conducting with precise, elegant movements and
never raising the baton or her hands above eye
level, she demonstrated a perfect acquaintance with
the Tasmanian Symphony Orchestra after three rehearsals.

Works of Mendelssohn, Litolff, Verdi, Rossini,
and Smetana, gave her the opportunity to demonstrate that she has studied with good teachers.
The tempos were right, the relationship between
the tempos faultless and there was ample proof
that preparations had been painstakingly thorough.
(Reprinted by permission of The Mercury.)

Conductor Atlas had a dream--a vision--and she dedicated her life to the study and time-consuming demands of
a professional career. Whenever she conducts a new composition she says, "I hear the entire score as I read poetry
or philosophy; I never listen to a recording of any composition until I have my own concepts very clear. My criterion
for repertoire is--if the music is good and has a message
to bring to the world, then I will identify myself with it and
perform it--no matter which style or period. "

Dalia Atlas had made several successful conducting
tours of England and Scotland over a period of years. She
is not able to accept all of the invitations she receives each
year to appear as a guest conductor, but in 1979 she completed an extensive tour of those two countries.

Reviewed by the Express & Echo on January 23, 1979
in Exeter, England:

MS. ATLAS CLIMBS THE ROSTRUM

The Bournemouth Symphony Orchestra has over the
years, developed a reputation for "first" in Exeter.
The latest concert at the University Great Hall
was no exception, when the rostrum was ascended
by a woman conductor, the Israeli-born Dalia Atlas.
Miss Atlas certainly demonstrated outstanding
talent and competence. She trained as a concert
pianist and went on to win leading international conductors awards. She has conducted for the B. B. C.
and the Royal Liverpool Philharmonic Orchestra,
as well as continental orchestras and ones in her
native Israel and the U. S. A.
The programme opened with the "Prelude and
Liebestod" from Wagner's Tristan and Isolde--a
wonderful start to any concert. The haunting motif
which dominates the music is a memorable one
which lingers on long after the music has died
away.

Great joy

The orchestra built up an exciting climax and Miss
Atlas caught perfectly the atmosphere of the excerpt, particularly the conclusion, which tells of
the death of Isolde. The orchestra responded well
to Miss Atlas's directing and achieved some magnificently atmospheric moments.
Other works were Haydn's Concerto No. I in D,
Pictures from an Exhibition by Mussorgsky and
final subject--The Great Gates of Kiev brought the
concert to a triumphal conclusion. (Reprinted by
permission of the Express & Echo.)

Reviewed by Anne Johnstone for the Evening Times,
Scotland, June 27, 1979:

DALIA AND HER MAGIC WAND

When a woman takes a man's job she has to be
not just as good as her colleagues but better than
most of them.
Promenaders at the Kelvin Hall witnessed a
proof of that old truism in the imposing form of
Dalia Atlas, who took the rostrum and the lime-
light at last night's concert.
Clad in a voluminous black and gold gown, she
coaxed and drove the SNO through her own choice
of programme, like a female magician working a
powerful spell.
To follow Verdi's taut energetic Overture, The
Force of Destiny, she picked Mendelssohn's Scot-
tish Symphony.
For fun there was Britten's entertaining Soirées
Musicales and to cap the lot, Ravel's arrangement
of Mussorgsky's monumental and unmistakenably
masculine Pictures from an Exhibition. (Reprinted
by permission from the Evening Times.)

Miss Atlas has made guest conducting appearances
with the Israel Philharmonic Orchestra and the Israel Radio
Symphony Orchestra. The Israel Philharmonic Orchestra
had a unique beginning. Unlike any other major symphony
orchestra in the world, it was founded outside the country.
The violinist Bronislav Huberman, a non-resident of Israel,
realized the musical needs of the Jewish people and at the
same time the rejection of the Jewish musicians by Nazi
Germany in 1936. He auditioned these musicians and made

arrangements for the best players to live in Israel. The
caliber of musicianship was very high. In the beginning
there were five former concertmasters. For many years
the Israel Philharmonic Orchestra used only guest conductors.
Now the permanent conductor and music director is Zubin
Mehta. When Dalia Atlas received an invitation to conduct
the Israel Philharmonic she joined an impressive list of prestigious world conductors that included among others Toscanini, Dobrowen, Sargent, Munch, Koussevitsky, Bernstein,
Ormandy, Dorati, and Abbado.

>   The Jerusalem Post, 1965:

>   ... a polished and vital performance ... a fine
>   example of concord between conductor and orchestra
>   ... she conducts with technical ease and proves
>   herself a gifted conductor, with interpretative spirit
>   and outstanding musicianship. ...

>   The Jerusalem Post, 1967:

>   Dalia Atlas has a sound approach to music in gen-
>   eral and to her craft in particular ... she drove
>   the orchestra without respite through all the storms
>   and into the dramatic climaxes. ...

Professor Atlas has been a member of the faculty at
Technion Israel Institute of Technology since 1964. She reflects in her teaching the dedication of a fine scholar and a
humanist philosophy. The students' respect and devotion to
her commitment to teaching is shown by their willingness to
meet outside of the regular class-period, to attend double
class-periods, or to make other efforts necessary to complete
course requirements when Dalia Atlas is away for guest conducting appearances. The students do not want a replacement. Atlas said, "The college cooperates in released time
and I am the type who never neglects my chores."

The Rittenhouse Square Women's Committee for the
Philadelphia Orchestra, in celebration of their twenty-fifth
anniversary and in honor of the eightieth birthday of their
esteemed conductor, established the Eugene Ormandy Award.
This award recognizes women conductors, composers, and
soloists. After a time-consuming search for talented women
musicians, conductor Dalia Atlas was the first recipient to
appear under its aegis in February, 1980. She said, "The
Eugene Ormandy Award was the most important prize I received in my career--it was a big surprise--they researched

me for three years and I never knew it. Here I am to share
the podium with such a great master like Eugene Ormandy--
it was a greater honor than winning the conducting competitions. "

On February 14, 15, 16, and 19, 1980 Atlas conducted
the Philadelphia Orchestra in the opening number, La Mer.
Reviewed in the Philadelphia Inquirer by Samuel L. Singer:

DALIA ATLAS SHOWS CONDUCTING STYLE

Miss Atlas who has conducted many leading orchestras in Europe, appeared as the first recipient of
the Eugene Ormandy Award, established last year
by the orchestra's Rittenhouse Square Women's
Committee.   She followed the footsteps of Nadia
Boulanger, Elaine Brown and composer Thea Musgrave, each of whom conducted part of a program
at the Academy.   [Sarah Caldwell and Eve Queler
have conducted entire programs at Saratoga.]
Miss Atlas proved herself entirely worthy of
such distinguished predecessors.   Conducting without a score, she led Debussy's La Mer, opening
number on the program, with assurance and mani-
fest knowledge of what results she wished, bringing fresh insight to this much-played music.   She
developed the opening "From Dawn 'til Noon on
the Sea" logically, made a vivid picture of the
"Play of the Waves" and detailed the "Dialogue of
the Wind and the Sea" with finesse to a natural
musical climax.   (Reprinted by permission of The
Philadelphia Inquirer.)

The Jewish Post and Opinion, reported her appearance
in Philadelphia on February 29, 1980 with an article and picture, noting "that although this was hardly her first appearance as conductor of an international orchestra, still it was
a feather in the cap of Dalia Atlas to share the podium with
Eugene Ormandy for four nights. "

Dalia Atlas' lifelong dedication to her art is inspirational; she has succeeded where few women dare to tread.
She has guest appearances scheduled with major orchestras
all over the world for the next several years.   The artistic
message she conveys as a conductor and as a true and gentle
lady will be strongly imprinted in the annals of twentieth-
century music.   The young Maestra Atlas' artistic phenomena
cannot yet be fully assessed because she will undoubtly open
new horizons.   Her baton is elegant and sure.

SARAH CALDWELL

Opera Impresario, Conductor, Producer

Impresario Sarah Caldwell's legendary huzza, "Ho!, Ho!, Ho!, it's magic time," precisely reflects the personality of this amazing artist. Her international reputation as an inventive producer of spectacular opera has spanned more than three decades and clearly places her in the forefront of twentieth-century artists. Sarah: opera; opera: Sarah-- the word and her name are synonymous. A list of adjectives does justice to America's musical phenomenon: unique, adventurous, courageous, ingenious, and imaginative. She rightly deserves the title "First Lady of American Opera."

Success was a combination of extraordinary effort and tribulation--the word "impossible" does not exist in Caldwell's vocabulary. No task is easy but the road to international recognition requires absolute dedication to every minute detail. Sarah Caldwell has devoted hour after hour, day after day, week after week, and year after year to opera. Music and theater are the "love potion" that keeps her ticking and kicking.

She was born in 1924 in Maryville, Missouri, and was raised in her early years by relatives and her single-parent mother. A bright and determined child, she was often alone and on her own. Her mother Margaret, although dedicated to the young Sarah and believing her to be gifted in both music and mathematics, continued graduate studies in music at Columbia University and so could not maintain a day-to-day relationship with her daughter. Considered a child prodigy, Sarah began the study of violin at the age of four. At five she was performing with adult groups and soon after was giving recitals. Margaret Caldwell remarried when Sarah was twelve, with her daughter, they moved to Fayetteville where her husband, Henry Alexander, was a political science professor at the University of Arkansas.

39

Sarah recalls with special fondness the Saturday after-
noons that she spent as a youngster at concerts and at the
theater which nurtured her innate ability to love and understand these two areas. Because her favorite day of the year
was the Fourth of July, she spent hours planning the staging
of elaborate fireworks displays in her yard. Older adults
can still recall with excitement the joys of firecrackers,
cherry bombs, sparklers, snakes, and the like, now outlawed
in many states. Every child saved her nickels and dimes
to purchase the "joys of noise." Sarah went one step further
with her collection of "goodies" when she created and produced exciting fireworks displays which she shared with relatives and friends. Talent reigned at that young age even
though the rules of her home did not permit her to bring the
fireworks paraphernalia into the house until the night before
the Fourth. Some parents might have stifled the creative
process, but fortunately Caldwell's mother permitted this
with small restrictions.

After graduating from high school at fourteen, Sarah
attended both the University of Arkansas and Hendrix College.
There was some pressure from her father, who encouraged
her to continue to study music and also to pursue the study
of psychology during her freshman year at the University.
Eventually her love of music won, and she arrived with a
fistful of scholarships in the early 1940's at Boston's New
England Conservatory of Music to study opera production,
stage design, and similar craft courses. She continued her
violin studies with the concertmaster of the Boston Symphony
Orchestra, Richard Burgin. Because Burgin was not particularly encouraging toward Caldwell's study of the violin, she
changed teachers and studied with George Flourel. In 1946
she won a scholarship to play viola in the student orchestra
at Tanglewood, the summer home of the Boston Symphony
Orchestra. Later she was offered positions in the string
sections of both the Minneapolis and Indianapolis Orchestras,
but refused them in order to pursue her love of theater and
music.

Following the completion of her studies at the New
England Conservatory of Music, Caldwell was offered the
opportunity to assist Boris Goldovsky, founder of the New
England Opera Company. She spent the next eleven seasons
working as his jack-of-all-trades assistant, including such
tasks as prop manager, stage director, translator, and chorus
conductor. Goldovsky shared his knowledge and love of opera
with the young assistant and he provided Sarah with her first
opportunity to conduct opera--Mozart's <u>La Finta Giardiniera.</u>

Some years later, reflecting on that period of Sarah's career, her fellow artists and musicians would generally agree that those years were filled with productive and provocative experiences.   She and Goldovsky exhausted their energies to bring opera and other musical performances to a height of professionalism unknown up to that time in Boston.   That this union was to dissolve within a period of years was a natural event--lives are lived in a series of plateaus and this was just one portion of life for both of these musical entrepreneurs.

During this same period Sarah Caldwell spent several summers at Tanglewood, first as a student, and later as a member of the Berkshire Music Faculty.   She was the only woman in the master conducting class taught by her idol, Maestro Serge Koussevitsky.   She never missed a performance when he conducted.   To Caldwell, "Tanglewood was a place where gods strode the earth."   It was in this paradise that she staged her first operatic production, Ralph Vaughan Williams's Riders to the Sea, a one-act opera based on J. M. Synge's play.   The success of this production, although she was not yet twenty, led Koussevitsky to recommend her for the prestigious faculty at Tanglewood.

In 1952 Sarah Caldwell was appointed director of the Boston University Opera Workshop.   During her eight years at the University she created the department of music and theater.   Her operatic directorial debut with the Opera Workshop was in 1953 with Igor Stravinsky's The Rake's Progress. In addition to producing numerous other operas, she presented the American première of Paul Hindemith's opera, Mathis der Maler.   Her tremendous success with the University productions made operatic history in Boston and built a solid reputation as an exciting and venturesome director.   She quickly realized that the fine performers she was training at the University had no opportunity to continue their artistic commitment in Boston.   Only abroad could their art afford them a professional living, but in the process they could lose their native style.

The need was obvious for a resident opera company in Boston.   Unfortunately, the city had not supported a resident company since 1914 and had just demolished the magnificent Boston Opera House to make room for a parking lot. It had boasted a spacious stage and the most advanced stage machinery when it was built in 1909.   Although there was not even a suitable building in the city to house a new opera venture, it was not a deterrent to Sarah's dreams.   Supported

by a small group of colleagues and friends, Caldwell founded
the Boston Opera Group in 1957.   With an abundance of determination, an expectation of high artistic level, and a mere
$5,000 nest egg, the company was launched and would soon
become the most exciting musical venture in the entire country.   The group was later named the Boston Opera Company
until pressured by the Boston Opera Association, the organization that sponsored the Metropolitan Opera in its spring
tour, with a possible court injunction against any other group
using the words "Boston" and "Opera" in succession.   Just
prior to the 1965-1966 season the young company officially
changed the name to the Opera Company of Boston.

Sarah Caldwell reminds one of the fable, "Stone Soup";
she is the cook bringing to boiling temperature a stone and
water, knowing full well that she will produce a sumptuous
soup.   Others will offer assistance, services, help, money,
and support, but only Sarah can mix the ingredients.   Through
her talent to select and direct the cast, choose repertory,
commission sets and costumes, conduct, and do whatever else
needs be done, she produces the final medium, always a
phenomenon in the world of arts.   Caldwell had the training,
the ability, and, most of all optimism--a key combination
for success.   The première production, Jacques Offenbach's
Voyage to the Moon, was presented at the Boston Arts Festival in June 1958.   It was hailed by the Christian Science
Monitor as a "masterpiece of whimsey."   Sarah and company
were elated by the standing ovation.

Numerous problems, including financial woes, complicated the operation during the first few fledgling years of the
company's existence.   A less determined individual might
have given up, but not Sarah Caldwell.   She devoted all her
energies, including some twenty-four-hour days, to make the
impossible happen: a resident opera company for Boston that
all could applaud.   During this period, numerous tales of
Sarah's personal trials and tribulations surfaced; some were
fact and others were fiction, but an adoring reading public
idolized her gutsy approach and many of the tales were blown
out of proportion.   When one is bringing to fruition a creative
venture most daily tasks are mundane by comparison.   Were
there times when Sarah slept in the theater, tried to pay for
scenery by check (the banks were closed), delayed the opening of a performance until stagehands were assured their
paychecks wouldn't bounce, and held in small regard her personal possessions?   In all probability the answer is "yes."

There have been innumerable attempts by friends,

managers, musicians, and music critics to change some of
Sarah Caldwell's so-called eccentric ways because she fails
to conform to society's expectations. She has established her
credentials for over thirty years. Though she has on many
occasions not met daily routine deadlines or has offended the
establishment , to expect Miss Caldwell to conform could
destroy those creative powers that have made her unique.

For almost twenty years impresario Sarah Caldwell
had to stage her productions in almost impossible makeshift
physical structures, including some outdoor performances.
In 1959 the Opera Group leased the little 500-seat Fine Arts
Theater; from then on, they leased other rental property,
such as the Back Bay, Aquarius, and Boston Schubert theaters. Performances were also given at Boston College's indoor track, MIT's Kresge Auditorium, and the gymnasium
at Tufts University. The company's permanent home for
several seasons was the 2000-seat Boston Orpheum Theater,
totally inadequate structure for opera productions. Yet Caldwell had the visceral ability to overcome the physical limitations of the theater's shallow stage (a mere twenty-six feet
in depth), and its lack of orchestra pit and backstage area.
Finally, just before the close of the twentieth season Caldwell
presented Puccini's Tosca in the company's new home, the
Savoy. With enough money to make the needed improvements,
it could become a substitute for Sarah's dream castle envisioned in the 1970's. At that time she had hoped for a
new opera complex in the city of Boston with three theaters
under one roof at an estimated cost in excess of ten million
dollars. Who but the daring Caldwell would even consider
the momentous task of partly demolishing the old Savoy Theater in ten days and renovating it to stage Tosca? Reviews
of Sarah Caldwell's prodigious career could fill an entire
book and it would make for interesting reading. Her operas
have fascinated musicians and audiences for years because
she follows her instincts to generate exciting innovations.
How then does one pick and choose which reviews to present
in one short chapter? The goal in this chapter is to present
an overview of some of the significant aspects of Caldwell's
long and distinguished career.

Sarah Caldwell's unique and exciting accomplishments
in the production of opera in America have made European
dependence somewhat obsolete. Opera was an orphan in the
music circles until Caldwell made it the most exciting new
adventure of its kind in the twentieth century in this country.
She had produced the American première of Arnold Schoenberg's Moses and Aron; Sergei Prokofiev's War and Peace;

Guiseppe Verdi's Don Carlos, the first five acts in the original French edition; Jean-Philippe Rameau's Hippolyte et Aricie;
avant-garde Italian composer Luigi Nono's Intolerance 1969;
and the first completely staged and uncut American première
of Hector Berlioz's The Trojans. She has successfully attracted many of the leading operatic stars to perform roles
in her productions, including such noted artists as Beverly
Sills, Nicolai Gedda, Régine Crespin, Marilyn Horne, George
London, Donald Gramm, Joan Sutherland, Renata Tebaldi,
and Jon Vickers.

          Before the American première of Arnold Schoenberg's
opera Moses and Aron there were numerous events presented
in the city of Boston to help college students, musicians,
and other interested people to understand his music better.
Noted artists and historians gave special lectures and demon-
strations relative to the twelve-tone idiom that Schoenberg
used in a variety of ways in his opera. On opening night
music critics from throughout the world were in attendance.
Winthrop Sargeant wrote a lengthy review for The New Yorker
on December 10, 1966, and a short excerpt is presented:

          Last week, on Wednesday, I went up to Boston to
          hear the American premiere of Arnold Schoenberg's
          opera Moses and Aron. This venture on my part
          was really mandatory, because Moses and Aron is
          as near a full-length opera as Schoenberg over
          wrote, because it was written late in his lifetime,
          and because recent performances in London and on
          the continent had been greeted with considerable
          interest. Wednesday night's opera was, as every-
          one knows, presented by Sarah Caldwell's Opera
          Company of Boston, and it was given in the old
          movie house on Massachusetts Avenue known as the
          Back Bay Theatre. Miss Caldwell deserves a
          great deal of credit--first, for putting on the opera
          at all and, second, for doing a splendid job of the
          production. (Copyright © 1966 Winthrop Sargeant
          in The New Yorker. Reprinted by permission.)

          Excerpt from the review by Michael Steinberg pub-
lished in the Boston Globe on December 1, 1966:

          Moses and Aron has been done in America now.
          It was high time, for this is a very great work,
          not just for its philosophical content, but even more
          for its luminous, powerful music. It is a tribute
          to Sarah Caldwell and the company that Moses and

Aron could be produced here in a non-theater and
with all the other limitations of resources to fight,
and produced in a way that made a tremendous impact.
    Moses and Aron is an opera of ideas.   Some
past productions have had the effect of leading the
audience away from the essentials, in fact, from
the idea to the golden calf orgy.   Sarah Caldwell
has given Schoenberg's work a production that actually invites us to listen to the words and to the
music.   Her great success with it has been to
make it perfectly clear to the audience what Moses
and Aron is about, and any impact it makes for
relevent reasons.   (Reprinted courtesy of The Boston
Globe.)

In 1967 Sarah Caldwell expanded her concept of giving
audiences a good evening of musical theater.   She formed a
national touring opera troupe named the National Opera Company.   The troupe consisted of over 100 musicians, singers,
and administrators.   They received a grant of $350,000
awarded by the National Council on the Arts.   This was the
first time the federal government had made a major contribution to underwrite opera; it provided Caldwell the means to
expand her Boston accomplishments nationwide.

The membership of the troupe which included a thirty-
six piece orchestra, consisted basically of young Americans.
Some singers were auditioned by Caldwell in Germany and
agreed to sign on with the company for the first season.   In
addition, a few members joined the company from the defunct
Metropolitan Opera National Company that had toured the
country the previous two years.

During the first half of the first season over thirty
cities across the country contracted with the group for performances.   Each city was allowed to choose from the company's repertoire the opera to be presented there.   The two
most popular choices were Tosca and Falstaff.

No touring company has ever been able to establish
lasting roots in this type of operation and, in spite of all
of Sarah Caldwell's energies and expertise, the company
found itself in financial trouble after the first season and had
to file a petition in Federal Court under Chapter XI of the
Bankruptcy Act, listing its liabilities as $840,000 and its
assets as $150,000.

Although the American National Opera Company failed
financially, there were many positive reviews, the productions
were warmly received, and audiences expanded during its
short period of existence.   The troupe's presentation of three
different operas within two days in New York City in 1967,
Puccini's Tosca, Verdi's Falstaff, and Berg's Lulu won these
comments from Winthrop Sargeant in the October 14, 1967
New Yorker:

> The visit of the American National Opera Company
> to the Brooklyn Academy of Music last Friday and
> Saturday was probably an eyeopener to many New
> Yorkers besides me.   This is a company with all
> the style of the world's finest opera troupes, and,
> in addition, it produces opera with more dramatic
> effect than most of them.   The mind behind its
> production is, of course, that of Sarah Caldwell,
> a lady who has recently put Boston on the operatic
> map and who is now engaged in touring the country
> with this admirable new group.   Miss Caldwell's
> extraordinary gifts as an operatic director are well
> known to every opera buff who travels from city
> to city in search of great performances, but this
> was the first occasion on which they have been ex-
> hibited here.   They include nothing in the way of
> eccentricity and everything in the way of bringing
> to light all the musical and dramatic subtleties that
> the score contains.   Opera issues from her hands
> as superb drama, but never at the expense of musi-
> cal or vocal elements, and her taste appears to be
> infallible.
> Of the three performances, she presented, I was
> struck by the Saturday matinee, devoted to Verdi's
> Falstaff.   It was perhaps the finest Falstaff I have
> ever heard.   At any rate, all the elements of stage
> business were coordinated with the precision you
> expect from circus acrobats, and all the characters
> were presented vividly as individuals--even the
> minor ones.
> Under Miss Caldwell's baton, everything was as
> light as sunshine and technically close to perfect;
> one must also place her among the finest operatic
> conductors currently before the public.   (Copyright
> © 1967 Winthrop Sargeant in The New Yorker.
> Reprinted by permission.)

To open the fourteenth season (1972) of the Opera Company of Boston, Sarah Caldwell tackled a challenging master-

piece, the full-length <u>Les Troyens</u> by Hector Berlioz.   Some
edited versions had been presented in the United States,
namely by the San Francisco Opera Company and by the New
England Opera Theater, but the great opera houses, including
the Metropolitan, had bypassed the mammoth and demanding
work.   Yet Caldwell not only staged the American première
but also conducted it, an amazing accomplishment.   Excerpts
from a review by Michael Steinberg in the <u>Boston Globe</u> on
February 7, 1972:

> Sarah Caldwell has done it again.   With the Opera
> Company of Boston, whose artistic director she is,
> she has staged and conducted the first complete
> performance in this country of Hector Berlioz's
> <u>The Trojans</u>, offering that huge work with a 21-
> hour intermission after the two acts Thursday that
> show the sacking of Troy.   The three acts that
> deal with the stay of Aeneas at Queen Dido's court
> at Carthage were presented Friday.   The two parts
> were repeated Sunday afternoon and evening.
>   The most impressive feature of Caldwell's stag-
> ing of <u>The Trojans</u> was the musicality manifest in
> her deployment of soloist and of the ample and well-
> prepared chorus over the wide-flung stage, offering
> maximal definition and clarification of Berlioz's
> way of building his musical textures by piling layers
> with plenty of air space between.   In both parts,
> space was remarkably used in the big scenes where
> it was badly needed.
>   It was a theater experience full of life.   And
> we have been able to see <u>The Trojans</u>, a work that
> is after all, one of the great moments in the history
> of musical drama.   (Reprinted courtesy of <u>The
> Boston Globe.</u>)

It was only natural that in time impresario Sarah Caldwell would receive invitations to guest conduct orchestras in
both America and Europe.   During the decade of the 1970's
it was fashionable, particularly in the United States, for orchestras to divide guest conducting invitations among the several notable women conductors--Eve Queler, Antonia Brico,
Margaret Hillis, and Sarah Caldwell.   It is often standard for
guest conductors to limit their programs to a particular repertoire that they have thoroughly studied, perhaps even mem-
orized, and to repeat a given selection several times in a
given season.   This is not true of Maestra Caldwell; she
rarely repeats an orchestral selection.   As with opera she
enjoys the challenge of conducting a variety of scores.

In 1975 the New York Philharmonic Orchestra's Pension Fund concert was given in association with Ms. magazine and was titled "A Celebration of Women Composers." Sarah Caldwell conducted a program she had chosen from some 150 scores she had studied that had been written by women. It was a tribute to Caldwell and the orchestra that they were able to play five totally new compositions with only four rehearsals. Even though she was recognized as the first woman to conduct the orchestra in a pension fund concert, she had been preceded on the podium by Nadia Boulanger and by Rosalyn Tureck, who, seated at the piano as soloist, commanded the orchestra in a subscription concert.

As expected, the concert played to a sold-out house, perhaps an indication that too little music composed by Americans in general, and women in particular, is programmed by leading orchestras. It is a rare occasion to have music written by women performed by prestigious orchestras in the United States, although this is not true in European countries.

Not suprisingly, the concert was reviewed by many leading critics, including Donal Henahan for the New York Times on November 11, 1975:

> Female chauvinism reared its head last night at Avery Fisher Hall, where Sarah Caldwell became the first woman to conduct a New York Philharmonic Pension Fund concert, and the first to lead a Philharmonic program exclusively devoted to women composers. But since it was all in the good cause of dramatizing how women musicians are catching up with history, the men in the audience did not audibly object. For at least one night, an armistice was declared in Thurber's War Between Men and Women.
>
> It was Sarah Caldwell's night to make or break, and it may fairly be said that the formidable founder of the Opera Company of Boston held everything together. Seated high behind the stockade-like walls of the box she favors as a podium, Miss Caldwell presided over one of the most ambitious and, finally, one of the most successful concerts of unfamiliar music that New York has witnessed in some time.
>
> To try to rehearse and perform five difficult works, all new to the orchestra, seemed more brave than circumspect. And, sure enough, Miss Caldwell had to drop three of the four movements of Ruth Crawford Seeger's Quartet for String Or-

chestra, contenting herself with presenting the Andante instead of the first performance of the original version of the whole piece (the string quartet
version turns up now and then).

As the program's centerpiece, Miss Caldwell
brought out Lili Boulanger's Faust et Hélène, a
cantata that won the Prix de Rome of the French
Academy in 1913 for the younger sister of the more
renowned teacher of composers, Nadia. It was a
revival that could have justified the entire concert,
for while Wagner and Debussy ("Pelleas," in particular) haunted the work, it convincingly blended a
high post-Romantic rhetoric and a vocal sensuous-
ness that made one most tolerant of a middle section that bogged down. Gwendoline Killebrew and
Lenus Carlson were splendid as Helen and Mephis-
tophetes, but the pleasantly light tenor of Joseph
Evans was often squeezed, and sometimes smothered.

The shining virtuoso of the night, however,
turned out to be a man, the clarinetist Stanley
Drucker (the women can hardly begrudge us that
smidgin of solace). He tore into the solo part of
Thea Musgrave's Clarinet Concerto--a New York
première--without apparent concern, putting his
instrument easily over every hurdle the British
composer's score set up for it. The concerto is
a strenuous, wildly scored piece that demands all-
out virtuosity from everyone concerned. Mr. Drucker moved about the stage from time to time,
playing from four different spots as a kind of traveling soloist with different bands and adding spatial
interest to a fascinatingly intricate piece.

Pozzi Escot's Sands, a United States première,
was built of Varèse-like blocks of sound in the
first and last movements and had sustained threads
of interwoven tone (duration determined by computer) as a middle section. An easily followed
work, but not one that would seem destined for
frequent performance, nonetheless. The same
might be said of Grazyna Bacewicz's Overture for
Orchestra, a 1943 piece that scuttled along ener-
getically but got nowhere in particular.

As an orchestra conductor, Miss Caldwell functioned efficiently, though she still has things to
learn about that specialized calling. While her
concert went off smoothly and with every indication
of precision, one had to question the need for such
unalleviated novelty. The program was sponsored in
collaboration with Ms. Magazine and carried the title

"A Celebration of Women Composers," but Miss Caldwell ought to have leavened the lump with something
familiar. As it was, she made her Philharmonic debut
under undue strain and frequently seemed to be simply
giving a literal reading of a score that both she
and the orchestra had only recently learned. (Copyright © 1975 by The New York Times Company.
Reprinted by permission.)

After the concert Caldwell's comments, in an article
written by Robert T. Jones were published in Opera News, Vol.
40, on February 14, 1975.

As far as I'm concerned, it's a little late to speak
of women in the arts, because that is not a new
phenomenon. I don't think of myself as a "woman
conductor," but as a conductor, and I hope my
abilities will speak for themselves.
I have been fortunate that I have never felt it
was particularly a handicap to be a woman. Maybe I haven't thought clearly enough, and maybe
I haven't been sensitive enough. I think it is dangerous to take one's own experiences as a norm.
There were certain things that were depressing to
me as I spent time studying a number of scores
for the Celebration of Women Composers concert
with the New York Philharmonic last November.
I found several very distinguished composers who
stopped composing, who were writing works just
for chamber music or smaller groups, because
they didn't think there was any chance of getting
anything performed. Certainly my thing is opera.
But my thing is also music and theater, and anything that sharpens or develops any aspect of it
leads into new paths in a very natural evolution.
My passion in life is opera. I remember being
told when I was quite young that the real trick of
living was to find something you like to do best in
all the world and find someone else to pay you to
do it. And I love what I am doing.
I had my moment of truth when I was a student
and got offers to play violin with the Minneapolis
Symphony and several other orchestras, but I turned
them down because all my life I've loved both the
theater and music. (Reprinted by permission of
the author and Opera News.)

Maestra Caldwell has been a guest on the podium of

the Milwaukee Symphony Orchestra, when she conducted the
United States première of Thea Musgrave's Memento Vitae,
and of the Philadelphia, Pittsburgh, San Antonio, New Orleans, and American symphony orchestras.   In addition, she
has made numerous appearances in Europe and had an extended stay in China directing the Central Opera Company of
Peking.

      When Sarah Caldwell conducted the American Symphony
Orchestra, the critics raved.   John Rockwell reviewed the
program for the New York Times on December 23, 1974
(partial):

        OPERA: RICH SAMPLE OF 'WAR AND PEACE'

        Sarah Caldwell's presentation of extended excerpts
        from Prokofiev's opera War and Peace with the
        American Symphony Orchestra yesterday afternoon
        at Carnegie Hall was a triumph for all concerned.
            It does say something about New York's preten-
        sions as a musical capital that it got excerpts in
        concert form only after Miss Caldwell had presented
        the complete opera on stage in Boston (American
        premiere last May) and at the Wolf Trap Farm near
        Washington this summer.   And it says something
        more about this city that yesterday's event was
        Miss Caldwell's long delayed concert debut here.
            Whether War and Peace will catch on internation-
        ally as a repertory staple remains to be seen and
        concerts such as yesterday's can provide no answer.
        But what yesterday did reaffirm was that in this
        opera Prokofiev composed some of his grandest,
        most touching music, and that this city will be re-
        miss in its most obvious debts to 20th-century
        opera until we can see it staged, most logically by
        the Metropolitan Opera.
            Miss Caldwell presented about two hours' worth
        of the music, accounting for about half of the score.
        Her cuts can only be called brilliant: music from
        every scene except two--the introductory epitaph
        was also excluded--was offered, and the three miss-
        ing scenes were clearly the most extraneous.   The
        opera itself is overtly episodic in form and Proko-
        fiev made many suggested cuts.   Miss Caldwell's
        condensation (presented without intermission) flowed
        logically and naturally.   One's only regret might
        have been the near-total abolition of the character
        of Pierre (vestigial in the complete opera in any

case) and the absence of a chorus (although the
massed solo singers did surprisingly well in filling
in).

Presiding over it all (on a podium as bulwarked
and draped as the Rayesky Redoubt before the battle
of Borodino must have been) was Miss Caldwell.
Her feeling for the music was apparent in every
bar and she led a performance of compelling sweep
and sensitivity.   She is herself a compelling per-
sonage, of course.   No doubt Boston and the New
England area as a whole needs her, and no doubt
her extramusical gifts are as valuable as her purely
musical accomplishments.   But after yesterday's
effort, one can only hope she will appear again
here soon as a conductor, and often.   (Copyright
© 1974 by The New York Times Company. Reprinted
by permission.)

When Miss Caldwell guest-conducted the Indianapolis
Symphony Orchestra in 1976, the diversity of the program
she chose was a credit to her widely recognized musical versatility.   The program included Corelli's Christmas Concerto
for Two Violins, Cello and Organ, Tchaikovsky's Symphony
No. I (Winter Dreams) in G minor, and the professional
world première of Alec Wilder's Concerto for Tenor Saxophone and Chamber Orchestra.   The great jazz musician,
John Haley (Zoot) Sims on saxophone, the Indianapolis Symphony Orchestra, the composer, and the talented Caldwell
received a standing ovation for the rare musical treat which
fused the world of classical music and jazz.

Although Sarah Caldwell had staged two operas for
the New York City Opera she became part of opera history
on January 13, 1976 when she was selected as the first
woman to conduct the Metropolitan Opera.   She conducted
eleven performances of Verdi's La Traviata, with Beverly
Sills in the role of Violetta in some of the productions.
Harold C. Schonberg's review in the New York Times on
January 14, 1976 (partial):

> Miss Caldwell, it need not be stressed, has become
> America's newest culture hero.   In Boston she has
> her own opera company, where she stages and con-
> ducts.   Last night she was the first woman to ever
> conduct at the Metropolitan Opera, which admittedly
> has been a rather conservative organization since
> it opened in 1883.
> Miss Caldwell thus was the focus of attention.

Miss Sills is, after all, a known quantity here,
and she has previously sung Violetta at the New
York City Opera. When the conductor made her
appearance, many in the audience rose to greet
her. It may have been more than coincidence that
the greatest number of risers were women. There
is a nice cartoon idea here: all the women in the
audience standing to cheer Miss Caldwell, all the
men sitting glowering.

But that was not the way it happened. Everybody seemed to like her conducting, as well they
should. It was well-organized, it was brisk but
not pellmell in tempo, it was accurate in rhythm.
But now, after all, Miss Caldwell has had much
experience in opera conducting. La Traviata is not
the most severe test, but whatever problems it
poses were expertly handled by Miss Caldwell.

Above all Miss Caldwell stressed clarity. The
instrumental articulation in the accompaniment to
"De miei bollenti spiriti" was a case in point.
Not often have the figurations been so etched. Another characteristic was an avoidance of emotional
heaviness. Miss Caldwell demonstrated that she
felt the music--the drama of the last act was eloquent testimony--but she did not find it necessary
to carry on high. (Copyright © 1976 by The New
York Times Company. Reprinted by permission.)

Sarah Caldwell is a deeply serious and intensely sensitive musician. She stands as an idol to many aspiring
women conductors who have seen her efforts make the impossible happen. The sexual barrier has been broken, a
triumph not only for Miss Caldwell but for all women; another door has been opened. One must quickly add that Sarah
Caldwell considers herself a conductor who happens to be
female and there should be no relationship linked between
the two. Some writers equate strength with physical size,
and strength with the male; hence, it was a man's profession
to conduct, which is to control and command. Society plays
strange tricks at times and one must learn to take ignorance
in stride. There are many fine women conductors throughout the world who have been successful not because of physical size but because of intellectual capacity.

Daniel Webster reviewed the première of Be Glad
Then, America by John La Montaine, produced and directed
by Sarah Caldwell, for High Fidelity/Musical America in
June 1976:

UNIVERSITY PARK

Penn State: LaMontaine première

The Bicentennial is developing a catalogue of musical theater events to delight historians a century
hence.   Among the first and what will surely be
one of the showiest was John LaMontaine's opera,
Be Glad Then, America, premièred February 6
at Pennsylvania State University.   Using the mas-
sive resources of the University and director Sarah
Caldwell's theatrical wizardry, the piece became
a grand, grand pageant of the Revolution and an
interesting try at becoming an opera without the
usual operatic means.   The composer developed
a work of high literary quality, and Miss Caldwell
found the means of giving it theatrical presence.
The music, by comparison, was of less importance
and tended to magnify William Billings, whose
Chester brought down the curtain and whose Anthem
for Fast Day was sung after the scene of the Battle
of Lexington.   Using writings and speeches, poems
and songs of the time, LaMontaine sought a "non-
fiction" opera in a sense, it was a baroque opera,
with historical sweep and the appearance of mythic
figures--in this case Sam Adams, Thomas Paine,
Patrick Henry, and King George III.   The piece
had innocent charm.   Who could resist a work that
has the Boston Tea Party for the first act curtain
and colonials firing across the orchestra pit at
redcoats at Lexington?   And no one could resist
the fervor of the fresh-voiced chorus members who
were the central feature of the piece.   Raymond
Brown's chorus joined the action from the auditorium and, magically, from lighted lofts behind the
steel screening that covers the sides of the auditorium.   They never lost their precision and rapport with Miss Caldwell and the Pittsburgh Symphony in the pit.
    Miss Caldwell devised a production that crackled
with excitement.   Projections made transitions from
scene to scene fluid, and she almost managed to
make the repeal of the Stamp Act theatrical.   The
rustics swept up the aisles and across the stage
like the waves of history, and Donald Gramm,
David Lloyd, and Richard Lewis--the patriot, the
town crier, and the king--moved easily in this context declaiming their sung speeches.   Odetta, the

only woman in the solo group, sang her song movingly in what was the main lyrical achievement for
single voice. This patriotic pageant emerged as
a coup de theatre, a cheerful, sparkling exercise
that ended with a trademark of the irrepressible
director: fireworks. (Reprinted by permission
from High Fidelity/Musical America, June 1976.
All rights reserved.)

Another first for Sarah Caldwell appeared in the headlines of The Boston Globe on December 24, 1978--First and
Best Again this time Caldwell does it with a recording. The
article by Richard Dyer is reprinted with every detail relative to the recording of Gaetano Donizetti's Don Pasquale,
written in 1843, and available on Angel label, number SX-
3871.

Sarah Caldwell knows what attracts publicity, so
she has built a career on firsts--on premières, on
first revivals, on artists making their debuts in
important roles, and, although she prefers not to
make much of it, on being the first women to accomplish a number of things like conducting at the
Metropolitan Opera. She has built the most substantial part of her reputation not on firsts, however, but on bests; the most colorful part of her
reputation comes from the irregular ways she has
sometimes arrived at the best or from the times
she fell short of that goal.
    Her most recent accomplishment to reach us is
her recording of Donizetti's "Don Pasquale" (a
two-disc set on Angel) and it manages to be both
a first and a best. That is, this is the first studio
opera recording conducted by a woman (Eve Queler
has a couple of recordings made from tapes of live
Carnegie Hall performances) and Sarah Caldwell's
own first recording.
    It is also the best complete recording of "Don
Pasquale".
    The superiority of the new set comes partly
from its cast. Donald Gramm is simply the finest
Pasquale on records because he sings the role
rather than shouting and sputtering it, and in singing, through singing, he is able to create the kind
of ridiculous and sympathetic figure one reads about
in the text and hears in the music but seldom sees
in the theater or hears on records.
    Alfredo Kraus has probably sung Ernesto more

often than any man alive, and there is not a moment of vocal or interpretive uncertainty in his performance. The lean and pointed sound of his voice may not make the immediate impact on a single note that some other tenor voices do, but all Kraus has to do is link two or three notes to display his superiority as a vocal technician, as a musician, as an artist; there is no more elegant singer before the public.

The baritone Alan Titus has a fresh and appealing sound and something of his engaging manner comes across on records, but he is certainly not in Kraus' or Gramm's class when it comes to finish of style and communication of a personality not his own but of a character; he could certainly apply himself with benefit to those records of de Luca.

Beverly Sills probably should not be making records any more, since in recent years the significance and the delight of her performances have come to depend less and less on the way she actually sings; on this recording there are several sustained high notes that sliver and shatter like struck glass.

On the other hand, that observation could be made about nearly every Norina on records, and no other Norina on records brings to the role the amount of charm and wit, sensitivity and musicality and sheer knowhow of Sills. If she must proceed with caution through her aria and through the dreamy duet with Ernesto, there are other moments that suit her; she manages a couple of two-octave jumps to great effect, and the irresistible tune of the rondo-finale finds her singing with the clear-toned nimbleness and neatness of her best years.

But most of all this is Sarah Caldwell's recording. Any orchestra player you talk to will tell you that Caldwell is a stage director, not a conductor, but I don't know a stage director in the business who could get a performance of the "Don Pasquale" overture, say, out of the London Symphony Orchestra, like the one Caldwell secures here--headlong in its impetus at the beginning, full of the most delicate, delightful and witty inflections later on.

The playing is wonderful throughout, and even the simplest um-chug-chug-chug accompaniments, like that to Dr. Malatesta's aria, have lift and lilt and life; the dance meters do actually dance. Best of all, this set, unlike nine-tenths of the operatic records made today, sounds like a performance-- this cast, with the exception of the vastly experienced Kraus, had performed the opera in Boston in Caldwell's staging before the recording was made, so there is a sense of ensemble, and of ensemble theater, that is simply missing from most rival recordings of anything. The recorded sound is generally excellent, though one is occasionally aware that dials are being twirled in the service of flattering Sills; there are mercifully few "staging" effects, though the most prominent is also the most damaging--Kraus' voice lacks presence in the magical last-act serenade; his voice may indeed by supposed to float in from beyond the garden wall, but it should not sound as if it were coming from within the garden well. (Reprinted courtesy of The Boston Globe.)

In January 1981 the adventurous Sarah Caldwell directed Shakespeare's Macbeth at the Vivian Beaumont Theater at New York's Lincoln Center. The invitation was received from Richard Crinkly, producer of the theatrical season and a friend and supporter of Caldwell's for several seasons. Undaunted by publicity and the rhetoric of the press that it was impossible for an operatic impresario to direct a successful and inspiring production of a "straight play" (it had never been accomplished before), Caldwell welcomed the challenge and brought to fruition her own artistic interpretation of the great classic. There were mixed reviews following the performance but the daring Sarah Caldwell had indeed startled the establishment as well as those superstitious theater professionals who had labeled the Vivian Beaumont Theater a jinx. This was simply untrue; successful productions can become a reality at that theater.

The summer of 1981 found the invincible Caldwell in Peking, conducting The Central Opera Theater in five sold-out performances of Verdi's La Traviata in Chinese. This is the only professional opera company performing Western opera in China. The thunderous applause and standing ovations following each performance attested to the fact that once again Sarah Caldwell had made the impossible happen.

Discography

Gaetano Donizetti's Don Pasquale, Angel Label no. SX-3871.

POZZI ESCOT

Composer, Theorist

Pozzi Escot is a unique individual who in spirit reflects
twentieth-century Renaissance qualities in her life as a composer, scholar, writer, and teacher. All of her output is
based on a brilliantly intellectual perception of the universe
and the needs of humanity. To be anything less would negate
the patrician French Huguenot tradition of which she is justi-
fiably proud.

She was born in 1933 in Lima, Peru, the fifth of six
children of the eminent French bacteriologist Dr. M. Emm.
Pozzi-Escot, at that time a diplomat sent to help advance
Peru's technology and science. Her mother was of Moroccan
descent.

Escot has great admiration for her father who molded
all of his children to aspire to be in control of their lives,
live up to their lineage, and be contributors who would help
benefit mankind. He protected his family from unnecessary
and mundane trivia by designing a home enclosed by twelve-
foot walls with specific rooms and furnishings that would
stimulate their intellectual and physical growth. He method-
ically provided all the children with a fabulous education, beginning with tutors at a very young age. Today all six children are highly trained and respected in their chosen fields.

Pozzi Escot was a happy child; there were no emotional crises, since none were permitted. Her education was
extensive and demanding. She says, "It is extraordinary what
a child can be trained to study and learn." She was raised
speaking French, English, and Spanish. She attended the
American International School with students from all over the
world, where students were required to take numerous demanding courses and pass rigid examinations. Among other
courses in high school, Escot took five years of mathematics,

four of religion and philosophy, two years each of physics
and chemistry, botany, zoology, anatomy, psychology, and
logic.   With a smile Escot said, "This may sound colossal
and funny, but I also learned three years of bookkeeping,
typing, and stenography!   I was provided with enormous resources that have enriched my life and at the same time
provided me with the ability to do many things."

During this same period of time one of her tutors
helped to develop her musical skills and she began studying
with the well-known Belgian-born composer André Sas.   Her
training in solfège, harmony, counterpoint, and fugue was
extensive.   Equipped with the necessary skills, she began
writing compositions when she was in her early teens.

In 1953 Pozzi Escot came to the United States with a
scholarship from Reed College where Ernest Bloch had seen
some of her scores and was quite impressed.   Unfortunately,
Bloch became seriously ill before she arrived on campus
and she was unable to study with him.   A year later she
transferred to the Juilliard School where she studied with
William Bergsma and Vincent Persichetti.   Before Escot
graduated from Juilliard, her composition Little Symphony
(1953) was performed by the Peruvian National Symphony,
and in 1956, at the age of twenty-three, she was named
Laureate Composer of Peru.

After completing her studies at Juilliard she was the
recipient of a German Government Grant, which provided
her with four years of advanced study.   She did post graduate
study in composition and musicology at the Hochschule für
Musik und Darstellende Kunst Hamburg with the eminent Professor Philipp Jarnach.   Escot related her experiences of
studying with Jarnach and living in Germany:

> The only furniture in my room was a bed and a
> night table on which I studied, read, and composed.
> Since there was no piano, radio, or such in the
> room I memorized all the sounds--I hear every-
> thing as I write or read a score.
>   Professor Jarnach was rather an austere human
> being and absolutely fabulously endowed with a vast
> range of knowledge.   As often as we sat together
> and talked he never told me that my music was
> great.   He always said that I had an unbelievable
> intelligence and a fantastic talent, but as a student
> I looked forward to him saying that my piece was
> good or great.

Clemens Kalisher

POZZI ESCOT

When I wrote <u>Lamentus</u> in 1962 (after my return
from Germany and at the MacDowell Colony) I sent
Jarnach a copy of the score. It was the first composition using rather crude topological sets and the
new notation I had devised. He sent me a letter
and I long regret that I did not keep it. He wrote,
"Like my own teacher (Busoni) I can now tell you

that you are a master." For me those were magical words.

In 1961 Escot returned to America and with a private
grant lived in New York, writing and composing. In 1963 she
moved to Boston and in 1964 was appointed to the New England Conservatory of Music to teach theory and composition.

Music notation varies with different periods and cultures, according to Escot, and since there has never been
a universal system she developed her own--a system that
attempts to provide the musician with enough clues to facili-
tate reading and performance. She says,

> Ever since I was sixteen years old I had avoided
> dynamic markings. I hated to mar the notes with
> anything extra. I composed the notes and I felt
> that the notes were to carry (imbued in them) the
> dynamics, modes of attack, articulation, etc. I
> was already conscious of how impure, so to speak,
> our notation was. Eventually I worked out a sys-
> tem that many have found to be precise to a de-
> gree, unique and visually satisfactory.
>   One can control sound and most composers do.
> I control every sound and every single detail of
> my music when I write. I design topological sets
> that use specific set numbers. I use many sets
> simultaneously, one controlling each musical as-
> pect. All of the aspects [are] synchronized through
> the presence of these parallel sets.

The noted music-critic-composer Virgil Thomson said,
"I admire sincerely the work of Pozzi Escot and respect her
integrity as an artist. Actually, I esteem her as to me the
most interesting and original woman composer now function-
ing." Her music is delightfully refreshing, sensitive, and
extremely expressive. Unusual sounds, unfamiliar timbres,
new musical structures provide a musical treat for performers and listeners alike. For those music lovers who are
unable to attend a live performance of Pozzi Escot's works
there are three recordings now available: Delos number
25448, Spectrum numbers SR-128 and SR-234.

Since 1960 Pozzi Escot has written only on commission; however, there have been numerous awards over the
years. She has never turned down a commission but there
have been times when she found it necessary to postpone the
commission for a period of time due to other commitments.

Most of the commissions she has received have specified
the instrumentation.   It took three years to complete A
Trilogy (1962-1964) since most of her composing is done
during the summer when her teaching responsibilities are
fewer.   During her four years of study in Germany she was
deeply affected by the recent events of World War II.   A
Trilogy was written as a tribute to the 6,000,000 martyrs
of Treblinka, Dachau, Mauthausen, Buchenwald, Auschwitz,
and Belsen.

   Lamentus, Cristhos, and Visione constitute the three
sections of A Trilogy.   Lamentus, written in 1962 and commissioned by the Inter-American Festival of Music in Washington, D.C., was premièred at the International Festival of
Madrid in 1964.   The chamber piece is scored for soprano
(Escot wrote the text), two violins, two celli, piano, and
three percussion.   J. Espinos writing in the newspaper Madrid commented, "Lamentus of Pozzi Escot for soprano, instrumental ensemble and percussion constitutes a page of
marked dramatic character, creating a climax akin to the
best Italian verismo despite its contemporary form and language."   Cristhos, written in 1963 and dedicated to the composer Ralph Shapey and painter Vera Klement, was premièred
at the Composers' Forum, Donnell Library, New York City.
The piece was scored for three violins, alto flute, contrabassoon, and one percussion.   Eric Salzman commented in
the Herald Tribune: "Cristhos was quite another story.   Its
relatively few sustained notes are squared away in defined
planes but they define a musical and expressive space."
Visione, written in 1964, was commissioned by the Hartt
Chamber Players, Bert Turetzky, conductor.   It was premièred at Judson Hall, New York City, and is scored for
contrabass, flute-piccolo-alto flute, alto saxophone, and soprano (again Escot wrote the text).   Paul Turok wrote in the
New York Herald Tribune: "The most satisfying works of
the evening were those for larger ensemble, where there
was more variety of tone color.   These were Arnold Fran-
chetti's Settimino and Escot's Visione."   The time duration
for A Trilogy is forty minutes; score and parts are available
from Publication Contact International for Lamentus and Dorn
Publications, Inc. for Cristhos and Visione (see end of chapter for addresses).

   When Pozzi Escot was chosen as one of the ten American composers by the National Television of Belgrade, Yugoslavia in 1974, for a series of films in celebration of the
Bicentennial, Cristhos was used as the basis of the film Raz-
apeti.   The film won first prize and was presented at the
Prix Italia International Festival of Florence, Italy in 1974.

In 1963 Escot was one of two composers honored by
the Composers' Forum of New York in a concert that was
followed by a discussion, moderated by Milton Babbitt.   Both
Cristhos and two Groups of Differences for piano were then
performed.   Both groups were commissioned by the late
pianist Howard Lebow; the first was premièred by Robert
Henry in Hamburg, the second, by Howard Lebow at the
Donnell Library Composers' Forum.   Both Eric Salzman of
the New York Herald Tribune and Theodore Strongin of the
New York Times reviewed the program.   Of Differences Mr.
Salzman said, "Escot's Groups of piano pieces, entitled Differences, are built up out of an unyielding body of material
blocked out in stiff planes, rhythmic groupings and registers,
everything carefully elaborated and convincingly so."   Mr.
Strongin: "Escot also offered two Groups of Differences for
piano, both extremely well organized."

Pozzi Escot is always inspired to write music and
her standards and expectations are of the highest caliber in
all of the endeavors she undertakes, whether it is teaching,
writing, composing, or lecturing.   Her life, as well as her
music, is highly organized and meaningful for she wastes
no time or effort in areas that are inconsequential.   She has
not attended concerts, even of her own music, since the late
1960's.

She has no patience with those composers who would
sacrifice standards just to have their works performed.   It
is a corrupt game that is played by some people for the sake
of publicity or money.   There is no room in the world of
outstanding art for such games.   Escot also feels that there
are many chamber groups which start with good intentions
but suffer because they do not have necessary funds to support their programs.   In some cases they ally themselves
with certain cultures or groups to become better known or
just to receive more financial support.   Again it is a game,
and Pozzi Escot is critical of all who would compromise
their standards.

When Lamentus was premièred in Boston on October
28, 1968, Michael Steinberg for the Boston Globe, wrote:

> Lamentus is a scena for soprano with violins, cel-
> los, piano and percussion, set to a text put together
> by the composer from various sources.   Few of
> the words are, in a conventional sense, intelligible:
> real words and phrases are mixed with contrived
> ones and with cries on syllables like au and aue.
> The composer, however, wants the text to be thought

of not as composed of syllables, but of words which belong to laments. Lamentus with its violent contrasts and abruptions, is a composition of unusually expressive intensity, marked by demanding fresh and telling writing for voice and instruments.

She received a commission from the government of Venezuela to write an orchestral composition for the 400th anniversary of the city of Caracas. The première performance was given in May, 1966 by the National Symphony of Venezuela. Although the commission was for orchestra, Escot did not score for the instrumentation that one generally associates with a symphony orchestra. She explained her reasons for the choice of instruments which she used, "As a twentieth-century composer I feel that orchestras are obsolete for they represent the culture of a hundred years ago and they do not fulfill the needs of our own culture today." Sands, composed in 1965, is scored for thirty-six instruments: five saxophones, electrical guitar, four bass drums, seventeen violins, and nine basses. Just to read the instrumentation used in the score whets the musical appetite of performers as well as potential listeners. Her music is for today; new, exciting, vibrant--and this also describes the composer, Pozzi Escot.

In 1975 Pozzi Escot was chosen as one of the five outstanding twentieth-century women composers whose works, ranging from romantic to avant-garde, were performed by the New York Philharmonic Orchestra. The other composers were Grazyna Bacewicz, an outstanding Polish composer who died in 1969; Ruth Crawford (Seeger), a noted American composer who died at the age of fifty-two in 1953; Thea Musgrave, a native of Edinburgh, Scotland; and Lili Boulanger, young French composer, who died when she was only twenty-three. The Pension Fund Concert, co-sponsored by Ms. magazine, was conducted by Sarah Caldwell, the first woman orchestra conductor for such an occasion.

The concert was titled "A Celebration of Women Composers" and performed to a sell-out audience. Although Escot understands the women's movement and is supportive of the cause, she, as a French Huguenot of upperclass birth, never felt any difference between male and female since both are very important contributors in society.

There were numerous reviews of the concert. Andrew Porter, music critic of The New Yorker, wrote the following on November 24, 1975 of Escot's Sands: "Sands turned out

to be an arresting composition, as direct as some of Iannis
Xenakis' most formidable mathematical constructions.   As
Messiaen once observed of Xenakis 'Les calculs préalables
s'oublient complètement à l'audition.   Le résultat sonore est
une agitation délicatement poétique, ou violemment brutale.'"
Joseph McLellan of the Washington Post wrote: "Sands by
Pozzi Escot is a fascinating study in textural contrast and
interplay."

     Escot did not even know that the concert was being
planned (she does not read newspapers) or that her music
was being considered until she received a phone call asking
if the parts were available for use.   Since she never attends
concerts she was at Avery Fisher Hall at Lincoln Center only
because she had promised Sarah Caldwell that she would be
there.   She said, "I did not hear the concert but instead
went to the coffee shop and asked my friend, the composer
Robert Cogan, if he would be so kind as to let me know
when the performance was over by waving from the corridor.
When the piece was finished I went to the balcony and acknowledged the performance."   Sarah Caldwell, interviewed in
the Daily News of New York, had said:

> I wanted to find composers for the Philharmonic
> concert who had a face, whose music spoke with
> a distinctive voice.   This concert celebrates five
> women whose talent has been recognized and whose
> works have been performed elsewhere.   I was con-
> cerned that this program be of the highest musical
> quality.

Of Escot's work, she said, "Sands got me, and I am thrilled
to be conducting her work."

     In addition to those honors already mentioned, Escot
is recipient of the following awards and grants: Reemtsma
Foundation Grant; Salzburg Seminar in American Studies;
MacDowell Colony fellowships; Guest Composer, Tanglewood
Festival; Ford Foundation grant; Radcliffe Institute fellow-
ships; Carnegie-Mellon University Composers Forum; First
International Festival of Madrid; First International Festival
of the Avant-Garde in Rio de Janeiro; Inauguration of IRCAM
at G. Pompidou Center in France; Germany's Bielefeld Uni-
versity Center for Interdisciplinary Research International
Conference on Non-Linearity; and Outstanding Educator of
America.

     Pozzi Escot's latest commission is from the Massa-

chusetts State Council for the Arts and the Groton School of
Arts. Professor Earl Kim of Harvard University, Donald
Martino from Brandeis University, and Robert Cogan from
the New England Conservatory share the commission with
Escot to write three minute chamber pieces for youngsters.
She said, "I find it a very special and extraordinary com-
mission." She is working on a piece for three solo violins.
Eventually other schools will use the material written under
this commission and the music will be published and recorded.

In the past eighteen months she has received five commissions. Her music is avant-garde and rare. Musicians
and listeners consider it challenging, interesting, unique,
and original. She said, "My music is of now--today. It is
whatever I have done, whatever growth I have gone through
or am going through. It is my profession." Ildi Ivanji,
music director of Belgrade Radio-Television in Yugoslavia
has written, "This music is conscious of the time in which
it originates. It makes use of all the techniques known until
now. It makes use of all knowledge experienced until now
to build up new techniques. This is music which was born
in the twentieth century and carries twenty centuries of music."

Escot's contributions as a composer, researcher,
lecturer, and writer are enormous. Her intellectual ability
and consciousness is at a level that only a few people in the
world attain. Her life is highly organized and each day is
spent in a meaningful and productive manner. She recently
commented about the musical scene:

> This is a country I feel very much a part of. Yet,
> I detest what Americans do to other Americans.
> It is incredible to think that we have no permanent
> American conductors with our major orchestras.
> There is a mania to think that Europe, or other
> countries, better train conductors. Orchestras do
> not hire American conductors, therefore they do
> not play American music. We get a Japanese
> conductor, we hear Japanese music. Composers
> are not attracted to write symphonic music because
> so little of it is played. There is a big difference
> when you travel to other countries. There is a
> tacit law that you have to perform national music,
> since there is a tradition, respect, and pride for
> it. Moreover the orchestras are supported by the
> national governments.

Composer Robert Cogan and Pozzi Escot have co-authored two books: Sonic Design: The Nature of Sound and Music, published in 1976 and Sonic Design: Practice and Problems in 1981.

Written on a commission from the Ford Foundation and the Music Educators National Conference, they worked over ten years to complete the manuscript. The textbook has been praised both here and around the world. It is scheduled for various translations and there is every indication that it will become a classic in its field. Sonic Design: Practice and Problems is a workbook for students that supports and expands the textbook.

Pozzi Escot was a member of the faculty of theory and composition at the New England Conservatory from 1964 to 1967 and has been a member of the teaching staff at Wheaton College in Norton, Massachussetts since 1972. She presently holds the rank of associate professor. She said,

I like teaching very much and I have done it for many years. I am extremely happy at Wheaton College and they are very supportive of my teaching, work, and my whole ideal of accomplishing a relationship with the students. The students are intelligent and I find teaching them a fulfilling challenge. I think one must get involved in the future of education. This issue is very important to me. The realization that global relationships are vital to survival is absolutely crucial. I try to stress this globality and interdisciplinary processes in my teaching.

In the time left, Escot works in those areas that she considers important to the teaching profession, including lecturing and editing the journal Sonus. First published in the fall of 1980, Sonus, a journal of investigations into global musical possibilities, is quickly becoming a world journal. It now has a subscription which includes Europe, Australia, New Zealand, and Japan. A semi-annual, it is available by writing to Sonus, 24 Avon Hill, Cambridge, Massachusetts 02140. The statement of purpose of the journal:

Sonus aims to respond to the unique challenges of musical life characteristic of the last quarter of the 20th century--challenges of music stretched out to global extremities. There exists no forum whose

mission is to deal with the sum of music's specific
fragments (early music, new music, etc.) or its
separate disciplines (composition, history, etc.)
Sonus strives to provide a forum for all of the man-
ifold facets and disciplines of music, and these as
they relate to other fields such as anthropology,
linguistics, mathematics, philosophy, physics, politics, psychology, as well as to the other arts. We
invite all as authors or as readers in realizing the
potential that whole epochs and realms of human
sensitivity and ingenuity have placed within our
reach.

Escot has lectured extensively on a broad range of
topics which includes: Creativity, Five Remarkable French
Women, the Quality of Being, Math and Music, Non-Linearity
in Contemporary Music, Towards the New Concept of Non-
Linearity, and Analyses of Noted Contemporary Composers.
Her lectures have been highly acclaimed by the subject composers. Roger Sessions commented followed her lecture on
his music, "I found it a very exceptionally discerning study
of my music. The best introduction to my music that I
know. I am impressed by the very keen musicality, the
choice of points, the illustrations of these points. The lecture hits the nail on the head squarely in terms of my most
abiding musical preoccupations."

With Robert Cogan she gave a series of lectures in
Germany under contract from the United States Information
Agency. She has lectured at Brown University; Rhode Island
University; the University of Chicago; SUNY at Albany; Uni-
versity of Indiana; Ethnomusicological Society Meeting at
Wesleyan University; College Music Society Convention in San
Antonio, Texas; Holy Cross College; the Association of Uni-
versity Composers Annual Meeting at the University of Cin-
cinati; and elsewhere. Her writings have been published in
Perspectives of New Music, Music In the Americas, The
New York State Theory and Practice Journal, and Sonus. Of
her writing Elliott Carter said, "the best I have read from
the point of view of intelligent commentary. There is a
crying need for writing such as yours." Milton Babbitt wrote,
"I have already heard glowing accounts of the lecture, and
my own reading confirmed the enthusiasm."

The diversity of her accomplishments have received
plaudits from many noted world authorities, yet she seeks
no success. Pozzi Escot is a genius; she gives to the world
because she was given so much--that is her mission in life.

Published Compositions

1959 <u>Three Poems of Rilke</u> (959) 9' for string quartet and
     reciter
1960 <u>Three Movements for Violin and Piano</u> (960) 5'
1961 <u>Differences Group I</u> for piano (961) 5'
1962 <u>Lamentus</u> (962) 15' for soprano, 2 vl, 2 vc, piano,
     3 percussion
1963 <u>Differences Group II</u> for piano (963) 5'
1965 <u>Sands</u> (965) 12' for 5 sax, electrical guitar, 4 bass
     dr, 17 vl, 9 bass
1968 <u>Interra</u> (968) 13' for piano, tape music, spotlights, film
1970 <u>Ainu</u> (970) 11' for 20 solo singers (plexiglass)
1975 <u>Fergus Are</u> (975) 8' for organ (acetate sheets)
1978 <u>Ainu II</u> (978) 7' for solo singer (plexiglass)
1980 <u>Eure Pax</u> (980) 7' for solo violin (acetate sheets)
1980 <u>Interra II</u> (980) 6' for piano left hand (acetate sheets)
1981 <u>Missa Triste</u> (981) 6' for women's chorus

All published by Publication Contact International, 24 Avon
    Hill, Cambridge, MA 02140

1963 <u>Cristhos</u> 15' for 3 vl, alto fl, contrabassoon, 1 per-
     cussion
1964 <u>Visione</u> 10' for contrabass, fl, pic, alto fl, alto sax,
     soprano, reciter with microphone, 1 percussion
1981 <u>Pluies</u> 5' for solo alto saxophone

Above published by Dorn Publications, Inc. , 1492 Highland
    Avenue #4, Needham, MA 02192

1978 <u>Neyrac Lux</u> 8' for 3 guitars, 1 performer

Published by Rocky Productions, 53 Ash St. , Townsend, MA
    01469

Discography

<u>Neyrac Lux</u>, guitar (12-string, classical and electric), per-
     forming artist Harry Chalmers, New events: Boston
    Composers of The '70's, Spectrum No. SR-128.
<u>Eure Pax</u>, solo violin, performing artist Nancy Cirillo, New
     Events II, Spectrum No. SC-133.
<u>Fergus Are</u>, organ, performing artist Martha Folts, Delos
     No. DEL25448.

Addresses of Recording Companies

Spectrum, Division of UNI-PRO Recordings Inc. , Harriman, New York 10926.

Delos Records Inc. , 855 Via de la Paz, Pacific Palisades, California 90272.

VIVIAN FINE

Composer, Performing Artist, Teacher

Uniquely distinctive among twentieth-century serious composers, Vivian Fine's artistic freedom and inspiration has
placed her solidly with the leaders of American contemporary
music. Her copious imagination began to emerge as a young
child, and at the mere age of five, she was recipient of the
first of many honors, a scholarship to begin piano studies at
the Chicago Musical College.

The daughter of Rose (Finder) and David Fine, she
was born in Chicago in 1913. A child prodigy, she later became a pupil of Djane Lavoie-Herz, who had studied with
Scriabin. Under her guidance the young girl studied a huge
volume of works for the piano that would in time inform her
artistic investigation. It was her mother Rose who influenced
the direction of her artistic life. She said,

> She was devoted to me and knew that I needed good
> teachers. Even though she had no training in the
> arts, she found these teachers for me. My mother
> was intensely interested in my development, and a
> parent plays an important role in a child's educa-
> tion. My mother was an immigrant and had to go
> to work as a very young person; she had no formal
> training in music but she was musical, and she
> provided me with the encouragement and training
> out of her own instincts--nobody told her.

Vivian Fine studied piano with Abby Whiteside in New
York, composition and harmony with Ruth Crawford (Seeger)
in Chicago and with Roger Sessions in New York. At the
age of thirteen she became Ruth Crawford's student and spent
the next four years of her impressionable youth with this
famous composer-teacher. Fine said,

Alex Brown

VIVIAN FINE

She encouraged me to write a piece of music, since
I had written for the piano--she liked the piece and
of course I liked it too. This was to be the beginning of my career as a composer. Of course having her as my role model was a great influence--
although in those days we didn't think in those terms.

But having as a teacher a person who was in the forefront of composing contemporary American music had a great influence on me as a composer. I would give Ruth Crawford (Seeger) principal credit for making me realize I had creative talent. She did not try to influence me to be a composer but she had the ability to impart and encourage the individual in personal growth.

At the age of eighteen Vivian Fine went to New York to begin her career. An excellent pianist, she could have had a career on the concert stage. She played brilliantly and beautifully, using her pianistic abilities to première new music in New York, including music of Carlos Chavez, Ruth Crawford (Seeger), Paul Hindemith, and Ives for the League of Composers, International Society for Contemporary Music, and other organizations. She became the piano accompanist for Doris Humphrey and Charles Weidman in dance recitals, studied composition with Roger Sessions, and orchestration with George Szell. This would also be the beginning of her work with various organizations for the propagation of modern music.

Vivian Fine composes for a variety of mediums including chamber, choral, orchestral, and modern dance. Her national acclaim as a composer for dance took place very early in her career. She said, "At eighteen years I earned my living as a dance accompanist and very soon realized I had a knack for that type of work and was offered many jobs. Then people began to ask me to write music for dance--I worked with all major dancers and took part in an historic period of American dance--I am happy with that, although it is not my principal work."

In 1937 she wrote her first large ballet, The Race of Life, for Doris Humphrey. Originally scored for piano at the première, it was performed some twenty years later with orchestra and the Juilliard Dance Theater, with Frederick Prausnitz conducting.

The composer eloquently relates her feelings as a writer of music for dance in an article published in Dance Perspectives, Volume 16, 1963 (partial):

Music and dance are two languages with a common source. They come out of the same stuff--the same stuff, as Shakespeare wrote, "as dreams are made on." Before an idea finds its way into form, there is the as yet unlabelled sensation--a sensation that one recognizes as the modest herald of a new work. Out of this basic sensation of movement the dancer creates choreography; the composer, music.

What is different in composing for dance is that the initial stimulus is not connected with a sonorous image. In writing for dance, the musical ideas are stimulated by ideas the dancer has conceived. These may be ideas of a dramatic nature or, as in the earlier works I wrote, the completed choreography. In either case, the body sensations that are the response to an idea (though one is hardly aware of them) are similar for dancer and musician.

This underlying sense of movement is the first expression of a feeling we carry with us always, but keep concealed from our awareness: the feeling of the inexorability of the time-flow. The relationship between music and dance might be called dialogue concerning silence. It is the silence that is the silent motion of the flow of time. We measure the passage of time by the motion of the stars: we see in this side-real movement a demarcation of the measureless universe, without beginning or end. Within their ordered measures are framed a portion of unending time and space.

Each art tells of this mystery with its own signs. Music speaks through symbols we hear; dance speaks to the eye. So the two sisters--one having no voice --can both speak at once, each telling us of their mysterious mother.

Evoked by imagery outside the contained world of sound the musician inhabits, music for dance has a special character. This can perhaps be described negatively as music not having the same intensity of articulation required for "absolute" music. Music for dance can "stand alone," but it still relies to some degree on the choreographic and dramatic ideas that inspired it. The composer articulates the dimensions of his sonorous universe through the musical resources at his command. His burden is less when the movements of dance articulate forms in space.

In modern dance it is not the metrical aspects of rhythm that unite dance and music. In the free interweaving of movement and sound there is a link to deeper rhythm. Free of superficial points of rhythmic contact, music and dance create patterns of inter-relatedness that enhance the total work.

Roger Sessions has said: "Music is a gesture."
In composing for dance one must have a willingness to absorb from the dancer his basic gesture
and to inflect the musical gesture with the imagery
of dance and theatre.

The above spectulations are strictly after the
fact. I have written for dance intuitively, without
theorizing. The problems were no different from
those of composing any other music--except that
the feeling of 'rightness' was related to something
outside, rather than to the conscience regulating
the sonorous world of the composer. (Copyright
© 1963 by Dance Perspectives Foundation, used with
permission.)

Vivian Fine composed five major works for dance
early in her career. The Race of Life was intended to be
humorous, for she said,

The problem was to capture the kind of comedy involved, the particular area of the human dilemma.
In addition, it was based on drawings by James
Thurber, had a story and definite characters. I
had to discover the serious musical stance from
which humor could be achieved.

I wrote the music for this dance after the dance
was composed, although not after the entire work
was finished. I would write a section as each new
part of the dance was completed. In composing
for choreography, there is the problem of developing a musical structure and continuity. I was able
to do this by not composing for individual movements or patterns, but by sensing the impulse that
moved the dancer.

Wallingford Riegger considered The Race of Life as
brilliantly scored for small orchestra and revealing an astonishing versatility. He suggested that Fine do as he had
done with a previously scored dance composition--rework the
material for a concert number.

Vivian Fine did this later in the year when she scored
The Race of Life for 2-0-2-1, 2-2-2-1 for tympani, percussion, piano, and strings. The orchestra version is some
twenty minutes in duration and published by Catamount.

The success of this ballet left such a strong impression with the talented Doris Humphrey that some twenty years

later she wrote the following article for the American Composers Alliance Bulletin, Volume VIII, No. I, 1958.   The
value of this article is important since it reflects the growth
and expression of American dance during an important era
in this country.

MUSIC FOR AN AMERICAN DANCE

Vivian Fine wrote a score for me some twenty
years ago: --it was quite a score and quite an experience.   She was a true collaborator in a field,
that of composing for dance, which is so different
from other kinds of program music that it calls
for unique qualifications.   The dance is an art which,
though a part of the theater, has its roots in physical and psychological sources which differ from
those of the opera, the film or the musical to a
marked degree.   All these forms, except program-
matic concert music, depend on the word for explicit meaning; consequently music does not bear
the full burden of the dramatic idea.   Not so in
dance, where words are rarely used and movements
and music carry all the responsibility of communication.   This means, among other things, that the
theme must be suitable and intelligible in these
terms--not everything can be danced to.   So the
first task in a collaboration of this sort is the
choice of the idea by the choreographer.
My enthusiasm for James Thurber led me to
select one of his series of drawings, at the time
brand new, concerning the adventures of a middle
class American family called The Race of Life.
Vivian and I both loved his dry and improbable
humor, and the episodes met all the requirements
for dance: plenty of action, and had subject matter
with a challenging range; The Beautiful Stranger,
Night Creatures, Indians, Spring Song, culminating
in the achievement of the goal, a mountain top
covered with the heart's desire--gold, jewels and
money.
Vivian Fine met all these moods with imagination and a full awareness of their Thurberian gau-
cherie and humor.   Even his Beautiful Stranger is
no chic adolescent, but plainly bears the germ of
the full-grown Thurber female, rather hard, aggres-
sive and blowzy.   To catch such a conception in
music was a very difficult feat.   She treated the
Indians with a very funny version of an authentic

pseudo-Indian popular song.   Both in the music and
the dance our Indians were phony, gaudy cigar-
store fixtures.   Night Creatures was handled with
grotesquerie, but still with a dreamlike delicacy.
At this point she added to the all-piano score a
Flextotone whose sliding eeriness exactly met the
requirements of the weird scene.   In its entirety
it was a notable score--bright, humorous, expert.
     Among many other pieces written for the dance
by Vivian Fine, Opus 51, composed for Charles
Weidman, stands out, but in all her undertakings
in the dance field she has an uncanny sense of what
to choose as sound and that sine qua non for dance
composers, a complete understanding of body rhythms and dramatic timing.

     Perhaps The Race of Life can be best projected by
John Martin's review published in the New York Times on
January 25, 1938.   Too lengthy to reprint in its entirety,
the following excerpts are offered:

HILARITY FEATURE OF DANCE RECITAL

Audience Sees Doris Humphrey And Charles
Weidman In Program Of Novelty

Both Offer New Works

When an audience leaves a dance recital laughing
gayly, as Doris Humphrey's and Charles Weidman's
audience left the Guild Theatre last night, that is
news.   As if deliberately to prove that the modern
dance is not necessarily devoted to solemnity, both
dances ostentatiously snubbed the tragic muse and
went in for unabashed hilarity.   Miss Humphrey
turned wholeheartedly to Thurber and farce in her
new work, Race of Life.
     Miss Humphrey's Race of Life is pure nonsense
based on the drawings and story by James Thurber
of a family bent on winning wealth.   With 'Excelsior'
written on the banner, they encounter Indians, mar-
ital infidelity and bad dreams, but eventually scale
the heights and gain apparently fabulous amounts of
gold.   As Dorothy Parker's program notes say
'Anything may be read into it or left out of it without making a great deal of difference. '
     Nor does Vivian Fine's musical settings miss a
single opportunity to be as disarmingly silly as the
stage doings.   Certainly Miss Humphrey as a char-

acter actress and farceuse has been keeping something from us all these years.

The audience was a very large one and mani-
fested its pleasure in no uncertain terms. (Copyright © 1938 by The New York Times Company. Reprinted by permission.)

During the decade of the 1930's Vivian Fine was to
compose her greatest volume of music for dance, including
Opus 51 for Charles Weidman, and Tragic Exodus and They
Too Are Exiles for Hanya Holm. Her compositions for Martha
Graham were done some twenty years later and will be in-
cluded later in the chapter.

Yet during the same period Fine's art song compositions caused concern and comments, especially in William
Treat Upton's Aspects of the Modern Art-Song. Her Comfort
to a Youth that had Lost his Love, scored for voice, violin,
and viola, written in 1933, was the source of his rage, since
she had shattered the ancient mold to fragments and he felt
the song emerged as a purely instrumental form. He did
concede, however, that as a piece of purely abstract atonal
writing this composition had certain individual attractiveness.
I asked Vivian Fine some forty years later if she considered
herself a revolutionary composer as had been stated in some
articles. She smiled and said, "There have been many
changes in my compositions; originally it was atonal, then I
developed a more tonal style, and now my idiom is free atonality but quite different from the earlier style. I certainly
don't feel revolutionary; I hope my music is still fresh and
interesting."

The listener will readily agree that Vivian Fine's
music utilizes twentieth-century techniques that are consistent
and inspiring. We live in a jet age, have micro-wave cook-
ing, and listen on the most sophisticated electronic equipment
ever experienced by humans. Should not the arts reflect a
freshness and vitality comparable to the age in which we live?
Vivian Fine represents contemporary musicmaking, winning
the admiration of musicians, performers, and listeners both
in America and abroad.

It has forever been true that there is strength in numbers and organization; thus in 1937 some forty-eight American
composers met in New York for the purpose of promoting the
cause of modern music. The American Composers Alliance,
born as the result of this meeting, included such pioneers as
Aaron Copland, Wallingford Reigger, William Schuman, Roy

Harris, Marion Bauer, Roger Sessions, Virgil Thomson, and
Vivian Fine. Fine said, "There was no organization for
serious composers, and this group became a type of a union
to establish and collect fees and discuss common interests of
the composers." Vivian Fine was active in the group for
many years, holding the office of vice-president for several
terms.

Since 1972 Broadcast Music, Inc. has acted as American Composers Alliance performance royalty collection agency
and all members belong to BMI. ACA functions as a complete
service organization for its members, many of whom do not
have an active relationship with a commercial publisher.
American Composers Edition, Inc. , the publishing division,
offers over 5,000 compositions of all styles and instrumenta-
tions in facsimile editions, making available for sale or rental
pieces that other publishers, who print in quantity, cannot
afford to handle. Except for the Special Editions series, all
music is printed to order on ACA's own ozalid process equipment and listed by category in six catalogues.

In 1954 ACA invested two-thirds of the seed money
needed to found a recording company that would serve the
needs of all contemporary composers. Composers Recording,
Inc. has since become the oldest and largest record company
in the world specializing in new music.

The most recent innovative step taken by ACA was to
help found an orchestra of sixty players with the purpose of
performing American symphonic music. The orchestra is an
independent, non-profit organization that gives three concerts
annually at Alice Tully Hall.

It was important to establish an organization of this
nature to recognize the creative talents of its members and
accord them respect in the concert halls and significant financial remuneration as well.

From 1931 Vivian Fine was active as a performer of
contemporary piano music for the League of Composers, the
International Society of Composers and Musicians, and the
Pan American Association of Composers. It was through her
talent and inexhaustible energy as a soloist in modern works
that many young composers were afforded premières of their
works. In addition she was a lecture-recitalist at many universities, including Notre Dame, Wisconsin at Oshkosh, Bard
College, and William and Mary.

Composer Fine and Benjamin Karp were married in
1935.   Their two daughters are musically inclined.   Nina is
pursuing a career as a singer and actress, and Margaret is
a fine pianist and singer, although she has not chosen a professional career in the field.

In addition to her work as a performer and composer,
Fine has pursued an active life in academia with appointments
at New York University in piano, Juilliard School of Music in
literature and materials, New York State University at Pots-
dam in composition, Connecticut College School of Dance
in composition for dance, and since 1964, at Bennington College in piano and composition.

Vivian Fine has received numerous awards and commissions including: Dollard Award, Ford Foundation Award
in Humanities, Yaddo Award, Wykeham Rise commission (instead of a graduation speech, Fine composed a chamber work
for string trio, trumpet, and harp), National Endowment for
the Arts grantee, Woolley Foundation, Rothschild Foundation,
and numerous ASCAP Awards.

On May 23, 1979 Vivian Fine was the recipient of one
of the most prestigious music awards in the world: the
American Academy/National Institute of Arts and Letters.
Her name and contributions will forever remain among the
musical giants of the twentieth century.   The citation reads:

> To Vivian Fine, born in Chicago, Illinois, in 1913
> who is widely known for her exciting dance scores
> for Martha Graham, Hanya Holm, Charles Weid-
> man.   Her chamber music and dramatic works have
> intensity and depth, enlivened by wit and an un-
> usual sensitivity to the foibles of contemporary
> society.

In 1980 Vivian Fine was elected to membership in the
Academy/Institute of Arts and Letters.   This prestigious association is limited to a membership of 250 American painters, sculptors, architects, composers, and writers.   Nomin-
ations made by the members are first screened by the appropriate department--of art, music, or literature--then they
are voted on by the whole membership.   Also in 1980 she
composed Music for Flute, Oboe, and Cello (commissioned
by the Huntington Trio); and a work for piano, violin, and cello
(commissioned by Mirecourt Trio of Grinnell College, Iowa).
She received a Guggenheim Fellowship for music composition in
1980-81.   Composer Fine joined such notables as Betsy Jolas

of France and Barbara Kolb of the United States as one of
the three serious women composers recognized.   In addition
to the award, a recording will be issued by Composers Recordings Inc. of her Quartet for Brass (1978), commissioned
by the Metropolitan Brass Quartet, and Momenti (1978), piano
solo performed by Lionel Nowak.   Fine commented, "It was
a very prestigious award and I was delighted to receive it."

Vivian Fine was musical director of the Bethsabee de
Rothschild Foundation from 1955 to 1961.   Rothschild was for
many years the chief patron of Martha Graham.   In addition,
she had a small concert hall which was used to promote contemporary music.   The concerts sponsored by this Foundation
were an important part of the contemporary music scene.
Under the direction of Fine, the programs represented a
broad range of nationalities, the result of her careful planning.   Among the composers presented were: Luigi Dallapiccola, Roger Sessions, Leon Kirchner, and Edgard Varèse.

It is necessary to highlight Vivian Fine's composing
career because of the enormous quantity of work she has
written.   She said,

> I composed for years using the piano, but for the
> last twenty years I have not used it for composing.
> I think a lot about the idea of a particular composi-
> tion--yes--I hear it as I write it down and know
> exactly how it will sound.   Commissions and grants
> often determine what I compose and I enjoy that;
> it is not a restriction at all.   I like being asked
> to write things and find it challenging.

In 1956 Vivian Fine was commissioned by the Rothschild Foundation to write a stage work which she scored for
tenor and soprano soloists and chamber orchestra.   She
titled this work A Guide to the Life Expectancy of a Rose.
Wallingford Riegger, who wrote extensively about Fine's
music, considered this piece to be one of the most successful numbers in what he considered the third period of her
compositional expression marked by a return to atonality,
tempered occasionally by key impressions.

Vivian Fine found the idea for this work in the garden
supplement of the Sunday edition of the New York Times in
an article bearing the title, written by S. R. Tilley.   Premièred in 1956, the work was also performed on February
7, 1959, at the Composers' Forum, Donnell Library Auditorium in New York City, with Bethany Beardslee, soprano;

William McGrath, tenor; and Carlos Surinach, conductor.
The performance was reviewed by Jerome L. Blum for the
New York Times, February 9, 1959:

> An entertaining horticultural chamber-opera by
> Vivian Fine, A Guide to the Life Expectancy of a
> Rose dominated the Saturday evening Composers
> Forum Concert ... Some of its appeal came as a
> result of a colorful and imaginative staging, pre-
> viously unannounced, by Martha Graham and others.
> Any ineptitudes in the piece-it took its text from
> the garden page of the New York Times--would
> have been lost in this visual splash and in the com-
> pletely engaging performance by Bethany Beardslee,
> soprano, well abetted by Carlos Surinach, conductor,
> and William McGrath, tenor.

Her String Quartet written in 1957 was premièred at
Vassar College by the Claremont String Quartet. It was
later performed at the Composers' Forum by the same group
and reviewed for the New York Herald Tribune on February
9, 1959 by Jerome L. Blum:

> In these works she showed herself to be a composer
> with great control over her medium, with a sensi-
> tive and accurate ear, and possessing considerable
> imagination.   The string quartet especially was not
> only technically proficient but also strong and warm.

Composer Fine said, "My composing is constantly
undergoing different kinds of changes, I don't seem to be
locked into a particular idiom." Her music reflects this
comment, for indeed she combines an individual intensity with
an organized technique that is always emotional.

Interest was shown in her career by several eminent
twentieth-century musicians including Henry Cowell, Dane
Rudhyar, and Imre Weisshaus.   Henry Cowell wrote,

> When I first met Vivian Fine, she was a Chicago
> girl of seventeen, writing in the grimmest of disso-
> nant styles.   She had developed a technique for
> elimination of concord that gave her work an angu-
> lar, unladylike manner, which, however was quite
> consistent.   She had an extraordinary native gift,
> good conventional training, and the ability to apply
> known principles of writing a new media, which she
> handled logically and uncompromisingly.   In the

course of her development since those earlier times
there have been many superficial changes--disson-
ance has been tempered with consonance and the
form has become more all-embracing, but the inner
qualities are the same--native gift technique and a
rigid lack of compromise with anything less than
her very best.

Mr. Cowell's statement reflects the musical genius of a talented twentieth-century composer who some twenty years
later still continues to compose the most accomplished and
individualistic works that diffuse elements in a highly personal
style.

Alcestis (1960) for chamber orchestra was commissioned
and choreographed by Martha Graham. Premièred to raving
reviews in New York on April 29, 1960, the composer created a suite from the original ballet for orchestra in the
same year. It was recorded by the Imperial Philharmonic
Orchestra, conducted by William Strickland (Composers Recording Inc. number SRD 145).

Notes on Alcestis were written for Composers Recording by Don Jennings:

This work was commissioned by Martha Graham,
who created the title role. The story is simple
and will be familiar to any student of Bulfinch (or
Gluck). Alcestis has sacrificed herself to Thanatos (Death) in order that her husband, Admetus,
King of Thessaly, might attain immortality. While
the house of Admetus mourns her demise, Hercules
arrives. As the news of Alcestis' death has been
kept from him (for reasons best known to the per-
petuators of mythology), Hercules indulges in a
heroic, might we say Herculean, bout of feasting
and drinking. When he learns, by the careless
words of a servant, of her death, he engages mighty
Thanatos in combat. Victorious, he returns Alcestis to her husband and her people.
   The four sections of the dance are: 1. Alcestis
and Thanatos, II. The Revelling Hercules, III.
Battle between Hercules and Thanatos and IV. The
Dance of Triumphs and The Rescue of Alcestis.
Each movement is an attempt to depict the dramatic
and emotional qualities of the myth, and avoids
descriptive or representational writings. The orchestra consists of double winds, a piano, harp,
percussion and strings.

This recording is a must for any music lover's library. Included on the recording are: Toccata for Orchestra, by Louise Talma; A Short Piece for Orchestra, by Julia Perry; Deep Forest, by Mabel Daniels; and Spring Pastoral by Mary Howe. The five contemporary composers presented on the recording are excellent examples of sensitive twentieth-century talented creators.

It was during the 1960's that Vivian Fine began to conduct her own compositions. She said,

> I don't think of myself as a conductor because I am not really interested in that aspect. Henry Brant, my colleague at Bennington College, encouraged me to conduct my own compositions and I found I could get the results I wanted. I do know the music and if you know what you want musically, then you can get the results from the orchestra. The ideal situation is to work with technically expert players, and it is comparatively simple to conduct skilled players. I prefer a skilled conductor (he/she) to direct my music because this conductor has the necessary training at realizing the intention of the composer.

There have been only a few occasions that an entire program of a particular twentieth-century composer's music has been performed, and Vivian Fine was honored in this manner in 1973. Even more rare is a positive review of such a performance, and this was accorded to Fine in April 17, 1973 by Donal Henahan, writing for The New York Times:

MUSIC BY VIVIAN FINE PERFORMED AT FINCH

> A complete program of anybody's music can be too much, even if the anybody is a Bach or a Beethoven who has been unlucky enough to attract a mediocre performer's undivided attention. But a concert of Vivian Fine's compositions at Finch College Concert Hall on Sunday night proved all too short, for two good reasons: She writes elegant and inventive works, and Jan DeGaetani thinks highly enough of them to pour her remarkable talent unstintingly into them.
> Miss Fine conducted the first performance of her Missa Brevis (1972) for four cellos and taped voice--or voices, rather, for the expressive mezzo instrument of Miss DeGaetani was heard on multiple-

track, singing duets and trios with herself. The
10-part mass was full of melismatic slides, micro-
tones and other currently popular devices but it left an
impression of distant times and cool cathedrals.

The composer also gave the first performance
of her Concerto for Piano Strings and Percussion
(1972), in which she functioned as a one-woman band.
Although heavily in debt to Cowell, Ives and Cage,
the Concerto was absorbing in its aural sensitivity
and in its tongue-in-cheek manner (a parody, perhaps, but of whom?)

Miss Fine's careful ear and telling way of setting
a text could not have a more sympathetic interpreter
than Miss DeGaetani, who sang The Confession (1963)
and Two Neruda Poems (1971) with pinpoint intona-
tion and an equal concentration on sense and sen-
suousness. The Neruda songs made a delicious
pair, La tortuga crawling along in hushed beauty
and Oda al piano closing the concert with a witty
microdrama.

The singer silenced the pianist (Miss Fine) by
gently closing the lid, removing the music and,
finally, dropping the key covering. The final chord
was played woodenly but expressively by Miss Fine,
a marvelous straight-woman. (Copyright © 1973
by The New York Times Company. Reprinted by
permission.)

In 1976 Vivian Fine was commissioned by The Cooper
Union, funded by The National Endowment for the Arts, to
compose Meeting for Equal Rights 1866 for orchestra, chorus,
soloists, and narrator. Miss Fine used a setting of excerpts
from post-Civil war debates on women's suffrage. Many of
these debates took place at Cooper Union Forum, where the
première was performed on April 26, 1976 with The Oratorio
Society of New York, Lyndon Woodside, conductor. It was
performed a month later because of the fine reception it received at the première. Reviewed by Byron Belt, critic-at-
large for the Long Island Press on May 21, 1976:

ORATORIO'S BICENTENNIAL SALUTE WITTY AND
NOBLE

Last night's Alice Tully Hall concert by the Oratorio Society of New York featured a Salute to the
Bicentennial, including music both witty and noble,
rich in humor for both God and man.

Lyndon Woodside, the Oratorio Society's splendid
music director, selected four a cappella works by

America's first great composer, William Billings,
offered a second 'première' of a recent work by
Vivian Fine and concluded with Anton Bruckner's
Mass in E Minor.

Vivian Fine's Meeting for Equal Rights 1866
proved a stirring and timely piece devoted to the
unhappily still struggling cause of Equal Rights.
Taking a feminist viewpoint that is full of righteous
rage--which is understandable--and compassion--
which is more important--Meeting for Equal Rights
1866 provides the first current artistic statement
for women's rights other than literature.

While various painters, choreographers and others
in the performing arts have made spasmodic attempts to portray the inequity of society's treatment
of women, Vivian Fine has selected the writings
and spoken words of both men and women and set
them to music that augments and dramatizes the conflicts and hopes of countless generations.

Lyndon Woodside and the Oratorio Society had
given an April world première of Meeting for Equal
Rights 1866 in the historic setting of the Cooper
Union Great Hall.   On that occasion the scoring
was for full orchestra.   The conductor wished to
repeat Miss Fine's important work, and asked the
composer to re-score it for organ, percussion and
winds, which she did--with tremendous success.

Vivian Fine's cantata is an eclectic score which
manages to be obviously descriptive of textual matters (by a hint of Brahm "Lullaby" when Horace
Greeley's words implying that a women's place is
in the home appear,) or more subtle but equally
devastating by setting to the most insipid, weak
romantic dribble a male chorus contention that women
should only be "Obedient, meek, patient, forgiving,
gentle and loving."

The chaos of discordant words is captured by
multiple texts being shouted, recited and sung, with
instrumental shrieks from the organ and winds aside
vivid color.

The Vivian Fine work, which we obviously found
impressive and moving, is a bit complicated for
general performance purposes.   It requires three
conductors (and they really seemed needed,) so
Woodside was assisted by Roberta Kosse and Joseph
Rescigno, a narrator and two vocal soloists as well
as mixed chorus, organ and other instruments.
(Reprinted with permission of Byron Belt Newhouse
Newspapers.)

When asked whether she felt women composers are discriminated against, Miss Fine thoughtfully and candidly offered the following personal statements:

> That is a ticklish question--I don't want to put myself in the position of saying--play my music because I am a woman--I don't want that. I usually put this question into a larger social context. Women are an inferior status in society as a whole-- that is--their salaries are lower, and the statistics are not good in this area. The general attitudes in society are not good toward women--just as there is racism in society there is sexism. There is no doubt these attitudes must have some effect on one's work as a woman but I do not want my music to be played because I am a woman. The societal problems are there--you can look at the statistics --but attitudes are more difficult to define--I don't find any offensive attitudes toward myself as a composer but I do find a great many sexist attitudes toward women in general. I certainly can't point to myself as one who has suffered--I have a fine career.

Vivian Fine is talented and demands of herself an artistic commitment to excellence that projects her as one of the century's leading serious composers. That she has the ability to share this talent with aspiring college students is to her credit--many artists can create but are unable or unwilling to assist another generation in developing potential resources for future artistic growth.

Fine says of Bennington College, "it has a unique program where everyone who studies music is involved in composing even if they don't plan to be a composer. We help the students to be aware of the materials of music--we do not teach theory separately. They immediately get the knack of how to use those materials themselves."

In 1978 composer Fine was awarded a National Endowment for the Arts grant and wrote a chamber opera for five singers and nine instruments. The work received its world première in San Francisco, on February 12, 1978, by the Port Costa Players, Alan Balter, conductor. Charles Shere reviewed the première for High Fidelity/Musical America in June 1978:

> Vivian Fine's opera The Women in the Garden drew capacity houses in its three first performances in

San Francisco and Oakland in February, and earned
standing ovations for its composer. Written with
the assistance of a grant from the National Endowment for the Arts and produced by the Port Costa
Players, a Bay Area new-chamber ensemble, the
production was handsomely staged, affectingly and
often brilliantly sung.

Described by Fine as "plotless" the opera places
Emily Dickinson, Isadora Duncan, Gertrude Stein,
and Virginia Woolf in a sort of Elysian garden; they
soliloquize, quoting their own writings, addressing
one another, often supporting and responding to one
another, they nonetheless pursue their individual
meditations. Despite the composer's statement, a
plot emerges: the drama of the individual woman's
response to the experience which shapes her sensibility. The result is of course, an opera of suggestion, of evocation, not dramatic gesture. The
libretto suggests extended recitative, and The Women
in the Garden is clearly in the operatic tradition of
Wagner and Debussy, not Verdi and Puccini.

In fact, the clearest musical influence on this
hour-long stage poem is Erik Satie's Socrate, that
gentle musical commentary on the death of Socrates.
Like Satie, Fine shapes the drama simply, setting
forth long extended sections with little internal articulation. The musical effect is cumulative; The
Women in the Garden does not pull the audience
along with a succession of contrasting numbers,
but convinces them with patient, logical, graceful
musical statement.

The tempos are generally slow walking-paced.
(More sensitive shading through small tempo fluctua-
tions would have helped the performances.) The
music is contrapuntal, the nine-man accompanying
orchestra stating lyrical melodies with tone implica-
tions in free juxtaposition. The opera alternates
between the sort of counterpoint and simpler melodic
statements with chordal accompaniment. In the
climatic section there is a sudden glimpse of hope,
expressed through Emily Dickinson's poem of faith
("The Sailor does not see the North--but knows the
Needle can"). The music becomes chordal expressing the joy of life and the will to live freely.
Throughout, rhythmic patterns proceed simply, now
falling on a common beat, not going their own ways,
following ideas in Messiaen and Ives to express the
mutual support of diverse voices.

The performance was extremely well realized.

Vicky Van Dewark took extended coloratura Isadora
Duncan with great clarity and assurance even in
the moving rage over her dead child.   Susan Rode
Morris alternated between intelligent reflection and
brittle insouciance as Virginia Woolf.   Anna Cain
Dudley sang with her usual richness, accuracy, and
tonal warmth as Emily Dickinson, perhaps the key
ensemble role, and Barbara Baker made a lyrically
meditative Gertrude Stein, John Duykers was the
fifth character, the Tenor who alternates among
all the necessary male roles in this quintessentially
feminine work.   Susan Paigen's set and lighting off-
set the somewhat schematic stage direction of Tony
Arn, and Alan Balter's conducting, while stiff, was
accurate and sympathetic. (Reprinted by permission
of High Fidelity/Musical America.)

Vivian Fine has generated a productive flow of creative
energy for many years.   She said, "In spite of all the changes
my music has gone through, I think my approach to music
has always been humanistic--human feelings are very important to me.   I am also tremendously interested in the structure and the intellectual aspects of music but the music must
convey a human message."

When one listens to or performs Vivian Fine's music
he/she is immediately aware of the freshness and freedom
from the strictures of the academy.   In this house of twentieth-century music there are many mansions; the architec-
ture varies as do the results; yet this has been true for cen-
turies--creativity can never be stifled.

I listen to Vivian Fine's music in a state of sustained
excitment because it offers to me a new way of hearing that
has placed her in the forefront of American contemporary
composers.

Selected list of compositions

(Unless otherwise indicated all are available from Catamount
Facsimile Edition, Box 245, Shaftsbury, Vermont 05262.)

1929   Solo for Oboe.
1930   Four Pieces for Two Flutes.
1930   Trio for Strings.
1931-   Four Polyphonic Piano Pieces.
1932

1933   Four Songs, voice and strings, published by New
           Music.
1937   The Race of Life, ballet, with piano score or orches-
           tra.
1938   Opus 51, ballet.
1939   Tragic Exodus, ballet.
1939   They Too Are Exiles, ballet.
1939   Prelude for String Quartet.
1939   Sonatina for Oboe and Piano.
1940   Three Pieces for Violin and Piano.
1938-   Four Elizabethan Songs.
1941
1940   Suite in E-flat, piano solo.
1939-   Five Preludes, piano solo.
1940
1944   Concertante for Piano and Orchestra.
1946   Capriccio for Oboe and String Trio.
1947   The Great Wall of China, voice, flute, cello and
           piano, published by Music Press.
1951   Divertimento for Cello and Percussion.
1952   Sinfonia and Fugato, piano solo, published by Laws-
           Gould.
1952   Sonata for Violin and Piano.
1953   Variations for Harp, published by Lyra Music.
1956   A Guide to the Life Expectancy of a Rose, soprano,
           tenor, chamber ensemble.
1957   String Quartet.
1959   Valedictions, mixed chorus, soprano, tenor, ten in-
           struments.
1960   Alcestis, for chamber orchestra.
1961   Duo for Flute and Viola, published by Carl Fischer.
1962   Morning, mixed chorus, narrator and organ.
1962   Fantasy for Cello and Piano.
1963   The Confessions, soprano, flute, string trio, piano.
1964   Melos, solo double bass.
1964   The Song of Persephone, solo viola.
1965   My Son, my Enemy, ballet.
1965   Concertino for Piano and Percussion Ensemble.
1966   Chamber Concerto for Cello and Six Instruments.
1966   Piano Pieces, four.
1967   My Sledge and Hammer Ly Reclined, mixed chorus
           and orchestra.
1969   Paean, brass ensemble, female choral ensemble, nar-
           rator-tenor.
1971   Sounds of the Nightingale, soprano, female choral
           ensemble, chamber orchestra.
1971   Two Neruda Poems, voice and piano.
1972   Missa Brevis, four cellos and taped voice.

1972	Concerto for Piano Strings and Percussion and One Performer.
1973	The Second Prophet-Bird, solo flute.
1975	Teisho, 8 solo singers or small chorus and string quartet.
1976	Meeting for Equal Rights 1866, orchestra, chorus, soloists and narrator.
1976	Romantic Ode, string orchestra with solo violin, viola and cello.
1976	Sonnets for Baritone and Orchestra.
1977	Three Buddhist Evocations, violin and piano.
1977	The Women in the Garden, chamber opera for 5 singers and 9 instruments.
1978	Quartet for Brass.
1978	Momenti, piano solo.
1979	For a Bust of Erik Satie, cantata in the form of a Short Mass, for soprano, mezzo soprano, narrator and six instruments.

Discography

(All produced by Composers Recording Inc. , 170 West 74th Street, New York, N.Y. 10023.)

Concertante For Piano and Orchestra, (1943-44) Reiko Honsho, Japan Philharmonic Orchestra, Akeo Watanabe, conductor, number 135 SD.

Alcestis, (1960) Imperial Philharmonic Orchestra, Tokyo, William Strickland, conductor, number 145 SRD.

Paean, (1969) Frank Baker, speaker; Estman Brass Ensemble; Bennington Choral Ensemble; Vivian Fine, conductor, number S 260.

Sinfonia and Fugato, (1952) piano solo, performed by Robert Helps, Two CRI, S 288.

Quartet for Brass, (1978) Ronald Anderson, Alan Cross, David Jolley, Larry Benc.

Momenti, (1978) Lionel Nowak, pianist.

KAY GARDNER

Composer/healer, Conductor of Women's Music, Performing Artist

Kay Gardner, the artist who dares to blaze a trail in a changing world, is clearly a complex woman. Her multiple talents place her solidly in the arena of twentieth-century artistic commitment as a composer/healer, conductor of women's music, and performer. Tranquillity has always been a consciously sought-after state of being, and composer/healer Kay Gardner's creative imagination is best described in her quote, "I write and improvise music. My music is meant to heal the soul." Trained as a classical flutist, she has in recent years devoted much of her energy to professional conducting. She said:

> The first time I ever saw a conductor was at the age of nine. I immediately decided I wanted to be one, but because it is the epitome of performance it has been denied women ... too powerful a position I suppose. Conducting, especially orchestral conducting, is the last stronghold of the musical patriarchy.

Born in Freeport, New York, in 1941, she was influenced by her parents Enez and Karl, both music lovers. They enjoyed light classical music, opera, musicals, and the comic operas of Gilbert and Sullivan. Her mother is an amateur pianist. Her father sings bass and admired the late Ezio Pinza. At the age of two, Kay Gardner began to play the piano. Her formal studies started at the age of four with a debut as a composer and performer at her first public recital. When she was eight, her parents encouraged her to study the most innocuous instrument that could be practiced in the house, and that was the flute. She said, "I took to it immediately, loved it, and the flute became my primary interest although I still continued with piano. I am

92

very pleased that my parents recognized my ability early and
gave me lessons with professional musicians from the first
lesson. "

The gift of a ukulele at the age of ten profoundly influenced her young creative mind, for with this instrument
she could compose, write the lyrics, and create extemporan-
eous songs. Not much later she took up guitar.

During her high school years she believed her destiny
would be orchestral conducting, although she had never seen
a female conduct an orchestra. She made her debut as student director of the band, since her rural school in Ohio did
not have an orchestra.

Kay Gardner matriculated at the University of Michi-
gan, enrolling in the instrumental music program with flute
as her major instrument. Recalling this experience, she
said,

> Not receiving any encouragement as the only woman
> in the instrumental education program, and although
> receiving an "A" in conducting class, I think my
> teacher Elizabeth Green realized from her own ex-
> perience as a female conductor that I would not be
> able to make a career in orchestral conducting and
> she did not encourage me. I lost heart and let my
> studies slip, and devoted all of my energy to per-
> forming and writing. Elizabeth, as one of the jud-
> ges at the 1978 and 1979 National Adult Conducting
> Competition, has done a turn-about and has been
> most encouraging in our correspondence.

The one exciting college experience for Kay Gardner
was writing and directing an original musical, the Junior
Girls' Play, an annual extra-curricular production. Breaking a long-established tradition of hiring a local union band
and doing a take-off on some existing musical play, the talented Kay Gardner composed the score for an original play.
Based on an Amazon society off the coast of Africa, the
plot dealt with the election of a new queen. All of the music
was composed and scored by her. Eventually she flunked
out of college, "not because I did not have passing grades,"
she said, "but the faculty felt that I was not living up to my
potential (which was true). I had given up. "

Kay Gardner married in 1960 but remained active as
a folk-singer in coffee houses in California for a number of

Alix Jeffry

KAY GARDNER

years.   She did research in women's folk music, although at
the time she did not really know why she was drawn to this
particular subject.   She played the flute in a women's chamber group, the Merced Chamber Ensemble (still in existence).
The musicianship was excellent, with many of the performers
holding master's degrees.   This, too, was a valuable experience.   At the age of twenty she made her professional
debut as flute soloist with the Merced Symphony Orchestra,
playing the Telemann Suite in A minor.

Following the birth of her two daughters she put her
music aside for several years and devoted all of her attention to their needs.   During this period of her life, the family spent time living near Minneapolis, Indianapolis, St.
Louis, and Norfolk, Virginia, where her husband held orchestral management positions.

In the late 1960's when Kay Gardner's children were
less demanding of her time and energy, her own need for
an avenue of expression became painfully apparent.   Her sensitive awareness of the few opportunities available to women

performers and/or conductors stimulated her effort to form
her own group. Through her initiative, the Norfolk Chamber
Consort in Norfolk, Virginia, was established. This sixteen-
piece instrumental group was dedicated to the purpose of performing little-heard chamber music from all periods. At
times the group performed on replicas of the instruments of
the period in which the music was composed, presenting the
programs as closely as possible to the original music. The
complete Scherzo-Musicale by Claudio Monterverdi for voices
and instruments, for example, was an exciting program performed on instruments borrowed from Colonial Williamsburg.

During this period of her life the musical dictum that
males were the best conductors weighed heavily on Kay Gardner's mind. Her duties with the Norfolk Chamber Consort
were as founder, music director, producer, flutist, public-
relations manager and, as Gilbert and Sullivan would say,
"Lord High Everything Else," but she never conducted the
group. She recalled, "I always hired men to conduct. I
was so put down from past experiences, and so unsure of
myself that I could not conduct, even though inside that was
what I wanted to do most of all." The experiences she had
encountered in the sexual caste system had a far-reaching
effect on her confidence that would take incredible courage
to overcome.

On the merit of her performances and duties with the
Consort and local symphony orchestras, despite her lack of
a college degree, she was hired by Norfolk State College and
Old Dominion University to teach flute and baroque ensemble.
She said of this experience, "I built the flute department at
Norfolk College from three students to fifteen; they came
from all over the state to study with me. We did some exciting pieces--Henry Brant's Angels and Devils, an excellent
work for multiple flutes. The teaching was inspiring to the
students as well as myself, and I found I matured and gained
confidence. At that time in that part of Virginia I was pretty
much the première flutist and when pianist Vladimir Ash-
kenazy asked me why I was in a small city like that and
why wasn't I out doing more--it turned by head."

At this stage of Kay Gardner's life she found her marriage souring because of her involvement in music, and her
desire to expand these activities. She had been flying to
New York to study flute with Samuel Baron. She called and
told him, "I am separating from my husband, and I want to
enroll in the college wherever you teach." Learning that he
was a professor at the State University of New York at Stony
Brook, she made arrangements to enroll there.

While studying at Stony Brook, she found the classes
and training a stimulating musical experience, especially as
a student of Samuel Baron.   A bonus was being in a master
class with Jean Pierre Rampal.   The lack of feminist consciousness, however, was appalling.   As a militant feminist,
she found exhilaration in escape from traditional/conventional
masculine-femine stereotypes, and dared to find a deep and
encouraging acceptance in unpopular places and philosophies.
During this period she frequently traveled to New York City,
where she found support and survival strength.   She said,
"I had just come from a marriage where I had been squelched,
and I wanted to use my creative energy in the women's
movement. "

The manifestation of the male and the subordination
of the female had reached a peak in Gardner's young life;
she had been robbed of her independence and composure.
Out of this vacuum of negativism and indignities would emerge
a new Kay Gardner, a stimulating person, musician, and
important contributor to new societal mores.   No passive
male ever offered major contributions for societal changes
nor will a passive female; both must be intelligent and assertive.

Kay Gardner was an exceptional student and, based
on her professional experience, was permitted to work on
a master's degree without the usual bachelors degree pre-
requisite.   A scholarship student, she proved her excellence,
graduating with a 3. 9 in a 4. 0 grade-point system.   In 1974
she was awarded her Master of Music Degree.   Her master's recital included works by three master composers:
Bach, Mozart, and Prokofiev, as well as works by three
women: Variations for Solo Flute by Ursula Mamlok, Quatro
for Piano and Flute by Daria Semegen, and Flute Quartet by
Netty Simons.   Her comments, "I used New York City freelance musicians in my recital and gave a very different and
exciting program.   I programmed the three contemporary
women composers as the result of my research as co-founder
of Women's Music Network, Inc. of New York, a service
organization for women in music. "

While a college student, Kay Gardner became a member of a radical feminist music group called Lavender Jane.
She played flute and wrote musical arrangements.   In 1973
the group released an album considered to be the first openly
lesbian LP and the first entirely produced by women with
Alix Dobkin, Kay Gardner, and Patches Attom called Lavender
Jane Loves Women (available through Ladyslipper Inc. , P. O.

3124, Durham, N.C. 27705, on Women's Wax Work label).
The cycle included serious and humorous songs and Alix
Dobkin's original lesbian compositions; The Women in Your
Life is You, Talking Lesbian, and View from Gay Head.

Following graduation she was uncertain as to the direction her career should take, so she attended the First National Women's Music Festival at Champaign-Urbana, Illinois.
In many ways this festival was a disappointment. There was
little if any feminist consciousness expressed in the songs
performed, little opportunity for other than amplified instruments, and since the emphasis was on vocal and folk music,
no opportunity for instrumentalists. As a result, she led a
takeover of the stage by seventy-five musicians who voiced
their complaints and then proceeded to "jam" for hours.

The festival also afforded Kay Gardner the opportunity
to perform on an open microphone as a vocalist and guitarist.
She performed some of the women's folk songs she had researched and sung years earlier as well as a few of her own
songs. After the festival she spent a period of five years in
the bosom of the women's community where, little by little,
her confidence returned. Of that experience she said, "I
removed myself from the patriarchal society. I wanted to
know what it would be like to be a creative woman. Since
most of my teachers had been male, I needed to remove myself totally from male influence and find out who I was as
a women and if indeed there was female form in music and
female consciousness in writing."

During these five years as separatist, Gardner became convinced that there is a female esthetic as long as
there is a sex role division in society, and a difference between male and female sensibilities. She developed what can
best be described as circular form which is related to the
rondo form although the climax, like women making love, is
more toward the center coming back thematically to where it
began again. Rondo is linear: ABACADADA etc. Circular
form is cyclical: ABACADACABA etc. During this period
she also became interested in the healing power of music,
and started to work with the engineer of the Lavender Jane
album, Marilyn Ries. It was also at this time that Kay
Gardner dropped out of the Lavender Jane group because it
became too political for her. She wanted to devote her energy
to her own music and to work with female forms and instrumentation indigenous to female composition. She began to
preach women's music as a separate and distinct entity which
often fell on deaf ears.

When Gardner met Laurel Wise, a vagabond musician
who had experienced women's music in a women's commune,
she finally found a sensitive musician who shared her be-
liefs.   Together they began to create music that was beautiful by communicating in a non-verbal and spiritual way.   These
two musicians met Jeriann Hilderley one evening in Green-
wich Village where she was performing on an all-women's
program.   Complete with a marimba, suspended cymbal, and
brass bells, she accompanied herself as she sang/chanted
her ritual piece, The House of Many Colors.   Said Gardner,

> We had never seen or heard anything like it.   Laurel
> and I sat transfixed.   Jeriann began singing in a
> strange, almost unpitched voice.   She stated a musi-
> cal theme, built on it, and in the middle was so
> into her expression that she cried out with a lengthy
> and almost other-worldly sound.   The only thing I
> could possibly compare it with was the woman's
> cry of intense orgasm or childbirth.   It was in-
> credible to hear.   The piece then returned to its
> opening mood.

Kay Gardner spent the following summer as a minstrel,
traveling throughout New England with Jeriann Hilderley.   They
performed their own music and listened for more women's
music.   At later concerts they were joined by Laurel Wise.
Of this experience Gardner says, "All concerts were unique
and exciting.   Our music healed and lifted spirits.   Our music made women move in spontaneous dances best described
as sensual, natural, and free.   Our music, women's music,
was new and ancient at the same time, an experience freeing
to the performers as well as to the audience."   That fall
they separated and Gardner went back to New York.

At age thirty-three when she began to compose again,
it was with relatively simple folk and oriental sounds.   As
she became more sure of her improvisatorial ability, she
was more and more freed, able to incorporate into her compositions large sections where she could improvise either on
voice or flute.   The compositions for her album Mooncircle
were written on guitar as she traveled throughout New England as a minstrel with Jeriann Hilderley.   These pieces
grew, and when she returned to New York to live with her
daughters, she wrote all the compositions on paper.   Encouraged by Marilyn Ries to produce an album, they co-
founded their own label, Wise Women Enterprises/Urana
Records.   They decided on the name Wise Women after the
song on the album of the same name.   The company is woman-

owned and operated and dedicated to the production of high quality records. Other functions of this company include record distribution and concert production. Address: Wise Women/Urana Records, 20 W. 22 Street, Room 612, N. Y., N. Y. 10010.

Mooncircles, released in 1975, is a hauntingly beautiful recording of eight compositions composed and performed by Kay Gardner on flute, guitar, autoharp, and vocals; Dora Short and Olga Gussow, violins; Nancy Uscher, viola; Martha Siegel, cello; Althea Waites, piano; Meg Christian, guitar; Juliana Smith, vocals; and Bethel Jackson, Jennifer Smith, and Angie Walls, percussion.

Kirsten Grimsted describes the album and reflects on women's music in a lengthy and well-documented article printed on the back of the album cover, Wise Women/Urana excerpts include:

> The sound of women's music with its subliminal power to inspire and change women's lives, values, consciousness has become one of life's daily necessities in feminist households and communities around the country. It is stunning to realize that only a few brief and breathless years ago this same sound was a rare and precious event experienced only by the fortunate few in Chicago or New Haven or wherever women musicians first began to forge the explosive union between their feminist values and their music.
> Women's music as a musical genre has also evolved steadily from its unpretentious beginnings when feminist content was simply infused into conventional popular music forms. While such lyrical innovations continue to inspire delight and raise consciousness, feminist musicians have begun the profound and far-reaching search for breakthroughs in musical form to correspond to the radical breakthroughs that are occurring daily in women's lives. The work of Kay Gardner on Mooncircles represents one of the first milestones in this search for modes of musical expression that can transform the elements of sound itself into an authentic vehicle for female content.
> While Mooncircles openly resonates with undisguised echoes of classical tradition, Gardner skillfully integrates these sounds with the materials, modes, instrumentation and rhythms of our obscure

female heritage which she has lovingly excavated.
"Composition is nothing more than sinking yourself totally into your environment, pulling out and
organizing the sounds that are already there.   I
have tried to immerse myself in all that women
have done to produce music based on what I've
found. "   Perhaps the best example of the result is
seen in Prayer to Aphrodite, a composition based
on a poem by Sappha [sic] and on the mixolydian
mode--an almost obsolete scale which, according
to Plutarch, Sappha invented.   The mixolydian mode
is built upon the fifth note of the traditional Western
scale which, again citing Plutarch, arouses the
passions.   Now what could possibly be more suitable
for a "prayer to Aphrodite composed in honor of
the great progenitress of lesbian love?"

For instrumentation Gardner has consulted Egyptian wall paintings and Greek urns and has found
that throughout the ages women have been depicted
as playing flutes, plucked instruments and small
percussion such as tambourines, hand drums and
finger cymbals.   In Prayer to Aphrodite Sappha's
favored instruments, the lyre and the flute, are
suggested by the use of pizzicato strings and alto
flute.

In Lunamuse throbbing rhythmic regularity is
combined with the gypsy-like wanderings of the
melody line to produce an overall musical sound
that can only be described as anciently new and
unmistakably female.   Images of primordial Amazon ancestors dancing in the moonlight irresistably
spring to mind.   This effect is reinforced by the
circular structure of the piece, a form inspired by
the work of Jeriann Hilderley who, with musician
Laurel Wise and composer Pauline Oliveros is one
of Gardner's "three muses. "

Mooncircles in its totality resonates with the ata-
vistic place in time of our origins, before the advent of patriarchy and patriarchal dichotomization;
the music itself was a vehicle for attaining ecstasy,
before being split into the sacred and the profane.
But this is above all not a nostalgic flight away
from the pain of reality but rather a journey into
awareness of the strength and wholeness in our
heritage, which fortifies women for the present
and gives impetus to our struggle to regain, come
what may, that lost wholeness in our future.

Transcending the image of woman imposed on us

by the patriarchy--woman as object, woman as
"other"--is the key to women's liberation. The
affirmation of female biology expressed in this
music makes the transcendence possible through
its message of reconcilation, healing of those ancient opposites, body and mind, within ourselves.
(Reprinted by permission of Kay Gardner.)

Mooncircles was reviewed throughout the entire United States,
with each music critic extolling its merits, profound musicality, and particular emphasis on the way it engages all
the senses, the flesh, the mind, the past, and the future.
When Kay Gardner produced this "feminine classic" in 1975,
she opened new doors to a long-needed musical awareness.
One will listen, perceive, and forever remember the compositions; Prayer to Aphrodite, Changing, Beautiful Friend,
Moon Flow, Wise Woman, Inner Mood I, Touching Souls,
Inner Mood II and Lunamuse. They are truly gems.

Reviewed for Grass Roots by Bob Newman in 1975:
"Mooncircles is the most exciting and important record to
come out of the feminist music circles. The production
is flawless ... might also be the best ... it's that good."

Reviewed for Women's News ... For a Change
New York, N.Y.: "A haunting, lyrical, sensual album
that at times is almost trance-inducing. Kay is a consummate musician whose melodic compositions evoke all
the earthiness and tenderness of a woman who loves her
music and plays it beautifully."

Gardner continued to explore new compositional avenues and found that she learned more from folksingers than
from standard composition repertoire--even though she was
able to play the most difficult avant-garde music on her flute
with excellent interpretation. She said,

I really feel my roots are in folk music and that
explains the simple melodies I write. I feel an
audience deserves to understand pieces; that music
should be accessible to the listener. Disjointed
music is a reflection of a very sick society. Women,
as healers, are obligated to write music that will help
heal the chaotic world situation. I do not write dissonant music unless I'm using it as a stress point.
My music is melodic and harmonic and I probably
would describe it as neo-Romantic. However, I

venture into more avant-garde as in <u>Atlantis Rising</u>.

For several years Kay Gardner has written a column for the magazine <u>Paid My Dues</u>, published quarterly by Calliope Publishing, Inc. The column is called "Colla Sinistra" and is devoted to the exploration of music as it applies to women and is designed to provoke controversy. The following is excerpted from Volume 11, No. 4, 1978:

> Colla Sinistra. A term used in piano literature meaning "to be played with the left hand."
> Occultists, mystics, and physical scientists of all times have recognized opposing forces--negative and positive, black and white, yin and yang, feminine and masculine, left and right, etc. Recognizing these polarities, the ancient wisdom teaches that one force balances out another to create a center, a focus. In other words, opposites must work together as a whole. What has happened in the past ten thousand years, since the advent of patriarchal thought, is that these opposites have been pitted against each other in a "versus" situation.
> The resulting theory was that when the patriarch assumed almost total world-wide power, the right or masculine side of the body was celebrated and the female, or left side, was not only diminished but virtually crippled by disuse. (Reprinted by permission of the author and publisher.)

Readers of Kay Gardner's thought-provoking columns are in general agreement that the material presented is long overdue in the musical establishment and that it serves as a catalyst for the understanding and presentation of woman as performer, composer, and conductor. Talented women musicians are finally receiving recognition for their contributions to the mainstream of twentieth-century music. Composer/healer Gardner incorporates healing into the realm of her music with a sound, defying categorization, that is innovative, haunting and mellifluous. She devoted a portion of her "Colla Sinistra" column in <u>Paid My Dues</u>, Volume III, no. 3, 1979, to the explanation and development of her talents as a composer:

> Last time, in answering a letter from a reader, I touched upon the theories of Pythagoras (600 B.C. Greece) and the chromatic scale. As I write this

I am traveling with sister musician Mojo, doing concerts all along the West Coast as well as doing "Music for Healing" workshops. I'd like to expand on the Pythagorean theories and show how we composers, healers, and songwriters can consciously use healing elements in the music we write and perform.

Music is made up of vibrations which travel through the air on sound waves. Rays, or colors, travel on wave lengths parallel to sound waves. Because of this parallel traveling, certain colors and tones are directly related, resulting in the "chroma"-tic scale.

Just as there are seven basic notes in the diatonic scale, so there are seven colors in the spectrum, and each tone with each color also corresponds with one of the seven chakras, our bodies' energy centers.

How does all of this relate to healing? If, for example, someone were to lie down and chant the note E for a long time, the vibrations would touch the solar plexus area in most cases and could be used to cure indigestion, ulcers, and other stomach-related ailments. To add to this, the color yellow, either visualized behind closed eyes or actually projected on a wall within sight, would make the healing potential even stronger. I used this tone as a vocal drone in "Lunamuse" (Mooncircles, Urana Records WWE ST80), and in performance I ask the audience to hum it for the length of the piece (nine minutes). I continue to get comments on the work's healing and centering powers.

This isn't just archaic theory. In a workshop in Astoria, Oregon, participants were asked to choose partners in order to get in touch with each others' auras (that electromagnetic field around our bodies). During the course of exploration, one set of partners came to me and hummed a note, the note they had discovered to affect their heart areas the most. "What note is it?" they asked. I found it on my flute. Sure enough, it was F. Only one incident of many.

Staying with the note F, if someone were suffering grief or had a heart ailment and needed healing energy sent to that area, it would make sense to put the person in a room where green was the focal color (plants, colored glass, or green walls) and have that person chant and/or hear the tone F,

or a piece of music with an F tonic--F major if
the heart area needed to be more active, F minor
if the heart area needed to be quieted.   So it would
be with the other tones and their color and chakra
relationships.

Many hues fall between the seven colors of the
spectrum.   These are related to the half tones of
the musical scale (and quarter tones too; etc.) as
well as to the physical areas between chakras.

Esoteric teachers tell us that with evolution of
spiritual consciousness, our vibrational sensitivity
has climbed.   Humanity began with very low tonal
consciousness and has evolved in octaves through
the ages to the octave I have illustrated.   Human
consciousness is now said to be close to the top
of that octave; for example, the ultraviolet ray has
only recently been "discovered."   Coincidentally,
the founding of the planet Uranus, which is related
to violet, has issued in the Age of Aquarius.   (Reprinted by permission of the author and publisher.)

When Kay Gardner's second album Emerging was released by Wise Women/Urana Record label in October 1978
it was greeted with instant success, projecting her as one
of the twentieth-century's leading music personalities who incorporates healing into the realm of her art.   It was an
artistic triumph with eight musically and intellectually stimulating compositions.   It includes Atlantis Rising, which she
believes is her strongest work in the avant-garde electronic
idiom.   Other pieces include: Crystal Bells, performed by
Gardner on flute; Susan Hansen, violin; Martha Siegal, cello;
Janice D'Amico, guitar and lute; a combined improvisational
and compositional work, Romance; Rhapsody; Mermaids;
Cauldron of Cerridwyn; and Anagram.   Althea Waite on piano,
Mojo on flute and alto flute, Sarah Cunningham on viola da
gamba, and Root on a baroque violin complete the ensemble
with a beautiful and absolutely marvelous performance.   Special credit must be reserved for sound engineer Marilyn Ries
for her artistic handling of three of the compositions which
combine natural and electronic sounds into exquisite and
exotic tonal combinations.

Susan Wilson writing for The Boston Globe in October,
1978 reviewed Kay Gardner's Emerging:

Master flutist/composer Kay Gardner has never
been easy to comprehend.   Like Keith Jarret, Gardner utilizes a stream of consciousness style in her

music. Unlike Jarret, Gardner generally has a
socio-political musical statement to play. "Emerging" is the second of Gardner's albums on her own
Urana label. While "Mooncircles" (1975) was simple and soothing, the new release is a complex
and extraordinary exploration--women's music at
its most avant-garde. The core of Gardner's current thought is the renaissance of women's culture
and subsequent emergence into the Age of Woman.
Classical Renaissance instruments and voices har-
monize and galvanize on the disc's introductory
side. Yet musical strains of pain, discord, and
growth are interspersed throughout--and are integrated with intricately timed natural and unnatural
wind and sea sounds that dominate later cuts. Gardner and her supporting instrumentalists deserve
praise for their innovative interpretations and improvisations. Yet the record is even more the
masterpiece of sound engineer Marilyn Ries, whose
technical manipulations have created an arctic,
eerie, and delicately disturbing aura, culminating
in the album's final and finest piece, "Atlantis
Rising." (Reprinted courtesy of The Boston Globe.)

Gardner's former teacher of flute, Professor Samuel
Baron of the Department of Music, State University of New
York at Stony Brook on Long Island, writes:

Kay Gardner is a highly gifted musician of enormous energy and dedication. I know her work as
a flutist best, for she did her graduate work here
at Stony Brook in flute. She was outstandingly
good.
But flute playing is only a small part of the
musical world she inhabits. Her compositions are
extremely original and personal. She eschews
highly technical procedures in favor of direct and
simple expressions. On close examination her
works are, in fact, not so simple but her commitment to a folk-like esthetic shapes her output in
this mold. Her music repays careful listening.
I can attest to one point about Kay Gardner's
conducting: her personality is galvanizing. She
has a true "green thumb" for getting people to
play, to play together, to adopt a specific style
and interpretation for a specific performance. Her
career in this field should unfold in a very satisfying way.

Kay Gardner decided in the fall of 1977 (when her children went to live with their father) that she would pursue her dream of conducting professionally. She went to Denver, Colorado, to apprentice with Maestra Antonia Brico, one of the world's first women conductors who was recognized as early as the 1930's. Gardner describes Brico's contribution to her career as a professional conductor: "Antonia Brico has been a strong influence on my conducting; she took me back to the basics of music, teaching me solid beat patterns, impressive and strong first beats, ear training, and score reading; and that was most important."

Gardner was so frustrated in 1974 at the first women's music festival (because as an instrumentalist she had no outlet) that she began protesting. Each year following she returned to the festival and presented programs that would give instrumentalists an opportunity to perform. This work culminated in 1978 at the festival with the first symphony orchestra performance, conducted by Dr. Antonia Brico. The National Women's Music Festival orchestra presented works by women composers as well as those of Mozart.

Rain Forest, Kay Gardner's composition for chamber orchestra, was premièred at this concert. It was well received by both the musicians and the audience, as was her debut as a promising orchestral conductor.

She was inspired by the results of the orchestral performance at the festival and in 1978 became one of the founders of the New England Women's Symphony, with Gail Perry, president; Nancy Barrett-Thomas, manager; Leslie D. Judd, personnel manager, and herself as music director and principal conductor. The initiators of NEWS were seeking to provide an opportunity for women composers and conductors to function, since women instrumentalists had made some growth in professional orchestras. There was an obvious and long-overdue need to provide for the artistic capabilities of composers and conductors and to inform other performing groups of their accomplishments. Based in Boston, the orchestra is open to musicians of both sexes by audition. Gardner states,

> The necessity for this organization was frustration; there was no outlet for female conductors and composers. I admit there were selfish reasons: it would give me an opportunity to conduct, but I don't conduct the entire program, we provide an opportunity for at least two other women conductors. The

orchestra premières at least one new composition
by a woman per concert, one work by an established living woman, and one from the archives
as researched by the staff. The purpose is to
make known that women composers and conductors
have existed, still do exist, and are good. We
tape each performance and make tapes available
to other orchestras wanting to hear a piece before
programming them.

The taping of compositions is important, not only for other
orchestras' accessibility but also for publication and competition.

The first concert was given on December 3, 1978 in
Sanders Theater in Cambridge, Massachusetts. The New
England Women's Symphony Orchestra was reviewed by Diana
Newell Rowan for Sojourner in January, 1979:

The New England Women's Symphony (NEWS),
founded this year as a showcase for the work of
women composers and conductors, held its première performance recently in Sanders Theater,
Cambridge. It was an appropriate setting, recalling the exhilaration of women's music festivals or
concerts held there before, and the mood of this
audience during the NEWS performance was as
robust and supportive as for the earlier, more
colloquial music.
It began on a slightly apprehensive note as Kay
Gardner strode onstage with a yellow rose in her
hand. She neither ate it nor conducted with it,
however, merely smiled and got down to business--
the serious business of making good music. There
were some visibly relieved smiles from the audience as the orchestra--the first of its kind in the
country--began its first selection. "A Chill Wind
in Autumn (1978)," by Pamela J. Marshall, with
mezzo-soprano soloist Dorothy May.
"Chill Wind," a spare and moody piece with
dark tonal shadings, takes its text from a series
of T'ang Dynasty poems, concluding "Over cups of
wine, beneath trees beside a stream/We talked until it seems there was no subject left untouched. /
And now from down the road, I turn my head to
see you once again/But you are lost to sight, my
friend, veiled in the autumn rain." Dorothy May
interpreted the lyrics with precise and sensitive

phrasing, only seeming to force a bit--giving her
voice a momentarily hard edge--when the orchestra
threatened to crowd above her. It settled back for
a moving resolution, the wistfulness drawn skillfully as a Chinese inksketch, and as unsentimentally.
Pamela Marshall, a graduate of the Eastman School
of Music, is currently a member of the graduate
program at the Yale School of Music.

Vivian Fine, on the faculty of Bennington College,
conducted her concerto, "Romantic Ode" (1976),
with the panache and energy of a dancer (it in fact
grew out of a section of the ballet <u>Alcestis</u>, written
in 1960 for Martha Graham who danced the title
role). Whether it was a problem in the leader or
the led, however, the orchestra proved a slightly
erratic partner in that pas de deux, falling behind
the beat or rushing the tempo at points, and what
was meant to be dissonant counterpoint emerged
at moments as thin discordance. The heart of the
piece was there though, and another time, it all
might coalesce so that its dignity and power can
show through. Vivian Fine has received commissions from major dance ensembles in America,
Doris Humphrey, Martha Graham, Jose Limon,
Hanya Holm and others. Some of her recent compositions were "Meeting for Equal Rights 1866"
(1976), a setting of American writings on the subject of women, for narrator, soloist, chorus and
orchestra, and the chamber opera, "Women in the
Garden" (1977).

Pauline Oliveros' composition "To Valerie So-
lanas and Marilyn Monroe; In Recognition of Their
Desperation" (1970) was a brilliant melding of unconventional musical 'scoring', placement of musicians, and use of other effects. Before the piece
began (judging from the program notes), the stage
business seemed as if it had to be more intrusive
than any musical effect could warrant; the orchestra
would be divided into three groups, ranged about
the upper balconies. The "score" not ordinary
notation, simply a set of instructions to the performers and conductors, would include music divided
into three sections, the duration of which would
be controlled by lighting, first red, then yellow,
and finally blue. Each player, evidently, would
independently select five different pitches, to be
played on cues from the colored lights. Highly
suspicious. Who's controlling those lights, one

wondered. The players, moveover, would improvise, varying the articulation, timbre, etc. , to
produce a blend of sounds "in which no one performer or group would dominate." Very politically
correct. But where would the music come in?

Right down through the rafters, somehow. And
up from the upturned faces of the women (and a
few men) in the audience. Some craned to watch
the small groups of musicians in the balconies,
barely visible in the first soft, darkly lit roselight;
others bent forward in their seats, eyes closed in
concentration. The smooth, sustained tones from
the instruments grouped antiphonally overhead lap-
ped at each other and rustled like night sounds,
were plucked into a singing voice. Then they col-
lapsed, almost humourously, into a breathy rattling,
underscored with sensuous hums, grew restless,
still melodic, but rimmed with anger and rising to
some undefined high keening.

The rose light focused on the empty stage seemed,
suddenly, to emphasize the poignancy of the empty
chairs. Simultaneously, it evoked an almost pal-
pable presence, full of wild grace--yet a presence
rooted in reality, in slow learning, self-discipline,
self-knowledge. The women leading the groups
above could be seen turning slightly, now toward
their musicians, now glancing back out over the
balconies, listening for each other. Their hands
flickered as they gave some subtle signal, then
poised motionless again. As the lights changed
and changed again, what the three women and their
groups created between themselves changed. And
what they created drew an even more intense and
listening silence from those below, until the light
drew itself down to a pin point and went out.

Pauline Oliveros teaches at the University of
California at San Diego's Center for Music Experiment. She has created multi-media productions,
involving a combination of film, taped and live mu-
music, dancers, actors, lighting effects and other
elements.

The last piece, "Deep Forest, Op. 34 #1" (1931),
conducted again by Kay Gardner, was a tribute to
its composer, Mabel Daniels (1879-1971), and performed in memory of the life and works of Margaret Mead. After the impact of the Oliveros piece,
one might have thought this musical landscape of
brooks and rills, of wind through the trees, would

seem a bit quaint.   No so.   The Oliveros left one
still craning into the darkness, trying to see, to
trace the outlines of something utterly undefinable.
Too much of that can result in eyestrain, hyper-
ventilation and other metaphysical ailments.

Mable Daniels' piece is earthy and delicate at
once, suffused with hints of that rose glow, and of
the other shades as well, in her love of, and ability
to express the beauty of the simple and the natural.
And it was beautifully performed, flowing free and
sure from conductor and musicians alike.   The two
selections, Oliveros' and Daniels' were a perfect
balance for each other.   (Reprinted by permission
of Sojourner.)

The New England Women's Symphony has kept its commitment to both women composers and conductors.   Kay
Gardner has shared the podium with such notable conductors
as Antonia Brico and Victoria Bond among others.   The following are three sample programs:

February 11, 1979   Sanders Theater, Harvard University

Piano Trio In G minor	Clara Schuman
D'un Matin de Printemps	Lili Boulanger
Lyric Piece	Miriam Gideon
Aure Volanti	Francesca Caccini
Two Poems by Emily Dickinson	Linda Ostrander
Night Chant	Kay Gardner

Conducted by Rachael Worby, Kay Gardner, and Sonia Pryor

April 29, 1979   Jordan Hall

Two Sinfonie	M. Grimani
Spring Pastoral	Mary Howe
Concertpiece for Violincello	
and Small Orchestra	Nancy Van de Vate
Concertino for Harp and Orchestra	Germaine Tailleferre
Singing Earth	Elinor Remick Warren

Conducted by Jean Lamon, Miriam Barndt, Antonia Brico,
and Kay Gardner

November 18, 1979   New England Consevatory of Music

In Memoriam

Nadia Boulanger
September 16, 1887 to October 24, 1979

Tonight's concert is lovingly dedicated to the memory of this century's greatest teacher of composition, Nadia Boulanger

C. A. G. E. D.	Victoria Bond
Suite en Forme de Valses	Melanie Bonis
Crosswinds	Barbara Kolb
Piece for Orchestra	Netty Simons
Night Music	Thea Musgrave

Conducted by Kay Gardner, Kay Roberts, and Victoria Bond

To Kay Gardner the New England Women's Symphony must continue for as long as there is a need for this type of organization and that will be when women composers and conductors take their rightful place in the mainstream of twentieth-century music.   Society has imposed this separatist system, and only when it is eliminated will American music reach its pinacle.   Artistic expression belongs to all musicians, to all listeners.   There should be no division of gender--only the final product should be judged on its merit. (Author's note: NEWS suspended operations indefinitely on November 9, 1979, in order to raise funds.)

In May, 1981 in Albuquerque, New Mexico the Southwest Chamber Opera offered the world première of Kay Gardner's Ladies Voices, an opera in four short acts, with the composer as conductor.   The libretto was by Gertrude Stein. The production was reviewed by Michael Sloper in the Albuquerque Journal on May 5, 1981:

TWO CHAMBER OPERAS IN FINE PREMIERES

On Sunday the Unitarian Church hosted the world première performances of two chamber operas, that successfully offered a happy mixture of profundity and charm, realism, and fantasy, new and old.
The guest conductor, Kay Gardner, composed the music for Gertrude Stein's libretto Ladies

Voices. Gardner set the opera in "Gert's salon
in Paris" during a tea party. The stream of dialogue flows according to its own logic, as one might
expect from snatches of unrelated conversations.
Ms. Gardner emphasized the differences between
the various Ladies' voices by changing the melodic
style and instrumental accompaniment for each new
fragment of chitchat. The effect is Cubist--we
sequentially see several perspectives of the one
event, which is revealed as a multifaceted unity.

The cast sang well, both separately and together.
Mary Greenslet-Hesse portrayed her role of Miss
Williams with more mannerisms than any other
salon guest. Michelle Carroll played the central
role of Gert, who was clearly the boss of the tea
party.

During Act Four the opera briefly became an
audience-participation oratorio. The ladies put
aside their tea and crumpets to stand and sing a
complex polyphonic setting of the questions. The
composer/conductor had instructed the audience to
sing along with part of the text or with a drone
ooh-ahh. We were all delighted to be in the choir.
(Reprinted by permission of the author.)

In 1981 Gardner's variations on an American blues
theme, The Rising Sun, was premièred by the Blue Hill Chamber Ensemble in Bangor, Maine. Designed for flute/alto
flute, oboe/English horn, clarinet/bass clarinet, piano,
harpsichord, and cello, it includes "Poor Girl's Song," "Gentle Warnings," "Dance," "Lament," "Dance" (Reprise), "Street
Life," and "The House of the Rising Sun." Robert H. Newall, arts critic for the Bangor Daily News, reviewed the première on September 11, 1981:

Much interest was riveted on the world première
of Kay Gardner's The Rising Sun variations for
flute and alto flute, oboe and English horn, clarinet
and bass clarinet, and piano, and harpsichord. My
first acquaintance with the original blues number
came through a vocal version by, I believe, Odetta.
The folksong is an apostrophe to one of the most
famous bordellos in New Orleans.

In any case, Ms. Gardner has combined her
instruments skillfully, securing in each variation a
splendid texture. At all times she was able to
produce a sound at once seductive and sensuous,
entirely appropriate to the piece. Further, the

writing is both graceful and grateful. A downward figure assigned to the harpsichord usually signalled the beginning of another variation on this haunting blues motif. The performers evidently enjoyed this music since they played it with such feeling and regard for its nuances. The score is suffused with the heady aromas of the Deep South. (Reprinted by permission of the author.)

Kay Gardner continues to express her artistic ability as a composer, working on pieces called "healing atmospheres," conducting in adult competitions, performing in exhausting tour schedules--including workshops, and reaching out to a society that is forever changing. She said,

I'm only now emerging out of a total women's community into the established community of music. I've had a wealth of background in orchestral music, but in the time when I was finding out who I was as a woman and finding out I could compose and wanted to compose and wanted to conduct, I realized that I want to participate not only in the women's community but with the women's community as the basis of my support and as the giver of my self-confidence as I move into more established circles.

Her tripodal contributions as a vibrant flutist, inspiring composer, and aspiring conductor have been considerable, yet there remains the final reckoning, for she is a young woman. Kay Gardner will need to make some difficult decisions. Time alone dictates the spectrum of musical accomplishment, and her cup of creativity overflows. She alone bears the full responsibility of channeling these artistic energies.

Kay Gardner's poetry can best summarize her direction:

Changing

Changing, changing, ever changing
Like the phases of the moon
Changing, changing
Life is changing
Ever near, ever soon

There's a woman in the moon

I can see her when she's whole
And she's bright (she's the moon)
And deep as the sea
And soft
And strong
As Can Be

Changing, changing, ever changing
Like the ripples on the sea
Changing, changing
Life is changing
Ever near, ever soon

There's a woman in the sea
I can hear her when she's whole
And she's bright as the moon
And deep (she's the sea)
And strong
And soft
As Can Be

Changing, changing, ever changing
Like the river and its flow
Changing, changing
Life is changing
Giving time to grow

And the woman deep in me
Is a river inside my soul
And it's bright as the moon
And deep as the sea
And strong
And soft
And Whole

There's a woman in the moon
There's a woman in the sea
There's a woman inside ...

In 1981, after working with Kay Gardner for several
years, she talked to me about her career: "I really don't
have a whole lot of interest in conducting the standard
repertoire!   Basically I just really want to conduct my
own works and those by other women ... which certainly
is not going to make a conducting career for me.   I'm never
at a loss for compositional ideas and I'm feeling more and
more that composition is the main focus of my energies."

List of Works

Opus 1   (1960)   Tcartsba, A Musical Play
                       (Lydia Mendelssohn Theatre
                       Ann Arbor, MI)

Opus 2   (1974)   The Victoria Woodhull March,
                       -band
                       (Sea Gnomes' Music)

Opus 3   (1975)   Mooncircles:
                         1.   Prayer to Aphrodite
                               -alto flute & strings
                         2.   Touching Souls
                               -alto flute, guitar, small percussion
                         3.   Did You Know That I Can Fly?
                               -SA and harp (piano), English horn,
                               violin, viola, & cello
                         4.   Moonflow
                               -vocalize with piano
                         5.   Lunamuse
                               -flute, guitar, cello, small percussion
                               & tape loop or audience drone
                       (Iris Publications/WWE)

Opus 4   (1975)   Energies for Flute, Oboe & Viola,
                       (Sea Gnomes' Music)

Opus 5   (1975)   Innermoods for Flute/alto flute & guitar,
                       (Sea Gnomes' Music)

Opus 6   (1975)   Thirteen Songs: Collection
                             -mezzo soprano & guitar or autoharp
                       (available separately)

Opus 7   (1974)   Changing,
                       -mezzo soprano & guitar
                       (available separately)

Opus 8   (1976)   Three Mother Songs,
                         1.   Mother Mountain
                         2.   Do You Remember?
                         3.   The Voice
                               -mezzo soprano & guitar
                       (available separately)

Opus 9   (1976)   Song of Our Coming
                             -mezzo soprano & guitar
                       (available separately)

Opus 10   (1976)   Romance,
                             -flute or altoflute, viola or cello, &
                             guitar
                       (Sea Gnomes' Music)

Opus 11   (1976)   Crystal Bells,
                             -flute, guitar, cello & others at random
                       (Sea Gnomes' Music)

Opus 12   (1977)   When We Made the Music,
                          -SSAA and piano (or English horn,
                          string quartet & piano)
                   (Iris Publications/WWE)
Opus 13   (1978)   Rain Forest for Chamber Orchestra,
                          -1221, 1000, strings, harp, glockenspiel
                   (Sea Gnomes' Music)
Opus 14   (1978)   Emerging:
                   1.   The Cauldron of Cerridwyn
                        -recorder, 2 violas da gamba, baroque
                        violin, small percussion & woman's
                        voice
                   2.   Sea Chantress
                        -voice, flute, hammered dulcimer
                   3.   Sailing Song
                        -flute/piccolo, violin, viola, 2 celli
                        or woodwind quintet
                   4.   Mermaids
                        -SSAA, flute, altoflute, cello, piano
                        and small percussion
                   5.   Altantis Rising
                        -flute/altoflute, violin/viola, cello,
                        prepared piano, wood chimes & elec-
                        tronic tape
                   (Iris Publications)
                   (available separately)
Opus 15   (1979)   Night Chant for Chamber Orchestra with
                   Women's Voices,
                          -1111, 2000, strings, 2 percussion, pi-
                          ano, soprano, alto, mezzo soprano, SSAA
                   (Sea Gnomes' Music)
Opus 16   (1979)   Seven Modal Improvisation Studies,
                          -piano or any bass instrument with any
                          treble or bass instrument
                   (Sea Gnomes' Music)
Opus 17   (1979)   Song Studies for Piano,
                   1.   First Easy Piece
                   2.   Simple Gifts
                   3.   Sioux Lullaby
                   4.   Mountains at Dusk
                   5.   Rhapsody in Sea
                   6.   Rain Forest
                   7.   Heart Healer in Green
                   (available separately)
Opus 18   (1979)   Winter Night, Gibbons Moon for 11 Flutes,
                   (Sea Gnomes' Music)
Opus 19   (1980)   Ladies Voices opera in four acts
                   (Sea Gnomes' Music)

Opus 20 (1981)   The Rising Sun, variations on an American
                   Blues Theme for flute/alto flute, oboe/
                   English horn, clarinet/bass clarinet, piano,
                   harpsichord, and cello, Poor Girl's Song,
                   Gentle Warnings, Dance, Lament, Dance
                   (Reprise), Street Life, House of the Ris-
                   ing Sun.

Addresses

Sea Gnomes' Music, Box 33, Stonington, Maine 04681

Iris Publications/WWE, 20 West 22nd Street, 612, New York,
    N. Y. 10010

Discography

Mooncircles, Prayer To Aphrodite, Changing, Beautiful Friend,
        Moon Flow, Wise Woman, Inner Mood I, Touching
        Souls, Inner Mood II, Lunamuse.   Olivia Records.
Emerging, Cauldron of Cerridwyn, Romance, Crystal Bells,
        Anagram, Rhapsody, Pisces, Mermaids, Atlantis
        Rising.   Urana Records.
Women's Orchestral Works, performed by the New England
        Women's Symphony, conductors, Antonia Brico, Kay
        Gardner, Miriam Barndt-Webb, and Jean Lamon.
        Galaxia Records.
Moods and Rituals, Saraswati, Mountain Melody, In the
        Temple of Ishtar, Soul Flight, cassette.   Sea Gnomes'
        Music.

Addresses

Olivia Records, a Division of Wise Women Enterprises, Inc.
        Distributed by Olivia, P. O. Box 70237, Los Angeles
        California, 90070

Urana Records, a Division of Wise Women Enterprises, Inc.
        P. O. Box 297, Village Station, New York, N. Y.
        10014.

Galaxia Records, P. O. Box 212, Woburn, Massachusetts,
        01801.

MIRIAM GIDEON

Composer, Professor, Humanist

Miriam Gideon--composer, professor, humanist--has helped
to pave the road for the acceptance of women as serious
productive artists in the twentieth century. Her works, based
solidly on intrinsic value, musical literacy, and sensitive
human potential have projected her artistic capabilities into
the mainstream of this century's contemporary music. She
is a leader of her contemporaries. She has been judged on
merit alone.

Miriam Gideon was born in Greeley, Colorado, on
October 23, 1906, daughter of Abram Gideon and Henrietta
Shoninger. Her father was professor of philosophy and modern languages at Colorado State Teachers College, and her
mother was a schoolteacher briefly before her marriage.
Miriam and her sister, Judith, had no opportunity to study
or even to hear music as children, since at that time there
were few recordings, no radio, and only limited opportunity
to hear live music. Fortunately, the public schools of Colorado provided excellent training for young children in reading music. Miriam recalls: "My sister and I were taught
solfège from the first grade. We used 'movable doh,' and
everybody learned this system until it became automatic,
which is the only way it can be useful. This has remained
a permanent help to me."

When Miriam was a young child, the family moved
first from Colorado to California, then to Chicago, and finally to New York. Wherever a piano was available she
would make use of it, and thus taught herself to play.

When she was nine the family moved to Chicago, where
she began to study piano with a cousin who was a musician.
She learned very quickly. The following year, when the
family moved to New York, she enrolled in the Yonkers Con-

servatory of Music.   Here, on a scholarship, she studied
with the eminent pianist Hans Barth, who later worked with
quartertone music.

During this time her uncle, Henry Gideon, an organist, choral conductor, and music director of Temple Israel
in Boston, often visited the family.   Miriam spent several
summer vacations with him.   He was impressed with her
ability to perform on the piano, read at sight, transpose,
and improvise.   When she was fourteen her uncle asked her
parents to allow her to make her home with him in Boston,
where her musical talents could be nurtured under his guidance and expertise.   She recalls many wonderful musical
experiences at this period, among them listening to the choir,
the services, and the organ; all this would later influence
her in the two services she wrote for the synagogue.   Continuing her piano study with the distinguished pianist, Felix
Fox, she attended the College of Liberal Arts at Boston University, where she graduated with a Bachelor of Arts degree
at the age of nineteen.

As a child Miriam fantasized about being a concert
pianist.   "I thought very little about composing," she says.
"Although I did write music, I didn't think it was very good.
Eventually the idea of being a pianist faded and I became
absorbed in composing.   I recall about the age of nineteen
reading a poem by an American poet, whose name I've forgotten.   I set it, and realized that for the first time I had
found my own voice as a composer.   From that time on, I
was 'hooked.'"

Following graduation from Boston University, Miriam
took courses at New York University to prepare for a career
in public school music.   While there she studied with Marion
Bauer, Charles Haubiel, and Jacques Pillois, a distinguished
French composer, who was relatively little known in the
United States.   Her professors encouraged her to develop
her talents as a composer.

For several years thereafter she studied composition
with Lazare Saminsky, a well-known Russian composer who
was active in the first half of this century in both Europe
and America.   He coordinated her studies in harmony, counterpoint, and orchestration, and allowed her to develop her
individuality as a composer.   It was on his recommendation
a few years later that she became a student of Roger Sessions.

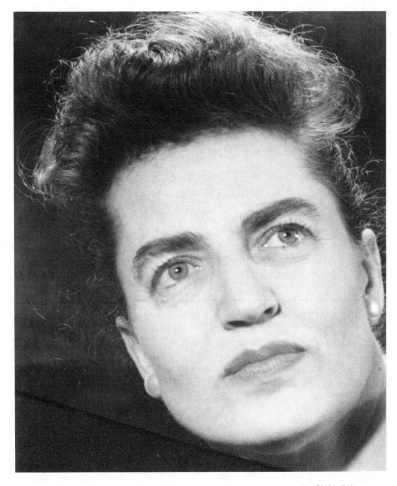

Judith Liegner

MIRIAM GIDEON

Gideon considers Roger Sessions the most important influence on her professional career. She recalls,

> Saminsky felt that either Roger Sessions or Arnold
> Schoenberg would be a good influence on my develop-
> ment. It was a generous gesture on the part of
> Saminsky. Since I could not decide which composer
> to study with, he suggested Sessions, since there

was every indication that he would remain in New
York, whereas Schoenberg might not. (This proved
to be correct--Schoenberg left New York about a
year later.)

Sessions taught very few students privately at
that time, preferring to work with a group, in
private studios or at the Dalcroze School. Composers who studied with him during this period included Vivian Fine, David Diamond, Hugo Weisgall,
Milton Babbitt, Leon Kirchner, and Edward Cone,
among others.

I studied with Sessions for several years. It
is difficult to define in specific terms his influence.
He gave me a perspective that was all-encompassing.

In 1939 Miriam Gideon went to France and Switzer-
land expecting to stay a considerable time, but the outbreak
of World War II aborted these plans, and she returned to
the United States to make her home in New York City. In
1946 she received a master's degree in musicology at Columbia University, and in 1970 the degree of Doctor of Sacred
Music in Composition, from the Jewish Theological Seminary
of America.

She now lives in an apartment overlooking Central Park,
where she and her husband, Frederic Ewen, have lived for
over thirty years. Her husband, a former professor (they
met when they were both teaching at Brooklyn College) is
a noted scholar and the author of several highly respected
books on Schiller, Heine, and Brecht. He is at present
working on a study of nineteenth-century European literature.
The devotion and love shared by this couple have nurtured
their creative talents.

Gideon has combined creative work with a teaching
career. She was a member of the faculties of Brooklyn
College and City College of the City University of New York
for many years and is at present on the faculties of the Jewish Theological Seminary and the Manhattan School of Music.
A composer who shares her talent and knowledge with future
generations, she has encouraged and inspired many young
students. "In working with young composers," she says,
"I try to encourage them to write what they really feel, re-
gardless of current fads."

The opportunity for public performance is an absolute
must in the career of every composer, if growth and develop-

ment are to flourish. It was through the efforts of Lazare
Saminsky and his respect for Miriam's compositional skills
that her first public performance was sponsored by the League of Composers in the early 1930's--Dances for Two Pianos.
She recalls her reaction to this occasion: "My heart was
thumping so hard I thought the whole row of seats would
collapse!" The response to this performance was positive
both in terms of the music critics and the audience. It was
the beginning of a brilliant and distinguished career.

Another of her early compositions to receive recognition was Lyric Piece for Strings, premièred in 1944 by
the London Symphony Orchestra, conducted by Hugo Weisgall.
In 1945 a version of this work for string quartet was broadcast as part of the celebration of the American Music Festival, and in 1961, the orchestra version was recorded in
performance by the Imperial Orchestra of Tokyo, William
Strickland conducting (Composers Recording CRI 170). In
Living Music of the Americas published by Howell, Soskin
and Crown, 1949, Lazare Saminsky writes of Dances for Two
Pianos and Lyric Piece for Strings:

> Clear trails of a radical tonal mind showed in even
> the earliest works of Miriam Gideon, born in Col-
> orado, reared in Boston, grounded in New York.
> Of her earlier music, Dances for Two Pianos was
> introduced by the League of Composers. Yet even
> then the youthful grimness of harmonic facade could
> not hide an engaging emotional essence wedded to
> a fine musical thinking. To be sure, a young com-
> poser's love for half-tones of harmony and all the
> polytonal bumps of the period are there. But
> through the Dances' willful atonalism glimmers at
> times a promising diatonic avowal. One recognizes
> the delicate creative self that will one day write
> a serene madrigal Slow, Slow, Fresh Fount to Ben
> Jonson's verse, a chorale of lovely stillness, dis-
> creet lyricism and handling of voices.
>   A Gideon piece heard in London and Prague, the
> Lyric Piece for String Orchestra is music somber
> and somewhat aloof. It is notable for its fertile
> thematic thought and fresh structure. In the open-
> ing sonata-like movement, Miss Gideon deploys her
> three main motives not in the usual dialectic-emo-
> tional play of contrasts, but after an order of her
> own. The andante closes on a dark, appealing
> threnody. (Reprinted from Living Music of the
> Americas by Lazare Saminsky. Copyright © 1949

by Lazare Saminsky.   Used by permission of Crown
Publishers, Inc.)

Lyric Piece for String Orchestra has had many performances
over the past four decades, including one by the New England
Women's Symphony on February 13, 1979, at Sanders Theater
in Boston. Writing for the Boston Globe on February 13,
1979, correspondent David St. George said of this work:

> The best by a considerable margin was the per-
> formance of Miriam Gideon's wonderful Lyric Piece
> for String Orchestra, conducted by Rachel Worby.
> The piece shows Gideon at the beginning of her
> career experimenting with the kinds of sonorities,
> textures, and contrasts in writing for massed strings
> that interested a number of American composers
> in the early and mid-forties, including Copland,
> Carter and Barber.   It was obviously a considerable
> challenge to the orchestra, and the players responded
> to the challenge and to Worby's direction with in-
> tense concentration and surprisingly beautiful re-
> sults.   (Reprinted courtesy of The Boston Globe.)

In 1945 Lazare Saminsky, who was then director of
music of Congregation Temple Emanu-El in New York, the
foremost Reform synagogue in the world, commissioned Miriam Gideon to compose a work for the celebration of the
centenary of the founding of the Temple.   Gideon says, "Some
of my most interesting commissions have been associated
with houses of worship.   This commission was particularly
gratifying to me."   She continues:

> The work is based on the poem The Hound of Heaven
> by Francis Thompson, and deals with conversion to
> Catholicism.   The few lines I chose to set, how-
> ever, had to do with overcoming life's strife and
> stress.   That might well be posed by the Jewish
> people in terms of their tragic history.   Saminsky
> understood the deeper implication of the words, and
> approved the choice.   The final lines I used were:

> > Designer infinite!
> > Ah!   Must Thou char the wood
> > Ere Thou canst limn with it?

The work is scored for voice, violin, viola, cello,
and oboe.   It is published by Columbia University Music
Press, distributed by Galaxy Music Corporation, and recorded
by Composers Recordings, Inc. CRI 286.

Assessing the reviews of this work over the years,
Gideon says, "It is revealing to see the difference between
the first review, when the piece was evidently considered
'difficult,' and later reviews, which see it in a different
light." A review of the première performance follows:

> Here the vocal line was of the ungrateful contem-
> porary variety, the idea being apparently that the
> voice is a tempered instrument which happens to
> be able to make vowels and consonants as well as
> tones. Romolo De Spirito did extremely well in
> singing this difficult piece; and the collaboration of
> Mitchell Miller on the oboe helped give suavity
> where it was badly needed. The work is not de-
> void of engaging effects, but the starkness of the
> idiom made a strange contrast to the Francis Thomp-
> son text, and in fact deprived it of much of its
> effect. (Reprinted with permission from the New
> York Herald-Tribune, March 24, 1945, by Paul
> Bowles.)

In the New York Times on January 16, 1956, Edward
Downes wrote concerning the performance of The Hound of
Heaven and Sonnets from Shakespeare given at Columbia Uni-
versity, New York City:

> The second large work was Miss Gideon's setting
> of selected lines from Francis Thompson's The
> Hound of Heaven.... Here, as in the three Son-
> nets, Miss Gideon showed a fine awareness of
> melodic line, and built to an effective climax, as
> they did with the final lines of The Hound of Hea-
> ven.

In an extensive article on the music of Miriam Gideon,
published in the Bulletin of the American Composers Alliance,
1958, Volume VII, #4, George Perle discusses The Hound of
Heaven (partial):

> The texture of this, as of most of Miriam Gideon's
> other works, is strikingly personal, characterized
> by lightness, the sudden exposure of individual
> notes, constantly shifting octave relationships. The
> unique quality of the texture, however, is not merely
> a subjective, idiosyncratic feature, but a conse-
> quence of her compositional technique. Individual
> intervals are isolated, contrasted, their components
> presented in all possible ways--simultaneously--

that is, by means of the successive juxtaposition
of separate lines. The larger melodic and harmonic components are generated from minimal
basic cells in this way. This is a technique that
imposes economy and the exclusion of irrelevancies
--a technique that may be indefinitely expanded
and within which a composer may grow, a growth
revealed in Miss Gideon's next large work, the
String Quartet.

I recall a conversation between Miriam Gideon
and a fellow composer who was complaining about
the composer's situation in the world today--a
world, he felt, in which it is impossible for a serious composer to find any proper motivation for
composing music. Miss Gideon replied, "If you
can relate tones to each other in such a way that
they belong together, that's enough of a reason for
composing." Her answer tells us a good deal
about her, as a person and as a composer.

During most of Gideon's career she was not aware of
discrimination against women in her field. But now that the
women's movement has made people very conscious of these
things she says, "I am beginning to think that there was,
and still is, discrimination, though now to a lesser degree
--particularly in judging competitions and awarding grants.
I've been a member of many juries and I'm aware of discrimination even in myself, so invidious is this attitude!
'Reverse Discrimination'--overestimating women's music is
part of this same picture!" She feels that women are doing
themselves an injustice to arrange concerts, broadcasts, or
recordings of women's music only. "How can their music
be judged objectively in such a situation?" she asks.

Miriam Gideon is probably the most recorded woman
composer at the present time. She speaks of recordings as
the greatest satisfaction of her career:

I am especially gratified by the response made by
people who have listened to my recordings, since
they have had the opportunity of hearing my music
more than the one time a live performance provides. One performance, even though it may generate a warm reaction in the listener, does not
really provide a key to what the composer is saying. Only repeated hearings can do that. I am
fortunate in having had excellent performers for my
recordings--the finest soloists and chamber players
a composer could wish for.

A complete discography of Gideon's music can be found
at the end of this chapter. The following was written in November, 1972 by Lester Trimble for American Record Guide in
which he reviews a recording of Gideon's Rhymes from the Hill,
settings of Christian Morgenstern's whimsical Galgenlieder
(Gallows Songs), and a recent recording of The Hound of Heaven.

MIRIAM GIDEON

Among the country's most gifted composers

Composers Recordings Inc. , CRI Sd 286.
Performance: EXCELLENT
Recording: EXCELLENT

It would be easy to begin a review of Miriam Gideon's
music by saying that she is "one of the United States'
finest women composers. " It would be more accurate
to say simply that she is one of our most gifted and
accomplished composers, period. Her setting for solo
voice and chamber group entitled The Hound of Heaven
(1945) I first heard in concert sometime in the Fifties
and I was impressed. It seemed an unusually sensitive and individual work, and a strongly expressive
one. It still does. But her later composition Rhymes
from the Hill (1968) shows such development of her
language toward an even greater fluency, even more
elegant and intimate lyricism, that it makes the earlier work seem more unyielding than it really is.
Rhymes from the Hill (from the "Gallows Songs" by
Christian Morgenstern) has a kind of coloristic and
lyrical inspiration that adds an element of naturalness
and frankness to the Expressionistic ethos, an ingre-
dient one does not expect. This has always seemed to
me one of Gideon's particular strengths as a composer:
her ability to take both the refractory twelve-tone
method and Expressionism in hand and make them the
servant of a very personal imagery. Hers is American Expressionism, not Central European. (Reprinted
by permission of Heldret Publications.)

Few composers of Gideon's caliber have the desire or
ability to write music for children. In 1960, she composed a delightful piece for voice and chamber group, The Adorable Mouse,
based on a French folktale. Contemporary music needs larger
audiences. What better potential than our children? Their enthusiasm and their ability to absorb new sounds is illimitable,
as well as their willingness to listen without prejudice.

Paul Kresh, writing for Stereo Review in December
1973, published the following review:

RECORDING OF SPECIAL MERIT

Gideon: The Adorable Mouse. John Reardon, baritone, and the Ariel Quintet. (The record is titled "For
Children and Sensible Parents." (Serenus SRS 12050)

If children don't wear this one out, their "sensible"
parents probably will; the texts, the readings, and
the music are all remarkable.
    The Adorable Mouse is a delight. Libretto and
music are by Miriam Gideon, who dares to experiment with the most modern dissonances in a way
that might even help prepare young listeners to enjoy more serious music of our time. Six instruments accompany the narration and singing of Mr.
Reardon to excellent advantage.

Gideon has been the recipient of many awards, honors,
and commissions. The first such recognition was the Ernest
Block Prize for choral music in 1948, given for a choral
work for women's voices with or without organ accompaniment.
Psalm 84--How Goodly Are Thy Tents won the award jointly
with a work by Norman Lockwood. In 1954 Hugo Weisgall,
composer-conductor, commissioned her to write Adon Olam
(Eternal Lord), a text in Hebrew, for chamber orchestra,
soloists, and mixed chorus. He conducted the première performance at Temple Chizuk Amuno in Baltimore, Maryland.
Gideon says, "The material was not traditional except for
the governing accentuation of the text, although I realized
after the completion of the work that I had used the same
four notes as the most familiar of all the traditional melodies
associated with these words."

Three Biblical Masks, written in 1958, was commissioned by composer-organist Herman Berlinski. Based on
cantillation motives from the Book of Esther, the composer
depicts the main characters in the Purim story: Haman,
chief minister of King Ahasuerus of Persia and the person
who secured a royal decree for the destruction of the Jews;
Esther, who frustrated this scheme; and Mordecai, who was
Esther's cousin. Written originally for organ and later re-
written for violin and piano, Masks has toured the United
States and Europe. It was selected as one of the contemporary works offered to contestants in the competition for
string players sponsored by the Rockefeller Foundation at the
Kennedy Center in Washington in 1980.

During the 1950's Gideon became interested in national musical traits.   An opera, Fortunato, based on the Spanish play by Serafin and Joaquin Quintero, was completed in 1958. A year earlier Gideon wrote Mixco, a setting of a poem by the Guatemalan poet, Miguel Angel Asturias.   Here the composer employed a bilingual setting: each stanza, in English translation, was followed by the original in Spanish, with a different musical frame for each of the two languages.   This procedure grew in fascination for her, and was used in later works: The Condemned Playground, where Latin, Japanese, and French were set, along with their English counterparts; and most recently, Songs of Youth and Madness, on poems of Friedrich Hölderlin, with the original German alternating with the English translations by Michael Hamburger.

Lester Trimble, writing for the New York Herald-Tribune on December 1, 1957, had this to say about a performance of Mixco in Carnegie Recital Hall, New York:

> Miriam Gideon's Mixco, which was having its first performance along with her To Music, revealed itself as an unusual creation in which the poem's stanzas were set in alternation, in English and in Spanish.   The music was lovely, and while stylistically consistent, made clear differentiation in its treatment of the two languages.

Written and premièred in 1953, Gideon's Symphonia Brevis for orchestra has had many performances and is recorded by Composers Recordings, Inc. CRI 128.   Jacques Monod conducts the Zurich Radio Orchestra in this recording.   Reviewed by Arthur Cohn, American Record Guide, November, 1960:

> Everything is concentrated, strongly wired by the scoring, avoids unhealthy abandon for the terse point of view.   Her music has a succinct way about it that makes one anxious to hear more of her output.

Eric Salzman's review of Symphonia Brevis, in the New York Times, May 8, 1960:

> Makes serious and impressive intellectual and emotional demands; its movements are so stark and concentrated that everything seems to come out of a tiny rhythmic and harmonic kernel.

Miriam Gideon was the winner in 1969 of the National Federation of Music Clubs National Award to an American woman composer for contribution to symphonic and chamber music.   One of her many compositions written during the 1960's, The Seasons of Time, based on Tanka poetry of ancient Japan, is scored for voice, flute, cello, and piano alternating with celesta.   Sponsored by the National Federation of Music Clubs, it is recorded on the Desto Label (DC 1717). Evocative and imaginative, it is dedicated to her late friend Otto Deri.   Another work from this decade, mentioned above, is Rhymes from the Hill, for voice, cello, clarinet, and marimba, on poems of Christian Morgenstern.   Philip L. Miller, writing an article for the American Record Guide in November 1972, titled "Over on the Distaff Side, mostly-- Miriam Gideon and Four Other Americans," reviews both previously mentioned recordings: The Hound of Heaven and Rhymes from the Hill, as well as The Seasons of Time, with which the review opens:

THE SEASONS OF TIME

Miriam Gideon opens the program with a cycle based on "Tanka poetry of Ancient Japan." There are ten songs, or sections, each leading into the next, and mostly comprising two-line epigrams; only the fifth runs to nine lines.   These are set for soprano with cello, piano, and flute.   Even with this small ensemble, the instruments are used sparingly to achieve a delicate and transparent texture.   The performance is a thoroughly happy one, with the sweet voice of Evelyn Mandac making the text clear and understandable; also, the instruments are in beautiful balance with the voice.

Despite its title, Rhymes From The Hill is a set of five poems from the Galgenlieder of Christian Morgenstern, in the original German.   The very name of this poet presages fun, and Miss Gideon has plenty of it with her little chamber group of voice, clarinet, cello and marimba.   It would not do to go into too much detail--and I suspect that I will discover even more with subsequent hearings--but little things like the cuckoo sounds in the Wiegenlied and the clock sounds in the third and fourth songs are quite delightful.   Of course the gifted Miss de Gaetani sings them all beautifully as part of this expert ensemble.   The Hound of Heaven is something else.   Composed as long ago

as 1945, using only a portion of Francis Thompson's
poem, it has more than enough seriousness to balance the Morgenstern humor. One thing the two
compositions have in common is textual clarity.
William Metcalf's singing is tonally attractive, and
he projects the text meaningfully. (Reprinted by
permission of Heldref Publications.)

Grants and commissions have been numerous during
Gideon's career, but she says "I can't really live on them.
However, most of my teaching positions have come about
because I am a composer." Gideon is Professor Emeritus
of Music at the City College of the City University of New
York, Professor of Music at the Jewish Theological Semin-
ary, and a member of the faculty at the Manhattan School of
Music.

The only woman to have written two complete sacred
services, and these for large and prestigious synagogues,
Miriam Gideon was commissioned by Cantor David Putterman
and the Park Avenue Synagogue in New York, as well as by
David Gooding, music director of the Temple, in Cleveland,
Ohio. Albert Weisser, noted composer-musicologist, whose
writings include The Modern Renaissance of Jewish Music,
is the author of two extensive articles reviewing Miriam
Gideon's two services: Sacred Service (a Sabbath Morning
Service), and Shirat Miriam L'Shabbat (A Song of Miriam
for the Sabbath). His depth of knowledge and keen percep-
tion justify presenting both articles in their entirety. Albert
Weisser wrote the following article for the Congress Bi-
Weekly, June 30, 1972, Volume 39, pp. 22-23:

MIRIAM GIDEON'S NEW SERVICE

Miriam Gideon's Sacred Service (for Sabbath Morning) which was given its New York premiere on
May 20 at, of all places, the New School for Social
Research, is a work of extraordinary significance.
Commissioned and first performed last year by the
Temple in Cleveland, the work is scored for cantor, soloists, mixed chorus, flute, oboe, trumpet,
bassoon, viola, cello and organ. It is easily the
finest service yet composed by a native-born Amer-
ican-Jewish composer, and very probably the most
important advance in the form since Darius Milhaud's Service Sacré (1947). Although the tonal
fabric of the work is related to the Schoenberg-
Berg orbit (which in the framework of the synagogue

alone would make it highly unusual), Miss Gideon's
style and approach to the liturgy is so deeply personal that its contemporary technical habiliment
proves no barrier at all to the sophisticated lis-
tener--or should one say worshipper if so one
should be inclined--and what one is mainly aware
of is a profoundly felt work of piercing beauty.

It is not an easy affair at this moment in our
musical and religious history for a serious composer to write a service in America--or even Israel
for that matter. With no universally shared Jewish
musical and liturgical tradition to draw upon and
the present fragmentation of what were once com-
paratively homogeneous Jewish cultural units a
clearly demonstrable fact, the composer for the
synagogue is bound to find pitfalls, false starts,
enticements and alarums on all sides. Thus it
must be quite evident by now that a dependence on
musical fads and fashions will simply not work for
long in the synagogue. Already, rock and jazz
services, which we were told only a few seasons
back were to prove our glory and salvation, are
now pretty much exhausted as viable forces--not
so much because these styles are inherently wicked
or liturgically unsuitable as some nearsighted souls
would have it. I personally find them capable of
enormous charm, gaiety, and vitality. The difficulty has been that they were used in the synagogue for purely ancillary and exploitive purposes--
instant religious experience, musical pabulum,
shock and titillation. In restrospect, every rock
service that I have heard seemed to be written
with a kind of tin-whistle technique.

Now Miss Gideon is a composer of genuine stature and delightful invention. She has that happy
facility of not making predictable artistic choices.
What is especially striking is the skill and total
freshness with which she has set the thrice familiar texts. So idiosyncratic is her craft here that
it were as though we were encountering the prayers
for the very first time and discovering new impli-
cations in them. One cannot but admire also the
lean, laconic quality of her work--there is not a
single wasted measure in it. In a field where ver-
bosity and the fustian seems too often to be the
accepted norm, hers is indeed a refreshing trait.
And although the work is surely of a piece, certain
sections do stand out--the haunting lyricism of the

opening prelude and "Ma Tovu," the drama of the
"Avot," the extraordinary power and elevation of
the "Kedusha," and the splendid anthem "The sun
and the moon, that is their paths" (text by Judah
Halevi).

I am quite positive that the question is sure to
arise in some narrow academic, journalistic and
cantorial circles as to the specific Jewish musical
complexion of the work. I can already hear the
tiresome and threadbare grumbling, "Where is the
nusach ha-teffillah?" and "I don't care what you
say, it just doesn't sound Jewish to me," which
of course has been the very same reaction after
the initial performance of every important synagogal
music art work from Rossi to Achron to Bloch to
Milhaud. The point of the matter is that Miss
Gideon is not a Jewish music literalist and it is
for this very reason that I find her work so fascinating and why I think it so very important Miss
Gideon certainly knows her Jewish musical sub-
stances--cantillation, psalmody, missinai tunes,
etc. But she has chosen to perform a really creative musical act. So, although a sensitive and
imaginative ear will be able to hear in her work
shofar calls, pentatonicism, asymmetrical rhythms,
melodicles and chantlike effects, all reminiscent
of numerous aspects and essences of genuine Jewish musical materials from a variety of traditions,
it should be noted that these are subjected to constant subtle and brilliant motivic and tonal trans-
formations. But I must insist that it is the emotional purity at the work's center that takes hold
of one.

It is, of course a sorry commentary on the
present state of affairs of synagogal music in New
York City that no synagogue saw fit to give this
unique work its first local performance. Is it
timidity, sloth, lack of taste, musical perception
or a general deterioration of musical energies?
What an irony, therefore, that a work of such
Jewish religious fervor and loftiness should be
first produced in the very center of Jewish culture
in the Diaspora by a basically non-Jewish, secular
organization--and to go totally unnoticed by the
local press. (Reprinted by permission of Congress
Monthly.)

The following article by Albert Weisser was published

in the Journal of Synagogue Music, November 1979, Volume
IX #3:

REVIEW OF NEW MUSIC

Miriam Gideon: Shirat Miriam L'Shabbat (A Sabbath Evening Service), Cantor, mixed chorus, organ. C. F. Peters Corp. , New York, 64p.

It is good to see Miriam Gideon's second service,
Shirat Miriam for Sabbath evening published in this
handsome format. A work of exquisite delicacy
and sturdy craft, it adds yet another ornament to
the American synagogue for which we must take
pride.

Miss Gideon is a singular voice in whatever
area she functions. Widely admired in contemporary American music for the high seriousness,
extraordinary power and uncanny sensitivity of her
chamber works and song settings, she brings to the
synagogue a musical personality ideally suited to
instill freshness and independence into its quarters.
Too often one has heard of late from composers,
musicians and discerning listeners whose critical
acumen one must respect, that they detect a deadly
flat, inbred sameness of sound and stylistic inert-
ness in many services of recent years.

Although it is primarily from the Second Viennese School, and especially its Alban Berg hub,
that Miss Gideon has derived her individual manner, there has always been in her musical personality an inquisitiveness and a spikey and restless will that made her move in whatever directions
her natural gifts could find invention and renewal.

It should therefore not suprise Miss Gideon's
followers that there is not a trace of Expressionism or atonal devices in Shirat Miriam. Instead
we have a work totally at ease with itself, with a
genuine sweetness and lyricism and of such decep-
tive simplicity--not innocence--that only a master
hand could have fashioned it--a hand entirely ac-
quainted, that is, with the most advanced contemporary techniques. Thus, this service's melodic
lines are always direct and clearly laid out. Free
and imaginative use is made of such Jewish traditional materials as cantillation, prayer modes and
folk songs. Textures which in the main are homo-
phonic, are silken and airy. I know of no other

work for the synagogue which has used quartal
harmony with such imagination and richness, and
I would advise every aspiring Jewish composer to
study that ravishing three measure cadence at the
end of "Ma Tovu."

Structurally, too, Miss Gideon has chosen to
organize her service in a rather unconventional
fashion. Each section is an individual unit, with
no recurring motifs. But as a unifying tactic she
has composed a prelude and three interludes for
organ, all based on recognizable Palestinian shep-
herd songs. Thus, psychologically, the work takes
on both Israeli and bucolic associations.

Although intimacy and conciseness of utterance
are the overall qualities of this work, the most
extended section of Shirat Miriam is the "Hashkivenu." It is also, externally, probably the most
emotionally stirring in the entire service and closest to traditional Ashkenazic song. One must admire how movingly Miss Gideon has set the utter-
ances of supplication for the Cantor and the contrasting dramatic bass solos with their striking
melismas. It might be noticed that the words
Hashkivenu and V'hagen Ba-adeinu use the same
melodic outline, though in different tonal centers.
And with what imagination and sense of imagery
she uses the melodic interval of the minor seventh
in setting the words L'chayim, V'hoshienu, V'cherev
and Yerusholayim. Here, too, her choral mastery
comes into full view with its polyphonic and anti-
phonal procedures. One is also startled how power-
fully her unisons can sound.

Shirat Miriam L'Shabbat was commissioned by
Cantor David Putterman and the Park Avenue Synagogue, New York, and given its first performance
in 1974. One clearly remembers that special
Friday evening when a wide variety of composers
of the avant-garde, middle of the roaders, minimal-
ists, neo-classicists, proto-Romanticists and what
you will gathered in separate clusters to hear Miss
Gideon's work. What was astonishing was almost
total agreement that what they had heard was moving and engendered a living religious experience.

There is little doubt in my mind that this service is the closest thing to a genuinely populist
work that Miriam Gideon has achieved. It should
be widely performed and cherished. (Reprinted by
permission of the author.)

In 1974, in observance of the one hundreth anniversary
of the founding of Boston University, Gideon was elected to
the Collequim of Distinguished Alumni, receiving this honor
in ceremonies marking this important date in the University's
history.

The same year she received a grant from the National
Endowment of the Arts for a work for voice and orchestra:
Songs of Youth and Madness, on poems of Friedrich Hölderlin.
The première performance took place on December 5, 1977,
at Alice Tully Hall in New York, with Judith Raskin, soprano,
and the American Composers Orchestra, conducted by James
Dixon. Raymond Ericson, writing for the New York Times
on December 7, 1977 says:

> SONGS OF YOUTH AND MADNESS
>
> Miss Gideon's setting of four poems by Friedrich
> Hölderlin for soprano and orchestra is quite un-
> usual. She has set them first in English transla-
> tion and then alternated this with the original Ger-
> man. The effect is of an emotional depth and
> color that would not be possible in a single-language
> setting. As sung by Judith Raskin, the music
> emerged nostalgic, troubling, beautiful.

Gideon composed Nocturnes in 1976, on a commission
from Mr. and Mrs. Sidney Siegel of New York City in honor
of their daughter Rena's eighteenth birthday. Scored for
voice, flute, oboe, violin, cello, and vibraphone, it is a setting of poems of Percy Bysshe Shelley, Jean Starr Untermeyer, and Frank Dempster Sherman. Gideon says, "The
poems I chose, and their transmutation into music, seemed
an appropriate evocation of youth and its awakening to the
magical forces of nature." The second performance was at
St. Paul, Minnesota, on February 22, 1976, with the St.
Paul Chamber Orchestra, John DeMain, conducting; and Judith
Raskin, soprano; John Harvey's review in the St. Paul Pioneer Press the next day stated:

> NOCTURNES
>
> A lovely, sensitive chamber piece. The vocal part
> moves mostly in smoothly lyrical lines and is ad-
> mirably attuned to both the inflections and sense
> of text. The instrumental setting is firmly and
> delicately woven through the vocal lines, and its
> colors beautifully evoke the atmosphere and imagery
> of the poetry.

Robert Herman's review, published in Gazette Journal, Reno, Nevada, on June 22, 1979, deals with recordings of Nocturnes and Songs of Youth and Madness, Composers Recordings, (CRI SD 401):

> Gideon offers two sets of hauntingly beautiful, emotionally charged and stylistically consistent songs, expressively and artistically interpreted by veteran soprano Judith Raskin.

> (Of Songs of Youth and Madness): Interesting and characteristic of Gideon are the bilingual settings (English alternating with German), which add dimension to the work.

Perhaps the most distinguished award for Miriam Gideon was her election to the American Academy and Institute of Arts and Letters in 1975. This prestigious group of American intellectual leaders has a membership of two hundred and fifty, forty of whom are composers. Only three of these are women: Louise Talma, Miriam Gideon, and Vivian Fine. The citation presented at the formal ceremony on the induction of new members on May 21, 1975 reads:

> Miriam Gideon, composer. For many years she has worked to build in her music a gracious, delicate and thoroughly convincing personal style. Every aspect of her work displays deep insight, as to her inspiration and her accomplishment. Her musical--poetic nature is both original and definitive.

In 1980 Gideon received an Elizabeth Sprague Coolidge commission from the Library of Congress for a work commemorating the fiftieth anniversary of the founding of the Music Library Association. Spirit above the Dust, a work for voice and eight instruments, on American poetry, was premièred in February, 1981 at Yale University and repeated at the Library of Congress in Washington in September, 1981.

Miriam Gideon has composed in all media, including works for orchestra, dramatic works, chamber music, with and without voice, and works for keyboard, solo voice, and chorus. Her music has been widely performed and recorded in the United States, Europe, and the Far East. Continued performance indicates not only recognition of her skill by performers and conductors, but also wide acceptance by audiences and critics.

Gideon reflects on the state of American music from her vantage point as one of the century's most productive composers:

> American composers, including women, are becoming more accepted and their reputation is growing. In spite of the temptation for young composers to write what will be assured of an audience--often striving to be in the avant-garde of the avant-garde, there seems to be a growing tendency for composers in general to draw on their genuine musical impulses, and to say what they alone can say!

Miriam Gideon is very modest and is quick to give credit to her contemporaries. Albert Weisser once wrote to her: "You are far too modest. For the fact still remains, with all our heady circumlocutions and splendid desire to be fair and speak justly, that you are unique both as a woman composer and as a composer intrinsically." This beautifully written observation of Miriam Gideon, the artist, is shared by this writer.

Scores Published

Orchestra

Lyric Piece for String Orchestra, (ACE, 1941)
Symphonia Brevis, (ACE, 1953)
Songs of Youth and Madness, on poems of Friedrich Hölderlin, for voice and orchestra (ACE, 1977)

Dramatic Works

Fortunato, Opera in 3 scenes, based on the play by Serafin and Joaquin Quintero (ACE, 1958)
The Adorable Mouse, a French Folk Tale, for voice and chamber group (General Music Corp., 1960)

Chamber music with voice

The Hound of Heaven, (Francis Thompson) for voice, vln, vla, vc, ob. (Col. Univ. Music Press, 1945)
Sonnets from Shakespeare, for voice, trpt., str. quartet (ACE, 1950)
Sonnets from "Fatal Interview" (Millay) for voice, vln, vla, vc (ACE, 1952)

The Condemned Playground, (Horace, Milton, Spokes, Baude-
        laire) for soprano, tenor, fl. , bsn. , str. quartet
        (Bomart, 1963)
Questions on Nature, (Adelard of Bath) for voice, ob, piano,
        tam-tam, glockenspiel (Bomart, 1965)
Rhymes from the Hill, (from the "Galgenlieder" of Christian
        Morgenstern) for voice, cl, vc, marimba (Bomart,
        1968)
The Seasons of Time, (Ancient Japanese Tanka Poetry) for
        voice, fl, vc, piano alternating with celesta (General
        Music Corp. , 1969)
Nocturnes, (Shelley, Untermeyer, Sherman) for voice, fl, ob,
        vln, vc, vibraphone (ACE, 1976)
Voices from Elysium, (Greek Poets)--voice, cl, vln, vc,
        fl, piano (ACE, 1979)
Spiritual Airs (Ewen, Trimpberg, Heine) for voice and 7
        instruments (ACE, 1979)
Spirit above the Dust, (American Poetry) for voice and 8 in-
        struments (C. F. Peters, 1980)

            Chamber Music without voice
Lyric Piece for String Quartet, (ACE, 1941)
Quartet for Strings, (ACE, 1946)
Sonata for viola and piano, (ACE, 1948)
Fantasy on a Javanese Motive, for cello and piano (Highgate
        Press, 1948)
Air for Violin and Piano, (ACE, 1950)
Biblical Masks, for violin and piano (ACE, 1960)
Sonata for Cello and Piano, (ACE, 1961)
Suite for Clarinet or Bassoon and Piano, (ACE, 1972)
Fantasy on Irish Folk Motives, for ob, vla, bsn (or vc),
        vibraphone (ACE, 1975)
Trio for clarinet, cello, piano, (ACE, 1978)

            Keyboard
Canzona, for piano (New Music, 1945)
Piano Suite No. 3, (Lawson-Gould in "New Music for Piano",
        1951)
Six Cuckoos in Quest of a Composer, (ACE, 1953)
Biblical Masks, for organ (ACE, 1958)
Of Shadows Numberless, suite for piano, based on Keats
        "Ode to a Nightingale" (ACE, 1966)
Sonata for Piano, (ACE, 1977)

            Solo Voice and Piano
Epitaphs from Robert Burns, (ACE, 1952)

Sonnets from "Fatal Interview," (Millay) (ACE, 1952)
Mixco, (Asturias) (ACE, 1957)
To Music, (Herrick) (ACE, 1957)
Songs of Voyage, (ACE, 1961)
The Seasons of Time, (General Music Corp., 1969)

Choral
Slow, Slow, Fresh Fount, SATB (ACE, 1941)
How Goodly Are Thy Tents, 3-part women's voices, with
        piano or organ; also SATB chorus (Mercury [Presser],
        1947)
Adon Olom, for SATB, ob, trpt, str (ACE, 1954)
The Habitable Earth, Cantata based on the Book of Proverbs,
        for soloists, mixed chorus, ob, piano or organ (ACE,
        1965)
Spiritual Madrigals, (Ewen, Heine, von Trimpberg) for male
        voices, vla, vc, bsn (Bomart, 1965)
Sacred Service, (Saturday Morning) (ACE, 1971)
Sacred Service, (Shirat Miriam L'Shabbat--Friday Evening)
        (C. F. Peters, 1974)

Publishers

ACE (American Composers Edition)--170 West 74th Str.,
        New York, N. Y. 10023
General Music Publ. Co.--Box 267, Hastings-on-Hudson, NY
        10706
New Music ⎫
Merrymount ⎬ Theodore Presser, Presser Place, Bryn
          ⎪   Mawr, Pa. 19010
Mercury   ⎭
Columbia Univ. Press, (Distributed by Galaxy Music Corp.)
        2121 Broadway, New York, NY 10023
C. F. Peters Corp.--373 Park Avenue South, New York, NY
        10016
Bomart Music Publ.--Hillsdale, NY 12529
Highgate Press--2121 Broadway, New York, NY 10023

Discography

The Adorable Mouse, (A French Folk Tale) voice and chamber
        group; Serenus Recording Inc. 12050
The Condemned Playground, (Horace, Milton, Spokes, Baude-
        laire) soprano, tenor, flute, bassoon, string quartet;
        Composers Recordings, Inc., CRI SD 343

Fantasy on a Javanese Motive, for cello and piano; Paradox
        (out of print)
The Hound of Heaven, (Francis Thompson) voice, violin,
        viola, cello, oboe; Composers Recordings, Inc.
        SD 343
How Goodly Are Thy Tents, (in "Choral Masterworks of the
        Synagogue") 3 part women's voices, 4 part chorus with
        organ; Westminster Recording XWN 18857
Lyric Piece for String Orchestra, Composers Recordings,
        Inc.; CRI 170
Nocturnes, (Shelley, Untermeyer, Sherman), voice, flute,
        oboe, violin cello, vibraphone; Composers Recordings,
        Inc. CRI SD 401
Piano Suite #3 (in "New Music for Piano"); Composers Re-
        cordings, Inc. CRI SD 288
Questions on Nature, (Adelard of Bath), voice, oboe, piano,
        tam-tam, glockenspiel; Composers Recordings, Inc.
        CRI SD 343
Rhymes from the Hill, (from the "Galgenlieder" of Christian
        Morgenstern), voice, clarinet, cello, marimba; Com-
        posers Recordings, Inc. CRI SD 286
The Seasons of Time, (Ancient Japanese Tanka Poetry),
        voice, flute, cello, piano alternating with celesta;
        Desto Recording DC 7117
The Seasons of Time, (in "The Vocal Art of Paul Sperry")
        voice and piano; Serenus Recording, Inc. SRS 12078
Slow, Slow, Fresh Fount, (in "A Garden Concert of American
        Choral Music"), choral, SATB; Golden Crest Record-
        ings CRS 4172
Songs of Youth and Madness, (Hölderlin) voice and orchestra;
        Composers Recordings, Inc. CRI SD 401
Symphonia Brevis, orchestra; Composers Recordings, Inc.
        CRI 128

Addresses

Composers Recordings, Inc., 170 West 74th Street, New
        York, NY 10023

Desto Recordings, Distributed by CMS Records, 14 Warren
        St., New York, NY 10007

Golden Crest Records, Inc. 220 Broadway, Huntington Sta-
        tion, NY 11746

Serenus Records, Inc., Box 267, Hastings-on-Hudson, NY
        10706

Westminster Records, 1330 Avenue of the Americas, New
    York, NY 10019

PEGGY GLANVILLE-HICKS

Composer, Music Critic, Internationally Renowned Artist

Peggy Glanville-Hicks has achieved an international reputation
as a composer, but more specifically, an opera composer.
In 1950, she was the first woman, and until recently the only
woman, to have ever received a major commission from a
major opera company in America. She has established her
unique status in many ways. The first woman to have her
music performed at the Music in Our Time Series in New
York in 1958, she has also won numerous awards. During
this time her compositions and trend-setting accomplishments
have had a tremendous influence on twentieth-century music.

Be aware that P. Glanville-Hicks never actively participated in the women's movement as it was known in the
decades of the 1960's and 1970's. In a letter dated February
25, 1978, she wrote to me:

> You will perhaps wish to put it on record that I
> utterly disapprove of all such books that separate
> the ladies from the gentleman! It encourages sep-
> aration in other matters. Presently, one is re-
> viewed, "very good, for a lady composer," there
> is nothing more annoying or misleading. To com-
> pete openly among the male composers, we all
> know that from start to finish there will be preju-
> dice and preference. If by greater gift--harder
> work, greater privation--one does succeed in "beat-
> ing the boys at their own games" then it is known
> and realized that "to win" it was not enough to be
> equal, perhaps a little better; to win--one must
> have been so much better that the judges could not
> look each other in the face and deny one the "prize."
> Don't think me bitter. I prefer it the hard way--
> rather than be considered, "really very good, for
> a woman."

142

One can only express respect and admiration for P.
Glanville-Hicks; she traveled a turbulent and most difficult
road in reaching a peak of international acclaim.

One readily agrees that there should be no need to
separate the sexes: merit should be based solely on quality.
Unfortunately this has not happened. Negativism should not
be accepted, but one must not fault society for its past history. It has been natural for one group of humans to consider another group of humans categorically inferior. The
important issue is to swiftly eliminate the inequities.

Born in 1912 in Melbourne, Australia, her creative
talents were recognized as a young child. She studied piano
and started to work in composition at the age of fifteen with
Fritz Hart, composer of some twenty operas and conductor
of the Melbourne Symphony Orchestra.

In 1931, at the age of nineteen, she won an open
scholarship to the Royal College of Music in London and
Studied for five years with Vaughan Williams in composition,
piano with Arthur Benjamin, and conducting , first with Constant Lambert and later with Sir Malcom Sargent. An impressive list of teachers for a gifted young musician.

On being awarded the Octavia Traveling Scholarship
in 1936-1938, she continued her studies in Vienna with Egon
Wellesz and in Paris with Nadia Boulanger. Other awards
include: Carlotta Rowe Scholarship, Royal College of Music
1931-1935; American Academy of Arts and Letters Grant
1953; two Guggenheim Fellowships in 1956-1957, and 1957-
1958; Fulbright Fellowship, Research in Aegean Demotic
Music 1961-1963; and a Rockefeller Grant for travel and research in the Middle and Far East.

When the International Society for Contemporary Music
was founded in 1922, the main aim was to cultivate contemporary music of value without regard to the nationality, political opinions, or religion of the composer. The Society's
goal was to protect and encourage those tendencies which are
experimental and difficult to approach. The concerts, held
in various locations throughout the world, include orchestral
and chamber music performances.

The first Australian composer to be represented in
the ISCM Festival was Peggy Glanville-Hicks in 1938. Her
Choral Suite, conducted by Sir Adrain Boult in London, launched
her career at the age of twenty-six. Considerable recognition,

BMI Archives

PEGGY GLANVILLE-HICKS

publication, and a recording resulted from this auspicious debut into professional musical life. The Choral Suite was recorded by Pathé in Paris.

Again in 1948, she represented Australia in the ISCM Festival in Amsterdam when the Concertgebouw Chamber Group performed her Concertino de Camera for flute, clarinet, bassoon, and piano, and it was recorded by Columbia in their

Contemporary Music Series.   Considered Poulenc-ish in style
by some connoisseurs of contemporary music, it is in reality
the composer's farewell opus to French neo-classicism, acquired in the Boulanger classrooms.

Peggy Glanville-Hicks married the English composer
Stanley Bate in 1938.   Together in London they founded, in
1940, the ballet company "Les Trois Arts," and she served
in many capacities--business manager, publicity director,
conductor, and arranger.   This opportunity afforded her a
variety of experiences that were to serve her well in her
future career.

She and her husband came to the United States in early
1940 and established permanent residency in New York.   She
became a United States citizen in 1948.

Following her arrival in America, P. Glanville-Hicks
rapidly won recognition as a composer of distinctive stature.
Although she has made her strongest impression in opera,
she has composed orchestral, chamber, and choral works,
for ballet and films.   Her list of works is extensive, but
by highlighting a few of her compositions one can get an idea
of the respect of the musical world that she garnered from
both music critics and an enthralled listening audience.

Nicanor Zabaleta premièred the Glanville-Hicks' Sonata
for Harp in 1952 at the Museum of Modern Art in New York
and performed the beautiful sonata again at Town Hall several
years later.   The composer wrote the sonata especially for
him.

P. Glanville-Hicks said,

It was hearing Nicanor Zabaleta play that convinced
me that the harp is a major solo instrument, and
one particularly suited to the purest esthetic of
modern musical thought.   The instrument is at its
best in music where expressive content and musical
idea are in the closest state of fusion; in the best
harp music, form is the point of focus, not in-
stumentation; it is the very heart of the musical
matter that counts, not the exploitation of the peri-
pheral factors, for with its fragile timbres and
tones there is room only for the very essence.

Her composition Letters from Morocco, written in
1952 and scored for voice and orchestra, was premièred in

New York on February 22, 1953, with Leopold Stokowski conducting and William Hess, soloist.   The text consisted of
letters she had received from Paul Bowles, author and composer.

P. Glanville-Hicks wrote, "The work (from actual
letters of Paul Bowles) carefully eschews oriental trappings,
taking from the East only the structual principle of a melody-
rhythm form, in place of the harmonic structure basic to
most European compositions."

Glanville-Hicks' status as composer was firmly established in 1953 with her opera, The Transposed Heads, the
first opera to be commissioned by the Louisville Opera Company of Kentucky with a grant from the Rockefeller Foundation.   This opera, with libretto by Thomas Mann, was premièred in Louisville in 1954, recorded thereafter by Columbia, and was first performed in New York in 1958 in a production presented by Chandler Cowles at the Phoenix Theater.

The Transposed Heads is a story with gruesome over-
tones; the two rivals for the love of Sita, her husband and
her lover, behead themselves.   When commanded by the god-
dess Kali to replace the heads on the bodies, Sita puts the
husband's head on the lover's body.   When the question of
the legality of her husband becomes enmeshed in obvious complexities, all three commit suicide.   The audience embraced
the opera enthusiastically at the final curtain of the première,
recalling the composer and cast repeatedly.

Peggy Glanville-Hicks' contributions as a writer and
music critic will be more fully developed at the end of the
chapter; the following article, however, published by the
composer in the New York Times prior to the New York
première, affords the reader an opportunity to understand
her artistic commitment in her first opera.

The New York Times, February 9, 1958 by P. Glanville-
Hicks:

A HINDU THEME

Composer Uses Oriental Style in New Opera

In connection with the New York première of my
opera, The Transposed Heads, the question is bound
to arise, just how and to what extent have Oriental
musical ingredients been used in this work?   Such

a query is pertinent, since it touches upon the vital
difference between 'arrangement' and synthesis--
the one superficial, the other an organic process.

Any parallel between my music and certain Oriental types lies more in an abstract principle than
in the use of specific detail, and was arrived at as
much from reflection on the dilemma of Western
music as on the music of the East. In The Transposed Heads, as in most of my recent pieces, I
used a melody-rhythm structural pattern almost de-
void of harmony that was evolved quite independently
of exotic subject matter.

Discovery of the Thomas Mann story and the
writing of the score The Transposed Heads brought
together two completely separate lines of activity
in my life that I had never expected to merge. On
the one hand a hobby--a lifetime addiction to archaeology and anthropology, with the comparative
study of folk music and musical remnants from antiquity as kind of a cue system in the treasure
hunt! On the other hand, my chosen profession
wherein as a scholarship student in the most sophisticated music schools of Europe I gained fair
mastery of twentieth-century composition techniques.

First Principles

The cause for this direction lies deeper than a
mere boredom with the expressive limitations of
dissonance, however; a distrust of composition 'systems' precipitated some years ago a searching re-
examination of music's first principles, of its primary inpulses and units, and a conviction grew that
melody and rhythm are our basic, perennial expressive and structural factors; that in harmony, the
vertical concept, we have come to an impasse.

Accordingly I threw out harmony, and with it of
course went dissonance. Structurally it left a gap,
for Western large-scale forms were evolved around
harmonic structure as was also our standard orchestral layout. Shed of its vertical prop, melody
gravitates naturally toward the self-sufficient equi-
ibrium of modality, while liberated from its position
as mere trimming and accent on chordal beats, percussion, the natural orchestration of rhythm, moves
to prominence as partner and polarity point to melody.

Arriving at this stage I began to realize that I
had developed a musical organism very similar to

the patterns of antiquity; a melody-rhythm element
of greatly enhanced freedom, so that the science of
intervals and meters as contained in Eastern music
(particularly in the still flourishing tradition of India), ceased to be merely a facet of my musical
archaeology, and became a highly relevent subject
for analytical investigation in Western terms.

Early Stages

Several preliminary works charted the earlier
stages of my new writing concept, and the idea of
an opera took shape, one to be written on a melody-
rhythm pattern where vocal melodic lines could
carry the whole form and pacing of the work, and
where rhythmic control could function as crisis
builder in lieu of piled up harmonic and orchestral
weight.
I looked for a story that would be timeless--or
at least that touched the timeless through the timely,
for this marks the difference between journalism
and literature, between a 'show' and an opera.
I looked for a plot whose unfolding was compre-
hensible from its observed events without the comment of arias, for even with the greatest prosodic
skill on the part of the composer, and perfect dic-
tion on the part of the singers, much of an opera
text is inevitably not heard.
I looked for a book whose events fell into scenes
in such a manner that musical, rather than literary
development brought about the apotheosis, and when
Thomas Mann's Transposed Heads came to hand the
advent seemed almost celestial. Not only did it
meet the structural, theatrical and literary needs,
but it was a Hindu legend offering an opportunity
to use actual Indian themes of folk and classic origins as point of departure for the music, and I
knew that I could now incorporate such material
without infringement of its essential nature and
without further amendment of my own style. (Copyright © 1958 by The New York Times Company.
Reprinted by permission.)

One of the most interesting of the many reviews of
this opera was written for the Cleveland Plain Dealer by Herbert Elwell, June 12, 1955:

Miss Glanville-Hicks is a composer who understands

the human voice.   She also understands what should
happen to the English language when it is sung.
This could scarcely be said of more than half a
dozen of America's top-ranking serious composers,
who--generally speaking--are not primarily interested in vocal music, and are miles behind the Tin-
Pan-Alley and Broadway show-tune composers in
the matter of prosody.

She places the open vowel sounds in strategic
spots; she preserves the vigorous rhythms of the
speaking voice to a remarkable degree.   She is
amazingly skillful in other ways too, particularly
in the building of exciting dramatic tensions, and
in the quickness of her transitions from one surprise
element to another.   In addition she has been most
canny in her choice of subject--a story of Thomas
Mann which is ideal for operatic treatment, combining as it does humour, exotic fantasy, violence,
passion, and even a bit of metaphysics.   (Reprinted
by permission of The Plain Dealer.)

Reviewing Chandler Cowles' Phoenix Theatre Productions, Robert Evett wrote in The New Republic, Feb. 24th,
1958:

The Transposed Heads ... introduced at the Phoenix
Theatre on Feb. 10th was not, technically speaking
a world première; nonetheless this first New York
staging was a grand affair.

The libretto drawn from a minor work of Thomas
Mann is a model of elegance. . . .   The texture of
the music is so light as to be insubstantial.   Two
things are emphasized; melody and rhythm. . . .
There are no fully developed arias in the conventional sense, but there are dozens of exquisite tunes
which, once they have been sung are expertly woven
into the fabric of the work.

The conventional instruments of the orchestra
are given minor jobs; it is the percussion section
(heavily augmented) that gives the music its sonority
and rhythmic drive.

Throughout her career, Miss Glanville-Hicks has
been in the vanguard of musical fashion ... ten
years ago she was effectively championing the highly
dissonant and volatile "advanced" styles. . . .   She
mastered those styles completely, and if she now
wishes to turn her back on them, her choice is
based on experience.

> The Transposed Heads ... is one of the richest
> outpourings of unencumbered melody in recent
> years.... While "originality" may be an over-
> valued quality, it is the quality that Miss Glanville-
> Hicks has developed, and the results have been
> most distinguished.
>
> Her opera is the only one I have seen recently
> that is likely to have any large or long-term sig-
> nificance. (Reprinted by permission of The New
> Republic, © 1958 The New Republic, Inc.)

World Theatre, a Quarterly Review published by the
International Theatre Institute with the assistance of Unesco,
Vol. VII, No. 2, 1958:

> Peggy Glanville-Hicks' The Transposed Heads with
> libretto by the composer consisting almost entirely
> of dialogue from the Thomas Mann novella, is de-
> void of all the "magnificent" encumbrances that
> attach to grand opera, but it is opera nevertheless
> --and in its way, a masterpiece.

Immediately following the première of her opera, P.
Glanville-Hicks was commissioned to write a ballet for the
first Spoleto Festival. This was The Masque of the Wild
Man, choreographed by John Butler and designed by Rouben
Ter Arutunian. It was performed at the "Festival of the
Two Worlds" in 1958. John Butler approached her to write
the ballet. She finished the score and had a tape ready in
twelve days so that he could take the work with him on the
day he sailed for Italy. P. Glanville-Hicks was in Spoleto
for the première and, as a result, many long discussions
with Butler took place. She said, "I had long regarded John
Butler as our greatest choreographic creator, but our collaboration in Spoleto and subsequent talks in Greece showed
him to be much more--a deep-thinking modern mystic and
a dedicated man of the theater in every sense."

The Masque of the Wild Man was singled out in the
June 12, 1958 edition of the newspaper Il Populo (Rome),
which reported:

> The accompaniment to the four ballets of Butler
> are all excellent. But the composition of Peggy
> Glanville-Hicks for The Masque of the Wild Man
> based on a melodic-rhythmic element, deserves
> special mention. The score of Glanville-Hicks fur-
> nishes valid cues for a choreography echoing back

to the medieval modes in an idiom genuinely based
on the principles of modern dance, and contributes
more than anything in eliminating the need for scenery and costumes.

In the 1950's P. Glanville-Hicks wrote a provocative
article published in the Bulletin of the American Composers
Alliance, VI, No. 4, 1957: "Some Reflections on Opera."
Her perception of the opera scene in America unfortunately
would still be true in the 1980's.   Although there has been
some progress, it has been extremely slow and frustrating
in essence and most of what she wrote three decades ago is
still true.   The following is an excerpt from that article:

> Opera of one kind or another is a matter of great
> concern to many American composers today, and
> it is clear from the bulk of our production to date
> that many of the basic principles of theatre drama
> have yet to be mastered and applied in our national
> idiom.
>
> American opera composers--aside from the one
> or two long associated with this form--will tend to
> be a new bunch of names yet to be developed and
> discovered, not those already known as symphonists.
> For the born opera composer is a different type
> from the symphonic man--rarer (as history has
> proven)--with a different, more varied, perhaps
> more comprehensive technique than the abstract
> forms demand.
>
> Most of this technique can be gained only by
> hearing--seeing opera in large quantities and by
> taking part in putting together operas in performance,
> neither of these opportunities having been part of
> the average training and background to date of Amer-
> ica's composers.
>
> Many of the perennial problems in operatic writ-
> ing can be studied in standard repertoire, through
> score--study is helpful more in the purely musical
> than in the dramatic and the spatial techniques
> which must be physically manifest to be realized.
> Basic problems of all kinds can be realized more
> immediately and more vividly for us by hearing
> them solved in twentieth century idiom, in the ter-
> minology of our own time: In short by hearing the
> works of our contemporaries of other countries,
> particularly countries like Germany where operatic
> tradition has been unbroken and the modern com-
> poser's work automatically takes its place in major

opera house repertory.   Where, as a result, the
composers--whatever their degree of creative gift
--at least have the technique, experience and authority in this form that we, by and large, lack.
The professional hearing of such works has never
been possible in New York--or indeed anywhere in
the U. S. --until recent years.   (Reprinted by permission of the American Composers Alliance.)

Since 1959 Peggy Glanville-Hicks has made her home
in Athens, where she owns a home on the slopes of the Acropolis.   In 1959-60 a Fulbright Research Fellowship and a
Rockefeller Grant made possible a comparative study of the
demotic music of Greece and the musical system of India already known to her.

The outcome of these years was Nausicaa, an opera
based on Greek demotic musical material, with libretto from
the novel Homer's Daughter by Robert Graves.   The libretto
was prepared by the composer and author in collaboration in
Mallorca in 1956.

After three years of work, Nausicaa was presented by
the Greek Government in the Athens Festival in 1961 before
an audience of 4,500 people in the ancient open-air theater
of Herod Atticus, under the Parthenon.   The première was
a triumph, achieving international recognition and coverage.

Following are excerpts from several of many reviews--
The London Times: "Nausicaa, modern opera by Peggy Glanville-Hicks, had an excellent reception"; The Guardian, England: "The highlight here was the world première of P. G. H's
fourth opera, Nausicaa"; Frankfurter Allgemeine Zeitung:
"She makes the daring--and dangerous experiment of reviving
the spirit of the ancient Greek Dramas within the means of
modern theatre"; Variety: "A ten-minute standing ovation
greeted the world première of Peggy Glanville-Hicks' new
opera"; Time: "Australia-born composer Glanville-Hicks, 48,
is one of the few women who have turned a successful hand
to opera"; Musical America: "It was probably the first time,
too, that an American composer wrote, cast, rehearsed, and
launched her own work. "

P. Glanville-Hicks said, "The composition and production of Nausicaa followed a kind of artistic journey to the
source of the river, both in musical idioms and in forms,
that led to a study of antique and folk material on one hand,
Greek theater concepts on the other.   It is a rather curious

turn of fate that a work begun in the Aegean, completed in
Manhattan and designed from the first principles of Greek
theater should have to face the acid test of a debut "in the
round" in a classical stone arena.

Review in Variety, New York City, August 30, 1961:

> A ten-minute standing ovation greeted the world
> premiere of Peggy Glanville-Hicks' new opera Nau-
> sicaa in the ancient theater of Herod Atticus at the
> base of the Acropolis in the heart of Athens. The
> cast of 150 won eight curtain calls from the capa-
> city crowd of 4,800 which overflowed into the aisles
> and represented the cream of Athens society, in-
> cluding such international figures as Madame Pan-
> dit.

Peter Gradenwitz writing for Frankfurter Allgemeine
Zeitung, Germany on August 31, 1961:

> In Nausicaa she makes the daring--and the danger-
> ous experiment of reviving the spirit of the Ancient
> Greek Drama within the means of the modern the-
> atre--and with the use of traditional (regional) musi-
> cal elements. This work was preceded by two
> years of study of Greek Demotic Music.
>   There was born an opera which will probably
> have a similiar effect on educated Greeks as Bizet's
> Carmen has on Spaniards at its first hearing ...
> The musical means are finely integrated, and result
> in a highly personal style of composition.
>   Style and subject in this opera seem in an odd
> way timeless. "Modal" materials are treated at
> times in a "serial" spirit, while the sound of the
> orchestra reveals a master of the modern composers'
> profession.
>   The effect of Nausicaa is not at all that of scien-
> tific research work in the fields of history and
> musical science. It is an opera with an individuality
> all its own--a work opening vistas to new modern
> roads in ancient spirit never trodden before. (Per-
> mission for this translation granted by author and
> publisher.)

Following this success, P. Glanville-Hicks was commissioned by the Ford Foundation, as part of its eight-year
program to encourage the writing and performing of American
opera, to compose a work for the San Francisco Opera. This

resulted in Sappho, an opera in three acts, with libretto from
the play by Lawrence Durrell. It was commissioned for
Maria Callas in the mezzo-soprano role of Sappho.

Composer of five ballets, she heard her new work,
A Season in Hell, premièred on November 25, 1967. It was
reviewed by Winthrop Sargeant for the The New Yorker:

> I was lucky enough to arrive in time for the ballet
> that preceded Golden Age--A Season in Hell by John
> Butler. This is a sober item indeed, about the
> trouble with poets is that they never get the girl.
> It was danced before an interesting backdrop--a
> sort of Milky Way with steel wires in front of it,
> devised by Rouben Ter Arutunian--and it has a
> score of unusual expressiveness by Peggy Glanville-
> Hicks. The two main roles were danced by Law-
> rence Rhodes and Brunilda Ruiz, both of them vir-
> tuosos of the first rank, while Dennis Wayne pro-
> vided the lure that attracts Miss Ruiz and left Mr.
> Rhodes in despair. As ultra-romantic ballets go,
> this was an absorbing one, though all the dancers
> were dressed abstractly and the sort of movement
> was mixed--part ballet, part Martha Graham. (Copy-
> right © 1967 Winthrop Sargeant in The New Yorker.
> Reprinted by permission.)

In 1966 P. Glanville-Hicks was commissioned by CBS
Color Television, resulting in her ballets, Tragic Celebration,
and Saul and the Witch of Endor. The first was scored for
tympani, percussion, harp, and strings--the second for trumpet, three percussion, and strings. Both were choreographed
by John Butler.

Her artistic accomplishments, as a composer will forever remain a part of the history of music. Her works,
published and recorded, are easily procured by the listening
public and performing groups. Her scope of achievement is
enormous, not least of all her organizational skills and contributions as a music critic and writer.

From 1954 to 1958 she was one of the outstanding
music critics for The New York Herald Tribune. As a colleague of Virgil Thomson, composer and music critic for
the same newspaper, she shared assignments that covered
the international world of music of interest to the reading
public. Shortly after the beginning of her tenure with the
Herald Tribune, she wrote a birthday greeting to Virgil Thom-

son, a composition for voice and instruments that used musical settings of excerpts from the reviews he had written.
Of course the title was Thomsoniana. Humorous, and a delight for both Thomson and the audience, it was likewise a
fine example of her artistic gift. Her articles have appeared
in: Musical Quarterly, Notes, Harper's Bazaar, Vogue, The
Juilliard Review, and Musical America.

Some twenty years ago Peggy Glanville-Hicks published
a lengthy article in The Juilliard Review, Spring 1958, No.
2. This should be read by every serious student of music,
for the depth of musical knowledge it reflects. The following is an excerpt:

> It is customary to discuss the art of composing as
> though its entire process and product could be ex-
> pounded in analytical discourse. Such elements as
> cannot be subjected to this process are considered
> somewhat esoteric--or at least as unproven, and
> therefore unreliable data.
>   Yet it is clear that in the arts the problem of con-
> tent versus form precipitates us right into the heart
> of the battle of tangible and intangible forces, so
> that a dual concept must be faced from the outset.
>   It has been said of the composer that his ma-
> terials lie in the territory of the physicist, his
> technique in the territory of the mathematician and
> his message in the category of the Prophet--since
> only time can establish its validity! Certainly the
> composer's span of awareness embraces two areas;
> the emerged level of the intellect wherein is culti-
> vated the technical skill and mastery, and another
> submerged level from whence springs his inspiration,
> and where an instinctive rather than a calculated
> choice appears to reign.
>   The whole is like an iceberg, whose submerged
> mass provides the stability supporting the emerged
> peaks. From the buried mass comes the eternal
> potency, while above the surface, like a long line
> of ancestors, are the forms and idiomatic patterns
> in all their geographic and historic variety in which
> this expressive volume incarnates. It is a duality
> of spirit and body, and the quality of greatness in
> art has a lot to do with the degree of poise and
> balance with which these two halves relate to each
> other and act together.
>   In eras such as our own where the arts are
> working their way through a phase of cataclysmic

change, it is illuminating to re-assess from time
to time the output of contemporary writers in terms
of two aspects: expressive content and technical
syntax.

The composer of the present day has inherited
as his point in time the end stage or final decadence
of a huge cycle of musical evolution, the cycle of
harmonic or vertical thinking which crystallized
around the tempered scale.

The turn of the present century witnessed an apparent revolution in the materials and moods of
music, whose tide carried away most of the certi-
tudes in technical and esthetic procedure, leaving
a chaos of new materials whose ordering is still
a matter of controversy. Inherent though it was
in the musical situation, the movement of the Twen-
ties came as a shock, this very shock aspect later
becoming a cult to haunt more serious and less
spectacular purpose.

It was in a sense a twofold revolution, the harmonic aspect being a European one, the rhythmic
aspect stemming largely from this continent and
from the impact here of native music of the Americas, not the least of which was that specialized
but impulsive Metropolitan folk art Jazz.

The two faiths, Atonalism with its head Church
in Vienna and Schoenberg as Patron Saint, and Neo-
Classicism in Paris under the spell of Stravinsky
were, from the point of view of advanced technique,
the choice for the younger composers twenty years
ago, and in the academic sense remain so today.

To be sure, Vienna and Paris have given way to
Los Angeles and Cambridge, Massachusetts, while
paradoxically, abroad, the German-speaking areas
have relinquished atonalism somewhat in favour of
neo-classicism, while France has embraced the
twelve-tone row, as though each had exhausted the
possibilities of its original favourite and had agreed
to exchange.

Both systems were easy to "package" for Academic life on account of the high degree of factors
on the tangible, analytical plane and the conveniently
low percentage on the intuitive level so hard to sys-
tematise for imparting in the classrooms. And as
a result, dozens of youngsters emerge yearly from
the Academies, fluent in these languages, imagining
that to be thus literate is to be a poet.

This situation had considerably eased during the

war years when, cut off from European thinking,
the patriotic search for 'Americana' discovered and
performed the wide swath of independent composers
who had either thrown off or never entered the
European schools of thought. Latterly, with the
resumption of communication abroad, a retrogression has again set in.

It is a fact that in countries or individuals,
when the inspirational quality wanes, the reliance
in intellectual formulae waxes. The creative fin
de siècle--or possibly, exhaustion--of Europe has
probably had a lot to do with their resorting to
systems, particularly the most highly intellectual-
ized one, atonalism. That this un-American blight
should spread over our own young creators is a
matter for regret; and there is an added subtlety
to the retrogression, Europe's composers were by
and large at a standstill for many war years. Their
history stopped at the point of dissonant experiment,
and they re-took it on from there in recent years.
The Americans during those same years worked
their way through maximum dissonance, evolving
regional styles of spontaneous individuality which
the European modernist, unaware of his own time-
lag, is apt to deride as 'old fashioned'. He fails
to see that this is the avant garde--in kind, at
least, if not degree--that he himself must reach
as he exhausts as we did the dissonant frontiers.

But such is the lack of faith in our own creators
here at home, and such the seemingly inextinguish-
able prestige of Europe, that the Academy and their
progeny take cover in an indiscriminate systematised
use of dissonance, being assured from afar that it
is the obligatory condition of both modernism and
originality.

To be a composer is a whole way of life, and
it is difficult to combine it satisfactorily with any
other way of life, especially if that other is geared
to a schedule without room for solitude and medita-
tion.

The real composer-artist who, endowed with the
spirit, will patiently build the Temple and await
the Muse, will find that the knowledge he has acquired, distilled into its final product, wisdom, will
inhabit the whole warp and woof of his musical ideas
so none can say which is technique, which heaven-
sent material with the germs of its own growth and
flowering contained therein. This is art, and this

alone is what the collectivity of people over a period of time always recognize, for this product of
true fusion is like an act of faith, and cannot be
counterfeited. (Reprinted by permission of The
Juilliard Review.)

Peggy Glanville-Hicks is also a humanist--her concern
and willingness to devote her time and energies to help those
artists in need of a friend and understanding must not be un-
derestimated. Following World War II, her position as a
delegate to the International Society of Contemporary Music
Festival in Copenhagen and in Amsterdam allowed her observation of the post-war plight of Europe's musicians. It was
her ideas and initiative, in collaboration with Carleton Sprague
Smith, that sparked the creation of the International Music Fund to raise $100,000 for the needy artists. She was
author of its first manifesto, and the on-the-spot reporter
at the Inaugural Benefit Concert given by Koussevitzky at
Tanglewood, in Lenox, Massachusetts.

The Tanglewood Parade Concert was a fascinating
story in itself--7,000 people were in the audience that raised
$10,000 for needy artists. It featured a gala six-point pro-
gram that included a parade of some 400 Berkshire Music
Festival students and ended with a fireworks display at the
close of the day. Students gave a program in the shed. On
the lawn in front of the original mansion were featured speakers who included Serge Koussevitzky, Archibald MacLeish,
Aaron Copland, and principal speaker Justice Felix Frankfurter of the United States Supreme Court. Operatic excerpts
were presented in the garden: students performed in the
chamber hall; opera students performed in the theater-concert
hall; and the chorus sang in the fields. Topping it all, the
Boston Symphony Orchestra performed in the big shed. The
entire program could be summarized as a musical mecca.
The unsung heroine was P. Glanville-Hicks, Executive Secretary of the International Music Fund, operating through
Unesco to assist European composers.

For a period of ten years, from 1950 to 1960, she
directed the Composers Forum in New York, organizing seven
concerts annually for young composers. Accounts of these
programs can be found in the leading New York newspapers,
now on microfilm in the leading libraries and universities in
the country.

She has been independently responsible for the recording of a dozen or more majors works by her colleagues.

These include not only premières, but the revivals of such pieces as Ballet Mecanique of George Antheil, the Concerto for Piano and Wind Octet by Colin McPhee, and the opera, The Wind Remains by Paul Bowles. All these works were neglected for twenty years until her efforts revived them.

Lou Harrison's opera Rapunzel was awarded the twentieth-century Masterpiece Prize in Rome but was not heard in the United States until P. Glanville-Hicks raised the backing and created the production for The Artists Company.

She devoted her energy to the performance, publication, and recording of the greater part of the music of author-composer Paul Bowles. She has also steadfastly sponsored in her writings that group of composers--Bowles, McPhee, Hovhaness, Harrison, El Dabh, and Surinach--who, like herself, use in some way the modes and methods of the Oriental or antique world.

In 1955 she co-chaired with Yehudi Menuhin the Museum of Modern Art series of concerts of Indian music and, because of her extensive knowledge of Oriental music, she has always been in demand as consultant in the East-West musical affairs that touch the United States.

Peggy Glanville-Hicks reminds us that compositional art rises above and beyond characteristics of the masculine or feminine--she is an artist who will always remain a part of twentieth-century music.

Selected List of Works

(Broadcast Music, Inc. 589 Fifth Avenue, New York, N. Y. 10017)

Operas

The Transposed Heads, opera in six scenes, text by Thomas
         Mann, for soprano, tenor, baritone, two speaking
         roles, chorus and orchestra (one and one-half hours).
The Glittering Gate, opera in one act, text by Lord Dunsany,
         for tenor, baritone, chamber orchestra and electronic
         tape (thirty minutes).
Nausicaa, opera in three acts, text by Robert Graves, for
         soprano, contralto, baritone, 3 tenors, bass, bass-
         baritone and orchestra (two hours).

Sappho, opera in three acts, text by Lawrence Durrell, for
        mezzo lyric-tenor, dramatic-tenor, baritone, bass-
        baritone, bass, chorus and orchestra (two and one-
        quarter hours).

Ballets
The Masque of the Wild Man, for harp, piano, percussion
        (2) and strings, commissioned for first Spoleto Fes-
        tival, eighteen minutes.
Saul and the Witch of Endor, for trumpet, percussion (3)
        and strings, twenty minutes.
Tragic Celebration, tympani, percussion, harp, strings, nine-
        teen minutes.
A Season in Hell, ballet after Arthur Rimbaud, strings and
        percussion, twenty minutes.

Orchestra
Etruscan Concerto, for piano and chamber orchestra, six-
        teen minutes.
Concerto Romantico, for viola and orchestra, twenty-one
        minutes.
Three Gymnopédie, Number 1, for oboe, harp and strings.
        Number 2 for harp, celesta and strings. Number 3
        for harp and strings, four minutes.
Sinfonia da Pacifica, tympani, percussion, harp and strings,
        fifteen minutes.
Tapestry for Orchestra, tympani, percussion harp, celesta,
        piano and strings, sixteen minutes.
Drama for Orchestra, percussion (3) and strings, seventeen
        minutes.
Tragic Celebration, tympani, percussion, harp and strings,
        nineteen minutes.
Letters from Morocco, for tenor and orchestra, text from
        letters of Paul Bowles, percussion (3), harp, and
        strings, sixteen minutes.
Choral Suite, for women's chorus, oboe and string orchestra,
        texts from poems of John Fletcher (1957), twenty min-
        utes.

Chamber Works
Sonata for Piano and Percussion, five percussionists, ten
        minutes.
Concertino da Camera, for piano, flute, clarinet and bassoon,
        eleven minutes.

Concertino Antico, for solo harp and string quartet, twelve
      minutes.
Musica Antiqua No. 1, for two flutes, harp, marimba, per-
      cussion (2) and tympani, eighteen minutes.
Sonata for Harp
Sonatina for Flute, or recorder with piano.
Profiles from China, five songs for voice and piano, poems
      by Eunice Tijens, also version for chamber orchestra.
Last Poems, five songs for voice and piano, Poems by A. E.
      Housman.
13 Ways of Looking at a Blackbird, thirteen songs to be sung
      without break, for soprano and piano.
Thomsoniana, five musical parodies, for tenor or soprano
      with flute horn, piano and string quartet, twelve min-
      utes.
Ballade, three songs for voice and piano, poems by Paul
      Bowles.
Pastoral, for women's chorus and English horn, text by R.
      Tagore.

Music for Films

Tel, cartoon for Film Graphics Inc. , 1950.
The African Story, from "All our Children" for the United
      Nations, 1956.

Discography

The Transposed Heads, Opera in Six Scenes. Text: Thomas
      Mann. Harlan, Pickett, conductor Bombard, Louisville
      Opera Co. and Orchestra, LOU 545-6.
Nausicca, Opera in three acts. Text: Robert Graves.
      Stratas, Modenos, Ruhl, Steffan, Athens Symphony
      Orchestra and Chorus, conductor, Carlos Surinach,
      CRI 175.
Etruscan Concerto, for piano and chamber orchestra, pianist,
      Carlo Bussotti, conductor, MGM Orchestra, MGM 3557.
Concerto Romantica, for viola and orchestra, violist, Walter
      Trampler, MGM Orchestra conducted by Carlos Sur-
      inach, MGM 3559.
Letters from Morocco, for tenor and chamber orchestra,
      Loren Driscoll, tenor, MGM Orchestra conducted by
      Carlos Surinach, MGM E 3549.
Sinfonia Pacifica, Carlos Surinach, MGM Orchestra, MGM
      E 3336.

Gymnopedie Nos. 1, 2, and 3, RIAS Orchestra, conducted by
        Jonel Perles, CRI 175.
Also, Carlos Surinach, MGM Orchestra, MGM E 3336.
Sonata for Piano and Percussion, Carlo Bussotti, piano, New
        York Percussion Group, Columbia ML 4990.
Concerto da Camera, Carlo Bussotti, pianist, New York
        Woodwind Ensemble, Columbia ML 4990.
Sonata for Harp, Nicanor Zabaleta, Esoteric E 5523.

Addresses

Louisville First Editions, 333 West Broadway, Louisville,
        KY   40202.

Composers Recordings, Inc. , 170 West 74th Street, New
        York, NY   10023.

MGM Records, 1350 Avenue of the Americas, New York,
        NY   10019.

Columbia Records, CBS Inc. , 51 West 52 Street, New York,
        NY   10019.

Esoteric Inc. , 26 Clark Street, East Hartford, Conn.   06108.

(Most, if not all these records are unavailable.)

DORIS HAYS

Composer, Performing Artist

Motivation is the phenomenon that probably stems from early
childhood and teenage experiences in which the environment
nurtures the creative growth and exploration that will flourish
through the artist's career.   That the truth will make one
free, but first it will make one miserable, is an experience
long accepted by an intellectual and creative society.

Doris Hays' dynamic energy as a composer and performing artist has projected her talents into the mainstream
of the international contemporary music scene.   She expresses an intuitive feeling when she speaks of her career as a
composer, "In 1975 I was upset by the disparity between
what I was composing (an enormous amount of electronic
music) and what I was feeling as a person."   The jolt in
thinking came from realizing that many of her creative endeavors stemmed from early life experiences and upbringing.
She was born in the South, weaned on church music, hymns,
lots of organ playing, fiddle tunes, country music, and of
course, the rock and roll music of the early fifties.   When
she premièred Sunday Nights for piano in 1976 at Carnegie
Hall, the obvious correlation from early life experiences and
background was immediately recognized.   This performance
signaled the beginning of the most productive period in the
creative life of the talented young composer.

Hays focuses on this première, a tremendous learning
experience, with total honesty when she says:

> The experiences of my Southern background have
> nurtured my creative output for over a period of
> five years and it is absolutely contrary to a lot of
> what I created prior to this time.   It is also con-
> trary to and it is still not quite accepted as "new
> enough" (the quotes made a point about what cate-

163

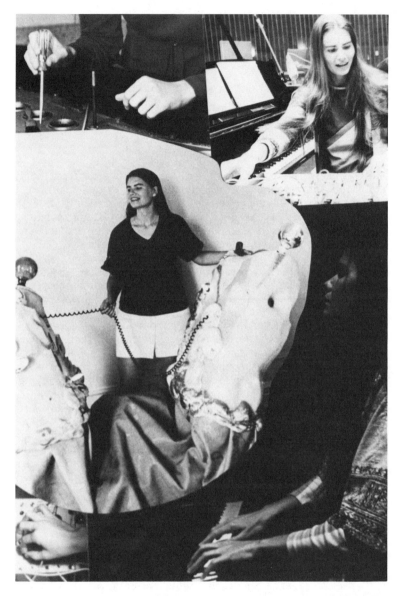

Self photo

DORIS HAYS

gorization it isn't) music which I find very interesting from the historical-sociocultural standpoint.
Categorization is irritating and limiting.
I still continue to write pieces based on my background but more on an intellectual and formal musical level. It has been increasingly more fun and
successful with audiences because it seems to touch
on something they can understand even if they don't
grasp it in its entirety. My parents passed on to
me their grit, stubbornness and independence. These
mountain, pioneer qualities are showing up in my
music.

Doris Hays, an independent thinker, composer, artist/
performer, and an authority on the keyboard music of Henry
Cowell, was born in Memphis, Tennessee, on August 6, 1941.
She is the daughter of Christina Doris Fair and Walter Ernest
Hays. Her mother is a homemaker and her father has his
own real estate business. The family of five (Hays has two
brothers) moved to Chattanooga when she was five. Hays
attended the local schools, beginning the study of piano when
she was six years old and continuing her lessons with the
same woman teacher for the next several years. At the age
of nine she wrote her first composition and states, "It was
not quite right, but my piano teacher, Helen Starnes, gave
me a medal at the yearly recital in recognition of my efforts
in composing and it was really reinforcing." She also credits
this teacher with a strong influence in helping her to develop
an excellence in rhythmic precision that has played an important part in her contemporary performance career.

She earned her Bachelor of Music degree from the
University of Chattanooga, Cadek Conservatory in 1959.
However, she had begun her keyboard studies with the Dean
of Cadek Conservatory, Mr. Harold Cadek, when she was
thirteen years old. She continued to study with him until
she was graduated at age twenty-one. Doris recalls her years
of study with Cadek,

He was a wonderful teacher; his parents came to
America at the turn of the century, and his entire
family, including a brother and sister, were (now
all deceased) musically active in many areas of the
South. He gave me support in any area that helped
me to develop my growth, although the emphasis
was on performance. When I wanted to write music
he supported my efforts and in addition, he suggested adventurous readings on everything from Zen

philosophy to piano building which directed my avenues of thought.   My parents had encouraged me to
read and explore things in early childhood, but
Harold Cadek was a primary influence in my musical and intellectual development for over eight years.

Doris Hays started to earn money as a pianist from
the time she was thirteen.   Her first paid job was accompanying a boys' choir.   She became an accompanist and choir
member at McFarland Methodist Church in Rossville, Georgia, among other solo and chamber performing jobs.   At this
particular stage of her life, nobody could imagine composing
as a possibility of a livelihood or even an activity.   The
standard avenue was to encourage women musicians to follow
the path of teaching as a career.   Hays admits, "I just didn't
fit into the agreed lifestyle.   It wasn't until I reached New
York and sold music I wrote, that people took my writing
seriously."

From 1963 to 1966 Hays studied in Germany, having
been influenced by many of her European-educated professors
at the Cadek Conservatory.   Without funds of her own, and
having just lived through a difficult period of life (she was
briefly married to a minister), she received a grant to go
abroad from the McClellan Foundation, a private family fund.
Fluent in German and encouraged by her teachers to go to
Germany, she went to Munich to continue her studies with
Friedrich Wührer at the Munich Hochschule für Musik.   She
received a Bavarian Ministry Fellowship for three years and
was awarded her Artist Diploma in 1966 with the Meister
Klasse designation.   Hays said,

> Although I was invited to remain at the Hochschule,
> I returned to the United States because the cultural
> life in Germany was alien to my Southern upbring-
> ing.   I've a deep respect for German love of music,
> and I am always well-treated as a creative and per-
> forming artist when I tour in Germany.   But the
> language and the habits and rituals I grew up with
> feed me.   I was starved for home-cooked ways of
> being after three years in Europe.

Following her return to the United States, Hays enrolled as a graduate student at the University of Wisconsin
in anticipation of a possible teaching career.   She chose Wisconsin because she wanted to study with Paul Badura-Skoda.
He proved to be the final Teuton.   Doris said, "Although he
is Viennese, with a little lighter touch, it just capped it for
me."   She received her Master of Music degree in 1968.

During this time Doris Hays decided that she needed a repertoire that made sense to her as an American in the 1960's.

> Something out of the American culture and out of my time and that is when I started playing the piano music of Henry Cowell. When I found this music in a friend's library, it appealed to me especially because of its seemingly rebellious nature. I developed the technique of performing Cowell's music entirely on my own, because none of my teachers or coaches could play it or would play it. Since I developed my own cluster technique it permitted me to perform his music well. It suited me and I made it my own. Sidney Cowell, his widow, loves the way I play it.

Today Doris Hays is recognized as an authority and a specialist on Henry Cowell's piano music as a performer, lecturer, and writer. Her techniques for the tone clusters used in this music include the use of the fist, palm, and forearm. Tom Johnson writing for the Village Voice on August 8, 1977, completed his review of two Doris Hays performances of Henry Cowell's piano music in this manner: "Only pianists with exceptional range could do justice to such a repertoire, and Hays is one of them. She can hammer out clusters like a wild animal, play intricate passages with fine control, and sound like a Chopin specialist at other times. "

Hays received numerous positive and exciting reviews with the release of her performance of The Piano Music of Henry Cowell recorded by Finnadar/Atlantic Disc, SR 9016 in 1977. The nineteen short pieces on this album were written by Cowell from 1912 to 1938. Two of the shorter reviews are as follows:

Critic at large--Newhouse Newspapers--by Byron Belt, Spring 1977:

> Doris Hays the pianist extraordinary. One evening in the early 1960's in Chicago, at a dinner party honoring Cornelia Otis Skinner, the late Henry Cowell sat down at the piano and enchanted a sophisticated gathering with a half dozen of his pioneering pieces. Tiny in length, but gigantic in their exquisite daring, Cowell's music has lingered in my ears through all the years since his passing in 1965.

Now for the first time, full justice has been done to Cowell's miniature delights. Fist-clashing tone clusters may sound wild in theory (and at one time they seemed to shock people), but they emerge as music with a Debussy-like luminosity, poetry and wit.

Doris Hays is a specialist on Cowell, and her love and brilliant virtuosity bring "The Piano Music of Henry Cowell" vividly to life on a beautifully recorded Finnadar/Atlantic Disc (SR 9016) that is destined to delight music lovers for a long time to come. Bravo! (Reprinted by permission of the author.)

Playboy, volume 24, No. 10--October 1977:

Doris Hays, who plays The Piano Music of Henry Cowell (Finnadar), is our favorite piano pit mechanic. Her keyboard is dandy, but she does her best work under the hood, where she scrapes and plucks and strums the strings of her concert-grand 88. On the short piece Sinister Resonance, composed by Cowell around 1930, Hays damps the strings with her fingers, creating a variable timbre from which the last sonorous shred of 19th Century Weltschmerz is gratefully stripped away. On The Banshee, she produces, by rubbing the finger tips, the scraping of fingernails and the strumming of fingers along the strings, an eerie ululation that for sheer horror beats hell out of the sound track of The Exorcist. To keyboard compositions such as The Voice of Lir and Tiger, she applies elbows, forearms and fists; in fact, she does everything to the piano but wrestle it to the ground and sit on it, in order to create what she describes as Cowell's "mystical muddiness of broad piles of massed seconds." (Originally appeared in Playboy Magazine; copyright © 1977 by Playboy.)

During the preparation for the Cowell recording, Hays was fortunate in having the opportunity to work with a very fine coach, Hilde Somer. She said,

Although Cadek was my early mentor, I want to mention Hilde Somer who became a strong advisor and friend later in my career. Her expertise and encouragement will always remain a strong imprint. She had a firm commitment to modern music, and

was the first woman pianist whose musical integrity
and warmth and humor I could enjoy in close association.   She died in late December, 1979.

Ms. Hays has appeared both as performer and composer
in concerts in America and Europe over the past years.   Her
performances concentrate on the music of twentieth-century
composers, including John Cage, Ruth Crawford (Seeger),
Cowell, Olivier Messiaen, as well as her own music.   The
Dutch weekly, Accent, reported the following, "Doris Hays
does not merely play, but presents the music in a clearly
penetrating manner.   It is as though she wants to bring the
audience into her work."   She has appeared in live performances at universities and in concert halls as well as in
radio and television concerts in Germany, Yugoslavia, Italy,
Holland, and the United States.

In the duality of Doris Hays' career many people who
know her as a performer are unaware that she is a composer, and people who know her as a composer often don't
realize that she is a performer.   Hays explains,

> I had to face the reality of life as a free-lance
> musician and composer--besides the fact that I en-
> joy performance enormously, it also pays money,
> and I needed to build that reputation to support the
> other aspects of my music-making.   Now that I am
> receiving more grants and commissions, my inten-
> tion is to spend more time writing.   However I
> won't stop performing since I get a kick out of it--
> that sense of completion of the musical act--very
> sexual!   That is how I started my recording career,
> and I think composing and performing are inter-
> woven.   My compositions evolve from my studies
> as an interpreter.

When Hays moved to New York City in 1969, she had
no job, $500 in the bank, a car, and a good friend.   She
supported herself with mundane jobs, including working for
a watchmaker, checking statistics for a business magazine,
teaching part-time in a music school in Larchmont, and
clerking for the American Society of Composers, Authors,
and Publishers.   It was while working (with flexible hours)
at ASCAP that she received the "breakthrough" in the big
city.   On her own time she had been writing short pieces of
electronic music and developing recording studio techniques.
By a quirk of luck, a fellow employee at ASCAP suggested
that she go to Peer-Southern Publishing Company to meet

Mario Conti and show him the electronic pieces that she had
been making.   Hays said,

> And sure enough they needed the music and bought
> it.   Here I was absolutely unknown and had never
> used a recording studio in my life until I came to
> the city and read a letter in the music section of
> the newspaper written by Hubert Howe, head of the
> Electronic Music Studio at Queens College.   I wrote
> to him explaining my background, since I had studied
> at The Center for New Music in Iowa, and asked
> to use his studio.   He said, "Sure."   I had the
> use of this studio sometimes for as long as eight
> hours per day and that developed my techniques in
> making tape music and sound engineering.

In 1971, although still struggling financially, the talented
and determined Hays borrowed $500 to fly to Holland to enter
a competition for performers.   Competing in Rotterdam with
the musically elite contestants, she was awarded First Prize
in the International Competition for Interpreters of New Music.
She was the only contestant to perform her program from
memory, which included a difficult and demanding composition
by Olivier Messiaen for piano from his "Catalogue d'oiseaux."
Her commitment to the music evidenced by the time taken to
memorize, plus her astounding performance of Henry Cowell's
cluster pieces, gave her a unanimous victory from the judges.

Upon returning to New York, she continued her career
in performance and composition as well as workshop presentations at various American colleges on new piano and electronic music.   In addition, she was consultant, composer,
and compiler of a chapter about composition for children in
a music textbook series published by Silver Burdett Company
in 1974.

Hays has been in educational music since the age of
thirteen when she began to teach privately, and this continued
throughout the years in addition to giving master classes,
workshops for music teachers, and occasional private coach-
ing.   For the past eight years she has been an occasional
composer, performer, compiler, and consultant for the Silver
Burdett Company on a freelance basis.   Some twenty of her
pieces are printed and recorded in the Music text series for
kindergarten through sixth grade published by this company.
She said, "I know how to write for children--short pieces
which are fun, compositionally sound and up to date.   They
are more free-form style than most children's music.   Chil-

dren are the freest--spontaneous, joyful, eager, imaginative, and original sound makers."

This Music series has a number of pieces, including Juncture Dance, Mouth Sounds, and Walkin' Talkin' Blues, that are open-ended which allow various rearrangements and unlimited repetition of parts.   There is a feeling of freedom for the children in her music that is similar to the freedom she extends to the performers in some of her adult compositions.   Hays comments,

> Children's music is wonderful training, to write
> to the point, complete, or define the idea and write
> for the pleasure of the music makers.   Children
> instantly know fakery, stupidity, and verbosity.
> They cut through it and eschew it.   They can be
> allowed and encouraged to create their own sound
> organizations.   I am proud that I played a large
> part in providing this freedom through these com-
> positions and my consulting in avant-garde music
> for the Music series.

The Silver Burdett series is used in the majority of American elementary schools that use a music series.   Hays' contributions to this series are important since children deserve and need the best and she has helped to provide this. She wrote and compiled much of the music for a special chapter in Music books V and VI, called "Working with Sounds." This chapter was also sold separately for children to take home, a "how-to-put-together sounds" booklet.   In addition to the music she wrote, which is also on the series discs, her picture at a synthesizer in the electronic music studio is the only woman composer of serious music pictured in the entire series.   A positive step--and certainly a picture that children should be able to see more often--women in professional roles.

When asked about compensation for this type of work, she said with a twinkle in her eyes, "One gets paid, not richly, but more than concert music, and of course there are the record royalties."

As a result of presenting a workshop for the Georgia Music Educators, she received an invitation from the Georgia Council on the Arts to visit the state as artist-in-residence for a four-month period in 1975-1976.

It was during the 1970's that Hays composed and pro-

duced the largest piece among her works, the multi-media
Sensevents.   It was scored for violin, viola, cello, flute,
horn, oboe and programmed lights, motorized sculptures,
with electronic music on cassettes.   She presented four versions of this piece on which she worked over a period of
six years.   Sensevents was premiered at Queens College in
its old cafeteria when students were constantly moving back
and forth, since it is the audience who determines the se-
quence of events and music by hitting the switches, thus
cuing instrumentalists to play.   The performers and sculptures were placed in the center of the room with the audience
walking around them and stepping on the switches to light up
the sculptures, which then began to move, thus motivating
the musicians and dancers as well.   Written as an hour-long
piece in an eleven-part suite, it has no formal beginning or
ending--indeed it is free-form and never the same from performance to performance.   This is exactly what excites the
audience as well as the performers.   They are all an active
part of a beautiful happening.

Some 3,000 people showed up at an Atlanta shopping
mall when it was presented in 1976.   The children discovered
that when they touched these switches, lights and sculptures
would go on, motorized ones would move, light patterns of
some one hundred lights would change, and musicians would
play.   According to Hays, "The children bounced their bot-
toms on the switches and the poor musicians had to play the
entire time."   The performance was made possible by a grant
from the Music Performance Trust Funds and co-sonsored
by the Georgia Council for the Arts through the co-sponsored
of the Atlanta Federation of Musicians.

The third presentation of Sensevents was held in Albany, Georgia, and Hays related,

> It was held in a wonderful art gallery, the Banks
> Haley Art Gallery, that had a rotunda.   Nine hun-
> dred school children were bussed to the Gallery in
> fifteen-minute intervals.   Because of the rotunda
> effect, the musicians and sculptures were placed
> down below.   The audience could touch the switches
> and walk around.   They could also view it from up-
> stairs thus giving a different perspective to the
> whole event.

The fourth performance was a popular offering at the
Lincoln Out-of-Doors Arts Festival in New York, sponsored
by the Exxon Corporation in 1977.   Kent Baker choreographed

the event for three dancers. Because of the difficulty of
coping with the large crowd, it was presented as a stage
performance with the composer working the switches. To
Doris Hays the music of Sensevents is still valid, but the
concept was part of the times and will never be produced
in the same manner again.

In 1977 Doris Hays received her first National Endowment for the Arts Grant of nearly $4,000. This com-
posing grant was encouraged by the Atlanta Ballet for her
idea of a story-ballet about a unicorn, to be scored for string
quartet, flute, tape, and chorus.

The ballet company, perpetually in financial difficulties, couldn't pay for the production of a première of Uni
Suite, but a concert version of the piece was premièred in
Manhattan in 1978 at the Mannes School of Music. Hays
likes to use parts of long compositions in different versions
removed from the original context. Uni Suite is a good example. Two of the choral and tape pieces from it are printed
and published to be performed separately from the rest of
the suite; a tape solo from Uni Suite is also heard as a separate entity.

Hays learned the craft of composing from her college
theory teacher, Arthur Plettner, whom she credits with being a marvelous contrapuntist. She still refers to his teaching. Professor Plettner must certainly be pleased with the
results of his teaching skills, since Hays' credentials, creative approaches, and receptivity characterize a style that
is uniquely contemporary as well as American.

Fascinated by the work of contemporary American
painter Richard Karp, Hays wrote nine brief sketches for
synthesizer and flute to interpret his art. Hays' eager curiosity generated the idea for the extra artistic dimension that
was the basis for the following review, written by "eu" in
Aufbau on May 13, 1977:

Painting Musically Interpreted

The music reviewer who is invited to the opening
of an art exhibition: it was on Tuesday of last
week in the Viridian Gallery (24 West 57th, Manhattan), no joke! More than a dozen of Richard
Karp's abstract paintings there led to instant musical compositions. About nine morsels, planned by
the young American pianist and composer, Doris

Hays, for synthesizer and flute, illustrated instruc-
tively the reciprocal actions that exist between the
two arts.

Many years ago in Vienna, Prof. Oskar Rainer
experimented with "musical graphics", the translation from sound into form, color, and graphic ges-
talt. Karp's paintings--mostly with closely thrown
together pigments (on paper or linen)--are very
similar to the notation of contemporary music (for
the uninitiated, meaning hieroglyphics). If then
Doris Hays regards this element as the beginning
point to a "graphic music"--who knows, whether
the idea will take root or not? She possesses her
own synthesizer with which already prepared tones
can be realized and varied, the electrotechnical
side of which the composer handles very proficiently.
She has appeared many times in public in Germany.
The flutist Andrew Bolotowsky did his famous teachers William Kincaid and Jean-Pierre Rampal
proud.

That which was heard sharpened the eye of a
completely unversed observer to this art which
operates in a sphere without definite subjects or
objects; so that little lines, points and circles in
bright colors began to sing many a song.

The uncritical recognition that painting and music
are sisters makes it worth relecting on the question whether hearing can make us see better. (Reprinted by permission of Aufbau.)

One of the highlights of Doris Hays' performing career
in 1978 was the United States première in Omaha and its
subsequent New York première of Henry Cowell's Concerto
for Piano and Orchestra. A thirty-minute television program,
which included an interview between the conductor and Hays,
highlighted the performance of the concerto in Omaha for
Nebraska Television. Cowell had given the world première
with the Havana Philharmonic Orchestra in 1930.

One of the reasons Hays chose Cowell's music was
"its seemingly rebellious nature," for he had been categorized
by many listeners and some music critics as the "bad boy
of American music" for his use of "tone clusters." One
could easily cast Hays in the role of the devil's advocate.
Based on her individual efforts as a performer/interpreter,
she has helped rid us of the debris of ignorance and inacces-
sibility that has been associated for too long with Cowell's
keyboard music. As an authority, she said, "Cowell's music

has rich inventiveness that comes from an instinctive feeling
for sound, and although he wrote clusters of sound, there is
always a melodic line. "

The following is part of a lengthy review written by
Theodore Price and published in High Fidelity/Musical America in February 1978:

OMAHA SYM: COWELL U. S. PREMIERE

Doris Hays performed the U. S. première of Henry
Cowell's Piano Concerto with the Omaha Symphony
Orchestra on October 12, almost fifty years after
Cowell's own first performance in 1930 with the
Havana Philharmonic.

Perhaps this national première awaited a capable
champion with a specialist's ability to provide a
fist, flattened-palm, and the forearm techniques
that Cowell's tone-clusters demand.   Tennessee-
born Hays, a Munich Hochschule graduate who won
contemporary interpretation credentials in Europe,
may be that torchbearer.   The release of her recording (on Finnadar/Atlantic label) of nineteen
Cowell solo pieces has already suggested such a
possibility.

Cowell's only piano concerto is a fascinating
compendium of the unusual expressive compositional
means he developed in the 1920's.   Spanning a
seventeen-minute arch in three movements--"Poly-
harmony," "Tone Cluster," and "Counter Rhythm"
--it bears traces of some lineage (Franckian chromaticism, a vivid taste of Stravinsky in the coda
of "Counter Rhythm").   But most pianistic details
render it unique in the concerto literature.   My
first hearing leaves an impression of having peered
through a thick stack of brilliant stained glass, a
curiosity to hear again, and an expectation that
Cowell's Piano Concerto--and Doris Hays--will win
well-deserved attention on other programs, especially if Cowell's creation mingles in equally distinguished all-American contemporary company.
(Reprinted by permission from High Fidelity/Musi-
cal America.   All rights reserved.)

Hays performed the New York première a month later
to the praise of music critics Byron Belt and Andrew Porter
and of conductor Victoria Bond.   Mr. Belt writing for Newhouse Newspapers in November, 1978 (partial):

Miss Hays offered the local première of the Henry
Cowell Piano Concerto, printed in Paris in 1931,
but introduced in America only last month by Miss
Hays--in Omaha, Neb., of all places.   The local
premiere came on the opening of the New Amsterdam Symphony, of which Victoria Bond is the expert conductor.

The orchestra is not a virtuoso ensemble, but
it played well, and Doris Hays is a virtuoso extraordinary.   She can play pithy tone clusters for
fist or full arm with the grace of a ballerina, and
she makes marvellous musical sense out of the
composer's rambuctious passages and sings the
lyrical portions with equal conviction.   The concerto is an authentic beauty and Doris Hays should
travel the world playing it.   (Reprinted by permission of the author.)

The internationally recognized music critic Andrew
Porter wrote for the New Yorker on November 20, 1978:

Here, a few days before the Druckman concerto
was done, Henry Cowell's Piano Concerto had its
New York première and (apparently) North American deuxième.   The composer played it with the
Havana Philharmonic in December, 1930; earlier
that year he had played just one or two movements
of it (authorities disagree) in New York with the
Conductorless Orchestra.   The score was published
in Paris in 1931, but--astonishingly--the work
seems to have been neglected until Doris Hays
played it last month with the Omaha Symphony,
and then in New York with the Amsterdam Symphony, conducted by Victoria Bond.   Miss Hays is
a Cowell specialist; a recorded recital on the Finnadar label demonstrates her command of his exuberant, extravagant piano techniques and her feeling for his exuberant yet poetic musical personality.

The concerto has three movements, titled Poly-
harmony, Tone Cluster, and Counter Rhythm.   A
good deal of the piano writing is for the forearms.
When a forearm is brought down on the white keys,
it suggests C major; on the black keys, F-sharp
major.   But Cowell avoids simplistic bitonality by
using his forearm clusters as color above or below
a chromatic melody, or by alternating distinct notes
and clusters with a sort of rapid oompah effect in
which the "oom's" define a tune and the "pahs" punc-

tuate it. Miss Hays is also adept at playing tunes
with her right elbow--striking the top note of a
cluster precisely.   It's not easy.   Just try it once.
The concerto is a dashing experiment.   It is quite
short--about seventeen minutes--and is exhilarating
to listen to.   It might be a hit at a Philharmonic
concert.   (Copyright © 1978 Andrew Porter in The
New Yorker. Reprinted by permission.)

When Sunday Nights for piano was premièred in 1976
it signaled the beginning of a new series of Hays' compositions that are scored for solo instruments, string quartets,
chamber groups, orchestra, and chorus.   Titles of the pieces
include: Sunday Mornings, Saturday Evenings, Tunings, and
Southern Voices. The originality, the imaginative aspects,
and the new dimensions illuminated in these compositions
project the all-encompassing revelations that Hays projects
in her writings.

Hays reflects on the compositions she wrote during
that time and still continues to write today:

Sunday Nights has enough tone-clusters in it that
people will say that it is kind of semi-Cowell and
that Cowell has influenced me.   At times people
will say it's kind of like Ives--those tonalities
against tonalities and hymn tune fragments--that's
O. K. with me.   Some listeners have to relate to
music from the past in this manner.
My growing up was so strongly influenced by the
church and by the conflicts of a very class-strati-
fied society.   All this begins to come out stronger
and stronger in my music.   I continue to make up
fragments of hymn tunes, fragments of rhythm,
bits of fiddle tunes and the quality of Appalachian
folk-songs that I love so much that I try to get an
essence of what they are to me and how I experienced them with both love and hate as I grew older
and felt the effects of religious repression.
After having studied in Europe for three years,
I came back to the United States because I love the
countryside and I love the South, and many of the
things that make up American culture.   An essence
in the language and feeling it was something I knew
when I was growing up I liked but I didn't know
why.   I have written numerous pieces in the past
five years but Sunday Nights was the firm beginning,
and there have been a number of other strong pieces.
since-recollection pieces, or affirmation pieces.

Sunday Nights has been recorded as well as having
had numerous performances.   Byron Belt, critic-at-large,
wrote the following review for The Jersey Journal on March
19, 1979 (excerpt):

> WOMEN'S MUSIC PROGRAM A HIT FOR THE BEST
> REASONS
>
> The Women's Interart Center is presenting its
> second festival of Women's music in the comfortable
> sonic setting of Christ & St. Stephan's Church at
> 69th near Broadway.
>   We attended the second program, which featured
> pianist-composers Ruth Schonthal, Doris Hays,
> Marga Richter and Judith Lang Zaimont.
>   It takes no reverse-chauvinism to state that the
> program was one of the most satisfying featuring
> contemporary music this critic has ever attended.
>   One factor that made the program of major new
> works so pleasant was the fact that romantic works
> by such underappreciated women composers as
> Louise Farene, Mary Bough Watson, and Cecile
> Chaminade were interlaced with the contemporary
> works.   The other major factors were the superb
> pianism of our composers, and a generally high
> level of quality in the recent works they presented.
>   Doris Hays, one of today's outstanding interpre-
> tors of modern music offered a thoughtful Momenti 4
> by Vivian Fine, contrasted with a sassy delightful
> Dishrag, (c. 1905) by Mary Bough Watson.   Of her
> own works, a short Sunday Nights was a blend of
> Ives and Cowell that jelled into a perfectly delight-
> ful piece that could be a hit on any recital program.
>   Hays' more experimental Wildflowers, using
> electronic devices seemed a bit long for its con-
> tent, but some of the sounds were fascinating.   (Re-
> printed by permission of the author.)

In 1980 Doris Hays recorded Adoration of the Clash
for Finnadar SR 2-720.   Included in the collection is the
music of Hays, Cowell, Peck, Mimarouglu, Feldman, and
Ornstein.   The following was printed on the record cover
and written by Ms. Hays in her poems Political Sounds.

Adoration of the Clash

a gun shot!
the crack of a brick falling on the sidewalk

from a broken building wall
crash of colliding stars--cars--
dissension within--and imagined--
gentle iron(y), bare cynic(ism)
adoration of the clash
hard edge tones overlap
fuse
torch
join
struggle
which sound comes out on top?

Tone clusters: ideal rebellious gesture to topple the sacred
Western muse off its sacred pedestal.   A forearm bang,
and the tedium of linearity is broken, its intractable logic
punctuated by the rude rough mass of second intervals--
fingered, palmed armed and fisted for the clash.

Hays' instrumental composition Tunings is scored for
string quartet, violin duo, or chamber combinations of either
strings and winds or voice, and is available for purchase as
indicated at the end of the chapter.   Tunings has an interesting heritage.   Hays' maternal grandfather was a circuit-rid-
ing preacher in Arkansas who lived to the ripe young age of
ninety-three.   She visited her grandfather summers and shared
his joy of writing poetry and gardening (she still enjoys her
penthouse terrace garden).   Grandfather Fair composed a
hymn tune when Doris was ten years old, but he was unable
to notate the music so she wrote it down for him.   Some
years later she rediscovered this hymn, written in the notation of a ten-year-old, and used it in Tunings along with
fiddle riffs.   The string quartet version written in a Bach-
like kind of counterpoint was premièred in New York City
by the Manhattan String Quartet and later performed in Char-
leston, South Carolina.   Frank P. Jarrell, staff writer for
The News and Courier wrote on May 29, 1980 in his column
Spoleto (partial):

MODERN MUSIC GETS OFF TO GRAND START

When I was playing in a high school symphony, our
director used to constantly make this awful joke about
playing a chinese song called "Tu Ning."   He even
put it on our rehearsal schedule.   Well, the work
performed by the quartet was something serious seemingly made from my band director's joke.
    Imagine a barn dance somewhere in the hills.   The
band is getting ready to play for a square dance that's

going to last late into the night.   Before the music
starts, of course, the group must tune instruments.
And that, to me, was the point of the quartet's piece.

Throughout the work's five movements, there were
returns to the sounds of the strings tuning.   Then
came embellishments, jig-sounding ditties, drones,
mellow passages, light passages--always returning
to the sound of tuning.

Many times I was reminded of the virtuoso fiddle
players of my West Virginia home area.   Tunings
was like a home-coming in a way.   (Reprinted by
permission of The News and Courier.)

Tunings received its European première at the Frau
und Musik Festival held in Bonn and Köln, West Germany,
in November, 1980.   The International League of Women
Composers was represented by a concert of works for string
quartet performed by the Crescent Quartet of New York.
Composers whose works for string quartet included Ruth
Schonthal, Sarah Aderholdt, Amy Marcy Beach, Gloria Coates,
and Doris Hays.   Reviewed by Gisela Glaglia in the Frankfurter Allgemeine Zeitung, December 13, 1980:

GENIALITÄT AND GLEICHBERECHTIGUNG

"FRAU UND MUSIK": EIN FESTIVAL IN BONN UND
KÖLN

... The excellent ensemble playing brought home the
point forcefully about the high standards of American
musicians with the Quartet's performance of works
by contemporary women composers from the United
States.   An original touch (accent) was set here by
Doris Hays (born 1941).   Her individualistic Tunings,
which played upon the elements of fiddle music and
of a chorale (hymn), revealed not only virtuosity-
mastered craft, but also a native musicality....

Doris Hays was last present at this festival as performer as well as composer.   She was on a concert tour
in Europe at the time.   She reported,

It was a wonderful experience.   For example, on
the evening of November 25, 1980, three different
concerts by American women were presented in Munich.   Hays performed piano works of Ann Silsbee,
Beth Anderson, Marga Richter, Mary Watson, and
her own music at six p. m. at the Amerika Haus; Ruth

Anderson and Anna Lockwood performed at eight p. m. in
an art gallery, and Pauline Oliveros presented her
program at ten p. m. in another space.

Hays continued,

> The festival inspired us all. This festival, though
> focused largely on historical music, with less con-
> temporary music, showed the tremendous change
> over a period of only a few years--the world has
> changed--women are being invited both as composers
> and performers, audiences are listening and they
> are interested. It was a fascinating four days full
> of music by women in itself and that made a point.

Hays' present project is huge. Entitled Southern Voices,
it is a series of pieces for various instrumental, vocal, and
tape groups that has received the support of the National Endowment of the Arts with a composers grant as well as a
commission by her hometown orchestra for its fiftieth anniversary.

In 1980 Hays spend over three months researching,
interviewing on tape, and collecting grass root sources
of material for Southern Voices. She spent considerable time
in Tennessee, Arkansas, Mississippi, Alabama, Georgia,
and the Carolinas. Her tapes include interviews with some
200 individuals in addition to visiting and taping Sacred Harp
Singers, a fiddlers convention, a cane fife maker (who has
a fife and drum band), school children, pottery makers, quil-
ters, and just plain people on the street.

The first composition to result from this work was a
version called Southern Voices, scored for tape with slides,
narration, and soprano. This sixteen-minute piece was premièred in October, 1980, at the Electronic Music Plus Festival at the University of West Virginia. She said,

> Southern speech is very musical, with the language
> often phrased poetically with graceful lilts. Lan-
> guage has a melodic character. In this piece I used
> fragments of speech in the way I have used fragments
> of melody in previous works, and I use them as
> melodic-rhythmic motifs. I also ran them through
> the synthesizer and picked up electronic signals trig-
> gered by speech rhythms. The collage of various
> voices used in the piece is arranged in paragraph
> groupings, representing the attitudes of Southerners
> about their community and its customs.

The orchestra première of Southern Voices will be by
Doris Hays' hometown orchestra, the Chattanooga Symphony
Orchestra.   She is presently working on the choral version
as well as a variety of short chamber pieces, again using
the same thematic ideas.   This immense project will culmin-
ate in a documentary film on which Hays is collaborating
with Southerner George Stoney, who was associated for many
years with the film and video department of New York University.

Doris Hays has been the recipient of numerous awards
and grants, including two National Endowment for the Arts
grants, numerous Meet the Composer awards, yearly ASCAP
Standard Awards, and a citation from the National Federation
of Music Clubs.   Being a freelance composer/performer
means that she has no permanent institutional affiliation and
no secure income, hence, grants and awards play an important part in her career.   The creative life has never been
built on security, but it is built on dignity and appreciation;
Hays' artistic accomplishments reflect this.

Her sensitivity to the adversities that impede the acceptance of women on a professional level has consumed a tremendous amount of her energies as a writer, speaker, or-
ganizer, and doer.   New acceptance and public awareness
by contemporary society of women composers has long been
one of the goals of the International League of Women Composers.   Hays is a member of the executive board, serving
as assistant chairperson.   Nancy Van de Vate is chairperson
of the League, and Hays considers her to be a superb tacti-
cian, diplomat, and excellent leader [see Van de Vate chapter
in volume I].

Doris Hays has written a number of articles promoting
the music of women composers and chiding various music
establishments for their failure to recognize such achievements.   The following excerpt was taken from Hays' article,
"New Publications" published in the Music Journal, February,
1978:

> The following 5 compositions [David Winkler's Inter-
> mezzo; Robert Pollock's Bridgeforms; George Ed-
> ward's Draconian; Thomas James's Variations and
> Pollock's Departure] from Mobart Music, Hillsdale,
> N. Y. , are on the repertoire list for the first com-
> petitions for performers of American music, which
> is sponsored by the Rockfeller Foundation and Ken-
> nedy Center, to take place next year.   Since the in-

clusion of a composition in a competition list auto-
matically renders the work significant (i. e. it will
be bought, studied, and perhaps performed and recorded) it seems worthwhile to ask what these pieces
are like. All were composed in the seventies. And
amazingly, all have a sound that suggests Schoen-
bergian disciples of the 1950's and early 60's. One
wonders what has happened in the 20 years between
--these composers, all young, must be convinced of
the efficacy of the serial idiom.

There are some 44 compositions on the Rocke-
feller-Kennedy American Music list, which is sub-
divided into pre-and post 1960. With the exception
of Bridgeforms, the Mobart Publications we've mentioned have not distinguished themselves by time or
prominence, and do not, to this reviewer appear to
warrant inclusion in inherent musical merit among
works of the scope and excellence of Cage's Etudes
Australes. There are certainly works of the short
size of Winkler's or the severity of Edward's which
have a newer interest and contemporaneous thrust
lacking in these works. One thinks of the piano version of Cage's Cheap Imitation, Russel Peck's Suspended Sentence, the various short, delicate works
of Morton Feldman, and the unique Action Music by
Alvin Lucier. One also has to question this competition's choice on other grounds--among all these
20th century compositions, only one woman composer
is represented. Women composers have come to be
recognized in increasing numbers since World War II
and we can say certainly that since 1960 numbers of
significant piano works have been published and performed. Just to mention a few--Betsy Jolas, Barbara Kolb, Vivian Fine, Miriam Gideon, and Ruth
Schonthal and of course, earlier in time, the excellent Preludes of Ruth Crawford (Seeger) ...

Doris Hays is a writer with many interesting and valuable ideas to communicate in behalf of the American
woman composer. The following letter to Mr. Howard Klein,
head of the Rockefeller Foundation, emphasizes her unique
ability to communicate, in a thought-provoking fashion, the
need to raise the consciousness of the male-dominated administration of major funding foundations. She said, "Changes
must come from both within and without the system." This
is a powerful and challenging letter:

April 17, 1978

Dear Mr. Klein:

Thank you for your letter of April 11, in attempting
to clarify how the repertoire list was made for the
Kennedy Center-Rockefeller Foundation Competition....
Unfortunately, your letter leaves me even more mys-
tified as to how compositions were chosen.

You wrote that compositions were selected by title.
But say if a Sonata No. I were listed, it could either
be Ives or Vivian Fine; if Six Etudes were listed
they could be by John Cage or Louise Talma.   Titles
must be backed up by a human creator in order to
be identified.   And how was the preselection of titles
arrived at, by whom and from what other list, which
titles were given to the repertoire selection panel?
As to the criteria of "stage worthy and neglected"
--the neglected women composers of this country
could provide you with enough stage worthy music
to complete an entire repertoire list.   If neglect is
one of your criterion, you failed utterly to take advantage of the obvious neglect and seeming discrimination which women creators encounter in finding
avenues of performance.

I should genuinely appreciate being enlightened about
the selection process for the competition repertoire.
Future competitions will produce other repertoire
lists.   Perhaps there is some way you can avoid the
present paradox of neglected women composers being
omitted from among the neglected titles by male
composers?

Sincerely,
Doris Hays

Doris Hays was a consultant for two years for the
Creative Artists Project Service, founded by the New York
State Arts Council, that grants monies to composers.   As
a consultant she helped to select the jury and screened all
the applications.   In 1980 only one woman received an award
out of the final twelve recipients.   However, only fifty-four
women out of some 300 candidates applied.   Hays comments,
"So it says to me that women are still afraid of rejection,
so they stop applying because they feel the heavy weight of
rejection, and because they don't apply, they have no chance
to be chosen."

Beth Anderson and Doris Hays coordinated the landmark series, "Meet the Woman Composer," held at The New School in the fall of 1976 as course No. 3610-0 for credit. The eleven concert sessions presented eighteen composers who were present and who sometimes performed their works and discussed their experiences in music. Hays said,

> There was enormous variety in the presentations, including artists as different from one another as Vivian Fine and Pril Smiley, and adventuresome artists such as Alison Knowles, Jill Kroesen, Anna Lockwood, Beth Anderson, and myself. There has been no series since that has had as much variety --there are more festival type events being presented today. The series was funded in the following manner: funds from Meet The Composer helped to provide a stipend to the composer, The New School paid for the cost of advertising and providing space, and mine and Beth's salary; and the student participants paid a small fee.

This was one of the important and exciting events of the seventies that promoted new directions for the woman composer.

It has often been said that if you give a busy person another responsibility, you can be certain that it will be completed in an expeditious manner. This held true when Doris Hays agreed to compile Expressions. A Radio series in behalf of the International League of Women Composers, it includes eleven one-hour taped programs with commentary by Doris Hays, narration by Loretta Goldberg, and tape production in the Hays studio. The programs provide tremendous coverage for women's music, with the listening potential of public and private radio. The present material is being used by American radio stations who pay a ten dollar fee on a two month loan for broadcast. The tapes are available from Doris Hays, 697 West End Avenue, Ph. B. , New York, N. Y. 10025. The series includes:

      I.   String Quartets
     II.   String Quartet/Quintet
    III.   Text-Sound and Electronics Using Voices
     IV.   Vocal and Choral Music
      V.   Piano and Piano and Tape
     VI.   Woodwinds
    VII.   Vocal Chamber Music
   VIII.   Solo Instruments

IX.   Chamber Music With Voices
X.   Electronic/Plus Voices, Orchestra
XI.   Orchestral/Chamber

Expressions has provided tremendous coverage for
women's music.   According to Hays, "The International League
of Women Composers supports projects that work within established systems.   We try to bring about changes within the
natural process, and it's a filter-down technique.   The League
is in no way a revolutionary group: we use lobbying efforts
to promote change, such as more radio coverage--and people
do listen."   Sometimes we give a strong nudge to the natural
process that might be called radical or unnatural.   Within
or without the system, we are making improvements in acceptance of women in music.

Doris Hays is an adventuresome composer, performer,
and artist.   It is in new and perhaps experimental forms that
women composers will have their greatest impact on American music.   This is a direction where women have done excellent work which is peculiar to their experience.   The old
forms of music hardened and set by men will not provide an
avenue of achievement for women composers, but they can
achieve in a new form that is pliable and can be influenced
by their expertise.   Hays' music abandons the convenience of
treating each new movement in the usual way.   She is prepared for the challenges ahead.   Doris Hays says,

> The challenges appear to include decreased public
> funding for music.   I am thinking of ways I can
> write the music I want to write and get it to a
> public, who will not only listen but also pay for
> it.   The conflict between my desires to explore
> the unlikely avenues of aural thinking, and the gen-
> eral public's tardy response to the new, and my
> desires to say what I want--that's a terrific chal-
> lenge.
>   In 1981, the directions for me are: music
> which can be played while dancers move, music for
> films, music for stage events, music for visual fan-
> tasy.   And all the time music for music.   My grap-
> pling fondly with my southern youth puts me close to
> human music--speech, lullabyes, humming, body
> pulses, and social sounds such as subways and wash-
> ing machines, in contrast to my rural childhood.

List of Compositions

[Key to Difficulty Level: E= easy; M= medium; D= difficult.]

Piano and Piano Plus
Saturday Evenings, 5', M-D, Quinska-Hays (1980)
Etude Bass Basses, 4', D, Quinska-Hays (1978)
Characters, for piano (or harpsichord), string quintet, 2 cl. ,
    oboe, 17', D, Quinska-Hays (1978)
Sunday Nights, 5' 15", D, A. Broude, Inc. (1977)
Past Present, 7' D, Quinska-Hays (1975)
Pamp, piano and tape and bird whistles supplied by composer,
    7', D, Quinska-Hays (1975)
Chartres Red, 3', D, Quinska-Hays (1972)

Harpsichord
Characters, for harpsichord (or piano), string quintet, 2 cl. ,
    oboe, 17', D, Quinska-Hays (1978)

Organ
For My Brother's Wedding, 4' 30", M, Quinska-Hays (1974)

Strings
Southern Voices--Sacred Harp Dance, 7', string quartet or-
    chestra, M, Quinska-Hays (1981)
Tunings, for string quartet, 13', D, Quinska-Hays (1980)
Tunings, violin duo, 3' 30", D, Quinska-Hays (1980)

Orchestra and Large Chamber Ensemble
Southern Voices, picc. , 3 flutes, oboe, English horn, 2 cl. ,
    bass cl. , bassoon, contrabassoon, 4 horns, 3 trum-
        pets, 3 trombones, tuba, per. , piano, strings,
        14', M-D, Quinska-Hays (1981)
Pieces from Last Year, 3 alto recorders (or flutes), 1 alto
    flute, ocarinas in G and E, vln. , vla. , strings div.
    in 3, piano, alternate version with wood winds and
    brass replacing alto flute, ocarinas, and strings,
    9', Quinska-Hays (1975)

Choral
Hands Full, 2-part chorus and tape, optional drums, 3', E,
    A. Broude, Inc. (1978)

Star Music, 2-part chorus, tape and bells, 5', Quinska-Hays
        (1977-78)
Dreams, Choral Scenes, from UNI Suite, 1. Chief of Police
        and Politicians, tapes and SATB, 3-5 choruses, 3'30",
        2. Park People (optional), 6' tape solo, 3. Uni's
        Dream, SATB and tape, 4'10", D, A. Broude, Inc.
        (1977-78)

        Vocal
Song of the Sky, 4 songs on Brian Swan's poetic versions of
        American Indian songs, for middle voice and piano,
        M, 8', Quinska-Hays (1981)
Hush, lullabye for medium voice, reco-reco, and snad blocks,
        5', M, Quinska-Hays (1981)
For Women, 5 songs for mezzo-soprano and piano, 11', D,
        Quinska-Hays (1976)

        Winds
Windpipes, for five flutes, 10', D, Quinska-Hays (1980)
Glub, for bass flute, piccolo and tape, 10', D, Quinska-Hays
Segments/Junctures, for clarinet and piano, 3', M, Quinska-
        Hays (1979)
Breathless, for bass flute, 3', D, Quinska-Hays (1978)
Winded, for c flute, 2', M, Quinska-Hays (1978)
For, A.B., clarinet and piano, 3', M, Quinska-Hays (1976)

        Tape and Live Electronic
Only, 2 or more tapes, or with 2 or more pianos, 8' plus,
        Quinska-Hays (1981)
Southern Voices, tape with/without narrative, soprano, and
        slides, 18', Quinska-Hays (1980)
Wildflowers, for Buchla Electric Music Box and Piano, Pip-
        sissewa, Pink Turtlehead, City Cedar, Trailing Ar-
        butus, Fire Pink, each c. 2-3', composer performance
        (1973-80)
In the Saddle, Cowboy Movie, tape, 40', Quinska-Hays (1980)
Glub, tape and bass flute and piccolo, 10', D, Quinska-Hays
        (1979)
Park People's Dream, from UNI Suite, tape solo, 6', A.
        Broude, Inc. (1978)
Hands Full, tape and chorus, 3', E, A. Broude, Inc. (1978)
Choral Scenes-Dreams, from UNI Suite, tape and SATB, 1.
        Chief of Police Dream, 3', and 3. Uni's Dream,
        4' 10", D, A. Broude, Inc. (1978)

Awakening, tapeized poem by Paul Ramsey on tape, 2', Quin-
　　　ska-Hays (1973)
Pamp, for tape alone, or piano, tape and bird whistles, 7',
　　　Quinska-Hays (1973)
13th Street Beat, Syn-Rock, Arabella Rag, and 15 other short
　　　electronic musics on tape and disc, from 40"-2',
　　　Southern Library of Recorded Sound, Peer-Southern
　　　(1972)

Multimedia
Water Music, for running fountain (supplied by composer),
　　　2-4 performance on melodic instruments, and tapes,
　　　optional film, 1 hour-?, M, Quinska-Hays (1980-81)
In-De-Pen-Dance, for chanter-actor and nylon strings, 10'-?,
　　　M, Quinska-Hays (1978)
Sensevents, for vln., vla., vcl., fl., horn, oboe, and pro-
　　　grammed lights, motorized sculptures, 30'-60', with
　　　optional electronic music on cassettes, D, Quinska-
　　　Hays (1973-77)
Hands and Lights, for piano, photocells, flashlights and flood
　　　lamps, 13', D, Quinska-Hays (1971)

Brass
Tommy's Trumpet, trumpet duo, 4', M, Quinska-Hays (1978)
Fanfare Study, for trumpet, horn, trombone, 4', M, Quinska-
　　　Hays (1976)

Chamber Ensemble
Tunings, for 3-10 of: solo violin, violin duo, viola, cello,
　　　double bass, clarinet, recorder, percussion, piano,
　　　soprano, flute, bassoon, all play 3-4' solos as well
　　　as in ensemble, many versions exist, including string
　　　quartet, string quintet, violin duo, flute/violin duo,
　　　duration 10'-60' plus, M-D, Quinska-Hays. (1979-81)
Lullabye, flute, violin, piano, 3', M, Quinska-Hays (1979)
Segments/Junctures, for cl., viola, piano, 12', D, Quinska-
　　　Hays (1978)

For Children
Look Out, choral canon, 1', E, Silver-Burdett MUSIC or
　　　Quinska-Hays (1974)
Mouth Sounds, 4-part chorus, 2', E, Silver-Burdett MUSIC
　　　or Quinska-Hays (1974)

O Susanna, tape and chorus, 3', E, Silver-Burdett MUSIC or
        Quinska-Hays (1974)
Clementine, tape and chorus, 3', E, Silver-Burdett MUSIC or
        Quinska-Hays (1974)
Juncture Dance, recorder, harmonica, triangle, autoharp,
        guitar, optional versions, flexible structures in dura-
        tion, E-D, Quinska-Hays (1974)
Walkin' Talkin' Blues, speaker(s) with or without double bass,
        flexible duration, E, Silver-Burdett MUSIC or Quinska-
        Hays (1974)
For Four, bongos, recorder, autoharp, paper rip, graphic
        notation, 2', M, Quinska-Hays (1974)
Sound Symbol Structures, for keyboard, non-traditional nota-
        tion, improvisation, flexible structures in duration,
        E-D, Quinska-Hays (1973)

Addresses:

A. Broude, Inc., 225 West 57th Street, New York, New
        York 10019

Quinska-Hays, 697 West End Avenue, Penthouse B, New
        York, New York 10025

Silver-Burdett Music, 250 James Street, Morristown, New
        Jersey 07960

                        Discography

Finnadar/Atlantic Records, Sunday Nights, piano, SR 2-720
Silver-Burdett Co., 250 James Street, Morristown, N. J.,
        record series of MUSIC text series, containing Junc-
        ture Dance, Walkin' Talkin' Blues, Mouth Sounds, and
        ten other children's musics, 74-183-04, 74-185-02,
        184-05
Southern Library of Recorded Sound, Peer-Southern Music
        Inc., 1740 Broadway, New York City, electronic music
        shorts including 13th Street Beat, Arabella Rag, Syn-
        Rock, on MOLP 38

FREDERIQUE PETRIDES

Pioneer Orchestral Conductor, Founder of Orchestrette Classique, and Editor of the First <u>Women in Music</u> Magazine

Madame Frederique Petrides' development and musical training, in the highest European cultural tradition, was the basis on which she built her reputation for excelling as conductor, writer, and editor. She possessed those unique qualities of temperament, intellectual capacity, and devotion that were necessary to firmly establish her credentials as gifted conductor and internationally recognized authority on women in music, with emphasis on women's work in the instrumental field. For over five decades her musical accomplishments have been reviewed by such leading critics and writers as H. Howard Taubman, Irving Kolodin, Olin Downes, Robert A. Simon, Jerome D. Bohm, Francis D. Perkins, Theodore Strongin, Robert Sherman, Harold C. Schonberg, and Raymond Ericson.

She was born in Antwerp, Belgium. Her mother, Seraphine Scbrechts, a former pupil of Jan Blockx and Peter Beriot, was a teacher at the Royal Conservatory in Antwerp, and a potential candidate for the prestigious Prix de Rome had she not been a woman. As composer, musician, and artist, she realized that her daughter, born with perfect pitch, was musically talented. This inherited gift was possessed by three generations of the family. Although piano was the first instrument Frederique played, at the age of seven she chose to study violin, a natural choice for a gifted child. Fortunately, her mother was aware of the necessity of providing her daughter with the finest teachers available in Antwerp and Brussels.

As a child she was a part of the family string quartet which often gave recitals; it included her mother and two brothers. Petrides and her brother played the beautiful Concerto for two violins of Bach. She was also a member of a

191

FREDERIQUE PETRIDES

large chorale group where the director used her ability of absolute pitch to start the singing correctly. She and her brothers were taken to many concerts to see and hear all the great conductors and soloists of the time.

When Petrides was a teenager, she was one of the three private students accepted by Mathieu Crickboon, Eugène Ysaÿe's assistant and second violinist in the famous Ysaÿe Quartet. He later took Ysaÿe's place at the Royal Conservatory in Brussels. Petrides said, "I can still recall, while studying with Crickboon in 1920, a telegram he

received from Eugène Ysaÿe, who was in America, asking
him to substitute in a concert for the Queen of Belgium in
honor of the 100th anniversary of the great composer Henri
Vieuxtemps. Crickboon played the performance."

Madame Petrides studied at the Royal Conservatory
in Brussels. The experience garnered from years of training, study, and exposure to the finest opportunities found in
European culture, provided the talented young woman with a
solid background. She said,

> I heard many of the great musicians during and
> after World War I: Fritz Kreisler, Engelbert Hum-
> perdink, Camille Saint Saëns, Pablo Casals, An-
> drés Segovia, Alexander Brailowsky, Ernestine
> Schumann-Heink, Alfred Cortot, and Elly Ney. Also
> I saw Isadora Duncan, the great dancer, and many
> of the great actors and actresses of the time. I
> went to all the museums and cathedrals in Belgium
> and Holland and heard many of the famous Quartets.
> I played in a quartet and became familiar with the
> great literature of chamber music.
> I was always dreaming of the various beautiful
> sounds I heard with great orchestras. My mother
> played the Sixth Symphony of Beethoven (on the
> player piano) when Antwerp was being bombarded.
> She had us listen to the different instruments and
> explained the beautiful passages. It took me years
> before I could study the score and years later be-
> fore I could conduct it. Even now when I hear this
> symphony I can hear the sound of the bombs hitting
> the targets and the response of our artillery trying
> to hit and scare the bombers away.

A born leader, Petrides developed exceptional organizational skills to complement her already acquired musical skills--
skills which led to her first European conducting experiences
while only a teenager. One of the conductors she idolized
was the famous German conductor, Felix Weingartner. She
observed, "I knew if I could learn to follow his techniques
that I could be a successful conductor." Some years later
at the invitation of Dimitri Mitropoulos, she devoted countless
hours as his guest at orchestra rehearsals of the New York
Philharmonic to watch and learn from this famous conductor
at work. He patiently answered her questions and encouraged
her development. When she stopped going to his rehearsals,
he wrote her a letter asking why she was no longer attending.

In 1923 because of illness and deplorable economic conditions in Europe, Madame Petrides came to America for three months to regain her health. The anticipated visit was extended and she made her permanent home in the United States.

On her arrival in America she lived with friends in Wilton, Connecticut, until she regained her health. During this period she gave violin recitals, violin lessons, and coached string quartet players. She said, "Although I was not interested in recital performance, I gave recitals and lessons because it was necessary in order for me to live."

Eventually Madame Petrides moved to New York City where there were more opportunities to build a conducting career. She enrolled in a conducting class at New York University because an orchestra was available there. Every conductor needs to direct an orchestra to develop technical skills. Her background was far in advance of other members of the class (America was still sending promising prospective conductors to Europe for training) so she was provided more opportunities to conduct than other members of the class. Membership in the orchestra was a combination of university students and professional musicians who were enrolled in advanced-degree programs. She said of this experience,

> Either you are a conductor who is a leader, or you are not. One can learn the elements of conducting 1-2-3 or 1-2-3-4, but it is up to the conductor as an artist as to what is made of these elements. The only advantage that I can find in taking a conducting class is that you have an orchestra to work with.

Frederique Petrides learned, as did other foreign and American women, that serious, ambitious, and accomplished musicians run into a sex barrier--no women conducted major orchestras in 1930. One of the avenues opened to aspiring women conductors was to establish their own orchestras. In 1933 Petrides founded a women's symphony orchestra in New York City--the Orchestrette Classique. Through her inspiration, as well as her direction and management, the orchestra grew from the original fourteen members to thirty-five.

In 1981, some forty-eight years after she founded the Orchestrette Classique Madame Petrides said:

I kept my orchestra small because I wanted quality musicians--most of the women in the group were studying at the Curtis Institute, and the Juilliard School. One must remember that at that time only a very few women played bassoon, oboe, horn, clarinet, and trumpet. Parents did not want their daughters playing these instruments because they were not considered ladylike. My idea was to keep the Orchestrette Classique small and show what could be accomplished by good musicians--I did not stress women musicians. They were talented and many of my players were trained by excellent teachers from the New York Philharmonic Orchestra.

The concerts were unique since I programmed little-known works by the great masters for small orchestras, as well as premièring new works by young American composers.

The concerts were usually given on Monday evenings because the Philharmonic Orchestra did not perform on that evening, and the music critics were available. We added a new musical dimension to the cultural life of the city.

During the twelve years the enterprising Madame Petrides conducted the Orchestrette Classique, later renamed the Orchestrette of New York, she was considered a prime mover in New York City's cultural affairs. Reading the numerous articles and reviews published in the many newspapers printed in the city at that time is a fascinating experience for musicians as well as music lovers. Robert Simon, writing in The New Yorker on December 12, 1936, best sums up the contributions of the gifted conductor Frederique Petrides when he wrote, "She concocts some of the best programs in town."

Petrides gives credit to her friend, the American composer Julia Smith, for helping her to form the orchestra. She said, "Julia, you are a composer and if you will help me to form an orchestra, I will program some of your music." It was through the efforts of Smith, who was at Juilliard, that the first group was formed. Today Petrides blushes when she recalls the first program. "The musicians were learning to play their instruments; their teachers would coach them on the parts, so when they came to me for rehearsal they were prepared. We rehearsed in the strangest places."

The persistence and determination of the members of

the Orchestrette Classique under the direction of their talented
conductor was recognized and supported by enthusiastic audiences and music critics from the first concert season.
Harold Taubman writing for the New York Times on November 5, 1935:

WOMEN'S GROUP IN RECITAL

The Orchestrette Classique, a chamber orchestra
of twenty-four young women directed by Miss Frederique Joanne Petrides, opened its third season at
Aeolian Hall last night. Without subsidy or endowment and without fanfare of publicity, this ensemble
has attended to its business of making music. In
other words, it has worked to perfect itself as an
orchestra, to develop a repertoire and to find an
audience.

On all three counts progress has been made.
Last night's concert was convincing evidence. In
the first place, the program was refreshing in its
exploration of rarely heard and new compositions.
It consisted of Sam Franko's arrangement of Pietro
Locatelli's Concerto Grosso for string orchestra,
Anton Rosetti's Symphony in G minor, a concerto
for cembalo written by Mozart at the age of nine,
an aria for oboe from Hasse's Piramo e Tisbe and
two compositions by young Americans: Syrtos--
Greek Folk Dance, by Julia Smith, and Ukrainian
Suite, for string orchestra, by Quincy Porter.

Secondly, the performances observed a standard
of competence. It is not necessary to advert here
to the question of whether women have the capacity
to operate the various instruments of the orchestra.
That has been proved affirmatively by other ensembles. Under Miss Petrides's clean-cut direction, the little orchestra played with unity, technical smoothness and a grasp of the various compositions. Some instruments were in better hands
than others. Some works were more fully realized
than others. The general impression was an ensemble that will grow by experience.

As for the last point, the small hall was filled
last night and there was an overflow audience in
the adjoining room. The ensemble, moreover, is
attempting by word of mouth and by mail to reach
an increasingly larger public. Miss Petrides and
her group are pursuing a wise and wholesome
course. (Copyright © 1935 by The New York Times
Company. Reprinted by permission.)

Conductor Petrides feels that her big mistake with the Orchestrette Classique was waiting until the end of the third season to seek financial support for the group.   She said,

> There were no national or state foundations at that time and one had to rely on wealthy patrons for support.   I waited until I had proved that the group was musically established and had received fine reviews before requesting financial assistance.   I received no help from the people I approached because they felt I had accomplished my goal in three years without help and would be able to continue based on ticket sales.   Of course I had many more successful seasons but we were never able to tour nationally because we had no funds.

The critics continued to rave.   "Music in Review," by Henriette Weber, was published by the New York Evening Journal on February 16, 1937:

ORCHESTRETTE PLAYS

> I like the Orchestrette Classique.   It's a women's orchestra of around 30 players who have stuck together for about four years under their ambitious leader, Frederique Petrides, and while a few changes in personnel have necessarily taken place, the majority have continued to play with "their" orchestra because of loyalty and pride.
>
> That's a spirit as unusual as it is fine where femininity reigns, and much credit is due their diplomatic conductress.   "I suppose we ought to say conductress?" (I got a letter yesterday from the "Chairlady" of a music committee.   It made me think of charwoman!)
>
> The orchestrette played to the edification of a good sized audience which required extra chairs for the Carnegie Chamber Music Hall.   The program, as usual, was selected with care and performed in the same way.   There was a Sinfonia by C. Ph. E. Bach, and that characteristic Holberg Suite by Grieg which in its piano solo form has been the delight of many a young pianist.   Helen Enser, one of the most earnest of these earnest young women, played the solo part of a French Horn Concerto by Mozart.   Modernism entered in with a suite all about lovers by Sibelius, and it ended with the cheery Clock Symphony by Haydn.

What could be heard of this attractive program
showed that Miss Petrides continues to have her
cohorts well in hand. It showed that they are practicing diligently and ever striving to climb higher
on the scale of fine ensemble. The playing at this
concert was a distinct gain even over their best of
last year.

In 1938 the critics praised Petrides' pioneering instincts in program making. During that season she presented
pianist Lonny Epstein in Mozart concerts unknown in this
country; Ruth Freeman flutist; the New York premiere of
composer Paul White's Sinfonietta; and the Sidney Lanier
Memorial Concert. She said,

I chose to commemorate Sidney Lanier's far-sighted
and daring attitude. As a poet-flutist, (1842-1881),
he was undoubtly the first noted American in the
last century to discern the merits of women as potential orchestral players and to advocate with enthusiam the studying of all orchestral instruments
by them. The concert was a wonderful success,
my players having taken it upon themselves to show
once again that Lanier was correct in his prophetic
sayings regarding woman's place in symphonic orchestras.

The New York Sun, January 11, 1938:

ORCHESTRETTE CLASSIQUE HEARD

The Orchestrette Classique resumed activities in
the Carnegie Chamber Music Hall last night with
Conductor Frederique Petrides inscribing the program to the memory of Sidney Lanier. This seemingly far-fetched association may be better understood when it is known that Lanier was one of the
first Americans in public life to champion the cause
of women musicians as orchestral players.
    With the admirable taste that she has demonstrated
in the past, Miss Petrides offered her listeners a
list of music that included Mendelssohn's Heimkehr
aus der Fremde overture and Italian symphony, the
first suite of Bach (in C), the Prokofieff Overture
on Yiddish Themes, and the D Major flute concerto
of Mozart. The soloist in the last of these was
Ruth Freeman, who performed her part with excellent tone, good musical understanding and substantial

command of the work's difficulties.   She used the
cadenzas of her mentor, Georges Barrere.   Both
here and in the Bach suite, the executive ability
of Miss Petrides was reflected in the smoothness
and sound technical competence with which the orchestra played.   (Reprinted by permission of Scripps
Howard Newspapers and Bell & Howell.)

During their eighth season the Orchestrette Classique
continued to play compositions by native or naturalized Americans which received support from the audiences as well as
the music critics.   Included were the first New York performance of David Diamond's Concerto for Chamber Orchestra, Julia Smith's Episodic Suite, Samuel Barber's Adagio for
String Orchestra, and Paul Creston's Partita for Flute and
Violin with String Orchestra and his Concerto for Marimba
and Orchestra.   Madame Petrides commissioned Creston to
write the marimba piece especially for the orchestra since
Ruth Stuber who played Bach and Mozart on marimba was
an exceptionally fine percussionist.   The program noted that
the marimba piece was the only serious work ever written
for the instrument.   It was designed to demonstrate the capabilities of the marimba as a solo instrument with orchestral
accompaniment, and was dedicated to Frederique Petrides.
Some forty years later Creston wrote to her and indicated
his pleasure at having written the piece, particularly since
he was still receiving royalties.

The World Telegram on April 22, 1941, highly praised
Petrides when it printed, "When Miss Petrides runs short of
standard material, she never delves among the sub-standard.
She seeks instead the new and unfamiliar, and not once in
eight seasons of concerts has she offered dullness as a substitute for guaranteed pleasure."

The New York Times on April 30, 1940 carried a review by Howard Taubman:

CONCERT OFFERED BY ORCHESTRETTE

Concertino for Marimba and Orchestra Featured at
the Carnegie Chamber Hall

Ruth Stuber is Soloist

Creston Composition Dedicated to Frederique Petrides, Conductor of Program

A concertino for marimba and orchestra--at first
blush, that might read like a manifestation of the
silly season. But don't laugh: it wasn't. Such
a work by the American composer Paul Creston had
its first performance last night at the concert of
the Orchestrette Classique, directed by Miss Frederique Petrides, at Carnegie Chamber Music Hall.
The soloist was Miss Ruth Stuber, who is tympanist
in the orchestra.

The program stated flatly that the concertino
"is the only work ever written for this instrument
in serious form." Until some musicologist produces
evidence to the contrary, the claim will be considered justified. It may not be the last work, because Mr. Creston made it an effective vehicle for
his ideas and because Miss Stuber played it with
skill as well as art.

Composition is Discussed

The marimba has its limitations as a solo instrument, but Mr. Creston wrote well within them.
He is, moreover, a composer with ideas and invention. Of the three movements marked Vigorous,
Calm and Lively--the first seemed the freshest and
the most original in thematic material. All three
are worked out with technical assurance, with the
marimba player receiving ample opportunity to display virtuosity. Mr. Creston writes with rhythmic
bite and variety and, occasionally, with delightful
lyrical strain.

Miss Stuber, looking trim and chic in a fluffy
yellow gown, was agreeable to behold as well as
to hear. She managed a delicately grated tone,
and she knew how to sustain a broad phrase and
how to skip up and down the length of the marimba
with grace and speed. The work was thoroughly
prepared. Miss Petrides and her players joined
with Miss Stuber in a smartly turned out interpretation. Mr. Creston was on hand to acknowledge the
applause.

Barbirolli Work Played

Miss Petrides, who has built her chamber orchestra
into a well drilled, responsive ensemble, has made
a habit of live programs. Last night she offered
Beethoven's Men of Prometheus Overture, Op 43;
John Barbirollis' skillful Concerto for Oboe and Strings

on Themes of Pergolesi, with Lois Wann as the
oboist; Bela Bartok's Rumanian Folk Dances for
Small Orchestra, Mozart's Serenade in D, and Haydn's
Symphony in D, known as the "Clock" symphony.
    The Bartok dances have a lusty vitality. The
seven movements are short and incisive and have
pleasant-like earthiness. The Orchestrette which
is almost all female, may have looked polite and
even demure, but the playing was appropriately
gusty. (Copyright © 1940 by The New York Times
Company. Reprinted by permission.)

The Orchestrette of New York (formerly the Orchestrette Classique) celebrated its tenth anniversary on May 3,
1942, with a concert at the chamber Music Hall. That the
Orchestrette has established a reputation for excellence and
originality of programs was to the credit of conductor Petrides. Her continued efforts each season to program many
worthwhile American works, which, in the opinion of some
music critics might not have been premiered by other orchestras, certainly helped the cause of American composers.
In 1935 there was only a few conductors who would undertake
the demanding responsibility of presenting contemporary works.
It is time-consuming to learn and interpret new scores continually and to present a polished performance. Conductor
Frederique Petrides should be congratulated for her pioneering efforts. Had more conductors in America shown this
initiative, the listening public would have been more in tune
to hear native music. It takes talent, energy, and guts to
present an unknown commodity.

    Review from the New York Times, May 4, 1943 by
R. L. :

NOVELTIES PLAYED BY ORCHESTRETTE

Four New Works by American Composers Heard
Here for the First Time

The American composer had his chance at the tenth
anniversary concert of Frederique Petrides's Orchestrette last night in Carnegie Chamber Music
Hall, with four "first performances." These included Paul Creston's Chant of 1942, opus 33; Haydn's Concerto in F major for violin and piano with
stringed orchestra, revised and arranged by Albert
G. Hess and believed to be the first performance in
this country; Rapsodia Sinfonica, for piano and or-

chestra, by Joaquin Turína, first public performance
in this city, and American Melting pot, by Henry
Cowell, first full performance anywhere.

Mr. Creston's work was described as the composer's emotional reaction to the contrasting hope-
ful and sorrowful events of the war in the fateful
year of 1942. The composer declares it is not a
picture or a story, but "a series of moods." His
intentions cannot be questioned, but the music
seemed definitely to be an objective picture in sound
of something especially toward the end, where one
thought of the Stalingrad fighting, although the surge
of the brass above the fortissimo of the rest of
the instruments did give the impression of what the
program notes called "hope in the nobler aspects
of humanity." Mr. Creston was present to hear
his new work, and was acclaimed by an audience
that filled the hall to overflowing.

Hinda Barnett, violin, and Vivian Rivkin played,
respectively, the violin and piano in the Haydn concerto, and did their work with real art. Miss
Barnett displayed a fine, full tone and an excellent
feeling for the composition, as did Miss Rivkin.
Turina's very Spanish work was played by Miss
Rivkin with dash and energy and the unusual feeling
for rhythm that the work called for. Despite a
tendency to force the tone, the technique was entirely adequate for the difficulties presented, and
the net result was one of unusual brilliance.

Henry Cowell's American Melting Pot consists
of five movements each in the style of some minority
group in this country--German, Negro, East Indian
and Near Eastern, Slavic, and South American.
The well-knit composition carried out its program
in a satisfactory and musical manner, although
without adding greatly to the music of the world.

Miss Petrides achieves fine results with her organization of women. In general the playing last
night showed excellent balance. The closing Mozart
Symphony No. 185 (Haffner), however, seemed a
little heavy-handed for the composer's style, lacking in the true Mozartean grace, lightness and
charm. The program began with Beethoven's overture, The Creation of Prometheus. (Copyright ©
1943 by The New York Times Company. Reprinted
by permission.)

An added note of interest--when Paul Creston was a

young composer and unknown, it was Frederique Petrides and
her orchestra that premièred many of his compositions. Eventually his works were conducted by Toscanini, Stokowski,
Ormandy, and others.   When he wrote Chant of 1942 Toscanini requested permission to première the composition.
Creston refused, saying permission would be granted only
after the Orchestrette of New York played it.   The piece
was dedicated to Petrides and he remained true to the conductor who had afforded him his early opportunities.   Eventually he added to the piece, and the New York Philharmonic
programmed the composition.   When Eugene Ormandy took
the Philadelphia Orchestra on its first trip to Russia, he included the Chant of 1942 on the program.

It was natural with the passing of time that women
instrumentalists would take their rightful place in the major
symphony orchestras.   Perhaps this was hastened by the Second World War, but in any case the time was right for the
Orchestrette of New York to close a golden era in the history
of American music.   One can only wish that the hundreds of
reviews it received during its tenure could be included here
for reference--unfortunately that is not possible.   Conductor
Frederique Petrides was a pioneer whose talents would continue to be shared with audiences.

During the years that she conducted her Orchestrette
she also edited and published Women in Music, the only such
publication available in America.   Her efforts in both areas
were supported for over forty years by her husband, Peter
Petrides, a publicity agent and a journalist with the Greek-
American newspaper and the National Herald.   Madame Petrides said,

> When I first met Peter, I had never met a Greek
> and I suppose I thought of Greeks as wearing togas!
> Peter was a fine looking gentleman, a lovely per-
> son, very knowledgeable in French, Greek, and
> American literature, and a friend of the great writer
> Theodore Dreiser.   I could never have done this
> work without his continuous encouragement and help.
> We spent countless hours researching the material
> for Women in Music, and since we had no children
> at that time, we financed the publication ourselves.

Women in Music was a monthly publication, with a
circulation of over 2,500 which specialized in the dissemination of news and facts pertaining to women conductors and
women's orchestras in America and abroad.   This venture

in musical journalism represented the first, and at the time,
the only publication of its kind in the world. The monthly
leaflet, published from 1935 to 1940, was sent to libraries,
universities, and other interested parties in both the United
States and abroad. Material from Women in Music was used
by many of the leading newspapers and periodicals of the
time and was often given front page coverage, including The
New Times, New York Post, New York Sun, Baltimore Sun,
New York World-Telegram, Chicago Tribune, San Diego
Union, Los Angles Times, and the Long Beach Press Telegram.

Madame Petrides spoke of this publication, "I started
to edit and write Women in Music because I wanted the members of my Orchestrette to know that they were part of a
tradition that went back to ancient Egyptian and Greek times.
In 1933 people would come to hear a women's orchestra with
a woman conductor, considering it a novelty, but we were
really a part of something that had gone on for a long, long
time. Mozart had declared that woman have more talent for
stringed instruments than men, a gift which he attributed to
the former's greater delicacy of touch and to the easier access to their emotions.

Sixty issues of Women in Music were published over
a period of five years. It is possible at this time to offer
the reader only a brief overview of the material available.
Women in Music July 1, 1935 (excerpt):

A LADY CONDUCTOR IN PEPYS' TIME

The First of the Batonic Species

(from his Diary)

"June 6, 1661 ... Called upon this morning by
Lieutenant Lambert who is now made captain of the
Norwich and he and I went down by water to Green-
wich, in our way observing and discoursing upon
the things of a ship, he telling me all I asked him,
which was of good use to me. There we went and
eat and drank and heard musique at the Globe and
saw the simple motion that there is of a woman
with rod in her hands keeping time to the musique
while it plays, which is simple me-thinks."

Women in Music Vol. 1, No. 7, March, 1936 (excerpt):

FOR THE RECORD!

Five hundred and twenty-two women musicians are affiliated with the eight women's orchestras which now function in America.   Listed in chronological order of their inception, these groups are:

Los Angeles Women's Symphony; 70 players. -- Philadelphia Women's Orchestra: 60 players. -- Women's Symphony of Long Beach, Cal. :   105 players. --Women's Symphony of Chicago: 100 players. --Orchestrette Classique: 34 players. -- Portland Women: 35 players. --N. Y. Women's Orchestra: 85 players. --Women's Little Symphony of Cleveland: 43 players.

The above list does not include women's jazz orchestras or chamber groups of less than fifteen players.

Women in Music Vol. II, No. 4, January, 1937 (excerpt):

VIENNA'S SURPRISE TO OLD NEW YORK

Throughout the twelve days which followed the evening of September 11, 1871, curious crowds of New Yorkers were rushing nightly and on matinee days to the Old Steinway Hall on Fourteenth Street.   The Vienna Ladies' Orchestra, the only aggregation of its kind to ever visit America, was the performing attraction, the big novelty.

The curiosity over the Vienna Ladies was well justified.   Those artists were professionals at a time when, with the exception of isolated cases, the day of the professional woman musician had not yet dawned in America.   Besides, their orchestra, not the very first all-feminine ensemble in history of music, was, nevertheless, the only one of its type heard in America up to that year.   Consequently, it stood out as something unique and almost incredible in that period of musical life in the New World.

The visiting group was composed of "twenty artists, most of whom were on the bright side of twenty years of age, generally graceful and good-looking, with sparkling eyes, flowing hair and nimble fingers. "   These musicians and Josephine Weimlich, their conductor, dressed with the most exquisite taste of their period.   They surrounded themselves

with "sundry elegant accessories such as roses,
white drums and a number of white bouquets of
regulation pattern." Their specialty was choice
waltz music, although their programs also featured
movements from light operas and symphonies. They
were brought over by a Mr. Rullman, the first
American to manage a women's orchestra on these
shores. Following their New York debut, they were
to play in various American cities.

Two short excerpts from Women in Music Vol. III.
No. 5, January, 1938 and Vol. III No. 7, April, 1938:

SHOP TALK

One of the first instances of women belonging to
a musicians' union is that of eight jugglers (jongler-
esses) who, together with twenty-nine men musicians' (ménestrels) combined in Paris in 1321 in
order to establish for themselves statutes, which
were sanctioned on the fourteenth of September of
that year. In New York, the musicians' Union
started admitting women to membership only in
1903, although it had been in existence for many
years.

When a Boston reporter asked Nadia Boulanger
how it felt being the first woman to ever conduct
the Boston Symphony, she answered: "I've been
a woman for a little over fifty years, and have
gotten over my initial astonishment. As for conducting an orchestra, that's a job. I don't think
sex plays much part."

Women in Music Vol. V, No. 3, February, 1940 (excerpt):

"In the hearts of ambitious women the world over
there is a special place for the Philadelphia Orchestra (and Leopold Stokowski),"--thus an item
in the N.Y. Times' Music Section. "For years
Mr. Stokowski proclaimed his belief in the ability
of the ladies to take their places competently in
symphony orchestras, and on several occasions he
has shown the world that he means what he says.
Today the Philadelphia Orchestra has four lady
members--a violinist, a cellist and two harpists"--
and now it "confirms its confidence in the sex"
choosing Elsa Hilger, its woman cellist, "to occupy

the first stand" in its Robin Hood Dell series this
summer.

"An Unusual Subject By An Unusual Woman," was the
title given a series of lectures presented by Frederique Petrides during the 1930's and 1940's. The lectures were presented for live audiences, as well as over stations WJZ of
the National Broadcasting Company and WOR. Her story of
women in orchestras and related information made a fascinating subject that sparkled with historical and timely interest.
In addition to lecturing, she wrote lengthy articles published
in the Family Circle in 1934; The Musical Review in 1935;
Pacific Coast Musician in 1935; The American Music Lover
in 1936; and, The Etude in 1938, among others. She covered
such topics as "Women in Orchestras," "Famous and Brilliant Conductors," "Some Reflections on Women Musicians,"
and "Outline of a Prejudice," this last published in Musical
Review September-October, 1935. It is reprinted in its entirety by permission of the author:

OUTLINE OF A PREJUDICE

Friends and apologists of women in music must
have been temporarily taken back in 1892, the year
when the American translation of Anton Rubinstein's
"A Conversation on Music" appeared in New York.
In the course of this book, the great pianist sneered
at woman's ability and accomplishments in the creative or the interpretative spheres of music. He
also read in the increase of women as instrumental
players or composers the signs of the downfall of
music.
    Rubinstein was neither the first or the last to
sound the tocsin on the subject of women in music.
Around 1880, Otto Gumprecht, a typical champion
of the status quo regarding barriers existing against
women musicians, was uttering loud protest in Berlin against the candidacy en masse of the fair sex
for virtuosoships. According to the mournful Teuton
such candidacies were characteristic of the "mor-
bid symptoms of the age."
    Even Shakespeare does not sound as if he had
much, if any, respect for feminine musical ability.
His words: "Will my daughter prove a good musician? I think she'll sooner prove a good soldier"
typify in part a widespread prejudice which lasted
for centuries. As long as that prejudice reigned
unchallenged, women were prevented from acquiring

a serious musical education. They were also being
discouraged from venturing outside the operatic field
for musical careers.

Since the days of Palestrina and up to the middle
of the nineteenth century woman was taught music
as a pastime and then only in its most elementary
forms. Her musical education seldom advanced
beyond playing the lute, the harpsichord, the clavi-
chord, the virginal and finally the pianoforte.

On the practical career side, the musically gifted
and at the same time daring and unconventional female was allowed to seek self expression as a singer
only about A.D. 1600, the period when opera was
introduced in Europe. But, women who had ambi-
tions for a serious study of music or who aspired
for a career as composers and instrumentalists
were more or less pitied, when not denounced, as
victims of some mental aberration. With few exceptions, those in the sex, who, urged by genius
or irrepressible talent, would now and then emerge
as composers or instrumental players, were doing
so at their own risk. Social laws and prejudice
were against them. For instance:

As late as the eighties to be told that a composition was the work of a woman was the equivalent
of its condemnation beforehand. This compelled
many women to use masculine pen names in order
to have their works published. After the gifted
Fanny Mendelssohn (1805-1847) had been dissuaded
by her famous brother from publishing her works
on account of her sex, she had some of her compositions appear as his own in his "Songs Without
Words." Anxious to get a musical degree, Elizabeth Stirling, the English composer and organist,
submitted in 1856 to Oxford her beautiful CXXX
Psalms for five voices and orchestra, her work was
accepted and praised. But the degree was denied
her "for want of power to confer same upon a
woman."

The history of professional women players between 1700 and 1850, shows that the class was
often censored for bad taste and affrontery for having chosen the piano, the violin, the cello, the
clarinet and other kindred instruments. "Our modern belles are determined not to be excluded from
exercising any department of art: all we now want
is a female virtuoso on the bassoon and trombone,
and we believe the list will then be complete." Thus

reads the sarcastic comment of a Munich critic in
1823 a propos of a concert given in that city by
the celebrated clarinetist Madame Krahmer.

The critics were full of hosannahs regarding the
genius and accomplishments of Signora Parravicini,
the great Italian violinist who was born in Turin in
1769. But they objected to her instrument. They
thought that the violin was "not suited to a female,
a fact universally admitted and which no skill or
address can ever get over with."

Sometime before 1774, Schmelling, the German
child prodigy who later became famous as the singer
Mara, gave a number of recitals in London. Immediately, various undoubtedly socially correct English ladies persuaded her to give up her instrument.
The ladies "disliked female fiddlers," an attitude
which impelled a contemporary critic living years
ahead of his time to write: "We cannot but regard
the exclusion of females from the violin as a prejudice and nothing but a prejudice."

There is little doubt that Mozart must have felt
a keen repulsion at this and other kindred discrim-
inations of his time against female musicians when
he declared that women have a more natural gift
for stringed instruments than males, a gift which
he attributed to their greater delicacy of touch and
also to a readier access of a conductor to their
emotions.

The prejudice against a serious musical education or careers for women in music kept waning
increasingly since 1850. In 1876, the English High
School of London began admitting for the first time
women students for the violin, Germany had already
admitted a woman as a Royal Professor in the Dres-
den School of Music. Between 1880 and 1882 the
Mendelssohn Scholarship in England went to a member of the fair sex. Women were now admitted at
the Royal Academy and the Royal College. They
could also enter the Cambridge examination for Musical degrees, an event which opened the doors of
more Colleges and Conservatories for them.

The isolated class of people who from the very
beginning had been favorably disposed toward women
in music had gained a good number of converts to
their viewpoint since the dawn of the nineteenth century. The eighties saw this element upholding with
fervor and even militancy the principle that woman's
musical genius and talents would develop in exact

proportion to the advantages for education and practical careers at her command. Naturally, those
on the other side of the fence could neither digest
nor accept meekly this principle. In the meantime,
the class of women who were winning regional or
international fame as concert artists and to a lesser
extent as music teachers was consistently growing
stronger and more impressive in Europe.
These developments exercised their practical
influences in the New World. Gradually the piano
ceased being the instrument par excellence for the
American girl. Between 1892 and 1900 the increase
of women actively engaged as music students, teachers or concert players under the American sky
demonstrated the fact that our women were quick
to appreciate their recently unfolded rights for equal
educational and professional advantages in the musical world.
Freed from the shackles and tatters of the old
tradition and prejudice, American and European
women in music are now universally hailed as important factors in the concert and teaching fields
and as promising and at the same time fast developing assets in the creative spheres of the profession.
Their development during the last thirty years in
all branches of music has already disproved the unfair prejudice expounded even by Shakespeare.
Futhermore, their record in the profession proves
that the signs which, according to Rubinstein, indicated the downfall of music, were in reality signs
of a fuller, abundant and representative musical
life for both sexes.

For a period of time Frederique Petrides slowed down
her professional career in order to devote more time to her
beautiful daughter Avra. She said,

I was happy to have more time to spend with my
daughter. I could tell when she was just a baby
that she had perfect pitch for she would always
sing a song in the key she had heard it in. Although she is not in music, she loves it (calls herself a former pianist) and is a very talented person,
and she has directed her creative energies as an
actress in stage productions and as a member of
the famous Actors Studio.

During the 1930's-1940's Madame Petrides headed the

string department at the Masters School at Dobbs Ferry-on-the-Hudson. This was an exclusive school for wealthy young girls who would receive the necessary training to take their places in the elite circles of society. With support from the headmistress, Miss Pierce, and Mrs. Elliott Speer, Petrides founded an orchestra of students and townspeople. The group rehearsed twice a week at the school and Petrides said,

> This was the first time the general public was ever invited to use the school's facilities. It also provided an experience for the students to play their instruments as well as providing the opportunity to become more informed about orchestral functions, as many of them would eventually become patrons of various orchestras in their hometowns.

This group would eventually be known as the Hudson Valley Symphony Orchestra with Frederique Petrides as founder-conductor.

Conductor Petrides would spend seven seasons as conductor of the Hudson Valley Symphony Orchestra in Dobbs Ferry. Under her skilled baton, her determination, and musical expertise, the orchestra was firmly established. Some four decades later it still continues to perform. A review published in the Dobbs Ferry Register on April 30, 1938 by Paul Creston:

> From the opening tones of Weber's Overture to Oberon it was immediately evident that Madame Petrides has a fine command of her instrument, the orchestra, as well as a clear understanding of the work under exposition. One can easily realize the problems involved in the unification of a heterogeneous ensemble of individuals only recently brought together, in the molding of a group into a homogeneous whole. Orchestras are not built in one season but Madame Petrides, being the experienced hand she is, has already attained commendable results with the Hudson Valley Symphony Orchestra.

Starting in the 1950's the talented conductor Frederique Petrides devoted her full effort to developing a series of outdoor concerts in the city of New York. These concerts would span a period of over twenty years. As a champion of good music for all the people, she offered all concerts free. Those who wished to donate money to help defray the cost of such an undertaking were welcomed, but equally welcomed were those individuals who could not afford to contribute. Some programs were sponsored by Local 802 of the American Federation of Musicians, by wealthy patrons, and by other community organizations.

On the surface, the idea of outdoor concerts would seem quite simple, but in reality the physical arrangements required many hours of work and considerable money. Under Mayor Wagner's administration, and with the full support of Parks Commissioner Newbold Morris, the operation was smooth. Needed lights, staging, speakers, chairs, and even on occasion, an acoustical shell, were all made readily available. No matter what difficulties might arise, the concerts did continue with audiences numbering in the thousands.

The first area in the city where Madame Petrides conducted an outdoor series was Washington Square Park. The orchestra included twenty-five members of the New York Philharmonic, with Michael Rosenker as concert master. Two reviews, one from the 1956 season and one from the 1957 season are included here to provide a sampling. In The Villager, August 23, 1956, and the National Herald, August 25, 1957, Paul Nord wrote:

CONCERT IN CHURCH BIG SUCCESS

Good Crowd Braves Rain--Hears Woman Conductor

Approximately 850 persons crowded into Judson Memorial Church, while another 500 had to be turned away for lack of space, last Tuesday night to hear the third in the current series of Washington Square Chamber Music Concerts. Rain on Monday, the regularly scheduled time, forced a postponement until the following night. More rain compelled the concert, for the first time, to be held indoors.
   Those who could get in, however, enjoyed one of the best performances held thus far. Frederique Petrides, woman conductor, and her ensemble made a smash hit.
   The concert opened with Concerto Grosso for Stringed Orchestra Op. I, No. 2 by Locatelli. The rendition was excellent, especially in the adagio and largo.
   This was followed by Concerto in E major for Violin and Stringed Orchestra by Johann Sebastian

Bach. Miss Anahid Ajemian, the attractive dark-
haired young soloist, was outstanding on the violin.
Her performance was distinguished by a broad,
smooth tonal quality. The orchestral accompaniment, under the direction of Miss Petrides, was
equally beautiful and effective.

In the Variations on a Theme from Tchaikowsky
by Arensky, Miss Petrides and the orchestra captured the romantic sentiment of the music. Miss
Petrides conducting has sure control and the instrumentalists played for her with great understanding, as she drew from each section what the music
demanded.

Wolfgang A. Mozart's Symphony No. 29 in A
Major, K. 201 was the final program selection.
Again, the ensemble, under Miss Petrides' dignified,
yet animated direction rose to the best expectations
of seasoned chamber music enthusiasts.

Modern Dance by Roger Goeb, first No. 2 and
then No. I were played as encores. American
dances, the first was delightful and captivating,
while the second was hard and brittle. Both were
applauded by the appreciative audience, which represented a cross-section of ages, types and tastes.
(Reprinted by permission of the publisher, The Byron Publication.)

FREDERIQUE PETRIDES TRIUMPHS IN WASHING-
TON SQ. CONCERT

An audience of some 5,000 music-lovers attended
the third concert of the Washington Square Chamber
Orchestra Series last night when Frederique Petrides
presented a well-chosen program of fine music.

Beginning with Benjamin Britten's nostalgic and
even witty Simple Symphony, Mme. Petrides led an
excellent Ensemble in such seldom-heard pieces as
William Grant Still's colorful and fiery Danzas de
Panama; Schubert's exquisite Polonaise for Small
Orchestra and Violin and Antonio Rosetti's captivating
Symphony in G Minor. The program also included
Tchaikowsky's Serenade for Strings and ended with
Johann Strauss' Voices of Spring, which was played
as an encore. Mr. Michael Rosenker was the
soloist in the Polonaise.

Throughout the concert, the conductor and her
orchestra were in excellent form. Under Mme.
Petrides' eloquent, sensitive and forceful leadership,

the orchestra did full justice to the evening's admirably balanced and taxing program. Its playing
was full of the artistry and the fine orchestral
shadings one associates with the best indoor concerts in this city.
    The large audience applauded enthusiastically
Mme. Petrides, Mr. Rosenker, her fine soloist,
and the orchestra.
    The New School for Social Research was the con-
cert's financial sponsor and the Washington Square
Association and the Concert Committee are spon-
sors of the series.

    For five years, beginning in 1958, Madame Petrides
organized and conducted a series of concerts at the Carl
Schurz Park in New York's fashionable upper East Side. The
setting was a lovely dell next door to Mayor Wagner's Gracie
Mansion. The orchestra's some thirty-two musicians were
mostly members of the New York Philharmonic. Speaking
of this experience, Petrides said,

    It was necessary to be well-organized because there
    was only limited time to rehearse. I talked very
    little but would get down to the business of rehears-
    ing immediately. A woman must be better than a
    man if she is to conduct prestigious groups, and
    I made it my career always to be 100 per cent
    prepared and know all the scores tremendously well.
    I never encountered any problem conducting all-
    male orchestras, and we always worked well to-
    gether.

Numerous accounts of these concerts are available, but only
the review of August 5, 1960, published in the New York
Herald Tribune, is offered here for lack of space:

FESTIVAL GROUP AT SCHURZ PARK

    The Festival Symphony Orchestra under the direc-
    tion of Frederique Petrides opened the third season
    of free concerts at the Carl Schurz Park last even-
    ing. Good weather and an interesting program drew
    a good-sized crowd to the park which, in addition
    to offering live music also boasts a most impres-
    sive view of the East River.
        Boat hooting and passing airplanes notwithstand-
    ing, the audience was treated to first performances
    of works by two contemporary Belgian composers:

Marcel Poot and Jacques Stehman. Both are highly
respected and much performed in their own country
and both are members of the Brussels Conservatory of Music.
    Listening to Marcel Poot's Divertimento for Small
Orchestra, one could immediately tell that the composer has been well schooled in the French tradi-
tion--there was elegance, urbanity, wit and charm
in his short work. Calculated to please, the Divertimento provided a gay march, an expressive
serenade, a somewhat overly somber movement entitled Melancollis (not really in keeping with the
piece) and spirited allegro.
    But of the two, it was Jacques Stehman's Sym-
phonie de Poche or Pocket Symphony which succeeded in being the more communicative work.
Eschewing the impressive, it made its point with
much simplicity and an ample dose of "tongue in
cheek" humor. It was really a miniature symphony
employing four short movements all of which contained wonderful lyricism and sustained sentiment.
    It cannot be said that either composer added new
dimensions to the contemporary musical scene--
neither breadth nor depth were present in these
works but, for what they were, they managed to
convey expressive musical ideas--and for a summer
evening, what could be pleasanter.
    The Overture to the Opera Euryanthe by Carl
Maria von Weber, Dvorak's Serenade for Stringed
Orchestra in E Major and Mozart's Symphony no.
41 (Jupiter) rounded out the program. Miss Petrides conducted with conviction and, while the orchestra could not always respond with complete
security, the spirit of each work was always maintained. --J. G. (Reprinted by Permission. Copyright © 1960. I. H. T. Corporation.)

Madame Frederique Petrides, conductor and founder of the
Festival Symphony Orchestra, drew enthusiastic audiences
for several seasons at the Carl Schurz Park. In 1960 she
organized and conducted a series at the amphitheatre at the
foot of Riverside Drive, near 72nd Street. It was an immediate success, for people came by the thousands to the beautiful, music-filled Riverside Park, a scenic spot of great
charm and beauty. "Tanglewood around the corner" was how
many listeners described the Riverside concerts. Petrides,
herself from the West Side, was aware that audiences at the
outdoor concerts were composed not only of neighborhood

people but also of people who came in increasing numbers
from other parts of the city or from the suburbs. Laudatory
notices in various newspapers and radio broadcasts on WNYC
were partly responsible for increased attendence, but partly
this was due to Madame Petrides' constantly acclaimed skill
and diversity in programming. Each concert given in the
season was reviewed by several music critics, and there are
numerous articles available on the series.

The New York Herald Tribune, June 19, 1962 carried
a review by Francis Perkins:

> WEST SIDE CONCERTS MAKE DEBUT IN RIVER-
> SIDE PARK
>
> The West Side Community Concerts made a promis-
> ing debut on the bank of the Hudson last night at
> W. 73 St. and Riverside Park when Frederique
> Petrides conducted her Festival Symphony Orches-
> tra in the athletic field at the south end of River-
> side Park before an audience that occupied all the
> seats in the enclosure and the neighboring grass
> and paths below the embankment of the West Side
> Highway.
>   Besides being one of the coolest spots in town,
> the area made an attractive amphitheater, and loud-
> speakers carried Weber's Euryanthe Overture, parts
> of Handel's Water Music, Haydn's Trumpet Con-
> certo, two Brahms Hungarian Dances and Beethoven's
> Symphony No. 1 to a generous distance.
>   Miss Petrides is an experienced conductor, and
> the 40 musicians under her direction gave spirited,
> balanced and thoroughly unified performances. The
> tones of Charles Schlueter's trumpet solo were both
> smooth and brilliant.
>   Acting State Supreme Court Justice Harry B.
> Frank, chairman for these concerts, said that this
> event represented the West Side as it should be
> depicted, and also read a congratulatory letter from
> August Heckscher, special consultant on the arts
> for President Kennedy. (Reprinted by permission.
> Copyright © 1962 I. H. T. Corporation.)

In The New York Times, June 25, 1963 Howard Klein
wrote:

> 4,500 HEAR CONCERT AT RIVERSIDE PARK
>
> A record crowd of 4,500 persons jammed the River-

side Park amphitheater last night at the first of
two concerts presented by the West Side Community
Concerts, Inc. Frederique Petrides, the founder
and conductor of the Festival Orchestra, put together an interesting program that was enthusiastically received.

There was Beethoven's Coriolanus Overture and
the Symphony No. 2 in D; Mendelssohn's Sinfonia No.
9 for stringed orchestra; Haydn's Symphony Concertante (Op. 84) and a premiere of Armin Schibler's Concertino for Clarinet and String Orchestra.

The Schibler work had William Lewis as soloist.
In one movement, it was somberly attractive and
well played.

Miss Petrides kept the music alive at all times
with her brisk, business-like beat. The Mendels-
sohn, a seldom-heard beauty, bubbled along nicely.
And the Haydn Concertante--which had as soloists
Harold Kohon, violinist; Leo Rostall cellist; Lois
Wann, oboist and Lester Cantor, bassoonist--was
clean and sprightly. (Copyright © 1963 by The New
York Times Company. Reprinted by permission.)

Miss Petrides offered only praise for the members of
the Festival Symphony Orchestra:

I had very fine musicians to work with, and I enjoyed the many hours of research I did to find interesting material for the programs. I read a
score the way many people read a book. I have
perfect pitch and I hear the music as I read it.
I read lots of music and I found many beautiful
works.

In 1967 the outdoor concerts were given in a new
acoustical shell at Riverside Drive and 103rd Street. The
shell was provided by the Department of Parks. Conductor
Petrides and her professional orchestra opened the new series
on June 17, 1967 and continued to perform until 1975.

Two reviews by Raymond Ericson for the New York
Times, appeared June 16, 1969 and July 30, 1975:

FESTIVAL SYMPHONY PLAYS TO WEST SIDE

The upper West Side has its only little summer
music festival in a park. Last night members of
the community gathered on the grassy slope facing
the Hudson River at the foot of 103rd Street to hear

the opening concert.   The Festival Symphony Orchestra was conducted, as it has been in the last
seven years, by Frederique Petrides.

Besides being a very able director, she is an
astute program builder, and the concert she provided was just right for the modest proportions of
her ensemble (about 40) and the outdoor setting.
The music was not too hackneyed; it was entertaining without being superficial.

There was a Flute and Oboe in C by Antonio
Salieri, a composer whom the Viennese preferred
to Mozart in the 18th century but who is just a
name in the history books today.   The work is
witty and charming, and it was brightly played by
the soloists, Lois Wann, oboe, and Harold Jones,
flute.

Then, quite properly, Mozart had his due, in
the orchestral arrangements that Tchaikovsky made
of four of his pieces and assembled under the un-
revealing title of Suite No. 4.   Panufnik's Suite of
Ancient Polish Airs and Dances, Von Rezniček's
Overture to Donna Diana and Prokofiev's Classical
Symphony completed the program.   (Copyright ©
1969 by The New York Times Company.   Reprinted
by permission.)

FREDERIQUE PETRIDES CONDUCTS ORCHESTRAL
CONCERTS IN THE PARK

In all this talk about women conductors, it is sometimes overlooked that Frederique Petrides has been
living and working here since she founded the Orchestrette Classique in 1933.   Nowadays her ap-
pearences are usually with the West Side Orchestral
Concerts, a series of four outdoor programs in
Riverside Park at 103rd Street.   The third of them
was given on Monday night, performed by a large
string ensemble.

The attractive program included a Vivaldi Concerto for Two Violins in A minor, with Jesse Cusi-
mano and Nanette Levi as soloists; a Boccherini
Suite in C: Arensky's Variations on a Theme of
Tchaikovsky; and Mendelssohn's Octet in E flat,
played by the full complement of strings.

If the concert suffered from the usual afflictions
of outdoor events, primarily amplification that was
either too loud and tinny or too soft, there was the
simple pleasure of sitting on a grassy slope and

watching the sun go down across the Hudson River
while listening to some exciting music.
Miss Petrides has long since proven that she is
an able conductor with a musicianly sense for the
right tempo. Her performances moved along neatly,
with all points effectively made. The playing was
variable, with long stretches of fine ensemble interrupted by ragged patches, but on the whole it
was acceptable. (Copyright © 1975 by The New York
Times Company. Reprinted by permission.)

Petrides conducted the Student Symphony Society of New York
City for eleven seasons beginning in 1950. She said,

The membership comprised students between the
ages of nine and nineteen, who attended either public or private schools. Auditions were held and
students were accepted solely on their musician-
ships. The Student Symphony Society appeared in
concerts, C. B. S. Television Broadcast, and over
radio stations C. B. S. and W. N. Y. C. Voice of
America devoted a broadcast to the group in November 1952.

Madame Frederique Petrides is a talented and dedicated pioneer conductor. She has the breadth and depth of
knowledge and perceptive ability to delve into little-known
scores and present new and different listening experiences.
That she was able to combine in her programs new music
with little-known classical compositions made a unique contribution to the American musical scene. Why would a conductor choose this direction? She answers,

I needed to attract attention in order to receive
the support of a listening public as well as support
from the higher echelon in the music circle of fine
musicians and critics. There was a wealth of music
on library shelves and it had not been explored.
There were fine works by classical composers and
these had never been performed in America. Modern works needed public performances, too. People
are instinctively attracted to new listening experi-
ences--how else can there be musical growth? I
continually accomplished this goal by offering something different.

One would readily agree, for the numerous reviews of her
work will speak far more persuasively than any interview
with this extraordinary musician.

Conductor Petrides is a charming lady who quickly
gives credit to the musicians, composers, and other members of the musical establishment for her success. But in
reality her success is firmly grounded in her own intellectual
capacity to comprehend, express, and inspire those around
her. She is truly a talented conductor.

MARTA PTASZYNSKA

Composer, Virtuoso Solo Percussionist, Teacher

Marta Ptaszynska is internationally recognized as one of the younger generation's leading composers. She is prominent as well as a virtuoso solo percussionist of contemporary music. Almost every recent Polish composition for solo percussion has been written for her and she has premièred many percussion works. Ptaszynska's compositions are sensitive and inspiring within a conceptual framework that is at times complex, yet persuasive for the aural simplicity of timbrels. She is an exceptionally fine musician and an intelligent, personable, creative artist.

One of two children of Juliusz and Romana Ptaszynska, she was born July 29, 1943, in Warsaw, Poland, during the city's devastation in World War II. Her father was an eminent engineer who rebuilt more than 300 Polish bridges destroyed during the second World War. He also played violin and composed many vocal and instrumental works. His cantata, The New Spirits, was dedicated before his death in 1980 to Pope John Paul II. Despite her country's difficult postwar years her musical talent, discovered when she was a young child, demanded education and training that were extensive, demanding, and arduous. Marta attended Podstawowa Szkota Muzyczna from age seven to age fourteen and the Liceum Muzyczne from fourteen to eighteen. The academic requirements were rigorous, for the Polish tradition of musical excellence is superior. She had thorough training in piano (every music student was required to study this instrument), harmony, theory, music history, analysis, and solfège as well as the required history, science, literature, philosophy, psychology, art history, and gymastics. She said, "There were times when I had so much to study, in so many different areas, that I could not do all the music I wanted to, but I had a fine education and appreciate it now."

Leon Myszkowski

MARTA PTASZYNSKA

Marta Ptaszynska studied composition under Tadeusz
Paciorkiewicz at the Academy of Music in Warsaw; music
theory with Stefan Sledzinski, Andrzej Dobrowolski, and
Witold Rudzinski at the Conservatory of Music in Warsaw;
and percussion playing under Jerzy Zgodzinski at the Conservatory of Music in Poznan. In 1968 she received three
Master of Arts degrees, with distinction in composition, percussion, and music theory. In 1969-1970 she received a
scholarship granted by the French government to study at
the Electronic Music Center à l'ORTF and, in addition to
complete her studies in composition under Nadia Boulanger
in Paris. She received the following recommendation from
the great Boulanger:

To Whom It May Concern

I certify that Miss Marta Ptaszynska worked on
composition under my direction during the year
1969-70.
She is an artist of great talent and great conscience.

As a young composer, her efforts have already been crowned with success as she has won several composition prizes. Miss Marta Ptaszynska deserves to be accepted this year in the summer course at Tanglewood. I repeat, she is a musician and an artist of unquestionable merit.

Ptaszynska said of her experience studying with Nadia Boulanger:

I loved to study with Nadia. First of all I did not come from Poland to her in order to receive from her the "recepies" for my new compositions, which is usually very common among young composers who expect to get them from their teachers. I just love her great knowledge of music, her experience, wisdom and her strength. These qualities are long lasting. Finally, I came to her not for the reason to learn the new twentieth-century techniques of composition, but learn from her whatever she could offer: a great musicianship, a great personality.

During 1970-1972 she was a member of the faculty at the Warsaw Conservatory. From 1972 to 1974 she stayed in the United States on a scholarship granted by the Kosciuszko Foundation at the Cleveland Institute of Music, where she received the Artist Diploma Degree in percussion playing. At the Institute she studied percussion with Cloyd Duff and Richard Weiner, and composition with Donald Erb.

Marta Ptaszynska returned to Poland in 1974 following her studies in Cleveland. She married a fellow countryman, an electrical engineer, Andrew Rafalski, and they are parents of a daughter, Julie Marie. In April 1975 she returned to America as guest lecturer and composer-in-residence in various institutions which included Bennington College in Vermont and the University of California at Berkeley and at Santa Barbara. At the present time composer Ptaszynska and her husband are permanent residents of the United States, living in Bethel, Connecticut, where he works for ASEA, the American branch of a Swedish firm.

Ptaszynska reflects on the role of a woman musician and composer in Poland, "Women are highly respected in all professional fields in my country including medicine, engineering, law, and the arts. I have never found any discrimination

as either a musician or composer, and my accomplishments
have always been readily accepted."

As a percussionist Ptaszynska specializes in solo performances of avant-garde works, including her own.   Her
large repertoire includes works by such composers as Schäf-
fer, Serocki, Stockhausen, Moszumanska, Meyer, Bargielski,
Rudzinski, Szalonek, Emma Lou Diemer, and Manuel Enriquez.   She has appeared in concerts in Warsaw, Mexico City,
Strasbourg, Breukelen, Paris, Royan, Poitiers, and cities
in the United States.   Her music has been performed throughout the world in many prestigious music festivals: the International Festival of Contemporary Music in Warsaw; the
International Society for Contemporary Music (ICSM); Aspen
Music Festival in Colorado; the New Music International Festival in Mexico City, New York, and San Jose, California;
the International Symposium of Percussionists Festival; and
the International Society for Music Education World Congress
(ISME).

Marta Ptaszynska said,

> I never studied composing until I was at the Con-
> servatory and every student of theory was obligated
> to write compositions for class and this was fol-
> lowed by a recital of students' works.   Many es-
> tablished composers came to hear these concerts
> and two noted composers, Grazyna Bacewicz and
> Andrej Dobrowolski, encouraged me to continue to
> compose after hearing my work as a student.   It
> was important to me to receive such encourage-
> ment.

A press review in the New Alsatian, 1967:

> Let's focus on the young Polish woman Marta Ptas-
> zynska, president of the "Circle of Young Polish
> Composers", and first-prize winner in competition,
> 1967.   Her preludes for vibraphone and piano dem-
> onstrate an almost classic structure; the sonorous
> effects alone are new and very pleasant to hear;
> they create an agreeable atmosphere.   The com-
> position is distinguished by perfect execution.   (Re-
> printed by permission of Le Nouvel Alsacien.)

From 1965 to 1970 she was acting chairman of the
Circle of Young Composers attached to the Polish Composers'
Union.   This organization was primarily responsible for the

presentation of music written by young Polish composers and performed throughout the country.   This was an important aspect of the cultural growth of the composer, for artistic development is dependent on hearing one's work in live performance and sharing this talent with audiences.

M. Komorowska wrote for Musical Movement Warsaw in 1969 on Ptaszynska's Variations for Flute Solo (excerpts):

> It is the correct opinion, that the best evidence of a talent, particularly composer's invention, is a monophony, the composition would give Ptaszynska a very good grading.

> This is a music narrative, dynamically developing, while giving a lot of freedom to the instrumentalist.

Tale of Nightingales for baritone and 6 instruments:

> The most interesting was the composition of M. Ptaszynska ... full of interesting, illustrative effects, every instrument had its own ascribed character ... percussion past was treated colorfully, a harp had an ostinato accompaniment, woodwinds were illustrating the text.   (Reprinted by permission of Ruch Muzyczny.)

In 1971 Marta composed Madrigals Canticum Sonarum, in memory of Igor Stravinsky, for wind, string quartets, trumpet, trombone, and gong.   She received a prize at the Young Polish Composers' Competition and the following review by G. Michalski was published in Musical Movement, Warsaw 1972:

> The concert's highlight was the world première of Two Madrigals by Marta Ptaszynska.... They are lively, dynamic, full of pleasant sonorities, although not necessarily consonances.   The listener is attracted to the very precise presentation of the smallest details in structure, articulation and orchestration.   These works must as well give great satisfaction to their performers.   (Reprinted by permission of Ruch Muzyczny.)

Having established her credentials as a composer and solo percussionist in Poland, she received acclaim in America soon after her arrival to do postgraduate work at the Cleveland Institute of Music in 1972.   Music critics and au-

diences voiced strong approval for her demonstrated agility
and excellent command of avant-garde styles in several performances over a period of two years.   In 1974 the Cleveland Orchestra and the Institute of Music presented a program featuring soloists and composers from the Institute in
Severance Hall.   Bain Murray writing for the Sun Press in
January praised her composition for orchestra, Spectri Sonori:

> The high point of the concert came with the per-
> formance of Spectri Sonori by Polish composer-
> percussionist Marta Ptaszynska.   Here is a new
> work with interesting textures and orchestral colors
> set forth in a meaningful design with a good sense
> of timing and dramatic impact.

Peter Craddock also reviewed this piece for the London Strad,
Vol. XC, September 1979, p. 371:

> Marta Ptaszynska.   Spectri sonori for orchestra.   A
> short sensitively textured work for largish orches-
> tra which was premièred by the virtuoso Cleveland
> Orchestra in January 1974 under the baton of Mat-
> thias Bamert.   Ptaszynska's style in this highly
> atmospheric score is almost impressionistic and con-
> siderable use is made of modern compositional
> techniques including graphic as well as conventional
> notation, multi-divided strings, aleatoric writing,
> and cluster chords.   The most intriguing colours
> in this $6\frac{1}{2}$ minute work emanate from delicate use
> of a large percussion section.   (Reprinted by per-
> mission of the author.)

Ptaszynska reflected on the concert:

> I still remember well the performance the Cleve-
> land Orchestra gave on January 22, 1974 with Mat-
> thias Bamert conducting.   I was enormously pleased
> with the quality of playing.   There was absolutely
> nothing I would like to suggest or to change in the
> performance.   The piece sounded just the way I
> imagined, even more colorful and more brilliant
> than I expected.

The dazzling virtuosity of Ptaszynska on percussion
has won plaudits in every country where she has performed.
Most people are completely unaware of the skill necessary to
be a fine percussionist; they merely think the performer just
bangs to make the sounds.   This is untrue, since the per-

cussionist is keenly aware of the variations of pitch as well
as the control and the tempering of the scale.   Imagine the
extremes that are possible with percussive instruments?   The
cymbal can be horridly loud and also quiet and hauntingly beautiful.   In recent years there has been an array of percussive
instruments added to traditional list of drums, tympani, triangle, temple blocks, bells, castanets, tambourine, and cymbals, and Ptaszynska is a master of all.   She completed a
five year course of study of percussion in three years.   The
following review written by Robert Finn was published in April
1974 in The Plain Dealer:

PERCUSSION BRINGS MOVING MOMENTS

It took percussionist Marta Ptaszynska a long ten
minutes to prepare for her performance of Kazim-
ierz Serocki's Fantasmagoria at Cleveland State
University Sunday night.
Moving drums, bells, cymbals, gongs, music
stands and herself around with finesse worthy of
Allied Van Lines, she built herself a sort of for-
tress from which to operate.
But the wait was worth it, for Serocki's piece
is a fascinating mixture of expressive content with
virtuoso feats by the percussionist and a pianist,
Nancy Voigt.
The imaginative and completely engrossing Serocki work came as a climax of a Cleveland Composers Guild program of variable effectiveness in
CSU's Main Classroom Building Auditorium.   The
oddly assorted evening contained two fun pieces,
two brief string quartets, two percussion works
(one of which features Miss Ptaszynska as both performer and composer) and other items.
Miss Ptaszynska, a visitor from Poland, has
been studying and performing at the Institute of
Music here this year.   Last night she proved beyond a doubt that she is a master percussionist.
She scurried about among a bewildering array of
instruments, drawing all sorts of sounds from them
--soft sounds as well as loud ones, be it noted.
The Serocki work pitted her against Miss Voigt
in a shifting relationship, now a contest, now two
independent lines.   Like most modern percussion
music, the piece moves spasmodically enough sonic
drama to make it continuously interesting.   (Reprinted by permission of The Plain Dealer.)

When Marta Ptaszynska was a young girl she studied
painting and art, reading many books on the subjects. She
was impressed by reading a book of Pablo Picasso's memoirs
and the suggestion he gave to young aspiring painters.
"Never to try to imitate yourself--for that is dangerous, you will
place yourself in a mold and this must be avoided at all cost."
Of course, this too can happen in music, since a composer
often has many commissions and a limited amount of time
to write. There is a danger of imitating material rather
than developing style and ideas. Ptaszynska said, "I use the
Picasso principle--when I start to create I try to forget what
I have previously written and I never check my old sketches,
although some composers do. I start completely from scratch
and my compositions are so completely different they don't
sound like they were written by the same composer."

Ptaszynska's music is unique; she has the uncanny
ability to compose with a variety of musical possibilities and
is committed to the individuality of the final product. Her
versatility as a composer in a variety of forms includes orchestra, opera, instrumental theatre, chamber works, solo
instruments, and music for children. Her works are vastly
admired for their overwhelming beauty that challenges the
musical complacency of listeners. Perhaps it is a fallacy
that an artist must create better and better works. Marta
Ptaszynska, however, continues to create works that uphold
her own high standards of artistic integrity. It is impossible
for her to maintain a consistent schedule of composition with
the numerous appearances as soloist, in guest workshops,
and with other responsibilities. She commented, "I absolutely
have to stop teaching for at least a year, for I need to compose. It is frustrating not to have enough time, and since
I travel extensively for guest residences and usually I am
faced with a busy schedule and a multiplicity of responsibilities, it is very difficult to compose."

One must hope that Marta Ptaszynska will always devote at least a small amount of her time and effort to teaching composition, for she is a master teacher and able to impart knowledge and encourage creativity without taking away
the individuality of the young composers. Her teaching is
never academic, but nutures the entire spectrum of the compositional modes. Invitations from universities and international organizations are abundant and often she must refuse
them because of an already demanding schedule. She said,
"I put so much energy into teaching that it's very successful,
but I probably spend more time than necessary to organize
and review my materials--but I like to do it this way." She

must be doing it right since she has received invitations time and time again to return to the same universities and colleges to continue to work with future composers.

Ptaszynska's compositions have won two prizes at the American Percussive Arts Society Competition in Indiana, first in 1974 for Siderals and in 1976 for Classical Variations. Siderals is scored for two percussion quintets and light projections. Marta Ptaszynska received the following comments in a letter from Nicolas Slonimsky after he had seen the score: "Some aspects of it evoked memories when I was working with Varèse on Ionisation, perhaps the progenitor of all works based on sounds of indeterminate pitch. But of course in the near half-century since that time, new indeterminacies have appeared, and your work represents the contemporary form of 'organized sound,' to use a Varèse word again." John Beck of the percussion department of the University of Rochester's Eastman School of Music wrote, "Congratulations on Siderals; it is an excellent work of major musical importance."

Marta's personal comments on this composition:

I came to the University of Illinois in Urbana, Illinois in the late Fall of 1973, on an invitation of Thomas Siwe the chairman of the percussion department at the University.
I was asked to write a piece for the University of Illinois Percussion Ensemble. When I saw the tons of percussion instruments I was terrified. I thought: "How I possibly could write a piece which will sound like music and yet, will use all these instruments and other strange objects called percussion"?
Tom Siwe gave me room to work at the University with a desk in front of which hung a big map of the world. Sitting at the desk and watching this map the idea of something universal, starlike or connected to the World came to my mind--something which will represent our Universe in the constellations and myriads of sounds. The piece was ready in sketches almost in two weeks(!).

Siderals has received numerous performances and many positive reviews since its première performance in 1974. Its appeal to audiences resulted in thunderous ovations and many positive reviews, both in America and in other countries. Two of the many reviews are as follows:

The Poznan Percussion Ensemble's Jubilee, reviewed
by Andrzej Saturna in Musical Movement, No. 5, March 2,
1975, Warsaw:

> The following works presented good instrumental
> workshop and fascinating playing by the performers:
> Toccatas by Carlos Chavez, Ritmi ed Antiritmi by
> Miroslav Istvan, and William Kraft's Momentum.
> But I was especially impressed by the three-part
> composition Siderals, by Marta Ptaszynska. This
> work, full of color and rhythmic "discoveries,"
> decidedly outshone the others. Besides having a
> fresh quality about it, Miss Ptaszynska's music
> absorbs the listener with its rich and easily as-
> similated expressive content. (Reprinted by per-
> mission of Ruch Muzyczny.)

In a review for the New York Times, April 29, 1975 Robert
Sherman wrote (partial):

> FIVE COMPOSERS HEAR BROOKLYN ENSEMBLE
> PLAY THEIR WORKS
>
> Morris Lang preaches at Brooklyn College what he
> practices as a member of the New York Philhar-
> monic, and the results were an impressive display
> Sunday evening at Alice Tully Hall, which was the
> first recital there by Mr. Lang's Brooklyn College
> Percussion Ensemble. The group's 12 student mem-
> bers played an astonishing array of battery instru-
> ments in superb synchronization, with the confident
> individual and collective expertise of seasoned pro-
> fessionals.
>   It was a significant tribute to the accomplish-
> ments of the ensemble that five of the six composers
> whose works were played--Irwin Bazelon, Elliot
> Carter, Jacob Druckman, David Loeb and Marta
> Ptaszynska--were present for the occasion.
>   Due praise having been given, however, this
> listener must confess that he found the cumulative
> effect of the program stultifying. All the scores
> had interesting and novel ideas, but with one ex-
> ception they exploded on far beyond the point of
> diminishing returns.
>   ... Miss Ptaszynska's Siderals made the greatest
> architectual sense. (Copyright © 1975 by The New
> York Times Company. Reprinted by permission.)

Marta Ptaszynska has been guest composer-percussionist at the University of California in Santa Barbara on two
occasions: the first in 1977, and, based on the quality of
her teaching and performances, again in 1980, when she was
invited to return. She shares a warm and respectful rapport
with her colleagues and has the unique ability to stimulate
the creative possibilities of her students. Her master classes
are a rare delight as she captures the attention of artistic
minds and helps mold and shape a creative process that is
both individually demanding and seeks new fresh idioms for
musical expression. She is a successful teacher who helps
the students to steer their own course; she never imposes
her personal style on them so that they can develop their
own individual traits. During her first visit to the Santa
Barbara campus her composition Epigrams, for twenty women's
voices, flute, harp, piano, and percussion, was commissioned
and premièred by the Dorians Chorale in an all-Ptaszynska
concert. It was reviewed by E. Van Ben Thuysen for the
Daily Nexus Vol. 57, No. 127 on May 12, 1977:

PERCUSSIVE CLASSICS SHINE IN DORIANS CHORAL
CONCERT

Those of you who feel that modern classical music
is formal, stiff, or doesn't have a sense of humor
about itself--you should have been at Lotte Leh-
mann last Sunday night to enjoy "An Evening of
Music For and With Percussion." It could have
been called "An Evening with Marta Ptaszynska,"
one of the foremost classical percussionists in the
world. Her inventive compositions, coupled with
her incredible energy onstage served as shape and
inspiration for the fine UCSB faculty and student
musicians in the program.
A lyrical mood was set immediately by the first
piece, Cadenza for Flute and Percussion (1971),
with Patricia Carbon on flute. I would not have
thought percussion lyrical or mystical--drums are
instruments of rhythm, not melody--but Ptaszynska's
combination of kettle drums, vibes and cymbals
lead the flute, eliciting questions and possible solu-
tions.
Space Model (1971), a solo piece, was like a
mathematical system for defining aural space by
continuous, energized rhythm of solo percussion
work within the physical space on stage. Ptaszynska filled the stage with three separate groupings
of instruments, which she moved very comfortably

between, creating a full juxtaposition of sound,
rhythm, and silence.
     A high point of Fantasmagoria (1970-71) involved
a tribal conversation between drums and piano.
The piano was played inventively and confidently as
per compositional instructions by pianist Carolyn
Horn, who variously plucked strings on the interior
of the instrument and muted some of those strings
to create a whispering effect when played conven-
tionally. Ms. Horn rose to the powerful interior
of the piece, using elbows and hands gracefully and
strongly.
     Tale of the Nightingales (1968) is a composition
for wind instruments, harp, percussion and baritone.
The lyrics of the piece were playful while maintain-
ing an artistic stance, asking serious questions.
Michael Ingham, baritone, is to be commended for
his excellent job as vocal interpreter on the Ptaszynska's words. The conclusion--geniuses? ... gen-
iuses?? was both lighthearted and pensive and drew
laughter from the audience and a final smile from
the deadpan vocalist himself.
     The UCSB Dorians seem to always be involved
in quality work. There are few choral groups today doing modern classical pieces, so the field is
open and they are actually sought after by composers. The final piece Sunday evening was their
combined effort with percussion, piano, flute, and
harp with Michael Ingham conducting. This was
the first performance anywhere of Epigrams, a
beautiful ritualistic piece, which was written especially for the Dorians. Ptaszynska shaped her
vocal arrangement around the poetry of Sappho,
Mossis, Xenophanes and Erinna. Beginning with
the Invocation of the Muses, the Dorians established
a weaving of voices in chant. The tempo, drawn
by Ptaszynska herself on percussion, moved as if
danced through heights of elation, pleading to the
gods with curious wonder of the world. The solid-
ness and dexterity of the Dorians, gathering inspiration from the words and movement of the piece,
were combined with the breaking of twigs, the sound
of blocks of wood together, finger cymbals, and
the hum of crystal glasses.
     The evening's ritual was completed with the hear-
ing of this piece, and the complete enjoyment of all
those who participated, as well as the audience, was
more than obvious. (Reprinted by permission of the
UCSB Daily Nexus.)

When Marta Ptaszynska returned to the Santa Barbara campus for the spring term in 1980 she was presented in a composer-percussionist faculty artist recital. Two of her works were performed, including Cadenza, for flute and percussion, and Mobile, for two percussionists. Also included in the evening program were two fascinating works by Bogustaw Schaeffer dedicated to Ptaszynska, Constructions, scored for vibraphone, and an instrumental theater piece titled Hieraklitiana, for tape and percussion. Emma Lou Diemer, a faculty member at Santa Barbara, joined Marta in Koji Takeuchi's Five Improvisions for vibraphone and piano. The recital presented Interpretations, for flute, percussion, and tape by the contemporary Polish woman composer Krystna Moszumanska-Nazar. The evening proved to be a delight for the audience which was captivated by Marta Ptaszynska's abilities as a composer as well as a performing artist of world renown. One California music critic projected her as the "unflappable Ptaszynska." How true this was for those in attendence!

As a younger colleague of Witold Lutoslawski and Krzysztof Penderecki, Ptaszynska has received numerous positive reviews in her native Poland. Her contributions at the seventeenth Poznan Spring Festival were reviewed by Olgierd Pisarenko in Ruch Muzyczny, No. 14 July 3, 1977, Warsaw:

> On the opening concert of the Spring Festival Marta Ptaszynska presented A Concerto for Percussion (performed by the percussion quartet of the Poznan Philharmonic Orchestra and the Poznan Philharmonic Orchestra conducted by Renard Czajkowski. This is an imposing piece not only of powerful sound and dynamic drive but also of uncommon conciseness and contact construction. These characteristics indicate the composer's taste and knowledge of the listener's perceptive possibilities as he is faced with an enormous mass of sound. (Reprinted by permission of Ruch Muzyczny.)

Beginning in 1975 Ptaszynska and Barbara Niewiadomska started to collaborate on a complete method of percussion training for young students. The book is to be published in five volumes by Polish Music Publications 31-111 Krakow, Poland. Volume I was issued in 1980. Comments by M. Ptaszynska:

> Colorful World of Percussion, is a handbook of percussion playing and the learning of music theory by

playing, not by reading about it. The purpose of
the book was to prepare children (age 5 and up) to
play traditional music (in measures) as well as new,
contemporary music with new notation (without measures). Therefore the material in the book is presented always in such a form as to not differentiate
between contemporary and traditional music. Contemporary notation appears on the very first pages
alongside pieces written in traditional notation.

There are no theoretical formulas, for theoretical presentations are abstractions and abstractions
are not understood by children well. It was quite
a puzzle for the authors to present the material in
the simplest possible form and at the same time
making it most applicable and relevant.

All topics of rhythm and percussion techniques
are illustrated by a great number of examples.
Each example is in itself a minature composition,
with a title. The book contains over 200 pieces
and is divided into two parts: a main section which
teaches the fundamentals of music with emphasis
on rhythm, and the additional part which is designed
for those studying playing techniques on many percussion instruments.

Because of the great amount of material the publisher decided to publish this method in five volumes.

Music critic Paul Hertelendy reviewed Siderals on
April 20, 1977 in the Oakland Tribune. The work was performed by the California State Hayward Percussion Ensemble:

Something approaching an entire orchestra of percussion made the rafters ring Sunday afternoon as
Cal State Hayward introduced a mixed-media work
by a very skilled 33-year-old woman composer of
the Polish school.

Here was no genteel "lady composer" tinkling
triple-time triads on celesta, but rather a forceful, contemporary composer who happens to be a
women. Nonetheless she is unlikely to become a
household name in the U.S.: her idiom is post
Varèse, her medium involves more percussion than
you can shake a drumstick at and her name is as
difficult to pronounce as it is to remember. Marta
Ptaszynska.

A one-time student of Nadia Boulanger, she is
now teaching at Bennington College in an assignment

that prevented her attending the West Coast premiere of her Siderals (although she had attended
rehearsals). A good-sized crowd came to hear the
20-minute-long piece for 10 percussionists on a
patchwork program including everything from tan-
gos to massed harps to Weber transcriptions.

Siderals has been played once in New York and
widely in Poland, but only the Hayward performance
realized the composer's intent of projecting abstract
art of specific colors during the performance. While
Jerome Neff was leading the Cal State Percussion
Ensemble and its arsenal of perhaps 100 instruments, his wife Jill was projecting slides of her
abstractions with Kandinsky leanings in design,
though painted mostly in earth tones.

Like the month of March, the piece comes in
like a lion and goes out like a lamb. Each of the
four sections sets up a cluttered ambiance, running
from the cicadas of a sultry summer night to clan-
gors like a freight train in a tunnel. Miss Ptaszynska often lets the musicians run off on different
tempos of their own, sometimes suggesting syn-
thesized music. In the absence of melody and harmony, the players conjure up modern and interesting sounds through bowed cymbals, plucked piano
strings and drum-blows that undergo glissando shifts.

Director Neff hypothesized that the invented work
Siderals referred to time, but there are other possibilities. According to the dictionary, the same
stem can allude either to stars (suggested in the
slow movement) or to iron (suggested by dozens of
instruments). (Reprinted by permission of the Oakland Tribune.)

Siderals has received numerous reviews, all of them
positive and a credit to the creative talents of an exciting
young composer. When it was performed as part of World
Music Days in 1978 at Helsinki the audience was elated, awed,
and inspired by this gigantic showpiece for percussion scored
for 117 different percussion instruments and requiring ten
percussion players. In addition there were projected pictures
of composer Marta Ptaszynska as well as pictures of the
American artist Jill Neff. It was a musical happening of
extended dimensions that stretched the imagination of the
listener to unknown limits.

During 1980 composer-percussionist Marta Ptaszynska
presented a percussion recital in Mexico City at the Instituto

Nacional de Bellas Artes. The program was part of the New
Music International Festival organized by Manuel Enriquez,
director of the Centro Nacional Musical of Mexico. In addition to this program she offered several seminars on "Percussion in Contemporary Music." The Percussive Arts Society's International Convention was held the same year in
San Jose, California, and during this convention five world
premières, including Ptaszynska's Dream Lands, Magic Spaces,
were performed. Paul Hertelendy wrote for the San Jose
Mercury News on November 15, 1980:

CONVENTION OFFERS THE BEAT OF DIFFERENT
DRUMMING

One of the year's most significant concerts was
brought to San Jose by, of all things, a convention
of percussionists. By the time the blocks and
chimes and drums died away Thursday night, the
Civic Auditorium had hosted five distinctive world
premières by composers from Poland, New York
and California.
    It wasn't your usual BOOM-bing-bang THUNK.
The pieces, mostly non-Western in inspiration,
were thoughtful and unorthodox.
    Lest you reach for your ear-plugs, percussion
compositions can be very gentle, genteel affairs of
intricately interwoven ideas. The perfect example
is Marta Ptaszynska's Dream Lands, Magic Spaces,
a shimmering chimera of sound around a violin that
plays a pointillistic concerto in cantabile style.
    The Polish composer uses a great array of
sounds that caress the ear tenderly: rubbed water-
glasses, whirled wind-hoses, miniature cymbals,
whistles, trembling glass touching a vibrating string.
At the center she puts a violinist and pianist--
Daniel and Machiko Kobialka, in this instance--and
produces great beauty of timbre, even in the absence of melody, harmony or rhythm.
    Miss Ptaszynska originally created the 24-minute
work for San Francisco violinist Kobialka to play
with Percussion de Strasbourg in France. But that
group was never able to schedule it, and Strasbourg's loss was very much San Jose's gain. It
is the kind of piece that could win a major composition prize, and it warrants repeating and recording, but in a much more intimate locale. (Reprinted by permission of the San Jose Mercury
News.)

It is difficult to predict the full impact that composer-
percussionist Marta Ptaszynska will have on the twentieth
and twenty-first centuries of music. She is certainly a leader
among young contemporaries; she has had strong imprint on
the compositional mores of the time, since her music seeks
new directions and inspired heights. She is a creative dis-
coverer in the musical culture and such expertise is limitless.
Ptaszynska's compositions traverse a broad expressive range
and provides the performer as well as the listener with a
profound musical experience. The passing of time and the
continued expression of her creative talents will eventually
determine her final place on the roster of leading contemporary composers.

Compositions

Symphonic Music
1968   Improvisations, for orchestra (score for sale)
1973   Crystallities, for orchestra
1973   Spectri Sonori, for orchestra (score for sale)
1974   Concerto, for percussion and orchestra

Chamber Music
1967   Passacaglia and Fugue, for organ and two percussion
            groups
1969   Transformation, for percussion quartet
1971   Madrigals Canticum Sonorum, for wind and string
            quartets, trumpet, trombone, and gong (score for
            sale)
1974   Siderals, for 2 percussion quintets and lighting pro-
            jection (score for sale)
1975   Mobile, for 2 percussionists (score for sale)
1976-   Epigrams, for twenty women's voices, flute, harp,
77   piano and percussion
1977   Un Grand Sommeil Noir, for soprano, flute and harp,
            to P. Verlaine's poem (score for sale)
1971   Cadenza, for flute and percussion, MLP (score for
            sale)
1970   Jeu-Parti, for harp and vibraphone, PPP (score for
            sale)

Instrumental Solo Pieces
1971   Space Model, for solo percussion, MLP (score for
            sale)

1967   Variations, for flute (for sale)
1969   Three Interludes, for two pianos (for sale)
1972   Arabesque, for harp (for sale)
1974   Touracou, for harpsichord (for sale)
1969-   Recitativo, Arioso e Toccata, for violin (for sale)
75
1974-   Two Poems, for tuba (for sale)
75
1976   Quodlibet, for double-bass
1975   Stress for percussion and tape, (E. Sikora 'tape) MLP
        (score for sale)

        Music for Children
1968   Suite variée, for percussion ensemble and piano,
        Leduc (score for sale)
1965   Preludes, for vibraphone and piano (score with part
        for sale, score for hire)
1967   Scherzo, for xylophone and piano (score with part for
        sale, score for hire)
1968   Little Mosaic, for percussion ensembles (score with
        parts for sale)
1971   Mexican Fantasy, for percussion and piano (score with
        parts for sale)
1977   Tunes From Different Sides, children's songs for per-
        cussion ensembles (score with parts for sale)
1975-   Colourful World of Percussion, a book in five volumes
78   for flutes, recorders, voices and percussion in-
        struments, co-author B. Niewiadomska
1980   Music of Five Steps, for flutes and percussion en-
        semble (for sale)

Addresses

Ars Polona, Foreign Trade Enterprise, Krakowskie Przed-
    miescie 7, 00-068 Warazawa, P. O. Box 1001 (Pub-
    lisher, sole exporter of Polish Music)

Edward Marks Co. , 1790 Broadway, New York, N. Y. 10019
    (Distributor of Ptaszynska's music)

MLP/Morris Lang Percussion Corp. , 200 Mercer St. ,
    New York, NY 10012

PPP/Paul Price Publications, 470 Kipp St. , Teaneck, N. J.
    07666

Leduc/A. Leduc Editions Musicales, Paris, France

Discography

Un Grand Sommeil Noir (A Great Dark Sleep) for flute, harp,
and soprano; words by Paul Verlaine, translated by Kate
Flores; 23 International Festival of Contemporary Music,
1979, Warsaw.   Polskie Nagrania SZ 18479

Polish Radio Broadcasting Corp. , Warsaw, Poland:

Madrigals (1971) for wind and string quartets, trumpet and
            trombone and gong.   perf. by Warsaw Philharmonic
            Chamber Players
Mobile (1975) for two percussionists, perf. by M. Ptaszynska
            and M. Szmanda
Recitativo, Arioso E Toccata per violino solo, perf. by Hanna
            Lachert
Space Model (1971) for one percussionist, perf. by M. Ptaszyn-
            ska
Cadenza (1971) for flute and percussion, perf. by Elzbieta
            Gajewska, flute, Marta Ptaszynska, perc.
Two Poems for tuba solo (1973-75) perf. by Zdzislaw Pier-
            nik, tuba

DARIA SEMEGEN

Composer, Associate Professor
and Associate Director of Electronic Music Studio

Daria Semegen, composer and "idea generator," revealed
her creative ability early. When she was seven, her parents
bought a piano not only as furniture, but also as something in which their children might become interested. She
recalled, "At my second piano lesson, I discovered that one
could write down the sounds of music and this really freaked
me out. It became a natural thing for me to do." From
that point on, Semegen devoted most of her piano practice to
notating sounds rather than practicing the instrument. The
satisfaction of creating, whether in music, painting, photog-
raphy, or some other medium, augments her drive to reach
out and produce new projects. She radiates creative energy
in an intriguing and fascinating manner that brings to fruition
an innate sense of curiousity. Semegen was born curious
and has devoted her life to the challenges and demands of
an inquisitive and creative mind.

Her parents, Wolodymyr Semegen and Olga Solocha,
were Ukrainians who escaped from their country when teachers, intellectuals, and artists were being discriminated against
during World War II. They managed to escape via Czecho-
slovakia and Germany by riding atop trains through various
places. In 1951 Semegen came to the United States as a
refugee with her widowed mother and brother.

Because she attended a private school that did not
have a music program, all her early musical training was
studying privately with two piano teachers who taught some
music theory.

During high school years she studied theory for four
years. By the time she graduated, she had written several
string quartets in classical imitation style and two orchestral

pieces. At the age of fourteen, her first string quartet was premièred. She said of that experience, "Although I had been playing my compositions for piano for a number of years, I had never heard someone else perform my music. Except in my fantasy I did not actually know what it would sound like. It was a fascinating and vital kind of experience for me."

There was never any question in Daria Semegen's mind as to what she would do with her life. "I had known for years that I would be a composer and there was never any doubt in my mind, although I didn't relate composing to teaching, for example, to earn a living."

Composer Semegen possesses excellent credentials. Following her private study as a young girl with Otto Miller and David Holden at the Chautauqua Institute she entered the Eastman School of Music. Her composition studies continued with Robert Gauldin, Burrill Phillips, and Samuel Adler. She received her Bachelor of Music degree in 1968. The following is her reflection of her studies with these three professors:

> I studied with composers or at least I was in their classes, I'm not sure how much one can really study composition. The most important aspect of these courses were the comments offered by the teachers who were very fine musicians--they gave their impressions and also hints which were very encouraging. In no way did they try to pressure one to write as they did or in any particular style (which I appreciated). I know far too many teachers who do just the opposite and want the student to pursue their way of thinking or embody certain trends. So, I was fortunate to have teachers who were classically trained, with solid backgrounds and who understood music. They were not coming from an academic background, they were from a practical background and they happened to be teaching in an academic enviroment.

All undergraduates are required to take specific courses, as was Daria Semegen. Although she was obligated to take certain courses, however, she concentrated intensely on writing pieces, copying parts, and getting her material played. This certainly was a propitious goal for an undergraduate student. She feels strongly that the cumulative experiences

DARIA SEMEGEN

garnered from a varied curriculum, although seemingly un-
important at the time, is most significant in developing an
attitude.   For instance, she reflected,

> I would not have become a teacher if I had not
> developed a certain attitude. Admiration for teach-
> ers I had worked with influenced my decision to
> combine a career in composing and teaching. My
> first two years in the field I couldn't teach a damn,
> due to inexperience--I had to get to the point where
> I could enjoy it and could fulfill a primary obliga-
> tion to continue a kind of apprenticeship system.
> Being a musician is really based on this system--
> one learns not from reading a lot of books but from
> someone who is a master of certain aspects of
> music.

Following graduation from Eastman School of Music,
she spent the following year in Warsaw as a Fulbright scholar,
studying electronic music at the Warsaw Conservatory and
the Polish Radio Studio, and composition as a private student
with Witold Lutoslawski.   The housing provided in Warsaw
offered an extra dimension of experience for Semegen since
the contemporary public housing had special features catering
to the needs of certain artists.   She lived with artists who
were working in the visual and plastic arts, thus offering an
excellent mixture of the work and the opportunity to exchange
ideas and experiences.   The electronic music courses that
she took were presented along the lines of the early Cologne,
Germany, radio studio schools.   In this respect the composer
does little except calculate pre-cognitive types of material
and the work is completed by a technician.   This method dis-
courages experimentation by precluding hands-on operation.
Creativity is stifled because one cannot hear the sound immediately, make revisions and changes.   The method is almost obsolete today and of course Semegen does not create
her electronic compositions in this roundabout manner.

Electronic equipment varies from studio to studio,
although today with voltage control devices such as synthe-
sizers, it is a matter of simply knowing the principle of
usage and applying it to a different vehicle.   Semegen observed, "It's similar to the automobile--you know how to
drive, but you have to orient yourself to the controls on each
different model."   Later in her career she became associate
director of the Electronic Music studio at the State University
of New York at Stony Brook.

While in Poland, she received a Yale University Fellowship and returned to the United States in 1969. At Yale
she studied composition and electronic music with Bülent
Arel, and theory with Alexander Goehr. Semegen completed
a Master of Music Degree in 1971 and found it to be a very
positive experience. She said, "Alexander Goehr and Bülent
Arel are excellent musicians. Arel is noted for his electronic music, although he is also a fine instrumental composer as well as a pianist and conductor."

In 1971, following a summer of study at the Columbia-
Princeton Electronic Music Center, Semegen directed all her
energies to electronic music. She received a Columbia University Scholarship and a Rappoport Scholarship from the
School of Arts, Columbia University, for postgraduate study.
During this period she was surrounded by all kinds of electronic music experiences. Semegen studied composition and
electronic music with Vladimir Ussachevsky and was a member of the teaching staff at the Columbia-Princeton Center
while the director was on a sabbatical leave. In addition,
she worked as sound engineer at the World Music Collection
of Columbia University and prepared historical recordings
for disc recordings. She also worked as technical assistant
to composers Ussachevsky and Otto Luening in the preparation of electronic music materials for disc recording on the
Composers Recordings, Inc. label. She also worked on
several of her own compositions during this time:

> To my mind there is no essential difference be-
> tween working with electronic music or instrumental
> music. Although the aesthetic treatment of elec-
> tronic and instrumental music is basically the same,
> the actual medium chosen to project an idea is
> seldom if ever interchangeable.
> For example, in 1969 I wrote Poème 1er: Dans
> la Nuit, with text by Henri Michaux. It is a large
> piece for baritone and chamber orchestra with very
> intricate parts. At the time I didn't know a con-
> ductor, an orchestra or a baritone to perform it
> and I didn't even get the rights to use the text.
> I didn't give a damn because I had to write that
> work at that point in time. I had to write it be-
> cause I had all the ideas and I had to project them
> in that particular medium and not in a string quartet
> or electronic setting.

It was not until some six years later that this piece
had its première performance at a Festival of Women's Music

at the University of Pennsylvania.   Later on it was performed
at the Eastman School of Music and the Cincinnati Conservatory.   Semegen is a unique individual--bright, determined,
and self-confident, with the willingness to recognize certain
detriments and to focus on their elimination or correction.
She is inexhaustible--a whiffle ball in a wind tunnel.

In the past several years her compositions have received over 150 known performances.   In 1970 she composed
Jeux des Quatres, a game for four instruments: B♭ clarinet, trombone, piano, and violoncello.   A recording of this
work is available on Opus One Records, number 59, Box
604, Greenville, Maine 04441.   Recording artists are Cheryl
Hill, clarinet; David Schecher, trombone; Martha Calhoun,
cello; and George Fisher, piano.

Jeux des Quatres contains five movements: Pourquoi
un Thême; L'Oiseau vermoulu; Variations sur l'Arbrecadavre;
Pacem in Terris; and Peutêtre une Musique.   Notes by the
composer are as follows:

> The work consists of five brief movements, of
> which the first and the last serve as parentheses.
> The music is structured around aleatoric means,
> relying both on specific notation of pitches and
> rhythms, and more free notation of gestures, reg-
> isters, dynamics, individual instrumental articula-
> tions, and blocks of sound within larger time-blocks
> measured in seconds.   The beginning and ending move-
> ments are built around a two-note theme: an or-
> dinary low pitch of long duration followed by a har-
> monic an octave and ninth above it.   The second
> and third movements introduce and develop various
> gestural materials.   In this case, the gesture may
> represent a rhythmic pattern, a pitch structure, a
> sequence of articulations, or any combinations of
> these, freely interpreted by the performers.   Move-
> ment four presents a dramatic use of piano timbre
> and sound effects achieved by playing inside the
> instrument, on the strings, with various percussion
> sticks and mallets while the cellist plays an obligato
> above the highly textured sound mass.   A special
> notation was devised for this movement.   The score
> is read in the ordinary manner from left to right
> by the pianist and cellist, while the two remaining
> players, who play on the piano strings, turn the
> score sideways and read the long notation closely
> resembling the types of gestures and attacks re-

quired for the performance on the strings. The
cello's drone begins the last movement and is occasionally interrupted by comments from other instruments. The initial two-note theme is reflected,
this time, by the piano in the coda of the work.

It is strongly suggested that interested musicians read
Ellen Lerner's thesis, The Music of Selected Contemporary
American Women Composers: A Stylistic Analysis, submitted to the Graduate School of the University of Massachusetts
in 1976. Chapter six of the thesis is devoted to a detailed
analysis, including excerpts, of the score of Semegen's Jeux
des Quatres.

The chamber piece has had numerous performances
in the past decade and was recently acclaimed most unusual
and intriguing by music critic Robert Croan when it was programmed along with the music of André Previn, William
Schumann, Lou Coyner, Gerlad Chenoweth, and Leo Kraft.
Robert Croan's review for the Pittsburgh Post-Gazette, December 1, 1980, is excerpted below:

A HARMONIOUS DIVERSITY BY NEW MUSIC EN-
SEMBLE

What a joy to see David Stock, Pittsburgh's leading
progressive musician, and André Previn, leader of
the establishment, together in the Chatham College
Chapel at last evening's concert by the Pittsburgh
New Music Ensemble.
By far the most unusual opus was Daria Semegen's intriguing Jeux des Quatres, a spare, pointi-
listic quartet that revels in aleatoric devices and
the sounds of silences. The visual element is important as well, when the cellist sits playing a
foundation while the others, including the conductor,
go to the piano with brushes and hammers to produce a quivering obligato of diverse, new sonics.
(Reprinted by permission of the author and publisher.)

In January 1974, Semegen joined the faculty of the
Department of Music of the State University of New York at
Stony Brook, Long Island, teaching composition, theory, and
electronic music. She is Associate Professor of Music and
Associate Director of the Electronic Music Studios. She
designed the University's Electronic Music Studios project,
which consists of three main studios and five editing studios

utilizing classic tape studio, analog, and digital systems.
Her sound system design also includes the department's professional Recording Studio System. She is an elected member of the International Audio Engineering Society.

With completion of this extensive project one must reflect on Semegen's career: from a Fulbright scholar in 1969,
who was disillusioned with the electronic music studio's limited opportunities offered in Warsaw, to recognition by America's distinguished circle of directors of electronic music
studios in less than a decade.

She discusses her work in the studio:

> I find that working in the studio on a tape piece is
> like doing a sculpture--it's there and does not need
> interpretation, it exists on its own. Doing this
> type of work versus writing instrumental pieces
> is quite different in terms of the psychological
> nuances involved. In studio work I am not depen-
> dent on a performance of the interpretation of the
> music. When I do work with instrumentalists, per-
> sonalities are involved and I enjoy performers'
> musical viewpoints on my music. In electronic
> music or plastic arts you just don't have this per-
> sonal human communication which varies with each
> performer and every performance. Lacking this,
> the electronic music composer must achieve a cer-
> tain independence and self-reliance in realizing a
> work as does the painter or sculptor.

Two prize-winning instrumental pieces, written early
in her career, were programmed in 1975 in New York.
Quattro, (1967), scored for flute and piano, was awarded a
Broadcast Music, Inc. prize that same year and Three Pieces
for Clarinet and Piano, (1968), won the University of Maryland and Southeastern Composers League Chamber Music
Competition Prize in 1978. The concert was reviewed by
Andrew Derhen for High Fidelity/Musical America in December 1975 (partial):

MOMA: WOMEN COMPOSERS

> 1975 is International Women's Year. Now is the
> time to test the male chauvinist notion that music
> composition is strictly a man's chore. A resolute
> effect to that end is being made by the League of
> Women Composers. This newly-formed national

organization hopes to make more commissions available to women composers, and to promote performances and recordings of their work. A sampling of League member wares, performed mainly by women musicians, was offered in the Summer-garden of the Museum of Modern Art on August 15. Despite poor amplification and the distraction of big city traffic, the evidence heard suggested that composing admits no sex barriers: women can compose just as well--or just as poorly as men....

More academically inclined were Quattro for flute and piano and Three Pieces for Clarinet and Piano by Daria Semegen. Both stress post-Webern pointillism almost to the verge of parody. Yet there is a certain appeal in the frenzy with which these works fulfill their quota of disjointed phrases and wide leaping intervals. (Reprinted by permission from High Fidelity/Musical America. All rights reserved.)

It is necessary to remind Andrew Derhen that music by women has been largely neglected and ignored by men who monopolized the culture by recording their own compositions.

In 1978 the International Society for Contemporary Music selected her Music for Violin Solo for performance at the World Music Days Festival in Helsinki (Sibelius Academy) and Stockholm. The work is recorded by violinist Carol Sadowski on Opus One Records number 59 and was competitively selected by Columbia University Press for publication in 1981. The composer recalls:

> Music for Violin Solo was first begun as a work for violin and piano. Gradually, the piano part began dropping out of the musical activity, while the violin was clearly becoming the more dominant character in an increasingly convincing manner. In an experiment to explore the possibilities of the music, some of the piano gestures were incorporated into the violin part. Suddenly, it became obvious the music gained fluency and strength within the context of the solo string instrument's linear continuity, while the same musical material was noticeably weakened and its intensity diluted when shared by the two instruments. This was more an intuitive rather than a rationalized impression, and it was a memorable moment of discovery which made the difference between a vigorous solo work and an all-

but-pedestrian duo.   Moral: sometimes less is
more; also, it is important to trust your instincts.

Semegen was previously a recipient of the International
Electronic Music Competition Prize in 1975.   Electronic Composition No. 1, realized in 1972 at the Columbia-Princeton
Electronic Music Center, was presented at the Competition
sponsored by the League of Composers of the International
Society of Contemporary Music.   The work is available on
recording: Columbia/Odyssey number Y34139.   It was reviewed by Lawrence B. Johnson on February 20, 1981, in
the Milwaukee Sentinel (excerpt):

> UWM SERIES CELEBRATES WITH A VINTAGE CON-
> CERT
>
> Tenth anniversary celebrations should be champagne
> affairs, and so it was Wednesday night with a vin-
> tage concert in the Music From Almost Yesterday
> series at the University of Wisconsin--Milwaukee.
> For ten years this project, created and sustained
> by Prof. Yehunda Yannay, has played a vital part
> in nurturing contemporary music in Milwaukee.
> Wednesday night's celebration devoted entirely to
> women composers, represented a stimulating series
> at its best. . . .
> Semegen's Electronic Piece No. 1 made a more
> rewarding impression, as backdrop to the variously
> athletic and sensual solo dancing of Susie Bauer.
> (Reprinted by permission of the Milwaukee Sentinel.)

Arc: Music for Dancers was commissioned for choreography by the Mimi Garrard Dance Theatre, New York
City.   It received a National Endowment for the Arts grant,
a New York State Council on the Arts grant and was realized
by Semegen at the Electronic Music Studios of the State University of New York at Stony Brook in 1977.   Semegen described it thus:

> It was an abstract non-problematic type of dance
> score that was highly organized in terms of phras-
> ings mapped out on huge rolls of graph paper.   The
> mapped graph paper contained the dancers phrasings
> and motions with five different tempi changes, basic-
> ally ABCBA, and it was complex.   The lighting
> which was extremely intricate was driven by a com-
> puter and the music had to be synchronized exactly.

I had very little choice on how I was going to
do the piece.   I had to give indications of the dance
beats in the music; there had to be a rhythmic
pulse, changes of tempi, and also changes of mood
according to the specifications of the choreographer.
I thought the final production was great!

A review written by Peter Frank of the recording that
included Semegen's Arc: Music for Dancers appeared in
Fanfare, the magazine for serious record collectors, in July/
August 1979 (partial):

> AREL: Mimiana I: Flux; Mimiana II: Frieze;
> Mimiana III; Six and Seven.   SEMEGEN: Arc:
> Music for Dancers; FINNADAR SR 9020.
>
> All four works on this album, three by a Turkish-
> born pioneer in "pure" (i. e. , wholly generated
> rather than collected and reorganized) electronic
> music and one by one of his most gifted students,
> were commissioned by Mimi Garrard.   Garrard is
> a New York based choreographer who is to my
> knowledge the foremost proponent after Alwin Niko-
> lais of visually oriented abstract dance....
>   The music Bülent Arel and Daria Semegen have
> realized for Garrard over the past decade is fittingly
> dance-y--that is, not just rhythmic, but clearly yet
> subtly oriented to corporal and especially pedal
> motion, and pronouncedly episodic....
>   I have never seen Garrard and company dance
> to the music by Semegen; to judge from Arc: Mu-
> sic for Dancers, this composer's music is equally
> apt.   It does have a character distinct from Arel's
> music, its range of sounds is some-what drier and
> more limited, and there is a greater dependency
> on traditional rhythmicality, on beat--something
> that Arel is prone to refer to, almost ironically,
> then to abandon in the progress of his episodes.
> The last Mimiana maintains certain jazzy rhythms
> for relatively extended periods, but nothing like
> the quick yet insistent beat passages that bustle
> through Arc, particularly past its midpoint, occurs
> in Arel's work.   Arc thus sounds more comical
> and readily choreographical than any of the Mimia-
> nas.   (Reprinted by permission of the publisher.)

Unlike some composers, Daria Semegen is willing to
discuss her art.   In addition she has published many inter-

esting articles on composing. When writing for instruments,
she begins by describing the nature of the instrument's meaning to her, and its capabilities, then writing these impressions on a yellow pad. She never starts to write a piece
until she has realized the kind of expression with which she
wants the piece to begin. She explained, "If I knew what the
piece was going to sound like from beginning to end there
would no more curiosity to give me inertia to write the piece."
She is particularily attuned to what she describes as present
day environment sounds like sea, sky, and others, but she
feels that a better word is contemporary resources:

> If I were to write an opera, then I would use tele-
> vision, film or a modern medium. I know people
> who are very happy writing classical pieces and
> that's part of their esthetic personality and I ap-
> preciate what they are doing. But I couldn't do
> that for myself--I would have to experiment be-
> cause that is part of the excitment of creating a
> piece. I have to set up things for myself to make
> it interesting. As living creatures we are con-
> stantly changing, our cells are changing, from one
> second to the next we are not exactly the same.
> Our chemical structure constantly changes, we go
> from one mood to another and that is partially a
> physical progression of the body chemistry which
> affects mental states and capabilities as well.

Composer Semegen wrote the following article that
was published on December 12, 1979, in the Statesman/Alter-
natives, expressing via the written word her thoughts and
feelings as one of America's exciting young contemporary
composers:

ONCE MORE, WITH FEELING

> Someone asks why do you compose music? Per-
> haps because I am perpetually curious about what
> will happen when various sounds are arranged in
> certain ways, because it is always interesting to
> deal with time as a working space because I want
> to. Indubitably, it is possible to add many intel-
> lectual, philosophical and high-minded reasons
> which betray one's background in academia. The
> encounter with music as a creative means of ex-
> pression came relatively early in life. At age
> seven my first piano lesson taught me that some
> sounds could be stored on paper via notation and

then rearranged in the manner of building blocks
to create different shades of expression with seemingly endless variation. The musical boredom of
some early piano etudes contributed to the necessity
to create something more interesting and challenging to play and listen to. From this childhood impression grew an ever present awareness that as
a composer I am the first listener to my own music
and beyond the myriad possibilities of cerebral compositional disguises and theories, the actual physical sound and the listener's own personal response
to it are what really counts ultimately. This is
the composer's real link with the world in the most
intangible and abstract of the arts which cannot be
seen or touched but exists as invisible sound waves
reaching the listener in an arcane and subtle communication.

Music as color and texture, gesture, and expression rendered in sound has analogous counterparts
found in the fine arts including drawing, painting,
sculpture, work combining various forms of media,
from the perception and appreciation of other art
forms are truly indispensable. Through their own
unique communication they provide the dimension,
perspective, and sometimes understanding which
revitalize a composer's work and enhance aesthetic
sensibility. Sometimes my working methods in
musical composition are rather closely related to
other art forms. The aleatoric or chance elements
in several of my works is akin to a similar device
found within the confines of an intricate three-di-
mensional mobile which retains the essential ratios
of its parts while they move randomly within their
assigned space creating various shapes, articulating
the total space. A whole which balances the same
ratios through different angular projections. Sharply
precise defined melodic lines, sweeping gestures
and stark, contrasting expressions of a solo violin
work may reflect similar qualities found in a pen
and ink drawing.

As a composer of both instrumental and electronic music, I am especially aware of technology's
contribution to extend beyond the timbral possibilities of musical orchestration without overshadowing
the acknowledged unique timbre and idiom of each
acoustic musical instrument. I find these new tools
do not change or solve the perplexing compositional
problems often encountered in creating each new

work, whose ultimate purpose is to communicate
with my audience--once more, with feeling.

Since 1973 she has been program director and founder
of the electronic music concert series at SUNY, Stony Brook.
She has hosted pre-colloquia that included guest composers
and performers Milton Babbitt, Samuel Baron, Harvey Sol-
berger, Rebecca La Brecque, Joel Gressel, Arthur Kreiger,
and Bülent Arel. The series continues because there are
relatively few electronic concerts available to the student body
and the public. Since the students are involved in electronic
music courses, it seemed only natural to Semegen that a
total experience be made available semiannually at least to
listen to the music and the comments of leading authorities
in the field. Confidence comes with experience and that is
exactly what an opportunity of this nature helps to develop.
There are times when this series programs instrumental
pieces with electronic pieces, thus offering interesting and
varying presentations. Plaudits to the director-founder.

Awards, honors, and grants have been numerous for
the talented Semegen--too numerous to list in their entirety.
They include four National Endowment for the Arts grants,
two Broadcast Music Inc. awards, Woods-Chandler and Brad-
ford-Keeley prizes in composition from Yale University,
fellowships from Tanglewood and Chautauqua, two from the
MacDowell Colony, three State University of New York Faculty
Research Fellowships, the National Composition Competition
Prize from the University of Maryland, an Alice M. Ditson
Fund grant from Columbia University, and over a dozen
Meet the Composer grants from the New York State Council
on the Arts.

Daria Semegen's name appears, despite her youth,
along with the contemporary musical giants of the twentieth
century in the following letter published in the New York
Times on September 11, 1977:

MUSIC MAILBAG

To the Editor:

Reading Harold Schonberg's article, "A fascinating
Document of Musical Futility" (July 31), I was dis-
turbed by the statement that "ASCAP still has a
headlock on most of the important American Composers." The 1971 edition of BMI Symphonic Catalogue (indicates) that BMI has its own roster of

very prestigious American composers that at least
equals the ASCAP top-drawer listing mentioned by
Mr. Schonberg.

We begin with the name of Charles Ives. The
most performed serious American composer in the
1974-75 concert season, Ives has more than 95
percent of his music controlled by BMI.

What is equally distressing is the list of American composers now affiliated with BMI who were
overlooked in the so-called ASCAP "headlock:" Walter Piston, Quincy Porter and Wallingford Riegger
(all three deceased and each a Pulitzer Prize winner): William Schuman, Norman Dello Joio, Elliott Carter, Robert Ward, Edgard Varèse, Leon
Kirchner, Milton Babbitt, Lou Harrison, Carlos
Surinach, George Crumb, Ernst Krenek, Roger
Sessions, Gunther Schuller, Allan Hovhaness, Karel
Husa and Henry Cowell.

BMI has its own special list of affiliated writers
of the younger generation--to name only a few:
Donald Martino, Mario Davidovsky, Charles Wuor-
inen, Leslie Bassett, Charles Dodge, Davie Amram,
Dave Brubeck, Donald Erb and Earle Brown. Among
the BMI affiliated black composers are such illus-
trious names as Ulysses Kay, Hale Smith, David
Baker and T. J. Anderson. Our roster of women
composers is equally striking: Peggy Glanville-
Hicks, Miriam Gideon, Netty Simons and Daria
Semegen, again to name only a few.

Through its affiliated foreign publishers, BMI
offers exclusive or near exclusive protection for
the works of Hindemith, Berg, Orff, Henze, Res-
pighi, Villa-Lobos, Penderecki, Ligeti, Frank Martin, Boulez, Busoni, Doonanyi, Stockhausen, Szy-
manowski, Milhaud and Berio. Again BMI is proud
of the opportunity to serve these Europeans who
have achieved high performance ratings in this country.

> Edward M. Cramer, President
> Broadcast Music, Inc.

(Copyright © 1977 by The New York Times Company. Reprinted by permission.)

A review in the <u>Performing Arts</u> in July 1981, Houston, Texas by Scott Sommers said:

Daria Semegen is an old hand at electronic music,

and her touch is among the lightest to be found.
Even when her sonic canvas is densely covered,
she manages to maintain a certain amount of stark-
ness and definition between sounds.

Society has portrayed the role of men as assertive in
nature and as human beings who are capable of solving the
woes of the world. This attitude has been accepted for centuries and only recently has there been some widespread acceptance of women's mental capacity to contribute to the development of a complex society. Ideally, in music there
should be no need to separate the sexes; merit should be
based solely on artistic ability. Unfortunately this has not
happened. It has become necessary for women, therefore,
to project their creative potentials by penetrating the establishment, thus seeking new avenues of attainment. Daria
Semegen has been an active participant in paving new roads,
not only as a musician but also as a human being. Her concerns:

1. Children are fed an audio drivel by the
people who are selling records. The media is cor-
raling the market for itself. They wean and condition teeny-boppers on material which guarantees
a future and continuing profit for the company.
Contemporary composers and musicians don't have
that clout. It is unrealistic to expect everyone to
develop a deep appreciation for new (or even old!)
music, but young people should have a chance to
hear it at least once if not several times.
2. Foundations that fund the arts are in need
of rejuvenation, some boards have tossed the same
ball for years--mainly in providing funds for the
same composers and same groups year after year.
This does not represent a growth process but stag-
nation. For example, there must be more funds
for recording of living composers--in this day and
age we must use the media if our music is to be
heard. Only a few people can even afford to go to
live performances, those who do, hear the piece
only once. And performances of new music are
not readily available outside of major metropolitan
areas or college campuses.
3. In academia problems exist because departments have become a product of over bureaucracy
--credentials and public relations have replaced
quality and values. Some consider a doctoral degree as a rubber stamp of excellence when indeed

many holders are incompetent. We have lost (if
we ever had) the ability to judge and appreciate
teachers on the quality of what they do. An evalu-
ation of an individual based primarily on accumula-
tion of credentials is a convenient substitute and
a way out for administrators and peers who are no
longer (if they ever were) capable of perceiving
and judging the quality of an individual's work, the
standard of values he/she espouses in a chosen
profession, and the all-but-overlooked commodity
of both personal and professional integrity.

In 1979 Semegen received a National Endowment for
the Arts grant, and a State University of New York Research
Foundation Grant.   During this period she realized Electronic
Composition No. 2 Spectra at the Electronic Music Studios at
Stony Brook.   The recording is available on Composers Re-
cording, Inc. number 443.   It was reviewed in July, 1981 in
The New Records:

ELECTRONIC MUSIC

Daria Semegen's Spectra warrants notice here. Re-
stricting herself to two contrasting sounds, one fil-
ligreed and made up of detached notes, and the
other a dense chordal pedal point, she achieves
variety and interest through the artful handling of
these sounds. (Reprinted by permission from The
New Records, 2019 Walnut St. , Philadelphia, PA
19103.)

One must admire the talent, capacity, and strength
of resolve that is apparent in Daria Semegen's creative endeavors.   In addition to her output in the field of music, she
is an accomplished photographer and painter--her work has
been exhibited at the Eastman Gallery.   Curiosity, discovery,
and directed energy combine to reap rewards in unknown ways,
as evidenced by her many accomplishments.   She does not
discuss lofty philosophies but rather explores the creative
phenomenon, bringing her creative talents to audio/visual
fruition.

Asked if she perceived her compositions differently
now from those early in her career, her answer was a simple,
"Nope," and continued:

I am very aware as to how we change from second
to second.   What I am doing now is just a natural

consequence of what I have been doing for years
and there is no explosion in my head when I get
a musical idea. Whatever is generated by my intuitive and creative capacities comes from assimila-
tion of the input of daily living experiences, ideas,
and the way I am.

Compositions

1981   Music for Contrabass Solo, Commissioned by New
        York State Music Teachers Association, premièred
        at Eastman School, American Composers Alliance
        (BMI).
1981   Music for Cello Solo, SUNY Research Foundation
        grant, ACA (BMI).
1981   Music for Viola & Tape, work in progress; com-
        missioned by the National Endowment for the Arts
        for John Graham, artist-in-residence, realization
        at Electronic Music Studios, SUNY-Stony Brook,
        ACA (BMI).
1980   Music for Clarinet Solo, commissioned by Jack Krei-
        selman, artist-in-residence, SUNY-Stony Brook,
        American Composers Alliance, (BMI).
1979   Electronic Composition No. 2: SPECTRA, National
        Endowment for the Arts grant, and SUNY Research
        Foundation grant, realized at the Electronic Music
        Studios, SUNY-Stony Brook, American Composers
        Alliance, (BMI).
1977   Arc: Music for Dancers, commissioned for choreog-
        raphy by the Mimi Garrard Dance Theatre, New
        York City, National Endowment for the Arts grant,
        New York State Council on the Arts grant, realized
        at the Electronic Music Studios, SUNY-Stony Brook,
        American Composers Alliance, (BMI).
1974-   Spectra Studies, National Endowment for the Arts
76   grant, experimental studies in timbral combinator-
        ialities using Buchla 100, 200 units, Synthi 1000
        (London, EMS), Steiner-Parker units, realized at
        SUNY-Stony Brook, Electronic Music Studios and
        Columbia-Princeton E. M. C. , Nat'l Endowment for
        the Arts library at the American Music Center,
        (BMI).
1973   Music for Violin Solo, commissioned by violinist Gen-
        ette Foster, Int'l Jury selection of Int'l Society for
        Contemporary Music, World Music Days, 1978 in
        Helsinki & Stockholm, American Composers Alliance
        (BMI), Columbia University Press, (1981).

1972   Electronic Composition No. 1, classic studio tech-
        nique, realized at the Columbia-Princeton E. M. C.,
        International Electronic Music Competition Prize
        (1975) of the Int'l Society for Contemporary Music,
        American Composers Alliance, (BMI).
1971   Trill Study, classic studio technique, realized at the
        Columbia-Princeton E. M. C., American Composers
        Alliance, (BMI).
1971   Out of Into, classic studio and synthesizer techniques,
        realized at the Columbia-Princeton E. M. C., Ameri-
        can Composers Alliance, (BMI).
1970   Jeux des Quatres, clarinet in B♭, tbn., pa., vlc., Publ.
        Journal of Scores of American Society of
        University Composers.
1969   Poème 1er: Dans La Nuit, text: Henri Michaux
        baritone voice, 1 picc., 1 fl., 1 ob., 1 tpt. in
        C, bass clar., pa., celesta, harp, 10 vln., 3 vla.,
        2 vlc., 2 c. bass, 4 percussionists, xyl., tamb.,
        sys. cym., hi-lo bongos, sn. dr., lg. tom-tom,
        gong, bamboo chimes, BMI Award, First Prize
        (1969) in western hemisphere competition, American
        Composers Alliance, (BMI), Penn State University
        performance grant.
1968   Three Pieces for Clarinet and Piano, University of
        Maryland & Southeastern Composers League Cham-
        ber Music Competition Prize (1978), American Com-
        posers Alliance, (BMI).
1967   Five Early Pieces, teaching pieces for the piano,
        American Composers Alliance, (BMI), New Eng-
        land Conservatory of Music preparatory department
        selection.
1968   Prayer of Hannah (1 Samuel 2), soprano, piano,
        Sacred Music Competition prize (1968), American
        Composers Alliance, (BMI).
1967   Psalm 43: O send out Thy Light, chorus, SATB,
        American Composers Alliance, (BMI).
1967   Poem; For:, text: Robert Sward, chorus, SATB,
        American Composers Alliance, (BMI).
1967   Quattro, Flute and piano, BMI Award (1967) in the
        western hemisphere competition, American Com-
        posers Alliance, (BMI).
1967   Lieder auf der Flucht, text: Ingerborg Bachmann
        soprano, fl., clar., F. hn., pa., vibr., sm.
        wdblk., lg. wdblk., sn. dr., trgl., vln., cello,
        eight players including 2 perc., BMI Award (1967)
        in western hemisphere competition, American Com-
        posers Alliance, (BMI).
1966   Triptych for Orchestra, picc., 2 fl., 2 ob., 2 B♭

clar. , 1B♭ clar. , 2 bsn. , 1 contra-bsn. , 4 F.
    hn. , 3 B♭ tpt. , 3 tbn. , 1 tba. , sn. dr. , bass dr. ,
    3 wdblks. , sys. cym. , 2 bngos. , 1 trgl. , lg. &
    sm. gongs, 1 xylo. , violins 1 and 2, violas, cellos,
    c. basses, Fourth Intramural Symposium selection,
    Eastman School of Music (1967), American Com-
    posers Alliance, (BMI).

1966   Three Pieces for Piano, piano solo, American Com-
    posers Alliance, (BMI).

1965   Composition for String Quartet, 2 vln. , viola, cello.

1965   Six Plus, tape, fl. , cello, F. hn. , harp, vln. , con-
    ductor, American Composers Alliance, (BMI).

1965   Silent, Silent Night, text: William Blake, tenor voice,
    piano, American Composers Alliance, (BMI).

1965   Suite for Flute and Violin, flute, violin.

1964   String Quartet No. 2, 2 vln. , vla. , cello.

1963   Fantasia for Orchestra, 2 vl. , 2 ob. , 2 clar. , 2 bn. ,
    4 F. hn. , 3 tpt. , 2 tbn. , 2 perc. , vln. solo, 1
    and 2 vlns. , vla. , cellos, c. basses.

1963   String Quartet No. 1, 2 vln. , vla. , cello.

Addresses:

American Composers Alliance, 170 West 74th Street, New
    York, New York 10023

Broadcast Music, Inc. , 320 W. 57th Street, New York, New
    York 10019

Discography

Electronic Composition No. 1 (1971-72) on Columbia/Odyssey
    Y34139, titled "Electronic Music Winners"; CBS Rec-
    ords, 51 W. 52nd St. , New York, NY

Arc: Music for Dancers (1977) on Finnadar SR9020, titled
    "Electronic Music for Dance"; Finnadar/Atlantic Rec-
    ords Corp. , 75 Rockefeller Plaza, New York, NY
    10019

Electronic Composition No. 2 Spectra (1979) on CRI SD443,
    titled "Electronic Music"; CRI Records, 170 W. 74th
    St. , New York, NY 10023

Jeux des Quatres (1970) on Opus One #59; chamber music--
    Cheryl Hill, clarinet; David Schecher, trombone;
    Martha Calhoun, cello; George Fisher, piano; Opus
    One Records, Box 604, Greenville, ME 04441

Music for Violin Solo (1973) on Opus One #59; Carol Sadowski, violin; OPUS One Records, Box 604, Greenville, ME 04441.

SUSAN SMELTZER

American Pianist, Composer, Poet

Susan Smeltzer, a child prodigy who performed her first solo
recital at the age of nine, has since appeared in concert
halls throughout the United States and Europe in solo and
chamber recitals as well as in guest appearances with orchestras. A gifted composer with over forty works, she
has received critical acclaim for both her compositions and
performances. As a young virtuoso she was awarded top
prizes in the most coveted national competitions and was also
the recipient of a Fulbright grant.

Born in 1941, the daughter of accountant Frank Smeltzer and his wife Mary Margaret, now commercial farmers,
she was raised with two brothers, James and Richard who
later became doctors. She described their home town in
Sapulpa, Oklahoma, as a strong progressive and open-minded
town that provided her many opportunities to perform concerts. As a child she was energetic, curious, and fascinated
with the sounds of nature, especially bird calls on which she
would improvise at the piano. Born with perfect pitch, she
continually improvised on the sounds of nature that she heard.
Observing this, her mother realized that the talented child
must have proper training. At the age of five she became
the student of Ina Ladd who directed her creative talent in
the proper channels.

In genealogy artistic traits can occur at different points
in the lines; these traits are found on both sides of the Smeltzer family. Her mother, who was graduated from Ventura
College, has written some lyrical religious lines and verse;
both parents are very creative. Her late ninety-nine-year-
old grandfather was a fine clarinetist; her great-great-uncle
was a well-known Greek scholar.

Influenced by the magical sounds of nature on her

Stan Begam

SUSAN SMELTZER

grandfather's farm, she began to compose musical pieces at
the age of five.   Since she did not know the proper rules
for notation at that age, she inprovised the difficult and elaborate sounds she heard and felt.   Ina Ladd helped the young
artist to formulate her ideas and to write them down properly.
She still has the book of marches with the principal themes
sketched out, written when she was six years old.   Her first
virtuoso piece for piano, Furious Wind, was written at the

age of eight.   She performed it a year later on Channel 2,
KVOO in Tulsa, Oklahoma.

Just before her tenth birthday, Susan performed her
first full-length solo concert at the YMCA in her hometown.
She ended the program with Grieg's Norwegian Concerto, an
auspicious debut for a talented young girl.   As a special preparatory student at the University of Tulsa from 1954 to 1959,
she studied with Dale Roller and Professor Boyd Ringo.

While a high school student she received scholarships
to study for two summers at the music festival in Gunnison,
Colorado.   She received a joint scholarship in piano and
clarinet, was principal clarinetist with the honor band, and
principal violinist in the beginner's orchestra.   During the
second summer she received first prize for her piano composition, El Matador, which featured bitonality and chromaticism.   This prize was the high-point of her youth.   Thoroughly
enraptured with life and the love of music, she felt certain
that she would have nothing but a solid career in music.
She said,

> I am very happy for the opportunities the festivals
> offered and the caliber of the musicianship as well.
> The staff included William Revelli, Dr. Rush, and
> Ferde Grofé.   I was so overwhelmed by the ex-
> periences that happened in my youth that I thought
> it would go on forever and ever, and that is a very
> embryonic view.   I reshaped that thought as I grew
> older but as I look back I was very strong and de-
> termined that there would be nothing else for me
> but a career in music.

Ms. Smeltzer received her Bachelor of Music degree
in performance from Oklahoma City University in 1963.   During her freshman year she gave up playing clarinet to concentrate on piano performance and to develop her compositional
skills further.   She had a close rapport with all her undergraduate instructors including Clarence Burg, Ernestine Scott,
and Robert Laughlin, now dean of the college.   As winner of
the Bloch Award, she made her first appearance with the
Oklahoma City Orchestra in 1963.   She had previously won
the Amarillo Young Artist and the Abilene Young Artists
Awards.   A graduate of the University of Southern California
in 1967; she received the Master of Music degree in performance, and the Master of Music Award in Piano.   A piano
pupil of Lillian Steuber, she was graduated magna cum laude.
Even in those seasons when she performed over forty con-

certs, she continued to compose. As she grew aesthetically
her compositions likewise grew; she attributes much of this
growth to her affiliation at USC with Lillian Steuber, Gregor
Piatigorsky, Rosina Lhevinne, and Ingolf Dahl, who taught a
tremendous course on Stravinsky's music.

A year before she was graduated from USC, she re-
ceived acclaim in Lens magazine with a featured article titled,
"A Salute to Genius." This magazine brings to public atten-
tion the achievements of young artists with exceptional talent.
In addition, the following review was published in The Daily
Oklahoman on January 17, 1966, written by W. U. McCoy:

PIANIST DISPLAYS MATURITY, POLISH

A young pianist who appeared with the Oklahoma
City Orchestra three years ago as a Bloch Award
winner returned Sunday night with more than three
years of maturity and polish.
Susan Smeltzer, OCU graduate now artist--pupil
of Lillian Steuber at USC, displayed impressive
facility with Beethoven's Emperor Concerto in E
flat in her appearance with the symphony for the
Fifth Oklahoma Showcase Concert at OCU's Fine
Arts Auditorium.
After the recording tape clicked off, audience
enthusiasm and Conductor Guy Fraser Harrison's
congratulations brought her back for three curtain
calls she well deserved.
Her poise and complete technical control were
unwavering from the first rhapsodic cadenza after
the orchestra's opening tonic chord.
Appreciation for her ability grew during develop-
mental passages and the cadenza after the crescendo
and pause. Her playing showed consistent clarity,
marked by an admirably fluid, liquid character.
Her concept of the work tended to the romantic
and rubato; the concept was held with conviction
and validity.
And so the adagio with the pensive second subject became some of her most effective material.
But the strength of her development of the rondo
in the finale raised Miss Smetzler above any sus-
picions of effete Beethoven. Her performance was
notable for its unity, shadings, rhythmic cohesiveness
and technical excellence.
The orchestra was splendid in the Brahms Variations on a Theme by Haydn, and in three other shorter

selections. (Copyright © 1966 by The Oklahoma
Publishing Company.)

Susan continued to compose even with a full performance schedule and a heavy teaching load. She said,

> Generally speaking, I am the combination of the
> Neo-Classical-Romantic periods, innovative with
> classical shapes, and I sometimes write with free-
> play fantasy with neo-classical and romantic forms
> sandwiched in between. An impassioned Romanti-
> cist, I have learned when to get my head out of
> the clouds in this constantly changing solar and
> computer age. Although not classified as an elec-
> tronic composer, I sometimes combined both new
> and older forms with special effects that edge over
> into the electronic areas. My writing style is con-
> sistently lyrical and according to the professionals
> it is appreciated for innovations and novelties in
> the score. I am a naturalist.

As a very young composer Smeltzer received recognition as
finalist in Oklahoma City Composition Competition with her
piece, Theme and Variation for Two Pianos.

In 1969 Smeltzer was the recipient of a prestigious
Fulbright grant for study at the Akademie für Musik, under
Dr. Joseph Dichler in Vienna. With an intimate group of
Fulbright scholars, she was accorded an impromptu invitation
by the Austrian Fulbright Commission to play on Ludwig van
Beethoven's grand piano in the Neue Hofburg Palace. It was
a delightful year for the young Smeltzer. Everything was
vividly marvelous including the study, the lifestyle, the people,
and the exciting concerts. Neglecting to wear snow boots on
a walk to mail a love letter caused a fall resulting in serious
injuries. The accident forced the cancellation of what would
have been her first international tour. The year in Austria,
however, led to her marriage to a fellow student there,
Philip Snyder (who was not the recipient of the letter). Later
the couple returned to Vienna in order that she might finish
her Fulbright work. She made her triumphant European debut January 16, 1974 in the world-famous Brahms Hall in
the Musikverein. She received numerous curtain calls for
her highly demanding program, later observing, "Playing in
that magnificent hall was a great moment in my career and
I was thrilled with the level of communication I reached with
the audience." After her debut, Smeltzer received the personal congratulations as well as the following note from Hilde-

gard Weidinger, cultural advisor to the United States Information Service and the American Embassy:

> I am convinced that you are a fine musician with
> a great understanding for the composers whose
> works you are playing, but you also show great
> technical ability and are certainly well-equipped to
> master even the most difficult scores. You have
> a touch that would qualify you to play with large
> symphonic orchestras any of the great concerti
> written for the piano.

Awards and honors have been numerous throughout
Susan Smeltzer's career. She was in the Van Cliburn Inter-
national Piano Competition as the United States Voice of
America representative. As one of the top five United States
pianists, she participated in the semi-finals of the National
Instrumentalist Competition. Her performances of Beethoven's
Concerto No. 2 and Concerto No. 5 with the Oklahoma City
Orchestra, Guy Fraser Harrison, conducting, were broadcast in the United States, Canada, the Armed Forces Over-
seas, Mutual European Radio stations, and the world-wide
Voice of America. In 1974 she was recipient of the third
highest national award, "Sword of Honor," at Dinner of Honors, Triennial National Convention, Kansas City, Missouri,
"for bringing honor and distinction to the Sigma Alpha Iota
Professional International Music Fraternity through exceptional
service and musical contributions as an outstanding artist."

The Sigma Alpha Iota presented Smeltzer in recital
at the University of Houston which was reviewed by Carl
Cunningham for the Houston Post on April 7, 1975 (partial):

MUSIC: PIANIST SUSAN SMELTZER

> A structurally clean and sensitively shaped inter-
> pretation of Aaron Copland's Piano Sonata was the
> most absorbing segment of a recital by College of
> the Mainland pianist Susan Smeltzer benefiting the
> Sigma Iota scholarship fund Sunday afternoon in the
> University of Houston's Dudley Recital Hall.
> Smeltzer played the sharply sculpted lines of
> the sonata's first movement with considerable au-
> thority and strength and gave a particularly thought-
> ful account of its poignant final movement, paying
> special attention to subtle coloristic voicings in its
> chordal passages. (Copyright © 1975 The Houston
> Post. Reprinted by permission.)

Susan Smeltzer's New York Carnegie Recital Hall debut received raves from critic-at-large Byron Belt who wrote,
"Idiomatic warm Chopin and a bravura climax to Debussy's
'L'isle joyeuse preceded an authentically exciting performance
of Aaron Copland's 1941 Sonata." Music Journal cited Smeltzer as "an uncommonly gifted pianist." The following review
was written by Robert Sherman for the New York Times on
April 20, 1975 (partial):

SUSAN SMELTZER ENERGETIC PIANIST

An energetic and talented pianist named Susan Smeltzer made her New York debut Friday night at Carnegie Recital Hall. According to the program
notes, the Oklahoma-born artist has won more than
21 competitions, and it is not difficult to see why:
she plays with a firm rounded tone, technical as-
surances and lots of dramatic fire.

The most compelling was Aaron Copland's Sonata
(1941). Miss Smeltzer projected a personal intensity that fit perfectly with the music; her well-
paced, finely modulated playing was equally successful in highlighting the playful and reflective moods
of the score. (Copyright © 1975 by The New York
Times Company. Reprinted by permission.)

Smeltzer established her credentials as a performing
artist long before she received recognition as a composer,
although she had been composing since the age of five. She
explained, "I have come to realize that as a composer and
pianist either you have all the necessary finances and money
needed to support a career but not the adequate credentials,
or you have superior credentials but not enough money for
support in important career areas. I have only met one exceptional artist in my life who had both. Part of the struggle
makes you what you are."

Susan Smeltzer commissioned herself to write Twelve
Mood Pictures in observance of America's Bicentennial Celebration and dedicated it to master pianist Vladimir Horowitz.
Deciding to do something different, she used interval-sets
based on historical years (1776 and 1976). The end result
was variations for piano on the theme of Yankee Doodle and
the interval-sets 1-9-7-6: 1-7-7-6. The work is highly demanding; Smeltzer gave its world première on January 18,
1976 in the Houston Museum of Fine Arts. This composition
portrayed what she had hoped, and she felt her mission completed.

When Smeltzer appeared on Artists in Concert, a series of live radio concerts featuring solo artists, she programmed five of the Twelve Mood Pictures: Fanfare, stating the interval theme; The Capricious Roadrunner, depicting the roadrunner who hears gossip about the revolution and then dashes out of sight; Triumphal March at Yorktown, presenting the Yankee Doodle theme in every other chord; Dance of the Fireflies, evoking a group of fireflies all dancing to "Yankee Doodle in 1776"; and Alleluia, feeling exultation with a jazz toccata complete with fireworks. Host and director of the series, Judith Kurz, lauded Smeltzer on interpreting a most interesting and beautiful recital which included not only the pianist's own composition but also music of Scarlatti, Chopin, and Debussy.

Smeltzer was guest artist on the WQXR Interview-Concert, "Listening Room," hosted by music critic Robert Sherman on July 5, 1977. Three of her own compositions were included on the program: Reverie, Kaleidoscope, and Twelve Mood Pictures.

In 1976 Susan Smeltzer's alma mater bestowed on her the Distinguished Alumni Award from Oklahoma City University. The citation reads, "In recognition and appreciation for her significant contributions made to her fellow man through creative composition of music and performance." Indeed, her contributions have been significant because her mission in life has been to understand the art of communication better. She has developed a deep sensitivity to other peoples' vibrations. Combined with her talent, this produces a winning combination.

Following the New York première of Twelve Mood Pictures at Federal Hall in the summer of 1977 Smeltzer was elected to the Board of Directors for the American Landmark Festival, headed by the enthusiastic concert pianist Francis L. Heilbut. The goal of this organization was to establish a series of concerts in various historical buildings throughout the country. She felt that both the handsome historical homes in Galveston and the buildings in Houston should be considered prime areas for concert series to sustain cultural growth.

Song, with text by Edna St. Vincent Millay, was written in a twelve-hour period during New York City's blackout. She dedicated the composition to the great operatic soprano, Eleanor Steber, on the occasion of her birthday. Smeltzer attended its celebration at the singer's home in Port Jefferson, New York, and later wrote, "I could not write a song for Eleanor Steber without thinking about the bel canto style and Eleanor Steber's magnificent artistry, feeling, and mastery of the line. I attended Eleanor Steber's concert in New York City last year and in listening to her many recordings of the great arias by Puccini and Verdi, two composers I adore, I was inspired to write this work for her."

Jonathan Richard, My Bicentennial Baby, scored for soprano, two trumpets, two flutes, drum, and piano was written in 1976 to celebrate the birth of her nephew. The world première was given in Texas in 1978, and in the words of the composer, "It's a lyrical ballad about a newborn baby and the mother's dreams of his future. The piece represents a new turn in my writing style. It is a folk ballad--lyrical, sweet, heroic and has a certain strangeness in some modal passages."

Since the Bicentennial celebration Smeltzer has made an effort to program some of her own compositions at each of her performances. She is open to using music written by her fellow-composers on her programs because she feels the importance of helping young artists to establish their credentials, necessary in garnering the needed support of the musical establishment. (How nice it would be if other established artists would share Susan Smeltzer's philosophy.)

In May of 1978 Susan Smeltzer performed Ravel's G Major Concerto with the Florida Symphony Orchestra in Miami, under the baton of British-born maestro Brian Priestman. The gala event on the Pops Concert Series was an all-Spanish evening at the Gusman Cultural Center. Smeltzer shared the program with flamenco guitarist, Carlos Montoya. The Lively Arts Review, hosted by Shirley Green over WAVS Radio commented on the performance, "Susan Smeltzer, an Oklahoma-born pianist did a handsome job with Ravel's Piano Concerto in G Major. Her forte was control. It's easy to run away with Ravel, or vice versa, but this young pianist didn't allow that to happen, and kept things under her educated fingertips where they belonged."

December 7, 1981 marked an important turn with the world première of her patriotic work, The Bald Eagle March, for choir, brass choir, and percussion. The two-hour concert was unusual in that it was a benefit concert in her hometown. The Sapulpa Historical Society needed funds for a large restoration project. The effort eventually brought $70,000 and matched funds given by Texas oil magnate, J. B. Saunders.

The record presentation of Susan Smeltzer's twelve artistic
roles variously included: a performance in opera (Pace,
pace, mio Dio, by Verdi); improvisations on clarinet with the
Sapulpa Banjo Band; her own comedy, Professor Stuffonisky
The Mad; violin performer; and conductor-composer of two
patriotic works: The Brotherhood March, and The Bald Eagle
March. The première was received with bravos and a spontaneous standing ovation. Restoration project chairman, Jim
Stewart, offered the following comments about Susan Smeltzer
via the Sapulpa Daily Herald, "Susan Smeltzer is the most
wonderful person I've worked with. She has created a new
interest in everything here in the museum and in the city.
I've never seen anyone work so hard and organize to get
things under control as she has with this program."

Although Susan Smeltzer started her teaching career
at the age of thirteen, over the past twenty-five years she
has held numerous full-and part-time positions as instructor
of piano and as a professional accompanist. Additionally
during this period she has designed festivals, special competitions, and programs that brought visiting artists to the campuses. She expended a considerable amount of energy in
establishing a piano department at one college. Top professionals have praised her for her teaching abilities and contributions.

Although presently not teaching, she found it a rewarding experience and has encouraged her students to strive to
achieve respected goals. She admires the positive thinker
and diligent worker.

Smeltzer has projected her creative talents beyond
performance and composition. She considers herself a space-
age person and often paints in fantasy. This is evident to
one who attends her art show in Los Angeles or visits her
Houston home to study the acrylic mural she has painted on
the wall and titled "Gateways." She said it's a "Picassoes-
que, kaleidoscopic design with fine lines and stain-like colors
and lights ... with the magnificence of our great Universe and
its future in the twenty-first century."

Her creative ability appears to be limitless. Two of
her poems "Acceptance" and "The Mad Man", will be published this year in New Hope International in England. She
has one book of poems published under the title Selected Orchestrations of Poetic Expressions. This inspiring collection
is a tribute to the artistic talent of the amazing Susan Smeltzer. The following two poems are printed by permission of
the writer.

At Sunset

The evening shadows begin to fall
Yet the wind and waves hurry inland
To greet the announcement of dusk
The sun shines sparingly through the haze
That captures the sea
As a prelude for night

My eyes peer through the thin, grey-green and blue hazy
   silky screen
On evening's ebb tide
As pink soft shadows
Kiss the earth goodnight

Summer, 1977
Westport, Massachusetts

A Dedication To Art

One artistic stroke or thought
Is one step further than the step before
That feeds the world with fine things
And a beauty that we only see
As history takes its toll with life

May 20, 1979
Houston, Texas

H. L. Prosser, author of fantasy short fiction with over 500 publications in that genre, recently said upon review of Susan's poetry that "Susan Smeltzer's poetry is creative, well-crafted, and above all else, reflects the soul of a sensitive woman." Smeltzer's book, Selected Orchestrations of Poetic Expression is available from the Sapulpa Historical Society, Inc., P.O. Box 278, Sapulpa, Oklahoma 74066. Price $4.00 (Tax deductible; including postage).

In 1980 Smeltzer was one of the fifty-five top United States delegates and dignitaries from forty-one countries attending the Seventh International Biographical Centre in Cambridge, England. The Congress on Arts and Communication was held in Amsterdam in that particular year. At the first session, Communication Through Music, she spoke on our kaleidoscopic times, survival of the artist, connecting our links, and building a bridge to a new era. She also participated in a special piano concert.

Designed for six high C trumpets, pipe organ, two natural trumpets, and two horns, An American Tribute for the Royal Wedding was a special fanfare in honor of Prince Charles and Princess Diana. Her composition combines the old and the new, using thematic material from her "super tune chart." It is designed so the set would be lyrical, though it's twentieth century and abstract appearing. She said, "The composition for the royal couple plays on the names of Charles and Diana and reflects Prince Charles' sense of humor and Princess Diana's compassion from the composer's own viewpoint, as these are special qualities she admired." The hand-painted illustrated borders found in the score were personally done by Smeltzer. The work will be formally presented at the Ninth International Biographical Centre International Congress On Arts and Communications at Queens College, Cambridge, England.

A member of the judging staff for the National Guild of Piano Teachers, she also holds memberships in Pi Kappa Lambda, Sigma Alpha Iota, Tuesday Music Club, National Guild of Piano Teachers, International League of Women Composers, American Women Composers, Inc., Broadcast Music Inc., Chamber Music America, International Biographical Association, F. I. B. A., and International Academy of Poets.

Susan Smeltzer's talents reflect the spirit of the Renaissance woman; her wide artistic capabilities reach out and encompass the beauty of performance, composition, poetry, and painting. A line of free verse from her many writings expresses her philosophy, "As far as I can see is as far as I would want to be. All beauty is held within this thing that holds me."

List of Compositions

1981   An American Tribute For A Royal Marriage, organ, 6 trumpets in C, 2 natural trpts., 2 natural horns, available from composer.

1980   A Doctor Date With Doctor Brute, soprano and piano, 12 min., available from composer.

1979   The Bald Eagle March, choir, speaker, 3 trpts., 4 horns, 3 trbs., 2 tubas, drum, timpani, cymbal, available from composer.

1979   Kaleidoscope, fl., ob., cl., hrn., bassoon, available from composer.

1979   Psalm, orchestra, choir, brass choir, available from
         composer.
1977   The Brotherhood March, choral work, 2 tpts., drum,
         cymbal/gong, available from composer.
1977   Song, soprano solo, available from composer.
1976   Music for A Midsummer Night's Dream, 2 fls., picc.,
         2 trpts., 3 hrns., 2 cl., bass cl., oboe, elec.
         organ, piano, triangle, woodblock, trb., bass trb.,
         female voices, available from composer.
1976   Twelve Mood Pictures, piano, available from American
         Music Center, The International Symphony for World
         Peace, Inc., United Nations.
1976   Jonathan Richard My Bicentennial Baby, soprano, piano,
         2 fls., 2 trpts., drum, available from composer.
1964   2 Studies, (3 part Madrigal and Motet) SAT and SA,
         available from composer.
1964   2 Studies for Harpsichord, available from composer.
1962-   Kaleidoscope, piano solo, available from composer.
68
1962   Reverie, piano solo, available from composer.
1962   What Child Is This, (arr.) choir and piano, available
         from composer.
1962   Intermezzo by Brahms, Op. 117, No. 3, (arr.) for
         piano, available from composer.
1961   Piece for Organ, available from composer.
1961   A Russian Theme and Variations, piano solo, avail-
         able from composer.
1961   Theme and Variation for Two Pianos, available from
         composer.
1961   German Chorale for Harpsichord, available from com-
         poser.
1961   Piece for Piano, available from composer.
1961   Study for Harpsichord With Romantic Touches, avail-
         able from composer.
1960   Come In, soprano solo, available from composer.
1960   Love, soprano solo, available from composer.
1960   Piece in 12-tone Style, 2 pianos, available from the
         composer.
1960   Christmas Fantasy, brass ensemble, 3 trpts., 3 horns,
         trb., bar., tuba, available from composer.
1960   Battle Hymn of the Republic, (arr.) available from
         composer.

Address:

Susan Smeltzer, 8102 Tavenor, Houston, TX 77075

Julia Smith

Composer, Musician, Author

Julia Smith's multiple talents have placed her in the forefront of contemporary American music culture for over four decades.

A native of Denton, Texas (1911), she is the daughter of Julia (née Miller) and James Willis Smith. She is one of seven children who received their first piano lessons from their mother, herself a graduate in voice, piano, and English from Baylor Belton (Texas) College for Women. Their father, later President of Hugh Perry School Book Depository in Dallas was Professor of Mathematics and Business Manager of North Texas State College. An amateur violinist, trumpet player, and choir singer, he encouraged the children to learn to play other instruments in addition to piano, and so a family orchestra was organized. This activity brought pleasure, creating a love for, and an interest in music that family members still enjoy.

Julia's first private piano teacher, to whom her mother sent her at about age ten, was Mary Anderson, a graduate of the Leipzig Conservatory and teacher at North Texas State College. As a young teen-ager Julia won a competition that provided a scholarship to study with Harold Von Mickwitz, a former Leschetizky student and classmate of Paderewski. Von Mickwitz proved a great inspiration to the Texas girl, both as a pianist and composer in her four years of study with him. She later dedicated her first opera, Cynthia Parker, to him.

At nineteen Julia Smith received her Bachelor of Arts degree from North Texas State College where she composed the school's Alma Mater song. She then attended the Juilliard School of Music studying piano with Lonny Epstein and Carl Friedberg, orchestration with Bernard Wagenaar, conducting

with Edgar Schenkman, and holding a composition fellowship
with Rubin Goldmark and Frederick Jacobi.

Carl Friedberg, her teacher at Juilliard when she was
an undergraduate, took considerable interest in the short compositions and songs she often brought to her piano lessons,
criticizing them and suggesting ways these pieces might be
improved.

Upon her graduation, as was his custom, Friedberg
discussed with Julia her future plans, aims, and aspirations.
He advised her not to pursue a career as piano virtuoso:
"The woods are full of good pianists." Urging her to consider being a composer, he stated, "There are few really
good American composers." He offered to recommend her
to Rubin Goldmark, teacher of graduate composition at Juilliard, if she studied fugue in the summer in order to pass
the required examinations.

This conversation resulted in Julia's enrolling in
courses at New York University that would lead to a master's
degree. In her orchestral conducting class she met Frederique Petrides, a young violinist, who had conducting aspirations. The two young women were invited to play Beethoven's
Two Romances for Violin and Piano on one of the University's
programs. This was the beginning of a lifelong friendship.

After receiving her Master of Arts degree in the spring of
1933, she applied for a composition fellowship that fall in the
Juilliard Graduate School. Julia's first meeting with Goldmark brought the young musician to her first confrontation of
women versus men as composers. "I have just decided not
to waste anymore of Juilliard's money on fellowships for
women," he said, "and only agreed to see you at Mr. Friedberg's insistence. All you gifted women composers come to
New York, study a few years, then go back home, get married, have children, and that is the last that one ever hears
of them as composers. Men will starve to become and remain composers but your sex has proved time and again that
you simply can't face the rigors of life alone."

Julia Smith said, "This one can; Von Mickwitz, Friedberg, and George Wedge believed in me, why can't you?"
Goldmark weakened, "If you turn out like most of my women
students this will be the last fellowship I will ever extend to
a woman." So Julia became a Goldmark student in 1933.

Meanwhile, her friend Frederique Petrides organized

John Pineda, Miami

JULIA SMITH

her first orchestra--one founded to give talented women opportunites to perform in an orchestra. She asked Smith to
invite some of her women colleagues at Juilliard to meet with
her to discuss ideas for an all-women's orchestra. As a
result, plans for this unique orchestra were formulated, auditions held, with Julia Smith becoming the official pianist
of the orchestra and frequently doubling on percussion instruments.

The chamber group was first called Orchestrette Classique and became a proving ground for Julia's first orchestral compositions.   In 1935-1936 her short chamberwork <u>Little Suite Based on American Folk-Tunes</u> was premièred by Frederique Petrides and her Orchestrette Classique at Aeolian Hall in New York.   This work was later revised with a title change, <u>American Dance Suite</u>, scored for theater orchestra; she also made a version for two pianos/four hands.

Early in 1934 Smith began to write an opera for the celebration of her native Texas' centenary, marking its independence from Mexico in 1836.   Her librettist, Jan Isbel Fortune, provided her with numerous radio scripts based on Texas history which Jan had written, and together they settled on a suitable story.

Goldmark discouraged her from undertaking the task, saying,

> Why should you write an opera?   I never wrote one.   Besides too many people can spoil it and cause the work to fail--the conductor, orchestra, singers, stage director, and finally the critics who will say, "no woman has ever written a successful opera."   Stick to the old sonata form and write chamber music and orchestral works.

Despite Goldmark's objections Julia began her opera. Later, because of his illness and eventual death, she became a student of Frederick Jacobi, Goldmark's successor.   Under Jacobi's guidance (he brought a more modern viewpoint to his pupils), Julia began in 1935 to get accustomed to his new compositional approach.   At Christmas time in 1936, receiving news of her father's sudden illness and approaching death, she hastened home to Texas.

On January 19, 1937 she notified Jacobi of her father's death and he wrote the following "up-beat" excerpt from a letter he sent to her in Texas, dated January 22:

> I am hoping for many reasons that you will come back to New York and work soon.   One's work is one's best consolation; and yours has been so promising recently that I have reason to believe that it will grow to be more and more of a satisfaction and happiness to you as time goes on.   I am hoping for fine things from you.

Assuaging her grief, Julia returned to New York, and plunged into her work with new determination to rise to her late father's expectations. Her first task was to complete the orchestration of her Episodic Suite. The piano solo version, dedicated to Muriel Kerr, had been played fourteen times by Kerr on her 1936-1937 Columbia Concerts tour. Julia's friend Frederique was intrigued with the score and programmed the work for performance April 26, 1937.

Francis D. Perkins reviewed the concert for the New York Herald-Tribune on April 27, 1937:

> The Orchestrette Classique, a woman's miniature symphony, played again last night under the direction of Frederique Petrides in Carnegie Chamber Music Hall. The program which, according to the laudable custom of this group, included a large proportion of unfamiliar old and new music, began and ended with Mozart....
> Julia Smith, the young Texas pianist of the ensemble, was called on for several bows after her well-scored Episodic Suite for small orchestra, which did not lack tunefulness and also included some discreetly contemporary harmonic coloring and pleasing touches of humor. (Copyright © 1937 by I. H. T. Corporation. Reprinted by permission.)

Julian Seaman, critic of the Daily Mirror, in his column of the same date wrote:

> Miss Smith's work is clever, adroit, compact, and is well scored. Intelligent scoring is not a virtue held in common by composers of her sex.

The composition was aired over CBS Everybody's Music Series, conducted by Howard Barlow on July 24, 1938. The same summer the piano solo version of the work was published.

Meanwhile Julia was striving to complete two works in larger form--her opera, and a concerto for piano and orchestra. She was unable to complete Cynthia Parker in time for the Texas Centennial celebrations in 1936, but a year later had completed a piano-vocal sketch and much of the orchestration.

Wilfred C. Bain was appointed the first Dean of North Texas State School of Music in 1937. Julia telephoned him

for an appointment to audition her new opera.   In short order
Dr. Bain brought together Julia Smith and the directors of
the college symphony, drama, and modern dance.   Together
they worked out a plan to produce the work.

From 1935 on, Julia Smith earned some of her living
expenses as a part-time music teacher at the Hamlin School
in New Jersey, served as music coordinator of records for
films at the Harmon Foundation in New York, spent one summer in Boston as an arranger of choral and piano accompaniments for an educational publishing house, and functioned as
pianist-arranger for a vocal trio, "The Mello-tones," which
presented weekly broadcasts over Radio Station WEAF, New
York.

Since 1933 Julia had known and enjoyed a close friendship with Oscar Vielehr, a friend of the Petrides' and an
engineer for the Sperry Company.   He was a staunch supporter of the Orchestrette Classique and always had season
tickets for the Philadelphia and Boston orchestra concerts
in New York.   Julia was his constant companion at these concerts.   Distinct opposites, Oscar was tall with dark hair and
eyes, while Julia was of medium height, slender, blonde,
and blue-eyed.

The two often spoke of marriage but Julia was convinced she could not fulfill the careers of composer, wife,
and mother.   Oscar, possessing an inventive, creative mind
agreed that they should be able to devote themselves to their
respective talents.   They were married at the Smith family
home in Denton, Texas on April 23, 1938.

Her opera, Cynthia Parker, premièred on February
16 and 17, 1939, launched her career as a composer.   Ernest Hutcheson, president of the Juilliard School, authorized
copying of orchestral parts and printing of these and the conductor's score to lower production costs of the opera.   The
Juilliard also contributed to the cost of players from the
Dallas Symphony Orchestra to augment the North Texas State
College Orchestra.   Jan Isbel Fortune wrote the libretto and
Metropolitan Opera soprano Leonora Corona, sang the title
role.   The event was chronicled by most of the nation's newspapers for news of the première was sent out over AP and
UP wires, with a Time Magazine photographer also covering
the première.

Headlines read: Cynthia Parker by Julia Smith Given
Much Applause, Corona Helps Texas Opera in Première,

Musical History Made at Denton, Julia Smith's Cynthia Parker
Moves Smoothly Before Big Audience.

An excerpt from a review by John Rosenfield for the
Dallas Morning News, February 17, 1939, revealed:

> Few excursions among the fine arts have so caught
> the fancy and stirred the interest as the first per-
> formance anywhere, of CYNTHIA PARKER by Julia
> Smith.
> The imported prima donna was in sumptuous
> voice, finding the music suitable to her ringing
> dynamic timbre and impassioned style.
> The musical content is consistently admirable,
> often inspired and never obviously derivative. The
> composer's young heart went into her Indian dances
> which contain the harmonic coloration we have
> learned to accept as American Indian, the traditional
> chanting monotone and the elusive single beat mea-
> sure. Arias for Cynthia arch widely through the
> scale and ride heroically on the orchestral tide.
> If the texture is Wagner, the pattern is Puccini.
> The instrumentation is mainly adroit and confident.
> (Reprinted by permission of The Dallas Morning
> News.)

Among the congratulatory telegrams received by Julia
Smith following the première were two which appeared to
offer wider audience opportunities for the new opera: the
first was from Manny Wolfe, head of the Scenario Department
of Paramount Pictures in Hollywood, who requested a copy
of the libretto and score to study with a view to motion picture production; and second, from McCann Erickson Radio
Producers in New York, for the Edison Hour who wished to
feature some of her music, and a personal interview with
her on their next broadcast: would she return to New York
by February 25, to go over the material?

Julia flew back to New York in time to appear on the
broadcast and to check the progress of rehearsals of her new
piano concerto at Juilliard. She wired Manny Wolfe that she
would go to Hollywood and audition the opera for him.

The reception at Paramount Studios was most cordial
and Manny Wolfe expressed great enthusiasm for Julia's
opera. However, his deep concern was the ending, for he
felt certain that only a change from the original tragic ending
to a positive "love-rescue" alternative would suit a film au-

dience. He said, "Do this, and I am certain we shall have a great box office success." Julia in no way agreed with the suggested change since she knew any distortion of the true story would be unfair to her art and to her native state. With true grit, she took her score and flew back to New York and her studies at Juilliard.

On March 18, 1939 the Juilliard Orchestra, conducted by Dean Dixon, and with Vivian Rivkin as piano soloist, premièred her Concerto for Piano and Orchestra in three movements. Although she had an offer from a French publisher at this time, instead she made extensive changes in the piano solo part over the years, so that the concerto was not published until 1971.

In 1940 Julia received a Columbia Broadcasting Commission to write a short orchestral work based on an American folktune chosen from a list of three tunes sent each participating composer under the editorial guidance of Alan Lomax. The twenty recipients of commissions included eighteen men, with Aaron Copland, Roy Harris, Bernard Wagenaar, and R. Nathaniel Dett among them; the two women were Ruth Crawford (Seeger) and Julia Smith.

Julia chose "Liza Jane" as her theme and received $50.00 plus having orchestral parts copied and given to each of the composers as part of the commission. This was her first paid commission. The work was premièred over CBS by Howard Barlow and the CBS Symphony of the Air. Liza Jane was to find its permanent place as Entr'Acte music in Smith's sixth opera, Daisy, premièred in 1973.

On March 11, 1940 Julia heard the first of many performances of her Episodic Suite, scored for large orchestra. She conducted this Suite with the Dallas Symphony on March 17 and 18 in the same year, the first guest conductor to appear with the orchestra.

John Rosenfield, Dallas News critic, wrote of the Suite on March 18, 1940:

> Earlier came the revelation--we are tempted to say the Ravelation--of the Episodic Suite by Julia Smith of Denton and New York with this young woman serving as guest conductor and exerting firm control over her forces. Miss Smith has long had our admiration for her uncanny gift of getting music written and then getting it played.

> The Episodic Suite, which pretends to do depths to
> greatness, is wholly worth a hearing and ranks
> without straining critical hospitality, among the
> better American works Mr. Jacques Singer has
> presented here. It has greater richness of ideas
> and more resources of orchestral color than the
> Five Miniatures of Paul White, once heard from
> Mr. Singer's finger-tips. (Reprinted by permis-
> sion of The Dallas Morning News.)

On April 21, 1940 Julia played the solo piano part of
her new Concerto for the first time at the Golden Jubilee
(Fiftieth Anniversary) of the founding of North Texas State
Teachers College. Miss Smith said that her concerto contained "something in terms of Texas, the Southwest, and
the 1940's." She dedicated the work to Carl Friedberg.

E. Clyde Whitlock, music critic of the Fort Worth
Star-Telegram, wrote of the Concerto on April 22, 1940:

> The Concerto is a studiously wrought work which
> "sounds" its first movement, the most conventional
> in form, uses for its main theme a modification of
> material presented in the introduction, which is
> flanked by two other strong themes. Miss Smith
> has a gift for appealing melodic trend.
>   The second movement, opening with a portentous
> theme for English horn, is romantic in mood, while
> the music of the third movement is agitated and
> terse. The instrumentation and the rhythmic de-
> vices are those of the best in a lighter field, al-
> luding legitimately to its Americanism. (Reprinted
> by permission of the Fort Worth Star-Telegram.)

The decade of the 1940's brought increased opportunities for the now professional young composer: joining the
faculty of the undergraduate Juilliard School; teaching harmony (written and keyboard) and counterpoint; founding and
heading the Department of Music Education at the Hartt College of Music--now affiliated with the University of Hartford,
Conn.; and teaching evening classes at New Britain State College.

The three-day-a-week Hartford experience enabled her
to attend lectures and discussions with such eminent musicians
as critic Alfred Einstein, Harold Bauer, Richard Burgin, stage
director Elemer Nagy, and Paul Hindemith. All this proved
stimulating to the young composer.

Miss Smith was still pianist for the Orchestrette Classique, now in its eighth season when Peter Petrides, husband of the conductor, requested she write an orchestral piece in support of the Greek war effort. At that time the tiny country was at the mercy of Nazi invaders. She obliged by writing Hellenic Suite, in three movements: Sirtos, Berceuse, and Saga.

Excerpt from the New York Times review by Ross Parmenter, dated March 4, 1941:

> Four works of Greek inspiration were performed here last night at the fourth concert of the season of the Orchestrette Classique at Carnegie Chamber Music Hall. Frederique Petrides, the founder and director of the ensemble, conducted, and one of the works, Hellenic Suite by Julia Smith, was dedicated to her.
>
> Miss Smith's composition, ... is based on Greek folk material. The final movement, Saga, utilized the song Helene of Preveze, the Dance of Zalongou, and the Greek national anthem and proved to be little more than a medley. But the first two movements--the former based on Sirtos, a folk dance, and the latter on a Greek lullaby--were attractively scored.
>
> The other Greek works were Beethoven's Prometheus Overture; La Mere Saronique (from Phaedre) by Arthur Honegger, and two songs in the popular Greek style by Georges Poniridy. It was an interesting and pleasant evening. (Copyright © 1941 by The New York Times Company. Reprinted by permission.)

Julia Smith's second opera, The Stranger of Manzano, with libretto by John William Rogers, was completed in 1943. Due to our country's involvement in World War II, production of the opera was delayed for two years. This gave the composer time to lengthen the work by adding an overture and ballet of three Mexican dances. The première of this one-act opera and at her suggestion, Hindemith's short work, Hin and Zuruck, were performed in Dallas, on May 1, 1946. Julia assisted in orchestra rehearsals for both works, since she had previously attended Hindemith's rehearsals and performances of his short opera at Hartt College. The Juilliard School again assisted in the funding of orchestral materials for the new opera.

The following partial review written by E. Clyde Whitlock, appeared in the Fort Worth Star-Telegram, May 2,
1946:

> With all the excitement of a première the North
> Texas State College School of Music produced the
> first performance anywhere of Julia Smith's new
> opera, The Stranger of Manzano and the First Texas
> performance of Hindemith's There and Back at Mc-
> Falin Auditorium in Dallas. The production was
> a project of the Variety Clubs of Texas, through
> whose generosity the works were heard by an in-
> vited audience. Conducted by Wilfred Bain, stage
> direction was by Mary McCormic.
>   The musical score is the focus of interest, to
> which the stage is something of a commentary.
> Miss Smith has given us a fine piece of craftsman-
> ship, steeped in the atmosphere of the Southwest
> and permeated by Mexican color and rhythm.   It
> is richly scored music, with plenty of good tunes,
> yet not too obviously in popular manner.   There
> are fascinating rhythmic and accompaniment figura-
> tions, and the vocal parts are singable, with a
> reservation as to the tenor part, which lies often
> too high for any except the unusual voice. (Re-
> printed by permission of the Fort Worth Star-Tele-
> gram.)

In comparison with the earlier opera, Cynthia Parker,
Whitlock was of the opinion that "the new opera is more confidently orchestrated, and probably carries more of a popular
appeal."

In 1945 Julia Smith gave up her teaching position at
the Hartt College of Music because it was too time-consuming
and the demands of her work as composer required more of
her creative energy.   Before she left the college, the Opera
Workshop commissioned her to write an opera for children's
audiences.   This resulted in The Gooseherd and the Goblin,
based on a play of the same name by Constance D'Arcy Mackay, with libretto by Josephine Fetter Royle.

Herman Neuman, Music Director of the Municipal Radio Station WNYC New York City, featured the Hartt College
production of the opera with a radio première during WNYC's
1947 American Music Festival.   Following this, the first stage
presentation was conducted by Moshe Paranov with Elemer
Nagy, innovative stage director, in November 1947, at New

London, Connecticut. In the next few seasons this little opera was to receive over thirty performances by the Hartt Opera Workshop in New England in addition to presentations by other groups in various parts of the country.

Julia Smith wrote her Folkways Symphony on a commission from the Friends of Music of the Toledo (Ohio) Orchestra. This work, approximately fifteen minutes in length, was modeled on the proportions of Prokofiev's Classical Symphony. Conducted by Hans Lange, the symphony received its première performance on January 31, 1949.

Excerpts from the review by Jean Aline Treanor, music critic of the Toledo Blade are taken from the issue dated February 1, 1949:

> Expectancy could be felt in the Peristyle last night as the stage curtains swung back on a concert of more novelties than Hans Lange had shaken a stick at in his two seasons and a fraction as conductor.
> Julia Smith's Folkways Symphony was a happy surprise. It was hard to believe she could rear such a solid symphonic composition from a handful of slight cowboy songs and fiddle tunes. As it turned out, their contribution was chiefly rhythm, that insisting, persisting regularity and syncopation that stamped the piece "Made in America."
> Hers was the major contribution of refreshing the tunes with variation, clothing them in just-discordant-enough harmonies, and pouring them, rhythm and all, into a fairly tight little classic mould. Not to be overlooked was the skillful orchestration that gave every choir and solo instrument the tunes most suited to its timbre. (Reprinted from The Blade, Toledo.)

Two of Julia Smith's best solo piano works were written in the 1940's--Sonatine in C and Characteristic Suite-- both premièred by Marienka Michna, in New York's Town Hall. Of the latter work Ross Parmenter, Times music critic, wrote the following under the dateline of October 31, 1947:

> Miss Smith's suite is written in the twelve-tone technique and she may have been poking fun, for she showed how a waltz, a march and other familiar forms sounded in it. But the technique, in its turn, lent oddity to her deliberately simple melodies. The

whole thing had a nicely satiric effect, as well as having musical worth in itself. (Copyright © 1947 by The New York Times Company. Reprinted by permission.)

There were many other performances in the 1940's of her music including Liza Jane performed in a Carnegie Hall Pop Concert by the New York Philharmonic-Symphony Orchestra June 4, 1946, conducted by Herman Neuman. He later led the piece in the Scandinavian countries and on the continent; Frederick Fennell conducted "Overture" to The Stranger of Manzano, with the Houston Symphony; and Julia Smith again played her piano concerto (with revisions in the piano part) with the Plainfield (New Jersey) Symphony Society, Louis Bostleman, conductor, on February 9, 1948.

In 1947 Miss Smith matriculated at New York University in a program leading to the Doctor of Philosophy degree --her thesis title: The Music of Aaron Copland. Among her teachers were Jack Watson, her research professor; Marion Bauer in composition; and music criticism with Virgil Thomson, then the leading critic of the New York Herald-Tribune.

The 1950's offered new avenues in musical expression for Julia Smith, including presentation of some of her works on the prestigious Composer's Forum, founded and directed by Ashley Pettis; commissions for an opera, piano trio, and a large work for chorus and orchestra; the completion of her Ph.D. and the publication of her doctoral thesis. Having studied all of Aaron Copland's works written up to that time, and having developed a special interest in his piano music, she presented these works in lecture-recital form throughout the United States and Latin America.

Miss Smith applied for presentation of her works at the New York Composers Forum for the season 1949-1950 and received a letter from Ashley Pettis, stating that she would share a program with the young composer, Lou Harrison. Each composer would be alloted forty-five minutes performance time, following which a forum would take place with questions from the audience for the composers.

Harold C. Schonberg's review of the concert for the Times, was dated April 17, 1950:

Two more dissimilar composers than the pair presented by the Composers' Forum on Saturday night

at the McMillin Theatre, Columbia University,
would be hard to find.

Julia Smith was extrovert in her music--breezy,
uninhibited and--alas--trite.   Lou Harrison was in-
troverted, delicate and sensitive.

Miss Smith dealt mostly in terms of symphony
and opera, with a few sketchy piano pieces, said
to be in the twelve-tone idiom, also in evidence.

Mr. Harrison's Suite for Cello and Harp, Suite
for Strings and Two Little Pastorals presented similar technical and compositional aspects.   The writing was quiet, lyrical, and strongly dominated by
modal and repetitive medieval elements.   Often a
polyphonic texture made itself felt, and the middle
movement of the Suite for Strings was an involved
canon, stunningly worked out.

On the whole, though, despite its thorough musicianship, feeling for texture and undoubted expressivity, the music remained weak and spineless.
This was the result of lack of emotional contrast.

Of Miss Smith's music, it can be said that she
enthusiastically used techniques that were unabashedly
obvious.   There was all the good will in the world
in her opera, The Gooseherd and the Goblin, and
also in her Folkways Symphony.   There was, unfortunately, not much else except academic work-
manship and "cute" themes of a neo-Disney character.   The libretto to the opera was along the
same lines.   Sample: I'll none of it!   I'll none
of it!   Away!   Away!   (Copyright © 1950 by The
New York Times Company.   Reprinted by permission.)

Long before the second women's movement was popular
and had wide support, Julia Smith played a key role in an
effort to have women's compositions performed.   She asked
Marion Bauer whether she ever had a concert of her works
presented to a New York audience professionally?   Bauer
replied: "No, I have not, though that has been my life's
dream."   Her reply ignited a spark within Julia Smith and
she immediately wrote the national president of Phi Beta
music fraternity (of which Prof. Bauer was an Honorary Member) to initiate plans to honor this composer and author who
would soon retire from teaching.

With Phi Beta's president taking the lead, the concert
took place at New York's Town Hall, May 5, 1951.   The
program premièred a new work for the occasion, Trio Sonata

II for Flute, Cello and Piano, one of the composer's last
works.   Bauer was one of the critics of Musical Leader magazine.   Her critical colleagues turned out en masse and all
made splendid comments on her work.

During this time Smith also insisted, as a member of
the Program Committee of the National Association for American Composers and Conductors, that a work by Ruth Crawford (Seeger) be performed in the Association's Chamber Music Series.   Seeger's String Quartet (perhaps her best known
work in 1981) was performed in 1953.   Regrettably, the composer had passed away shortly before the concert.

At the Second Annual Orchestral Concert of the NAACC,
chaired by Julia Smith, the first New York orchestral performance of Ohio composer, Elizabeth Gould, took place on
March 20, 1954.   Of five composers presented by the augmented Little Orchestra Society, conducted by Thomas Scher-
man, Gould made a tremendous impression as soloist in her
Concerto for Piano and Orchestra.

Smith first visited Puerto Rico in 1950 by invitation
of her ASCAP friend and colleague, Arturo Somohano, to
participate in his orchestra concerts at the Casino de Puerto
Rico in San Juan.   For this appearance she wrote a set of
six piano variations, published under the title Variations
Humoresque, using as a theme Somohano's well-known and
popular song "Dimé" (Tell Me).   On later visits she introduced her Episodic Suite, for piano, as well as works by Hector
Campus Parsi, a young native composer who had studied with
Copland at Tanglewood.

In 1955 she brought her friend Cecile Vashaw, violinist, to the island and they presented a number of joint recitals, appeared on television, and broadcast an hour's program of mostly American contemporary music that was heard
throughout the West Indies.   They also inaugurated the very
first concert of the Cruzan Concert Society on July 25 at St.
John's Hall, Christiansted, Saint Croix, Virgin Islands.

During the same period Smith appeared with maestro
Somohano and orchestra at the Pan American Union in Washington (D. C.) and later repeated this concert at the Depart-
mental Auditorium in a program celebrating Puerto Rico's
Seventh Anniversary as a Commonwealth.

Julia and her husband knew that her book on Aaron
Copland would be published in December of 1955.   They awoke

to a very happy New Year's Day on January 1, 1956, for
when her husband, Oscar Vielehr, picked up The New York
Times at their apartment door and turned to the Book Review Section, there it was, on page two! All smiles, he
came to the breakfast table saying, "The book's in with the
headline 'Scored for Americans' and it's reviewed by Taubman himself. Brava, Julia!"

There were numerous reviews of her book throughout
the country, appearing in Musical America; Saturday Review;
Evening News (Buffalo); The Blade (Toledo, Ohio); Tennessean
(Nashville); News (Birmingham, Alabama); and The Christian
Science Monitor among others; all were positive. The complete title of her book is Aaron Copland: His Work and Contribution To American Music (E. P. Dutton, New York).
Head music critic Howard Taubman of the New York Times
wrote an extensive review from which the following excerpt
is taken:

> Miss Smith's book makes clear the vital importance
> of Mr. Copland's role as composer and proponent
> of the music of other composers. She has done a
> thorough job of research on her subject's life and
> works, and she brings forward a great deal of
> fresh information about the composer. She has
> done a good job of digging up the facts, and she
> has provided thorough analyses of Mr. Copland's
> various styles and of all his significant composi-
> tions. Her enthusiasm for her subject is admir-
> able. Mr. Copland deserves a book of this scope.
> (Copyright © 1956 by The New York Times Com-
> pany. Reprinted by permission.)

Jules Wolffers, Christian Science Monitor, July 19,
1956:

> Miss Smith's book is a worthwhile addition to the
> Copland literature. Although the author writes
> from an obviously partisan point of view, her de-
> tailed and well-documented study is factual and al-
> most completely free of sentimentality. Regarding
> the compositions, Miss Smith presents not so much
> a critique as a comprehensive analysis and des-
> cription. The place of each work is painstakingly
> given in relation to the composer's development.
> Listing of Mr. Copland's compositions, recorded
> music, books, and articles complete a study which
> might be called indispensable for any person in-

terested in contemporary American music. (Re-
printed by permission from The Christian Science
Monitor. Copyright © 1956 The Christian Science
Publishing Society. All rights reserved.)

Following publication of her Copland study, Smith prepared pianistically all his solo piano works (to that date) for
concert-lecture performances. During the fall of 1956 she
gave four performances at her alma mater, North Texas
State University; at Forth Worth and Dallas public libraries,
and at the Lecture Hall of the Toledo Museum of Art. Appreciative audiences helped build her confidence so that she
felt prepared to present Copland's piano music in New York's
Town Hall the following spring.

New York critics were generally friendly in their
recognition of her efforts to make Copland's piano works
better known. Jay S. Harrison of the Tribune wrote that
he attended the lecture-recital devoted to the collected piano
works of Aaron Copland presented by Julia Smith, "an acknowledged expert on the subject and the author of a book dealing
with Copland's influence on the music of America." He
thought that very few composers were able to bear up under
the pressures of a program consisting solely of their works,
but that Copland's music "stood the test with admirable firm-
ness." In his March 11, 1957 review Harrison further stated:

> The concert was mainly of interest for outlining in
> detail the fantastic alternations of style that have
> characterized Copland's growth from his derivative
> and exploratory early years to the years of his supreme
> maturity.
>   Miss Smith knows the scores to the marrow and
> treats them with affection.... Her effort is a noble
> one. More power to her. (Copyright © 1957 I. H. T.
> Corporation. Reprinted by permission.)

Mary Craig of the Courier termed the recital-lecture
of Copland's Piano music "a must for conservatory and university concert series" (April, 1957). "To put it simply,"
she continued, "Julia Smith plays well, she explains and presents her chosen material in a pleasantly communicative
style, and the results are educational and enjoyable, a rare
combination."

Meanwhile Julia Smith's own compositional efforts during these years had continued and included performances of
her one-act opera, Cockcrow (libretto by C. D. Mackay),
Three Love Songs (Lyrics by Karl Flaster), Two Pieces for

Viola and Piano, a piano trio, and the choral work, Our
Heritage (poem by Arthur M. Sampley), scored for large
chorus and large orchestra.   This last work was commissioned by George Bragg, director of The Texas Boys Choir.
It received its première performance on March 5, 1957 in
Oklahoma City and was conducted by Guy Fraser Harrison
as a feature of one of the Oklahoma City Symphony's regular
season's concerts.   This work proved a big success and the
composer was requested by her publisher to prepare at once
a version for chorus and symphonic band and a version for
chamber orchestra and chorus suitable for touring.

     Highlights of the 1960's included: publication of her
second book, Master Pianist--Carl Friedberg; première of
her fifth opera, The Shepherdess and The Chimneysweep; her
collaboration with Cecile Vashaw in a published string method
series; two works for symphonic band; commission to celebrate the inauguration of Lyndon Johnson as 36th President
of the United States; several concerts in Texas and one in
New York of her representative chamber music works; fifteen
performances of Our Heritage for small orchestra and chorus
by the choir and orchestra of Lebanon Valley College (Ann-
ville, Pennsylvania) conducted by James M. Thurmond in the
annual spring tour of the group; the mixed chorus and symphonic band version of the same work performed by the four-
hundred-and-ten member Ohio State University chorus and Buck-
eye band conducted by Jack O. Evans prepared by Louis Diercks
in Columbus, Ohio; and the Arkansas première of the fairytale
opera The Gooseherd and The Goblin in two performances with a
third as a feature of the First High School Opera Workshop sponsored and convened at the University of Arkansas (Fayetteville),
under the direction of Kenneth L. Ballenger.

     Both the two-piano and orchestral versions of the
American Dance Suite enjoyed numerous performances during
this period.   Of the latter, those by the Cleveland (Louis
Lane), Dallas (Donald Johanos), Norwalk, Conn. (Dennis Russell Davies), Orchestras were particularly outstanding.

     On March 28, 1965 Julia Smith appeared as pianist
in a New York concert of her principal chamber music works.
The next morning a review signed L. S. appeared in the
Herald-Tribune, a portion of which is quoted here:

> Julia Smith, the Texas-born composer whose prolific
> output has had its share of performances by major
> American musical organizations, gave a do-it-your-
> self concert of her chamber works before a friendly au-
> dience yesterday afternoon in Carnegie Recital Hall.

The varied compositions, ranging over a twenty-years span, had in common an earnestness and care in construction, within the frame of several periods and styles, that somewhat compensated for a lack of particular urgency in the music itself. Most successful were the Trio, which showed invention and humor in its variations section, and the concluding new Quartet, which, took on increasing thematic and rhythmic interest as it progressed. (Copyright © 1965 I. H. T. Corporation.   Reprinted by permission.)

Smith's opera, The Shepherdess and The Chimneysweep, a Christmas opera in one act, was completed in 1963. "Conceived originally for television," she said, "I was unable to interest a producer in presenting it at least once instead of the perennial Ahmahl, so I began to think of a theater production. "

It was premièred on December 28, 1966 and five performances followed presented by the Fort Worth Opera Association, Rudolf Kruger, conductor, and Robert Telford, stage director.   Excerpts of a review by E. Clyde Whitlock, critic of the Fort Worth Star-Telegram, appear below:

> A Christmas fantasy with the ingenious charm of the fairy story from which it was derived was the seasonal contribution to the city on the part of the Opera Guild of Fort Worth and the Fort Worth Opera Association Wednesday night at the Wm. Edrington Scott Theater.
> The engaging little piece is The Shepherdess and The Chimneysweep suggested by the Hans Christian Anderson story, from which dramatist C. D. Mackay fashioned a libretto considerably more appealing than the original story.
> The music is the work of Texas composer Julia Smith, who knows what she is doing stagewise since this is her fifth opera.
> Miss Smith has a background of exceptional tutelage, the experience of a record of performances in many mediums and the craftsmanship to handle a full orchestra; also the judgment not to write a Christmas fantasy with Wagnerian complexity....
> The skilled simplicity of the writing is its greatest charm.   (Reprinted by permission of the Fort Worth Star-Telegram.)

When Julia Smith and Merle Montgomery, co-chairmen of
the Musicians Club of New York (Program Committee) planned
a concert of chamber music works by American women composers, little did they realize the national repercussions this
event would create.   Mme. Serge Koussevitzky (Olga), President of the Musicians Club, suggested dedicating the concert
to the National Federation of Music Clubs for its efforts in
1967-1969 on behalf of women composers.   The concert was
co-sponsored by the Music Performance Trust Fund, American Society of Composers, Authors and Publishers (ASCAP)
and the thirtieth Annual WNYC Festival of American Music
which broadcast the performance live.

The five composers whose works were performed represented various sections of our country and were chosen
from a list of Ten American Women Composers named by
the National Council of Women of the United States in 1963.
They were Elizabeth Gould, Toledo; Mabel Daniels, Boston;
Louise Talma, New York; Elinor Remick Warren, Los Angeles; and Julia Smith, Texas-New York.

Julia Smith's responsibilities as co-chairman included
press release coverage of the concert.   She was contacted
by Joy Miller of the Associated Press who requested an interview with the composers.   Smith arranged a luncheon for
the composers and the reporter where a lengthy discussion
on the lack of opportunities for performances of their music
and the unconcerned and uninterested attitude of nearly all
conductors were stressed.   Reporter Miller attended the concert and reception and proved a most sympathetic listener
and questioner.   The morning after the concert her story
was carried by over sixty-five newspapers:

> NEW YORK (AP)--The distinguished woman composer
> smiled thinly.   "They think they're paying me the
> highest compliment when they tell me after a per-
> formance of one of my works, 'My, it sounds just
> like it was written by a man!'"   said Elinor Remick
> Warren of Los Angeles.
> A pretty, reddish-brown-haired mother of three,
> Mrs. Warren was one of five composers presented
> in a concert here Tuesday evening that one of the
> women called the best concentrated effort ever made
> in behalf of women composers.
> Of the five composers, only Mabel Daniels, now
> in her 89th year and still composing, didn't make
> it to New York to hear her work performed.
> The capacity audience of about 250 that crowded

into the auditorium of Donnell Library Center applauded all the compositions enthusiastically.

Said Mrs. Maurice Honigman of Gastonia, N. C.
president of the National Federation of Music Clubs,
at a reception after the concert: "Women have been
considered second-rate composers for too long.   If
men composers heard this program they'd soon
change their minds."

Composers Talma, Smith, Gould, and Warren--
with international reputations and perhaps more
prizes won abroad than at home denied personal
discrimination.

But Miss Smith voiced a general plaint: "Women
don't get the opportunities for performances or
commissions that men do.   Opera houses, for example, don't seem to mind having flops with men
composers--so why can't they take a chance with
women?" (Reprinted by permission of The Associated Press.)

The 1970's saw both Women's International Year and
The Decade of Women.   Prior to this decade, the National
Federation of Music Clubs had issued in 1955 a recording
of orchestral music by women under Composers Recording
Inc. (CRI) label, conducted by William Strickland and performed by the Imperial Philharmonic Orchestra of Tokyo.
Composers included Louise Talma, Vivian Fine, Julia Perry,
Mabel Daniels, and Mary Howe.   This recording (CRI SRD
145) was made during the presidency of Ada Holding Miller
(1951-1955), but little else was accomplished for women composers until the dynamic presidency of Maurice (Hinda) Honigman (1967-1971).   President Honigman, in support of the
International Woman's Movement and in tribute to Ada Holding Miller, announced a program of awards to American
women composers, in two parts under the leadership of
Marion Morrey Richter and supported by ASCAP.

Three $1000 prizes were presented: Hansi Alt, for
the best piano teaching material; Emma Lou Diemer, for her
choral and instrumental compositions for high school and
college level; and Miriam Gideon in concert and symphonic
literature.   The second part of the award was to afford wider
hearing and stimulate public appreciation and knowledge of
works by American Women Composers under the leadership
of the Senior Clubs and Senior Affiliated Organizations of the
National Federation of Music Clubs.   A prize of $50.00 was
awarded to one club in each of the fourteen districts.

Although this was a new approach to an old problem, there still existed the need for published music by women composers, particularly in large forms. A request was made to presidents of each State Federation to send in names and addresses of active composers, classification as to genre of their works, and publishers (if any), to Marion Richter, American Music Chairman. Julia Smith was asked by Honigman to compile and edit the collected materials for book publication by the National Federation of Music Clubs.

Julia Smith said, "Such a formidable task presented a great challenge, but it also meant temporarily ceasing my own compositional activities." After a long discussion with President Honigman of the benefits for women composers as a whole, Julia Smith consented to do the work, completing the task within a few months. Titled Directory of American Women Composers, this sixty-page book was the first and best recognized source for locating American women's music for almost a decade. Smith, named the first chairman of American Women Composers by Honigman, said, "I shall always cherish that title."

Another accomplishment under Honigman's administration, in cooperation with The Ford Foundation, was the release of a recording in spring of 1971, Four American Composers, under the Desto label; the composers were Mabel Daniels, Miriam Gideon, Louise Talma and Julia Smith. This music was now available in both published and recorded forms for listening, study, and performance.

During this time Smith wrote to the National Endowment for the Arts and learned that no woman had ever received an outright grant in music although some few had received small amounts for copying of parts. "Something had to be done about this state of affairs," said Smith and she made an appointment in Washington in fall of 1971 with Walter F. Anderson, Program Director for the National Endowment of the Arts.

Why had no woman received a grant when the Federation's Directory listed over 600 active composers? After considerable discussion, Anderson suggested that Julia Smith and the succeeding Federation president, Merle Montgomery (1971-1975), devise a list of twenty women they thought were qualified to receive such grants, and this they did. When the first sizable grants from the National Endowment were made to women composers in June 1974, at least eighteen names among the twenty-five grantees had appeared on the National Federation's list!

Anderson was to demonstrate further interest in American women composers when he invited Vera Brodsky Lawrence, collector and editor of the complete Scott Joplin and Louis Moreau Gottschalk piano works, and Julia Smith to a meeting of notable American composers. The rest were men! It took place in a large conference room at the Juilliard School in 1972, the first time women were included in such a gathering. The meeting's purpose was to determine the most practical and efficient way the National Endowment of the Arts might contribute to American composers' interests.

When Montgomery assumed the presidency of the National Federation of Music Clubs she used her promotional fund for American music to provide interested radio stations with free recordings of "serious" American music for broadcast. Smith and Montgomery sent letters to a selected list of 200 radio stations throughout the country; they received seventy-two positive responses for two series of thirteen weeks of Contemporary American Composers' music. Recordings of the music of twenty women and twenty-two men were assembled and shipped out with a suggested order of programs and notes in a package of twenty-five records: Series I devoted entirely to the music of women; Series II to an equitable division of music by both men and women.

Robert Sherman, program director of WQXR, the New York Times Radio Station, premièred the announcement of the series in October 1971 by interviewing Louise Talma, Margaret Harris, and Julia Smith and by playing a recording of each. Smith wrote him a letter of thanks for his cooperation in getting the series underway over so prestigious a station. The following is his reply, dated November 4, 1971:

> Thank you so much for your gracious and most flattering note. Needless to say, it is we at WQXR who are grateful to you, as well as the Misses Harris and Talma, for giving us such a provocative broadcast.
> I certainly hope that your planned series of broadcasts goes marvelously--the fact that you have pulled together 72 stations already is quite something--the whole Metropolitan Opera network is not much larger than that! And if there is anything more that I can do specifically, please don't hesitate to call.

Arturo di Filippi, artistic director of the Opera Guild

of Greater Miami (Florida), approached Julia Smith to write
an opera about Juliette Gordon Low, founder of the Girl
Scouts of the United States of America. He enclosed a libretto approved by both the Girl Scout National and Miami
Local Councils. Upon reading the libretto and finding it non-
stageworthy, Julia Smith replied that she would be interested
in writing such an opera if she could choose her own librettist. That being agreed, Smith wrote her friend, the celebrated novelist, Bertita Harding, and contracts for librettist
and composer were signed in early 1971.

The opera would be titled Daisy after Juliette Low's
familiar name. The writing and production of the opera
were filled with tragedies: di Filippi's death postponed the
opera production for a year and Bertita Harding's failing health
and eventual death left the burden of responsibility for completing the libretto to Julia Smith (she completed this task
with the assistance of Kenneth Ballenger). A request by
stage director Jack Nagle for a ballet as part of the production, just a few weeks before rehearsals were to begin,
added to the burden.

In spite of these almost overwhelming difficulties the
opera was premièred on November 3 and 4, 1973, by the
Florida Family Opera in affiliation with the Opera Guild of
Greater Miami, Warren Broome, conducting. The reviews
were enthusiastic, with headlines reading: Future's Bright
for Daisy, New American Opera 'Daisy' Treat from Start to
Finish, Opera Daisy is a Spirited Charmer, Daisy light Opera
Magnificently American and Opera's Good Deed.

A lengthy review by James Roos was published by
High Fidelity/Musical America in April 1974 from which the
following excerpts are quoted:

> Frankly, I never expected to get mixed up with the
> Girl Scouts, except perhaps to buy a box of cookies.
> But how was I to know that notable organization
> would end up commissioning an opera from the
> Opera Guild of Greater Miami, no less? Yet there
> was Daisy in its world première, superbly decked
> out as Miami's first indigenous production, from
> the glittering sets up. Happily it turned out to be
> a charmer.
>   Why Daisy Gordon? Why the Girl Scouts at all?
> Well, for many a season the Scouts worked closely
> with Miami's opera guild, planning educational pro-
> grams, especially for the company's federally aided

Florida Family Opera. How better to reciprocate
than to honor the Girl Scouts' 60th Anniversary by
commissioning a work to lure the uncaptured young
to opera? So thought Arturo di Filippi, Miami's
late director. So it was belatedly carried out,
one year after the anniversary.

No matter. Operatic quality is what counts,
anniversaries notwithstanding, and Daisy plainly
had that. For one thing, it had the right composer
--a woman with historical, fairytale and Christmas
operas to her credit.

Daisy was a colorful, spirited show, part opera,
part Broadway musical, and pure pleasure, for
most of the distance. And that's no small achievement considering the threadbare drama of Juliette
Low's life.

After all, what can you say about this lady that
makes for two hours of engrossing stage play? ...
Yet with mellifluous tunes, some lively dances,
and a libretto to match, the audience was held in
the music's thrall. (Reprinted by permission from
High Fidelity/Musical America. All rights reserved.)

Daisy, written by two women and starring a woman
as the central theme, was an artistic and musical success
with more than thirty performances by 1979. It was presented by opera companies in Miami, Detroit, and Charlotte,
fourteen performances in the Fulton Opera House at Lan-
caster (Pennsylvania), and Allentown (two additional), Birmingham, and elsewhere.

A grant from the Ford Foundation Recording-Publishing
Program made possible a 1976 recording of Highlights from
Daisy, issued by Orion Master Recordings. The piano-vocal
score, dedicated to Roberta Rymer Balfe, co-founder and
chairman of the Florida Family Opera, is published by Mowbray Music, New York, and distributed by Theodore Presser,
Bryn Mawr, Pennsylvania.

The succeeding NFMC president, Mrs. Frank A.
Vought, (1975-1979) widened the Federation's sphere of interest in furthering the music of women composers and stres-
sing the need of opportunites for women conductors. This
marked a step forward in the recognition of creative women
musicians both internationally and in the United States.

On November 7, 1976, a gala orchestral concert cele-

brating Women's International Year was presented by NFMC
and conducted by Victoria Bond at Columbia University's Mc-
Millin Theatre featuring works by composers from Great
Britain, France, West Germany, and the United States.   John
Duffy, executive secretary of Meet the Composer, said to
Julia Smith: "Now that NFMC has proven (that women can
produce) orchestral scores of merit and enjoyment for audiences, we would be interested to hear some outstanding
theater works by women to which we would again contribute
support."

Following Duffy's suggestion, the NFMC Board of Directors on the recommendation of President Vought authorized
the presentation of a triple bill of one-act operas performed
on December 2 and 3, 1978 at Hunter College Playhouse,
New York City, in celebration of the third year of The Decade
of Women.   These operas, all by American composers were:
The King's Breakfast (1973) by Joyce Barthelson; The Shepherdess and The Chimneysweep (1963) by Julia Smith; and
The Nightingale and the Rose (1972) by Margaret Garwood.

Julia Smith best summed up the entire event in her
report to the NFMC 40th Biennial Convention at Portland,
Oregon in 1979, a portion of which reads:

> I am certain that this is the first time anywhere
> that three competently composed one-act operas by
> women, conducted by a woman, staged by two women
> directors, one of whom is also an outstanding chor-
> eographer, with an orchestra of 31 players whose
> manager is also a woman, in a proper theater with
> an orchestra pit, an adequate stage with modern
> lighting equipment, with beautiful but inexpensive
> costumes and scenery and presented in a thoroughly
> professional manner, with top-notch singers in the
> musical capitol of the United States, if not the
> world, have ever before been heard under such ad-
> vantageous conditions.   NFMC and its outstanding
> and courageous president who was willing to take
> this artistic and financial risk are entitled to the
> greatest praise for this tremendous effort.

American composer, writer, and concert artist Julia Smith
is a champion and a prime mover in the search for recognition of serious women composers.   Through her own artistic commitment, her proliferation of articles and lectures on
the subject of women composers, and her decades of effort
to program the compositions of women, place her solidly as

a leader among her contemporaries.   Few artists are willing
to give of their time and energy for the development and
promotion of other artists.   Her imagination and dedication
attest to her unselfish quest to give women composers their
due.

Partial list of Compositions

Published by: Mowbray Music Publishers, P. O. Box 471,
Cathedral Station, New York, N. Y.   10025; Theodore Presser
Company, Bryn Mawr, Pennsylvania 19010, sole distributor.

Piano Solo

1935   Episodic Suite, (Yellow and Blue, Nocturne, Waltz
                for 'Little Lulu', March, Toccata).
1943-   Sonatine in C.
44
1949   Prelude, (Recital Piece).
1949   Variations Humoresque.
1949   Characteristic Suite, In Serial Style, (Canon, Waltz,
                Passacaglia, March, Toccata).

2 pianos/4 hands

1936   Revised 1966 American Dance Suite, (One Morning in
                May, Lost My Partner, Negro Lullaby, Chicken
                Reel) Originally for small orchestra and titled
                "Little American Suite."
1938-   Revised 1971 Concerto for Piano and Orchestra, (2-
39   Piano Reduction Published).

Organ Solo

1968   Prelude in D Flat, (Originally for piano solo, dating
                from 1932).

Chamber Music

1944   Two Pieces for Viola and Piano, 1. Nocturne 2.
                Festival Piece.
1946   Sonatine for Flute and Bassoon.
1947   The same arranged for Flute and Piano unpublished,
                music with composer.
1955   Trio--Cornwall for Violin, Cello & Piano.
1964   Quartet for Strings, (2 vlns. , vla. , cello).
1980   Octet for Winds, (2 obs. , 2 clar. , 2 horns, 2 bsns.).

1981   Prairie Kaleidoscope, song cycle for soprano and
       piano, (Autumn Orchestra, Captive, Prairie Wind,
       Answer, Wakening), lyrics Ona Mae Ratcliff, Pres-
       ser Catalogue Rental.

Vocal Solos

1954- Three Love Songs for Solo Voice & Piano, Lyrics by
55   Karl Flaster, (I will Sing the Song, The Door That
       I Would Open, The Love I Hold), Complete Set
       MM-104B Medium, MM-104C Low Voice, MM-104A
       High Voice.
1967   Invocation for Solo Voice & Piano, Text by J. S.,
       (Chosen as the official Invocation by National Feder-
       ation of Music Clubs) Published for Medium High,
       and Low Voice.

Choral Music

1949   To All Who Love a Song, (SSA & Pno.), Lyrics by
       Mary A. Donovan.
1956   Our Heritage (SSAATB & Pno.), Poem by Arthur M.
       Sampley.
1966   Glory to the Green and White, (SATB & Pno.), Text
       by Charles Langford.
1966   The same arranged for (TTBB a Cap. with Pno. for
       rehearsal only).
1967   Invocation (SSA & Pno.), Text by J. S.
1969   Enrich Your Life With Music (SSAA & Pno.), Poem
       by Kathleen Lemmon.
1974   God Bless This House (SSTB & Pno.), Poem by Anna
       H. Branch.

Band

1964- Remember the Alamo for Band & Optional Narrator
65   & Mixed Chorus, (with Cecile Vashaw), 3-2-7-3-5-
       sax., 4-2-3-3-3 cornets, timp., perc., str. bass,
       Full score, parts for Full Band, Symphonic Band.
1966   Sails Aloft--Overture, (with Cecile Vashaw), Full
       score, parts for Full Band, Symphonic Band 3-2-5-
       2-4-5 sax., 4-2-3 bar., 3-3-3 cornets, timp.,
       perc., plus vib., c-b op., condensed score avail-
       able.
1971   Fanfare for Alma Mater, (Full Band, condensed score
       & parts), 3-2-5-2-4 sax., 4-2-3 bar., 2-2 cornets,
       timp., perc., vib.

String Method
Work And Play String Method, (with Cecile Vashaw).
1964   Book 1: Teacher's Book, Violin, Viola, Cello, Bass.
         Book 2: Teacher's Book, Violin, Viola, Cello, Bass.

Note: All rental and perusal requests should be sent to:
         Theodore Presser Company, Rental Dept. , Presser
         Place, Bryn Mawr, Pa. 19010

Operas
1935   Cynthia Parker, Revised 1945 (2 Acts with Prologue),
         Libretto by Jan Isbel Fortune, Perf: Solo SSAT-4B.
         Choruses: SA, TTBB, SATB; ballet: Male & fe-
         male; 10 supers; Piano-vocal score available for
         perusal.
1943   The Stranger of Manzano, (1 Act with prologue &
         ballet), Libretto by John W. Rogers; based on a
         tale of old New Mexico by Frank Applegate.   Piano-
         vocal, orch. score & parts.   Perf: Solo SAT-5B. ,
         choral SSAATB; 1-1-1-1; 2-2-1-0; timp. , perc. ,
         plus xylo. , vib. celesta, hrp. , str.
1946   The Gooseherd and The Goblin, (1 Act with Prologue),
         Libretto by Josephine Fetter Royle on Play of the
         same name by Constance D'Arcy Mackay.   Solo
         SSAT; Choral SSA; Pno. -vocal; score & parts:
         1-1-1-1; 1-1-0-0; perc. , pno. , str.
1953   Cockrow, (A fairy-tale opera in 1 Act), Lib. by C. D.
         Mackay.   Perf: SSSA, TT, BB, 1 Super, Pno. -
         vocal; score & parts: 1-1-1-1; 1-1-0-0; timp. ,
         perc. , pno. , str.
1963   The Shepherdess and The Chimneysweep, (Christmas
         opera in 1 Act), Lib. by C. D. Mackay based on
         a story by Hans C. Andersen.   Pno. -Vocal score
         pub. by MM. Orch. score & parts on rental.   Perf:
         Solo STB, Choral SSAA; 2-2-2-2; 2-2-2-0; timp. ,
         perc. , plus xylo. , vib. , celesta, chimes, hrp. ,
         str.
1973   Daisy, (2 Acts, with dances), Lib. by Bertita Hard-
         ing, based on life of Juliette Gordon Low, founder
         of Girl Scouts of the U. S. A. Pno. -Vocal Score
         pub. by MM. Perf: Solo 4S-4A-T-Bar-B; choral
         SSAATB; dancers, orch. score & parts: 1-1-2-1;
         2-2-1-0; timp. , perc. , plus xylo. , celesta, hrp. ,
         pno. , str.   Recording: "Highlights From Daisy"
         50 min. 2 sides, Orion 76248.

Orchestra

1963   American Dance Suite for theater orchestra, (revised)
       Chicken Reel, Negro Lullaby, Lost My Partner,
       One Morning in May.   Score & parts: 1-1-2-1;
       2-2-1-0; timp. , perc. , pno. , (or hrp.), str. Origi-
       nal version from 1935-36 and titled "Little Ameri-
       can Suite"; Also version for 2 pnos. 4 hands, MM-
       109.

1936   Episodic Suite for large orchestra, (Parts cued for
       small orch) Yellow & Blue, Nocturne, Waltz for
       "Little Lulu" (cartoon character), March Toccata.
       8' Score and parts: 3-2-2-2; 4-2-3-1; timp. ,
       perc. , plus xylo. , hrp. , str. Orig. pno. solo.

1967   Eposodic Suite Ballet version for 10 Players, Same
       titles as above Perf: 1-1-1-1; 1-1-1-0; drum
       traps; pno. -conductor, str. bass.

1971   Concerto For Piano & Orchestra, (revised), 22' score
       & parts on rental: 2-2-2-2; 4-3-3-1; timp. , perc. ,
       str. Original version dates from 1938-39.

1940   Liza Jane For Theater Orchestra, 4' score & parts:
       1-1-2-1; 2-2-1-0; timp. , perc. , str. (Commissioned
       by Columbia Broadcasting Symphony 1939-40).

1940- Hellenic Suite for large Orchestra, based on Greek
41   folk-melodies; Sirtos (Dance), Berceuse, Saga. 15'
       score & parts: 2-2-2-2; 4-2-3-1; timp. , perc. ,
       hrp. , str.

1943- Overture and Mexican Dances from The Stranger of
45   Manzano for Theater Orch. , 21' Overture; El
       Jarabe, La Botella (Valse), Le Virgen y Las Fieras.

1948   Folkways Symphony for small orchestra, (based on
       Western themes).   Day's a-breakin', Night Herding
       Song, Cowboy's waltz, Stomping leather.   14' score
       & parts: 2-2-2-2; 2-2-1-0; timp. , perc. , hrp. ,
       pno. , 4-hands, str.

1956   Our Heritage for Solo S. , Chorus SSAATB and large
       Orchestra, Poem by Arthur M. Sampley.   10'
       Score & parts: 2-2-2-2; 4-3-3-1; timp. , perc. plus
       temple blks. , glock. chimes, tom-tom.   Choral
       octavo published MM125.

1958   Our Heritage for Solo S. Chorus SSAATB and small
       orchestra.

1959   Our Heritage for Solo S. Chorus SSAATB and sym-
       phonic band.

1965   Remember the Alamo! for large orchestra, same
       instrumentation as for band with added string parts
       and conductor's score (with optional Narrator) and
       Chorus SSAATB.   121/2 For Band and/or Orchestra

Festivals; may be performed with band, orchestra and chorus combined.

<u>Note</u>: The following simplified Published vocal music is available only from: Girl Scout Council of Tropical Florida, 11347 S. W. 160 Street, Miami, Florida 33157

1974   Vocal Selections from <u>Daisy</u>, (Solos and Duets with Piano) from ACT one.

1974   Scenes from <u>Daisy</u>, (Soprano, Alto, and Narrator, with Piano).

1974   The Girl Scout Promise and Whene'er You Make a Promise-from Daisy, SSAA and piano acc.

Discography

Four American Composers: Mabel Daniels, Miriam Gideon, Julia Smith, Louise Talma. Desto Records, Stereo DC7117 distributed by CMS Records, Inc. , 14 Warren St. , New York, N. Y. 10007. Quartet for Strings by Julia Smith performed by the Kohon Quartet: Harold Kohon, violin; Isadora Kohon, violin; Eugenie Dengel, viola; W. Ted Doyle, cello.

Highlights from Daisy. Orion Master Recordings, Inc. , 5840 Busch Drive, Malibu, Calif. 90265; ORS 76248. 50 minutes. 2 sides from the Opera Daisy in Two Acts (90 min.). Based on the life of Juliette Gordon Low, Founder of the Girl Scouts of the United States of America. Performed by The Charlotte Opera Association, conducted by Charles Rosekrans, Charles Starnes, Chorus Master with Elizabeth Volkman, Soprano in the title role; David Rae Smith, bass-baritone; Linda Smalley, Contralto; and Larry Gerber, Tenor and Orchestra and chorus of the Charlotte Opera Association. (See Operas listing for instrumentation used.)

Books

1955   Aaron Copland (New York: E. P. Dutton, 336 pp.)

1963   Master Pianist: Carl Friedberg (New York: Philosophical Library, Inc. , 183pp.)

1970   Directory of American Women Composers (Chicago: National Federation of Music Clubs, 60 pp.)

ELINOR REMICK WARREN

Composer, Performing Artist

Elinor Remick Warren is generally acknowledged to be one of America's foremost contemporary composers, and one who achieved distinction early in her career. In a survey of five major U. S. orchestras published by High Fidelity/ Musical America in 1975, she was recognized as one of the five most performed women orchestral composers of the past decade. With over 185 published compositions in her catalogue, the talented Warren has been described by music critic Martin Bernheimer of the Los Angeles Times as "an undeniable mistress of her métier."

She was born in Los Angeles in 1905, the only child of Maude Remick Warren and James Garfield Warren. By the age of four her parents recognized her talent when she continually went to the piano and picked out tunes. Her mother was a fine non-professional pianist and an excellent musician who wrote down the pieces. There was always music in the home and Elinor Remick Warren recalls as a youngster getting out of bed to sit on the stairs many evenings, listening to her father sing with her mother as accompanist. Her grandmother and great-grandfather lived with the family and her childhood was always filled with love even though there was a very strict home atmosphere.

At the age of five Elinor began piano lessons with Kathryn Cocke, who remained her music teacher until Elinor was graduated from Westlake School for Girls. She said, "Miss Cocke was wonderful to me and I had a very quiet, happy and industrious childhood, and I was writing music all the time. I learned to write musical notation from the first lesson, and loved it. Miss Cocke provided me a solid background in music for which I am most grateful. My mother sat by me when I practiced, so I was never allowed to practice mistakes. Consequently, I played very well--for a child."

William Hennegin, Los Angeles

ELINOR REMICK WARREN

        As a freshman at Westlake School for Girls, Warren's
compositions were principally featured on a program presented by the school.   She was studying theory, harmony,
and form with composer Gertrude Ross, who encouraged her
to send her music to a publisher.   As a sophomore Warren
sent A Song of June, for voice and piano, to the prestigious
publisher G. Schirmer; it was accepted for the munificent
sum of fifteen dollars.   This became the first of many pub-

lished songs.   During her senior year she became the young-
est member of the Dominant Club, a group of professional
musicians in Los Angeles.   Her music was often performed
at the monthly meetings of this club, of which she is now an
honorary member.

Warren attended Mills College in California for one
year before going to New York City to continue her musical
studies with Frank LaForge in the art of accompanying, Ernesto Beruman in piano, and Clarence Dickenson in musical
form, theory, counterpoint, and orchestration.

Although a fine professional pianist and accompanist,
she rarely wrote for the instrument.   Her first loves were
singing and poetry, and she realized that as an accompanist
she would acquire the knowledge of vocal expertise more
sensitively.   She traces her love of poetry to childhood, when
her mother read to her numerous books of poems among other
literary classics.   When she was studying with Frank LaForge,
he was much impressed with her keyboard ability and arranged a number of tours of her with outstanding Metropolitan
Opera singers of the era.   She toured as accompanist and
assisting artist solo pianist with Lucrezia Bori, Florence
Easton, Grete Stueckgold, Richard Crooks, and Lawrence
Tibbet who all featured her songs on their programs.   She
said, "I loved these associations, as well as the travel." Her
songs were also in the repertoire of Kirsten Flagstad, Rose
Bampton, Helen Traubel, Dorothy Kirsten, Bidu Sayao, Jean-
ette MacDonald, Nelson Eddy, Igor Gorin, and Eileen Far-
rell, among others.

These concerts took her to many parts of the United
States, and she received the plaudits of the musical establishment as well as those of the critics.   During this same time
her choral works were beginning to be widely sung throughout the country, but soon her interests turned increasingly
to writing for orchestra.

In December 1936, Elinor Remick Warren married
Z. Wayne Griffin, a man of broad interests; a producer of
major radio shows, television, and motion pictures; and a
person deeply interested in music.   Although a prominent
businessman he was also active in civic affairs and community
development.   For the next forty-four years, until his death
in 1981, Wayne Griffin would be her loyal supporter, encouraging her to continue to develop her skills as a composer.
Although a mother of three children, James, Wayne Jr. , and
Elayne, her devotion to her family did not preclude her com-

posing career.   In fact, her husband urged her to take a
period of time to study in Paris with the world-renowned
Nadia Boulanger.   This she did in 1959, spending a concentrated four-month period of private daily study with this mentor of many famous composers.

Reflecting on this period of study, she observed,

> Nadia Boulanger was a tremendous influence in my
> life.   You don't study how to compose--you study
> the building blocks, the craft of it.   I learned a
> great deal about orchestration from her, and much
> from our long talks.   She was marvelous, and crys-
> tallized so many of my questions.   I visited her
> classes on two occasions, but she embarrassed me
> by insisting that I stand up in a roomful of her
> students (and one didn't refuse what she requested)
> and said, "Now I want you to look at Elinor--she's
> worked harder and accomplished more in four months
> than <u>any</u> of you have in a whole year!"   Mlle.
> Boulanger was amazed at the solid foundation
> [which] I had received as a young child, she had
> found this lacking among many who came to her as
> professional composers to seek her advice.

We remained friends until her death.   Boulanger loved
my husband, too, and whenever we went to Europe we always arranged to see her in Paris, even if it meant making
a special trip to Paris for this pleasure.   I carried on years
of correspondence with her and have saved all of her letters,
which I will always treasure.

In the early 1940's when Elinor Remick Warren's reputation as a composer had increased, with more and more of
her works being performed by leading artists and orchestras,
she decided to devote her time to composition, and from that
time seldom appeared as pianist professionally in public except in performance of her own works.   She frequently wrote
settings for the words of poets Carl Sandburg, Tennyson,
Walt Whitman, and Edna St. Vincent Millay.   She comments,

> I compose the way I <u>feel</u> and must express myself
> honestly.   My musical style evolves around growth
> and change; some of my works can be classified
> neo-romantic in style.   I look at my earlier com-
> positions (now long out of print) that gave promise
> of what I wrote later.   I am not avant-garde, elec-
> tronic, or ultra-modern; these styles are fine;

they are just not <u>my</u> métier. A composer is influenced by ideas, impressions, and sounds. I
can best explain myself and my music with Tennyson's lines, "I am a part of all that I have met."
I am happy with my life as a composer and find
it very rewarding.

The Los Angeles Philharmonic Orchestra and chorus,
conducted by the late Albert Coates, premièred Warren's
choral symphony, <u>The Legend of King Arthur</u>. The première
was given a national broadcast over the Mutual Network in
1940. This is one of her largest works for chorus, orchestra, and soloists; it is also published with piano reduction.
It appeared in a new, revised edition in 1974. A work of
considerable magnitude, its text from Tennyson's <u>The Idylls
of the King,</u> it embodies the dramatic aspects of the powerful legend, as well as bringing out the pathos and the lyrical
beauty of the story. Though the text was a product of the
last century, its philosophical concept is entirely modern.
It has received two notable performances by the Los Angeles
Master Chorale of 200 voices, with orchestra.

A review by Walter Arlen in the <u>Los Angeles Times</u>,
February 1, 1971 said, in part:

MASTER CHORALE AT PAVILION

In setting up the season's third Master Chorale
program at the Pavilion Saturday night, Roger Wagner opted for warm-hearted, full-throated music
that thrived on juicy parts for the singers and big
sounds for the Sinfonia Orchestra. The composers
in question were Zoltan Kodaly and Elinor Remick
Warren.
   For Miss Warren the occasion must have been
doubly special: It marked the third Los Angeles
hearing since 1940 of her <u>The Legend of King Ar-
thur</u>, and had among its audience the man who conducted the cantata's previous local exposure in
1954, while he was the Los Angeles Philharmonic's
music director--Alfred Wallenstein.
   Once again the work was in excellent hands.
Wagner led a remarkably smooth performance. It
had drive, nuance, fine balances and a cohesion
that brought formal design clearly to the fore.
   The 30-year-old piece wears well. Its frankly
conventional idiom has lost little of its youthful
freshness. The unabashedly direct romanticism

which underpins the vocal writing (words by Alfred
Lord Tennyson) with splashes of lush orchestral
color still teases the senses and demands respect
for the skill that created it.
   Because of Miss Warren's clear textures the
Master Chorale had an easy time of it.   The soloists, too, had good reason to be appreciative. Both
William Chapman (King Arthur) and George Met-
calfe (Sir Bedivere) had ample opportunity to let
their attractive voices shine.   (Reprinted by permission of the author.)

   Warren's Suite For Orchestra was premièred on March
2, 1955, by the Los Angeles Philharmonic Orchestra, Alfred
Wallenstein conducting.   The Suite in four movements was
inspired by the views of the sky over the high Sierra Nevada
as seen from the composer's Corona del Valle Ranch.   According to Warren, "There is no program or story, but a
few lines of the poet, John Gould Fletcher, indicate the moods
of each movement.   These are: Allegro moderato (Black
Cloud Horses), Andante molto tranquillo (Cloud Peaks), Scher-
zino (Ballet in the Midsummer Sky), Moderato (Pageant Across
the Sky)."   The tightly knit work is neo-romantic and skillfully orchestrated.   Patterson Greene writing for the Los
Angeles Examiner describes the work: "Prismatic orchestral
coloring makes telling use of an extensive instrumental pal-
ette ... orchestral hues spread over a deftly woven texture
of thematic lines."   Suite For Orchestra has been recorded
by the Oslo Philharmonic Orchestra, William Strickland,
conducting.   It is available from Composer's Recordings,
Inc. #172, 170 West 74th Street, New York, N. Y.

   On a commission in 1958 from Occidental College,
Elinor Remick Warren wrote a cantata, Transcontinental,
scored for mixed chorus, baritone soloist, and chamber orchestra or piano.   It is brillant in style with impelling rhythms, which Warren describes as "a zestful piece of Americana."   Text: A. M. Sullivan.   The work was premièred
at the college with Dr. Howard Swan, conducting.

   Transcontinental was reviewed by Music Clubs Magazine
in September 1958 by Martha C. Galt as follows:

NEW MUSIC

For between Seasons, Looking forward to Fall

Larger Choral Works:
A most unusual and impressive composition is to

be found in <u>Transcontinental</u>, Elinor Remick Warren's most recent contribution to choral literature,
written for baritone solo and mixed chorus.   The
text, by A. M. Sullivan, is unique and outstanding
in quality, showing a kinship to Walt Whitman in
its Americanesque content.   It is brilliant in style
and the piano-vocal score requires a good accompanist.   The impelling motion of the train, and the
American traveler's continuous reaching out to a
greater distance as he crosses a continent, sans
customs, sans language or currency barriers, but
traveling in a great democracy--all of this is found
in all the music and the text, as the soloist calls
stops en route.   Orchestral accompaniment and
vocal score for this thrilling score is available on
rental from the publisher, Theodore Presser.   (Reprinted by permission of the National Federation
of Music Clubs, Feb. 6, 1982.)

Warren's tone poem for orchestra, <u>The Crystal Lake</u>,
received its United States première in 1958 by the Los Angeles Philharmonic Orchestra, Alfred Wallenstein, conducting.
It was later introduced in Canada by Sir Ernest MacMillan
with the Toronto Symphony Orchestra.   Performed widely
throughout the United States and Europe, the <u>Los Angeles</u>
<u>Examiner</u> reviewer wrote on November 26, 1958, "deserves
inclusion in the repertory of all major symphonies ... lim-
pid timbres appropriate to the title stimulate the imagination
and serene beauty of glowing orchestration." Some sixteen
years later <u>The Crystal Lake</u> was programmed twice by the
New York Philharmonic orchestra conducted by Andre Kostelanetz in Avery Fisher Hall.   Other composers represented
on the program were Rachmaninoff, Shostakovich, and Hovhaness.   In the same year, 1974, the Detroit, Milwaukee,
and Minnesota symphony orchestras also performed the tone
poem.   Ms. Warren wrote the program notes:

In an isolated place ten thousand feet high among
the snowy peaks of the High Sierra mountains lies
the shining, jewel-like Crystal Lake; it can be found
only after a long climb up lofty ridges and over
snowfields. The panorama of beauty that burst before my eyes when I first came upon it could never
be forgotten, and for me could only find expression
in music.
In free form, the tone poem is scored for woodwinds, brass, strings, harp and percussion.   It
began with the impression made upon me by the

high, lonely eerie characteristics of the scene, expressed by tremelo strings and woodwinds, in the high registers. Soon the horns enter, and as the drama of the changing elements of nature unfolds, the full orchestra is brought in with strong rhythms and vigorous movement. As the piece draws to a close, there is a repetition of earlier themes, and as the music takes on the former quality of enduring serenity, finishes as it began, with divisi strings, soft woodwinds and horns. The piece does not endeavor to put into music the sounds of the elements as much as to create the impression made upon me by the scene.

Warren's major works for chorus and orchestra have received numerous performances, a testament to her talent and the quality of the compositions. The reviews presented in this chapter provide only a minute overview of some of the many performances of her works. It is interesting to note briefly here a few of her compositions for voice, keyboard, and instruments. Theme for Carillon, commissioned by the Hollywood Bowl Board, was performed at every concert of the season and at every performance at the Dorothy Chandler Pavilion of the Music Center for the past twenty years. The Mormon Tabernacle Choir of Salt Lake City often sings "More Things Are Wrought By Prayer" over ABC network telecast and CBS radio network broadcast. In January 1981, it was sung by the combined choruses numbering over 600 at the Christian College's Sacred Music Festival conducted by Howard Swan, at Harding University, Arkansas. Singing Earth for high voice and orchestra, based on poems by Carl Sandburg, was premiered at the Ojai Festival in California, the only contemporary American work to be played at the 1952 festival. In 1955 a performance of much interest was held in the ancient Herodicus Atticus Coliseum, at the foot of the Acropolis in Athens. The soloist was Metropolitan soprano Nadine Conner, with the Athens Orchestra conducted by Andreas Parades. Reviewed in Vrathyni, "The composition is characterized by noble romanticism and sensibility, revealing a serious composer possessing all the secrets of technique." The Harp Weaver, for women's chorus, baritone, harp soloist, and orchestra, with text from Edna St. Vincent Millay's famous poem, was premièred in 1936 in New York City with Antonia Brico, conductor. It has received many performances through the years. Some twenty years after the première, the women's section of the Los Angeles Master Chorale, conducted by Roger Wagner, performed it on several occasions and on tour; it continues to be widely sung by col-

lege and professional choruses. Warren said, "It maintains
wide popularity; the poignant feeling of the music and poetry
lead to a stirring climax." Awake! Put on Strength was
sung by the 160 mixed chorus members attending the Associated Musicians Workshop at Columbia University.

   During the 1960's, Elinor Remick Warren's major
works for chorus and orchestra received international recognition. Many of her friends and colleagues considered it
unwise to write for full orchestra because of the difficulty
in getting performances. Not so for Warren, since she had
many performances and said, "I love to write for all the
colors of full-orchestra."

   Abram In Egypt, for mixed chorus, baritone soloist,
orchestra, was commissioned by Louis Sudler, Chicago baritone and music patron. He sang it first as a solo cantata
in Chicago under the baton of Thor Johnson. Its performance
in its present form was premièred soon after, in 1961, at
the Los Angeles International Music Festival to represent
the United States, along with Stravinsky, Piston, and Harris.
Donald Gramm was baritone soloist and Roger Wagner conducted his own Chorale. The work had notable performances
at the Israel Music Festival in 1976 in Jerusalem and Ce-
sarea. It was later recorded by the Roger Wagner Chorale
and the London Philharmonic Orchestra, conducted by Roger
Wagner with Ronald Lewis, baritone. It is available from
Composer's Recordings, Inc., #172, 170 West 74th Street,
New York, N.Y. According to the composer, the music is
written in a style combining the modal influence with modern
idiom, although not employing any actual ancient themes.
The words of Abram are sung by the baritone soloist, with
the chorus singing the narration. It is not sectional, but
continues the dramatic and poignant story unbroken to the
stirring climax. Elinor Remich Warren's detailed description of the text provides interesting and informative information:

      The text is compiled from one of the ancient Dead
      Sea Scrolls discovered in 1947 in a cave near the
      Dead Sea where they had remained hidden for cen-
      turies, and from the Book of Genesis in the Bible.
      While both sources deal with the same subject, the
      Scroll reveals for the first time why Abram urged
      Sarai (later commanded by the Lord to call them-
      selves Abraham and Sarah), to conceal her true
      identity, and adds many touching and absorbing de-
      tails found neither in Genesis nor in other ancient
      writings.

The greater part of the material used for the present work comes from one of these poetically powerful scrolls, written in ink unknown today, on thin, light brown leather, the sheets sewn together with tendons, all dangerously brittle from more than two thousand years of entombment. The Scroll was in fragile condition, some of it having decomposed, and was deciphered by scholars who are authorities on ancient languages, only after lengthy, painstaking efforts. The Scroll was rolled, inside it a sheet of thin, smooth, white material, evidently there to protect the writing.

As the narrative in the Scroll is in the first person, it was necessary to change the excerpts from Genesis from the third person to the first, for the sake of continuity. Otherwise the text follows the narrative as found in Genesis and the Dead Sea Scroll.

The script of the Scroll helps to date its composition. It would seem to be attributed to the fourth, third, or second centuries B.C. The Scroll, along with others found at the same time, was purchased for the State of Israel. They were committed to the care of a specially established institution, Heikal ha-Sepher (the Shrine of the Book), headed by the President of the State of Israel.

This Scroll is described as the earliest literature of its type that has come down to us. It not only helps us to reconstruct and understand obscure passages in early Aramaic literature during a decisive period in its development. It is a powerful contribution to the world's storehouse of literature, a monumental link with the early beginnings of our culture and theology.

The portions of the text from the Dead Sea Scrolls, as published in A Genesis Apocryphon, were translated from the original Aramaic into Hebrew by Dr. Nahman Avigad and Dr. Ygael Yadin, and from Hebrew into English by Sulsmith Schwartz Nardi. The composer gratefully acknowledges permission given by the Heikal ha-Sepher at Jerusalem, to use this material.

Along with many of her other works Abram in Egypt has had major performances in the music centers of America and Europe and was the prizewinning work in an international contest held in Germany in 1961. Numerous reviews are available on this work which is hailed as a major contribution for mixed chorus and baritone, conceived in the contemporary vein. Patterson Greene writing for the Los Angeles Examiner on June 9, 1961 said:

'GREATS' APPLAUD GREAT FESTIVAL

Another stimulating concert in Royce Hall Auditorium on Wednesday night justified the Los Angeles Music Festival in adding to itself the designation of "International."

In the programming, Iain Hamilton of England and Darius Milhaud supplemented U. S. A. composers Elinor Remick Warren and Roy Harris. All but Miss Warren conducted their own works. An alert audience, numbering many of the great names in music, crowded the hall to its limits.

Taking the items of the evening in order of performance....

There was no confusion in Elinor Remick Warren's oratorio, Abram in Egypt, in its world première. Its idiom stemmed from tradition, but there was freedom and unconventionality in its exercise. Its orchestration underlined the chorus and baritone solo passages with coloration that was achieved by an artful simplicity.

The text, taken largely from the Dead Sea Scrolls and partly from the Book of Genesis, deals with the episode of the sojourn of Abram and Sarah in Egypt.

Notable were Abram's description of his dream, accompanied by solo cello and woodwinds, and his rhapsodic account of Sarah's beauty, with a choral obbligato to the baritone narrative. Soloist was Donald Gramm, resonant of voice and musicianly of style, and the chorus was the Roger Wagner Chorale. With Wagner conducting, the ensemble achieved a splendor and amplitude of sound in the finale that was monumental. (Reprinted by permission of the Los Angeles Herald-Examiner.)

When Elinor Remick Warren first met Edna St. Vincent Millay a good many years ago, she had already set her narrative poem, The Harp Weaver, as a chorus, with baritone, harp soloist, and orchestra. The poet heard it at a festival in the East, during one of her lecture tours. When the two artists met they discussed music and poetry and she suggested that Warren should write a musical work based on her book, Fatal Interview, a story uniquely told in the form

of fifty-two sonnets. Warren said, "To select only a few
for a song-cycle, I chose one from each phase of the story
--numbers 7, 11, 35, and 50.   I felt the poetic and deeply
moving poems were particulary suited to strings, and set
them for quartet or string orchestra, with soprano, in which
form the work has had numerous performances.   Later I
scored it as well for string orchestra." Four Sonnets For
Soprano and String Quartette by Warren was premièred in
1963.   A review in the Los Angeles Examiner, April 30, 1963;
said in part:

NEW WARREN WORK SCORES

> A striking new work by Elinor Remick Warren was
> the feature item in the Sunday night concert of the
> chamber music series presented at the California
> Institute of Technology by the Musart String Quartet
> with Bonnie Murray as soprano soloist.
> In Four Sonnets for quartet and soprano, Miss
> Warren has taken unusual texts from Edna St. Vin-
> cent Millay, and transcribed them musically with
> stirring individuality and power.   The moods were
> etched with swift, bold strokes in a style that com-
> bined a modern idiom with tonal beauty.
> Miss Murray sang them with the affection and
> care properly bestowed upon important music, her
> sure intonation and fine musicianship making the
> difficult vocal lines and demanding intervals seem
> deceptively easy.
> Her voice is of lovely timbre that can float ex-
> quisitely, thrill challengingly or lull sensously at
> will.   These facets, and all their gradations as
> well as instrumental accuracy, were demanded by
> the four selections, respectively emotional, reflec-
> tive, poignant and tragic.
> The quartet, composed of Ralph Schaeffer and
> Leonard Atkins, violins, Albert Falkove, Viola,
> and Emmet Sargeant, cello, gave a finely balanced
> presentation.   The composer was present for a
> bow.   (Reprinted by permission of the Los Angeles
> Herald-Examiner.)

Although focus is primarily on Elinor Remick Warren's
larger works, she has composed an enormous amount of
sacred music, which she thoroughly enjoys writing.   Among
many works is the anthem, "Sing to the Lord, All the Earth."
It is impossible to speculate the number of performances
these works receive.   She has received numerous awards,

commissions, and recognition in this field, including many prizes in the Biennial Competitions of the National League of American Pen Women. She has been an honored guest on music station KFAC Los Angeles, interviewed by Director Carl Princi in a discussion of women in the field of composing. In 1972 Abram in Egypt and Suite for Orchestra were heard in a series sponsored by National Federation of Music Clubs titled "American Women Composers." A total of seventy radio stations in thirty-four states were included. She has been a recipient annually since 1958 of a special award bestowed by ASCAP "for significant contribution to the cultural growth and enrichment of our nation's musical heritage."

On a commission from Roger Wagner, Warren composed a Requiem for chorus, orchestra, soprano, and baritone soloists; the liturgical text is in Latin, with English translation. The world première was conducted by Roger Wagner on April 3, 1966; the performance brought acclaim and a standing ovation from a large audience in the Dorothy Chandler Pavilion in the Music Center in Los Angeles. Reviewer Martin Bernheimer said in the Los Angeles Times on April 4, 1966 (partial):

> Fine craftsmanship, poignantly lyrical--a stimulating evening at the Music Center. In the Requiem (her most ambitious work to date) Miss Warren has proven herself an undeniable mistress of her metier; choral writing is superbly idiomatic--mezzo soprano and baritone solos are grateful for the singers and beautifully integrated, the orchestration equally effective and colorful.

Symphony In One Movement was commissioned by Stanford University and premièred there in December 1971 by the University Orchestra, conducted by Samdor Salgo. The Palo Alto Times wrote, "Score is outpouring ... big surging themes through the first section, a smoldering slow movement, building up in rising power to an impressive, big sonority." Warren was guest of honor at a dinner given by Wallace Sterling, President Emeritus of the University, on the occasion of the première of the work. In 1973 Symphony was performed by the Los Angeles Philharmonic Orchestra conducted by Gerhard Samuel, and followed by performances throughout the country.

Good Morning America was commissioned by Occidental College in California and further supported by a grant from

the National Endowment for the Arts. It is a powerful work
along broad lines, set to Carl Sandburg's famous poem.
Scored for mixed chorus, narrator, and orchestra, it is
also published with piano reduction. It was performed in
1977 by the Honolulu Orchestra conducted by Robert LaMar-
china with Efrem Zimbalist, Jr. as narrator, and has had
numerous performances since its première.

Her latest publication is a Collection of Twelve Songs,
for voice and piano, published by Carl Fischer in book form.
This collection is a fine addition to vocal repertoire and will
prove to be of great interest to concert singers, students,
and voice teachers.

She has been named "Woman of the Year in Music"
by the Los Angeles Times, and also by the National Federation of Music Clubs. Warren is the recipient of an honorary
Doctor of Music degree from Occidental College.

Elinor Remick Warren is an American composer who
has helped pave the road for the acceptance of women composers. She is already a part of the musical heritage of
America, to which she continues to contribute. Along with
raising a family and participating in her husband's activities
through the years, she has, with her family's cooperation,
been able to organize her life to gain time to express her
own great talents as composer and performer. In all her
compositions, whether major works on a large scale or art
songs of sensitive detail, her consummate skills prove her
dedication to the high goals she has attained.

Selected List of Compositions

Choruses for Women's Voices
The Night Will Never Stay, SSA, publisher, Lawson-Gould.
White Iris, SSA, publisher, Theodore Presser.
Windy Weather, SSA, publisher, E. C. Schirmer.
Songs For Young Voices, SA, publisher, Lawson-Gould.

Mixed Voices, a capella
More Things Are Wrought by Prayer, publisher, H. W. Gray.
Rolling Rivers, Dreaming Forests, publisher, Carl Fischer.
To My Native Land, (full), publisher, E. C. Schirmer.

Mixed Voices, with Organ, or Piano

Awake! Put on Strength!, publisher, Concordia.

God Is My Song, publisher, Boosey-Hawkes.

Let The Heavens Praise Thy Wonders!, publisher, H. W.
        Gray.

My Heart Is Ready, publisher, Lawson-Gould.

Night Rider, publisher, Lawson-Gould.

Now Thank We All Our God, publisher, Fred Bock.

Now Welcome, Summer!, publisher, Lawson-Gould.

Our Beloved Land, publisher, Theodore Presser.

Praises And Prayers, publisher, Neil Kjos.

Sanctus, (from Requiem), publisher, Lawson-Gould.

Time, You Old Gypsy-Man, publisher, Neil Kjos.

To the Farmer, publisher, Carl Fischer.

Organ Solo

Processional March, publisher, G. Schirmer.

Works for Orchestra

Along The Western Shore, (The Dark Hills, Nocturne, Sea
        Rhapsody), performance time 12 minutes; Carl Fischer
        Rental Library.

Symphony In One Movement, performance time 17 minutes;
        Carl Fischer Rental Library.

The Crystal Lake, performance time 9 minutes; Carl Fischer
        Rental Library.

Scherzo, performance time 2 minutes, Fleischer Library.

The Fountain, performance time 4 minutes; Fleischer Library.

Suite for Orchestra, four movements, performance time 17
        minutes; Carl Fischer Rental Library.

Intermezzo, from The Legend of King Arthur, performance
        time $4\frac{1}{2}$ minutes; H. W. Gray Rental Library.

Works for Soloist and Orchestra

Singing Earth, Text: Carl Sandburg, with soprano or tenor,
        performance time 16 minutes; Carl Fischer Rental
        Library.

Sonnets For Soprano and String Orchestra, or Quartet; piano-
        vocal score on order for purchase or rental, Carl
        Fischer.

All orchestral scores and parts are available from the indicated publishers on rental.

Songs for Voice and Piano

King Arthur's Farewell, from the Legend of King Arthur;
    publisher, H.W. Gray.
Snow Towards Evening, (in Songs by 22 Americans), pub-
    lisher, G. Schirmer.
For You With Love, publisher, G. Schirmer.
More Things are Wrought By Prayer, publisher, H.W. Gray.

Elinor Remick Warren's Collection of Songs for voice and
    piano, publisher, Carl Fischer, includes: "Sailing
    Homeward," "Lady Lo-Fu," "Heather," "If You Have
    Forgotten," "White Horses of the Sea," Lonely Roads,"
    "Christmas Candle," "Who Loves The Rain"; (and
    From Singing Earth:) "The Wind Sings Welcome,"
    "Summer Stars," "Tawny Days," and "Great Memories."
    (O-5096)

COMPOSITIONS

Chorus with Orchestra, or Piano

All orchestrated parts in the Rental Library of Publishers.

Abram In Egypt, Text: Dead Sea Scrolls and Book of Gene-
    sis, Full chorus, baritone soloist, with orchestra or
    piano or two pianos, performance time, 23 minutes;
    publisher, H.W. Gray.
Requiem, Latin and English Texts, mixed chorus, mezzo-
    soprano and baritone soloists, orchestra or piano,
    performance time, 53 minutes; publisher, Lawson-
    Gould.
Transcontinental, Text: A.M. Sullivan, mixed chorus, bari-
    tone soloist, and chamber orchestra or piano, per-
    formance time 12 minutes; publisher, Theodore Pres-
    ser.
The Harp Weaver, Text: Edna St. Vincent Millay, three-
    part women's chorus, baritone and harp soloists, with
    orchestra and piano, performance time 12 minutes;
    publisher, H.W. Gray.
The Legend of King Arthur, Text: Tennyson, full chorus,
    baritone and tenor soloist, with orchestra or piano,
    performance time one hour; publisher, H.W. Gray.
Good Morning America! Words: Carl Sandburg, full chorus,
    narrator, orchestra or piano, performance time 17
    minutes; publisher, Carl Fischer.

Addresses

G. Schirmer, 866 3rd Avenue, New York, NY 10022.

Concordia, 3558 S. Jefferson Avenue, St. Louis, MO 63118.

Boosey-Hawkes, Inc. , 30 West 57th Street, New York, NY
    10019

Niel Kjos, Inc. , 4382 Jutland Drive, San Diego, CA 92117.

Theodore Presser, Bryn Mawr, PA 19010.

Carl Fischer, Inc. , 56-62 Cooper Square, New York, NY
    10003.

H. W. Gray, 159 E. 48th Street, New York, NY 10017.

Discography

Abram In Egypt, London Philharmonic Orchestra, Roger
        Wagner Chorale, Roger Wagner, conductor, Number
        CRI 172.
Suite For Orchestra, Oslo Philharmonic Orchestra, William
        Strickland, conductor, Number CRI 172.

Address

Composer's Recordings, Inc. , 170 West 74th Street, New
    York, NY 10023

JUDITH LANG ZAIMONT

Composer, Performer, Teacher

Judith Lang Zaimont, the vibrant young American creative
artist, possesses a musical instinct that predicts a notable
future for her works.   Her compositions extend and rejuven-
ate that concern with beauty and form characteristic of the
nineteenth-century master composers' techniques.   Yet Zaimont has squarely confronted this century's creative crisis,
remaining adamant in the conviction that music whose only
appeal is structural will never survive the test of time.   Her
own works have frequent and responsive hearings, both on
live programs and in recordings, largely due to her ability
to communicate through music and poetry her most personal
emotions.   Her works have been awarded twenty-six prizes
and honors, and they have been performed throughout the
United States, England, France, Australia, and Germany.

Born in 1945, the eldest of three children of Bertha
Friedman and Martin Lang, she was raised in Queens, New
York.   Her father was a New York City official; her mother
was a music teacher who occasionally composed popular music
of the Cole Porter variety, writing entire musical shows for
the music schools where she taught.   Judith Lang Zaimont
said,

> My mother was the musical root in the family.   In
> our upbringing the thrust was performance: she
> taught both my sister and myself piano until I re-
> ceived a scholarship (at age twelve) from the Juil-
> liard Preparatory School.   This division of Juilliard
> is a Saturday program for children, and my sister
> and I studied piano there with Rosina Lhevinne and
> her associate Leland Thompson; theory and duo-
> piano with Ann Hull, who was the keyboard partner
> of Mary Howe.   Naturally, we played a great deal
> of Mary Howe's music.

Although her mother had not encouraged her to compose, she did realize that Judith displayed signs of creative
talent when the young girl, around the age of eleven, wrote
two compositions for piano. From this point on, she became a strong supporter of her daughter's compositional
skills.

Judith and her sister, Doris Lang Kosloff, aged twelve
and eleven respectively, were teamed together to play duo-
piano recitals. They received national recognition, appearing as individual soloists on several Lawrence Welk shows,
later playing as a team on three Mitch Miller television programs, and also performing in numerous concerts throughout the country. The recital and orchestral performance
schedule arranged for the girls by their manager was exhausting. Composer Zaimont states flatly, "I hated to tour."
Despite this, to further their seven-year joint professional
career, they made the first American recordings of Francis
Poulenc's Sonate, Leland Thompson's Two Masques, and
Robert Casadesus' Six Pieces Pour Deux Pianos for a disc
still available on the Golden Crest label, Concert for Two
Pianos, CR 4070.

A review written by Edward Tatnall Canby and published by Audio January, 1964 comments:

> Judith and Doris Lang--Concert for Two Pianos
> Golden Crest CR 4070 mono.
>
> I must say, I was so bedazzled by these two young
> sisters' pianistic sounds that I didn't even notice
> the disc was mono.
> The girls made their whirlwind debut with old
> Mitch Miller, the bearded Satan, on bigtime TV.
> That's just how they sound here, but nicely so I'll
> admit. High powered, incredibly skillfull, tuned
> to each other like one mechanism, full of bounce
> and enthusiasm, these sisters project on two pianos
> the American Ideal, just like the ads--let's HAVE
> FUN! Let's run hand in hand down the beach,
> straight into the surf; let's idle under a green
> waterfall (smoking Pool or something), or lean
> rakishly into a red sunset out of a red super-con-
> vertible. That's it! These girls have it!
> Nevertheless, they are pianists to contend with
> in any league. They've long since solved all the
> technical problems they'll ever run into, their co-
> ordination is the best I've ever heard; their forte

Leni of Long Island

JUDITH LANG ZAIMONT

chords sound like a dual trip hammer and their
piano sounds are nicely soft--and they know all
about bringing out planes of melody and accompaniment in the often complex 20 fingered music they
play.   Their feeling for the snazzy French music
of Milhaud and Poulenc is wonderfully spontaneous
--it's their stuff, all right.   Fine rhythmic verve,
too, throughout.

> As youthful performers, zestful, peppy, full of
> bounce, the sisters can't now be beat.   But, Golden
> Crest airily announces, "the future looks bright for
> Judith and Doris Lang."   Future with Mitch?   May-
> be.
>   P. S. and by the way: the Lang girls, it says,
> practice two pianos by remote control, one piano
> in the living room and the other downstairs in the
> playroom.   Papa Lang, an engineer, rigged a sound
> system so that "at a flick of the switch" each girl
> can hear the other.   Feedback anyone? (Or may-
> be they play with earphones.) (Reprinted by per-
> mission of Audio.)

The sisters made their New York debut with the Little
Orchestra Society in Carnegie Hall in 1963.   They continued
their professional appearances in concerto and solo performances through 1967, when they disbanded following their
entry into graduate school.

Judith received her Bachelor of Arts degree in music
magna cum laude from Queens College, CUNY (1966), where
she studied composition with Hugo Weisgall.   At that time
the college didn't offer a theory course in twentieth-century
compositional techniques, so she completed a private tutorial
in this area with Leo Kraft.   Zaimont also holds an Artist's
Diploma--Master in Piano from the Long Island Institute of
Music (1966) and a Master of Arts in composition from Columbia University (1978).   During her graduate years she studied
composition with Jack Beeson and Otto Luening.   This ver-
satile young woman is also a member of Phi Beta Kappa, a
Woodrow Wilson Fellow in composition, and a MacDowell
Colony Fellow.

Reflecting on her composition teachers she said,
"Weisgall and Beeson may have influenced me, since I write
a tremendous amount of music for voice, and they both are
heavily concentrated in vocal music.   Luening gave me a
wonderful sense of "anything goes"--one need not wear a
stylistic straight-jacket."

Judith Zaimont was still a teenager when she first
received recognition for her compositional ability through
awards in four Junior Composers Competitions sponsored by
the National Federation of Music Clubs: two New York State
First Prizes, a Charles Ives Scholarship, and a National
First Prize.   As New York State's first-place prize winner
she went to Washington, D. C., at the age of fifteen, to per-

form her Portrait of a City, a suite for piano that is descriptive of New York City.   At age seventeen she received
the National Federation of Music Clubs' first prize for a
composition for flute and piano.

During her junior year at Queens College, she wrote
Four Songs for Mezzo-Soprano and Piano to texts by e. e.
cummings, which later won a Broadcast Music, Inc. Student
Composers Award.

In 1971 she was awarded the Debussy Fellowship of
the Alliance Française under which she spent a year studying in Paris with André Jolivet.   She said,

> Jolivet received me as a colleague rather than as
> a student--an exhilarating change in status.   I
> worked with him particularly to study orchestration;
> my experience of orchestration study in American
> universities had been dismal, since there were
> never actual orchestras at hand to perform what
> the students wrote.   Being a pianist, I didn't have
> the orchestral musician's background, and I needed
> to establish in my inner ear the infinite variety of
> mixed orchestral tone colors.

During her stay in France she wrote several compositions,
including the thirty-minute Concerto for Piano and Orchestra.

After returning to America, Zaimont felt she should
continue to study orchestration and spent the next two and
one-half years on a program of self-study.   Thousands of
hours were spent with the scores of Ravel, Stravinsky, Bartok, and Britten, and with the writings of Piston, Forsyth,
and Rimsky-Korsakov, among others.   The musical nourish-
ment taken in during this period created a climate that encouraged the utmost freedom of expression, based on her
intellect and instinct.   The fruits of this study experience
may be found in the Sacred Service and in the later chamber
music--all notable for their sensitivity and ingenuity in the
assignment of instrumental colors.

Although Zaimont has toured the United States as a
pianist, she insists that her career is basically that of a
composer.   As a professor, she has held faculty positions
at Adelphi University and Queens College.   When commissions and grants became large enough, however, to enable
her to resign her teaching positions, she did so in 1978.
She returned, nevertheless, to the classroom in 1980, joining the theory faculty at the Peabody Conservatory of Music.

Gregg Smith, conductor of the Gregg Smith Singers, has commissioned Zaimont to write for his group on several occasions. The first occasion was in 1974 when she wrote Songs of Innocence (premièred at the Gregg Smith Salon Concerts at New York City's Cubiculo Theatre). A setting of four poems by William Blake, the piece is scored for soprano, tenor, flute, cello, and harp. Conducted by Roger Nierenberg, it is recorded on Golden Crest Records ATH 5051. Conductor Smith said of Judith Lang Zaimont:

> I consider Judith Zaimont to be a woman of extraordinary talent as a composer and pianist and one of the most musical individuals I have known. She writes music that has a great deal of expressive strength and rhythmic vitality. In the field of choral music, she has written several excellent works that in addition to the above qualities also show a true innate skill in vocal writing.

On March 30, 1978, at its performance in Memphis, it was also reviewed by staff writer Michael Donahue for the Memphis Press-Scimitar (partial):

DEPARTURES ARE MUSICAL DELIGHT

> As much of modern art is a departure from standard art form, most of the modern music performed at the New Music Festival IV presented by the Memphis State University music department was a departure from simple song melodies and simple usage of musical instruments.
> The high point of the evening was several songs performed by a tenor, soprano, flutist, cellist and harpist under the heading Songs of Innocence composed by Judith Lang Zaimont, of Floral Park, New York.
> Gently Swaying, one of the four tunes in the set, showed great depth and feeling, and all of the tunes conducted by Jim Richens were beautifully performed by soprano Nancy Dolph; Carl Gilmer, tenor; Bruce Erskine on flute; Lisa Neaf on cello; and Marian Schaffer on harp. (Reprinted by permission of the Memphis Press-Scimitar.)

As a composer with a strong performance background and as an experienced teacher, Zaimont has given numerous lecture-demonstrations throughout the country. She has been in demand on the chicken-à-la-king circuit because of her uncanny ability to explore through words and performance the

maze of contemporary music.   One of her favorite subjects
is Tonality Revived, a discussion of the post-serial tonal
music of the '70s, particularly the neo-Romantic music of
composers such as George Rochberg and herself.   As she
notes,

> In past decades, many composers confused novelty
> with progress, endorsing innovation at any or all
> cost.   The composers of the present have relaxed
> enough to mull over the pioneering efforts of the
> past, and now feel free to amalgamate the best of
> the old with the new.   This does not mean that we
> cannot use the tools of the structuralists; but musi-
> cal form, repetition of previously-heard materials,
> contrasts, variety of pitches, etc. , continue to be
> valid in expressive power and should not be dis-
> carded.

In 1975, in honor of Otto Luening's seventy-fifth birth-
day, a special concert was planned for the "Hear America
First" series in New York City.   Premièred that evening
were Luening's Sonata for Piano: In Memoriam Ferruccio
Busoni and a new Zaimont song cycle.   In the New York
Times on November 20, 1975, Raymond Ericson wrote:

> The evening also offers Judith Lang Zaimont's
> Greyed Sonnets, a fine setting of five poems by
> Edna St. Vincent Millay, Sara Teasdale, and Chris-
> tina Rossetti for soprano and piano.   The music is
> strongly emotional, suiting the texts, yet carefully
> constructed, and it was well performed by Elaine
> Olbrycht, soprano, with the composer at the piano.
> (Copyright © 1975 by The New York Times Com-
> pany.   Reprinted by permission.)

Asked to reflect about this composition, Judith stated,

> I am very particular about what texts I set: I'll
> go to the library and take out an entire shelf of
> poetry anthologies just to find three or four individ-
> ual poems suitable for use as lyrics.   I chose the
> poems for Greyed Sonnets after being introduced to
> the writings of Edna St. Vincent Millay.   As a
> modern Romantic, I felt akin to many of her senti-
> ments.
>   Very often on the first encounter with a text, I
> will hear in my head a linear contour, a rhythmic
> setting--in short, the whole musical setting, com-

plete. I try to develop vocal lines independent of the instrumental parts, and I pay particular attention to the rhythmic scansion.

An interesting song from this standpoint is the second song from Greyed Sonnets, a setting of Sara Teasdale's "Let It Be Forgotten"--a very clear eight line, two-stanza poem. The motto, "Let it be forgotten," appears just once in each stanza, but the rhythmic motive of "forgotten"--an unusual tri-syllable--intrigued me: The first line of the song is simple unaccompanied recitative in which the singer repeats the text three times, using three differing melodic contours and three different rhythmic settings, as if she cannot get just the right emphasis: "let it be forgotten; let it be forgotten; let it be forgotten."

Always, I try to create a musical environment that embodies a specific reading of the poem, knowing full well that any single musical setting cannot stand as a definitive reading of the line, but can yet be the most satisfying setting for that line as it stands within the context of a particular musical work.

Greyed Sonnets is available on Golden Crest ATH 5051, with Elaine Olbrycht, soprano; and Judith Lang Zaimont, piano.

In a review of a New York performance on April 15, 1980, the New York Times' Raymond Ericson said, in part:

> Miss Zaimont's avowed purpose in her Greyed Sonnets was to match the ambiguity of the poems she had set to music, a fine quintet by Edna St. Vincent Millay, Sara Teasdale and Christina Rossetti, and she did this successfully while creating an effective wide-ranging vocal line. (Copyright © 1980 by The New York Times Company. Reprinted by permission.)

Zaimont has been associated with the Great Neck Choral Society for many seasons, both as accompanist and composer-in-residence. The group is conducted by George Rose, an adventurous musician who delights in presenting new music commissioned periodically by the organization. When composer Zaimont's work, Sacred Service for The Sabbath Evening, was premièred by the Great Neck Choral Society, Paul Kwartin, the conductor of Cantica Hebraica of New York City

wrote, "Judith Lang Zaimont has brought a new and exciting
voice to liturgical music. Her ideas are fresh; her combination of voice with text, added to her considerable skills in
choral and orchestral writing create memorable compositions."
Written on a commission from the choral society, the work is
scored for solo baritone voice, chorus, and orchestra. She
orchestrated it while a MacDowell Fellow, with help from a
Composer's Assistance Grant from the American Music Center. Anita Kamien reviewed it for The Great Neck Record
(New York) in June 1976 (partial):

GN CHORAL SOCIETY PERFORMS NEW WORK

Credit must be given to the Great Neck Choral
Society and its conductor George Rose for premièring Judith Lang Zaimont's ambitious Sacred Service
for the Sabbath Evening. Occupying the entire
second half of the program, the work was designed
for concert performance rather than as an integral
part of a religious service. It employs a predominantly English text sung by chorus and baritone
soloist, supported by an orchestra and piano.

Ms. Zaimont is a thoroughly professional composer whose tonal style is both lyrical and dramatic. Her sonorities are somewhat reminiscent of
Stravinsky, Copland and Bloch. Most attractive
and original were the orchestral sections where
Ms. Zaimont's sensitivity to instrumental timbres
was beautifully demonstrated.

The performing forces were handled capably by
Mr. Rose. In particular, he elicited some lovely
sonorities from his orchestra assembled for the
occasion. The baritone soloist, Robert Shiesley,
sang pleasantly and accurately. (Reprinted by permission from The Great Neck Record.)

The first time Judith Lang Zaimont was asked how
she felt as a woman composer (when a guest on Listening
Room with host Robert Sherman) she said,

I didn't know what to say--I didn't realize then that
I was a "woman composer." After a brief pause,
I just said, "I am a composer and biologically I
happen to be a woman." After becoming educated
in the politics of the current musical establishment
however, I now feel it is probably helpful at this
particular time to be considered as representing
some special interest group. The music of women

composers has been generally neglected, and if
the opportunity to hear it is not provided then how
will anyone know whether it's good, bad, or in-
different? I'm not a great feminist but I have been
active in women's music organizations, and I am
exhilarated at all the activity going on with my sister composers. The quality of the work, and the
variety of "languages" being spoken by women is
so impressive that it cannot be ignored. If it's
useful at this point to group women composers together for programming or for scholarship purposes, in order to awaken general audience interest
in the repertoire, then for the time being, sure
let's do it.

In 1972, when Zaimont wrote The Chase for mixed chorus
and piano, she based it on a narrative poem she had written,
founded on Greek Mythology. The legend of Atalanta's race
tells of a maiden who refuses to marry unless her suitor
could outrun her; those suitors who tried and failed were
sentenced to death. The hero, Hippomenes, enters a race
with her and, during the race, drops three golden apples
along the path. Just as Atalanta stops to retrieve the apples,
he speeds by her and wins the race. Not so, however, in
Zaimont's own reinterpretation of the myth:

In my reading of The Chase, Hippomenes tries
three times with three golden apples to distract
the beautiful Atalanta, and she refuses to be dis-
tracted. After the third try he bemoans the fact
that he will lose the race--only then does Atalanta
catch his eye, smile, and stop voluntarily, thus
allowing him to win. As I see it, Atalanta made
a conscious decision to let him win. If she was
as sharp a lady as I think she was, this was the
way it really must have happened!

Zaimont spent five years of her young life (1973-
1978) writing A Calendar Set, her most widely performed
work. It is the most popular recording of the several discs
of her compositions available. (Leonarda Productions, Inc.
number LPI 101 Stereo). The FM Radio Stations in America
continually play this delightfully exciting recording performed
by Gary Steigerwalt, piano. Also included on the label are
Chansons Nobles et Sentimentales (1974) and Nocturne: La
Fin de Siècle (1978), performed by the composer. David
Moore comments in the American Record Guide, March 1980:

A new record company makes its debut with these
two discs of contemporary music, most of it by
less than wellknown contemporary composers.   In
a deliberate redress of the balance usually shown,
the majority of the composers and performers here
are women, and they make a fine showing as performers and/or composers.

Judith Zaimont (b. 1945) has amassed an impressive list of awards and recorded a choral disc on
Golden Crest.   The present works, mainly for
piano solo, show a sensitive, romantic temperament
with a healthy dash of dissonance and humor.   A
Calendar Set is a group of 12 preludes which not
only represent the months of the year, but were
written during the month described, a new twist.
They are attractive, demanding miniatures, played
with gusto and a variety of approach by Steigerwalt.   There are a couple of Ivesian melanges of
popular tunes for July and December, a difficult,
windy etude for October, ice for February, all
with quotations to further clarify the composer's
intent.   The set lasts 26 minutes and is never dull
or trivial, as Tschaikovsky's model sometimes
seems to be in the wrong hands.   These are the
right ones; both composer and interpreter serve
the cause well, and the recording is excellent.

Overside, the composer shows her own considerable ability as a pianist, accompanying the redoubt-
able Charles Bressler in an atmospheric song cycle
to five poems by Baudelaire, Verlaine, and Rimbaud, and performing a lyrical Nocturne in homage
to the French piano composers of the turn of the
century, Fauré, Debussy, Ravel, et al.   Since
the poets used in the song cycle were the composers' contemporaries the works chosen show careful planning.   Even the recorded sound changes for
the Nocturne; though the disc was entirely recorded
in Golden Auditorium at Queens College.   The Nocturne has a warmer sound, not entirely attributable
to Zaimont's touch, which is, however, plangent
and romantic.   This is a disc of evocative music,
excellently performed and recorded.   Bressler is
at his expressive best in the song cycle, and his
French is satisfyingly clear.   (Reprinted by permission of the author.)

In speaking of the Nocturne the composer notes:

This piece is my personal 'valentine' to the great
composer-pianists of the high Romantic age. It's
cast in three parts, slow, fast, slow and opens in
an uncertain A minor. The two outer selections
sound improvisatory with an arching, yet hesitant,
melody spun out above a harmonic bass that moves
in constant eighth-notes. By contrast, the mid-
section scurries darkly--quasi doppio movimemto--
rising to a series of sequential peaks, each of
which spills over and rapidly breaks apart. The
final peak dissipates in the high register, and the
eighth-notes slowly resume, bringing with them a
reprise of the opening material; the piece closes
in G# minor.

In an article written by Peter G. Davis in The New
York Times on June 7, 1981, titled "Pianos Still Stir Composers' Souls" he offers the following on A Calender Set
(partial):

Not all contemporary music written for solo piano
attempts to make the sort of earnest statements
that most of the above works strive for. One
curse that beset composers in the 1950's and 1960's
was the masterpiece syndrome--an ironic residue
from the Romantic age when every note on paper
had to be of cosmic significance. A lot of music
written today seeks only to charm the ear, instruct
the fingers and pass the time in an agreeable civi-
lized fashion.
    Judith Lang Zaimont would probably make no
extravagant claims for her A Calender Set, 12
preludes describing the months of the year (Leonarda LPI 101), but they are exquisitely crafted,
vividly characterized and wholly appealing. Gary
Steigerwalt plays them to perfection on this release,
which also contains Miss Zaimont's atmospheric
song cycle Chansons Nobles et Sentimentales sung
by Charles Bressler. The composer is the expert
pianist here and on the disk's envoi, Nocturne:
La Fin de Siècle, a personal valentine to the great
Romantic composer-pianists of the gilded age.
(Copyright © 1981 by The New York Times Company. Reprinted by permission.)

Judith Lang Zaimont's music is controlled and passionate at the same time, reflecting both her temperament

and her intellect.   She thrives on having great technical limitations imposed on her, compositionally speaking, and is
stimulated at the thought of extrapolating a good-sized musical work from two or three bits of material.

Most of her compositions are the result of commissions.   She usually works in conjuction with the commissioner to discuss and revamp certain ideas so that they are
equally valid for both the commissioner and herself.   Like
many of her contemporaries, she feels a commission that
includes performance, publication, and recording is a real
bonanza.

She is presently working on <u>Devilry</u>, a theater piece,
that includes lighting cues.   It is scored for eight solo
speaking voices, twelve choral voices, and eight tambourines.   Zaimont explains,

> I'm looking to expand my color palate and this
> piece is coloristically far beyond what I have writ-
> ten previously.   I am not yet looking to electronic
> sounds because I would rather squeeze the juice
> out of our traditional instruments and voices to get
> them to sound different or new.   That intrigues
> me most at the moment, and I consider it part of
> my growth cycle.

Another work concerned with the coloristic possibilities of percussion timbres and voice is <u>The Magic World:</u>
<u>Ritual Music for Three</u>, scored for bass-baritone, various
percussion instruments, and piano (keyboard and strings).
The texts are fragments and snippets that the composer chose
from English translations of American Indian poems, spells
and chants organized into a twenty-minute cycle of six songs.
Zaimont notes that "the texts alone exerted an enormously
hypnotic pull.   They have a spare, unique beauty all their
own--it was a long process to discover the appropriate musical setting for each of these terse, beautiful poems."   What
results is a composition bold and subtle by turns, the direct
and basic statements alternating with sections composed of
hints and suggestions only.

> The heart of the cycle is songs 2, 3, 4.   Song 2
> uses as text three delicate fragments, each trans-
> lated three times into English phrases of subtly
> differing meanings; the accompaniment is glocken-
> spiel, finger cymbals, and piano strings.   Song 3,
> "The Whirlwind," is appropriately tempestuous and

gusty, using tambourine, jingle bells, triangle, and vociferous keyboard figurations; Song 4, "Ghost Dance Song," steps out hypnotically in overlapping and shifting 'walking' rhythms for all three performers (keyboard, woodblocks, cowbells, claves).

Framing these three are songs 1 and 5, two versions of similar musical material using virtually the same text. Song 6 begins with quotations from actual Indian songs (in three different meters, three different tempi, all overlapping) using tubular bells, hand-held tom-tom and keyboard, followed by a brief reprise of the music of song 1, and closes with a floating coda punctuated by the Chinese bell-tree. As a whole the cycle resembles a shell, or similar natural formation, that serenely, securely folds back in upon itself.

All artists are not humanists, but Judith Lang Zaimont certainly is, as has been noted many times over the past years. She has often expressed her concern for the manner in which music is taught in the United States. In her opinion, it would be more important to stress the music of the present time to children when they are young and have open ears, then gradually introduce them to Chopin and Mozart. She is concerned that music is basically thought of as a "museum" art by the general public, not a living, evolving art. In her view, the composer as a craftsperson should begin to work with the materials of his/her craft on a regular basis, as soon as theory studies are well under way. For example, every individual who studies an instrument should be encouraged to write a little music, to explore, to create different musical environments and textures, and to develop mood. Zaimont's ideas and suggestions are worthy of consideration, for indeed, many of our American composers have been deprived of their musical birthrights. Is it still necessary for young composers to go to Europe for training that could essentially be obtained in their own country?

Composer Judith Lang Zaimont emerges in the 1980's as a brilliant young artist. Her compositional skills project a freshness and excitement that have indeed been recognized and make a strong imprint on American twentieth-century music. She is an impressive artist who possesses an abundance of creative talent that will continue to flourish and produce compositions of lasting value. One cannot predict her place on the roster of American composers; essentially only time and continued performance and recordings will establish this position. However, based on past accomplishments, one can predict that she will surely be on the roster.

List of Compositions

[Selected works are available from the American Music Center, 250 West 54th Street, Room 300, New York, N. Y. 10019]

Chamber and Solo Instrumental Works

1967   Two Movements for Wind Quartet, flute, oboe, horn, and bassoon.
1970   Grand Tarantella, for violin and piano.
1971   Capriccio, for solo flute.
1971   Trumpet and Piano Sonata.
1971   Music for Two, for any two treble wind instruments.
1972   Valse Romantique, for solo flute.
1980- De Infinitate Caeleste (Of the Celestial Infinite), for
82   string quartet.

Solo Piano Works

1976   Calendar Collection, 12 prelude-etudes, published by Alfred Publishing Co. , Inc.
1973- A Calendar Set, 12 Preludes, published by Leonarda
78   Productions, Inc.
1974   Judy's Rag, published by Tetra Music Corp.
1961   Portrait of a City, suite in 5 movements.
1974   Reflective Rag, published by Tetra Music Corp.
1977   Solitary Pipes, published by Yorktown Music Press in The Joy of Modern Piano Pieces.
1979   Sweet Daniel.
1981   Stone.
1968   Toccata.
1966   White-Key Waltz.

Piano, Four-Hands

1972   Snazzy Sonata.

Solo Instrument With Orchestra

1972   Concerto for Piano and Orchestra, written with a Debussy Fellowship from Alliance Française de New York. Available through the Fleisher Collection, Philadelphia.

Vocal Works

1971   The Ages of Love, 5 songs for baritone voice and

piano. Composed while a MacDowell Colony Fellow, published by American Composers Alliance.

1974   Chansons Nobles et Sentimentales, 5 songs for high voice and piano to texts of Baudelaire, Verlaine, and Rimbaud; commissioned by Michael Trimble, Cleveland Institute of Music; published by American Composers Alliance.

1970   Coronach, 5 songs for soprano voice and piano.

1965   Four Songs for Mezzo-Soprano and Piano, (e. e. cummings).

1975   Greyed Sonnets, 5 songs to texts of women poets, for soprano voice and piano; first song published by Galaxy Music Corp. Available from American Composers Alliance Library.

1980   High Flight, high voice and piano, (John G. Magee, Jr.).

1978- The Magic World, 6 songs to American Indian texts,
79   for solo bass voice, piano, and percussion.

1974   Songs of Innocence, 4 songs to texts of Blake, for soprano and tenor voices, flute, violincello, and harp; commissioned by Gregg Smith.

1978   Two Songs for Soprano and Harp, commissioned by the New York State Music Teachers Association.

1977   A Woman of Valor, for mezzo soprano voice and string quartet; commissioned by Cantica Hebraica; published by American Composers Alliance.

1978   Psalm 23, for bass-baritone, flute, violin, cello, piano.

Choral Works

1972   The Chase, for mixed chorus and piano. Text: a narrative poem by the composer; commissioned by Great Neck Choral Society.

1968   Man's Image and His Cry, for solo baritone and alto voices, chorus, and orchestra.

1975   Moses Supposes, 3-part Canon for treble voices and percussion; published by Tetra Music Corporation.

1976   Sacred Service for the Sabbath Evening, for solo baritone voice, chorus, and orchestra; commissioned by Great Neck Choral Society for the Bicentennial; Orchestrated as a MacDowell Colony Fellow, with a Composer's Assistance Grant from the American Music Center; published by Galaxy Music Corp.

1974   Sunny Airs and Sober, 5 madrigals for chorus, a cappella; commissioned by Waldorf Singers; published by Walton Music Corp.

1979   The Tragickal Ballad of Sir Patric Spens, SSAATTBB, piano.

1966   They flee from me ..., for flute solo and mixed chorus.

1969   Three Ayres, for mixed chorus, a cappella; commissioned by Great Neck Choral Society; published by Broude Bros., Ltd.

Works in Progress

String Quartet, Commissioned by the Primavera String Quartet.

Wind Quintet, Commissioned by the Prevailing Winds.

Devilry, for 12 voices and eight tambourines.

Trio, for flute, oboe, and cello; commissioned by the Huntingdon Trio.

Addresses of Publishers

Alfred Publishing Co., 15335 Morrison Street, Sherman Oaks, CA 91403

American Composers Alliance, 170 West 74th Street, New York, NY 10023

Broude Brothers Ltd., 170 Varick Street, New York, NY 10013

Galaxy Music Corp., 2121 Broadway, New York, NY 10023

Tetra Music Corp., 225 West 57th St., New York, NY 10019

Walton Music Corp., c/o Lorenz, Box 802, 501 East 3rd Street, Dayton, Ohio 45401

Yorktown Music Press, 33 West 60th Street, New York, NY 10023

Edwin A. Fleisher Collection, The Free Library of Philadelphia, Logan Square, Philadelphia, PA 19103

Available Recordings

Three Ayres, (SSATB) published by Broude Brothers, Ltd.; recorded on Golden Crest ATH 5051 by the Gregg Smith Singers.

Sunny Airs and Sober, (SSAATTBB) published by Walton Music
      Corp.; recorded on Golden Crest ATH 5051 by the
      Gregg Smith Singers.
Greyed Sonnets, soprano and piano published by American
      Composers Alliance; recorded on Golden Crest ATH
      5051, Elaine Olbrycht, soprano and J. L. Zaimont,
      piano.
Songs of Innocence, soprano, tenor, flute, cello and harp
      available through the Edwin A. Fleisher Collection of
      the Free Library of Philadelphia, recorded on Golden
      Crest ATH 5051 by Elaine Olbrycht, Price Browne,
      Pat Spencer, Barbara Bogatin, Nancy Allen, Roger
      Nierenberg, conductor.
Chansons Nobles et Sentimentales, high voice and piano pub-
      lished by American Composers Alliance; recorded on
      Leonarda Production LPI 101 stereo.
Nocturne: La Fin de Siècle, solo piano, published by Galaxy
      Music Corp.; recorded on Leonarda Productions LPI
      101 stereo, J. L. Zaimont, piano.
A Calendar Set, published by Leonarda Productions, Inc.;
      recorded on Leonarda Productions LPI 101 stereo,
      Gary Steigerwalt, piano.
Two Songs for Soprano and Harp, recorded on Leonarda Pro-
      ductions LPI 106 stereo, Berenice Bramson, soprano,
      Sara Cutler, harp.

Addresses of Recording Companies

Golden Crest, 220 Broadway, Huntington Station, New York,
      NY 11746

Leonarda Productions, Inc., P. O. Box 124, Radio City Sta-
      tion, New York, NY 10019

ELLEN TAAFFE ZWILICH

Composer, Musician

In 1975 the Juilliard School conferred its first doctorate degree in composition to a woman, thus ending the sacrosanct myth of the male composer. The recipient was the vibrant and gifted composer-musician, Ellen Taaffe Zwilich. The nurture of a creative mind is an elusive process that combines unexpected as well as effective elements that help the artist to communicate feelings and emotions. If one admires talent and capacity, then one will thoroughly enjoy the music of Ellen Zwilich.

She was born in Miami, Florida, on April 30, 1939, and adopted by Ruth (Howard) and Edward Taaffe. Since her father was a pilot, the family enjoyed many exciting escapades during her childhood. She said,

> My parents were wonderful people, although they
> were not musicians and didn't quite know what to
> do with me at times. There was a piano in my
> home which I discovered before I learned to walk
> and I spent a good part of my childhood at the
> piano, improvising and making up pieces. This
> seemed to me as natural an activity as breathing.
> At some point I made a transition and began to
> notate what I was inventing.

Her first music teacher was a neighborhood piano teacher, but it was not until she was thirteen years old that she found her first really inspiring music teacher. He was Bower Murphy, a trumpet teacher, who was not only well-versed in the technique of his instrument but also helpful in encouraging his students to transpose, to learn the orchestral repertoire, and to perform chamber music. He would write a special etude for the student who was having a particular technical problem. He also encouraged the young Ellen in her composition; she considered him a model of the

working musician. Later in life she would dedicate her
Clarino Quartet for trumpet, to his memory.

She attended Coral Gables High School, where she
served as concertmistress of orchestra and played trumpet in the band. She also functioned as student conductor
for both the band and orchestra and wrote arrangements for
the band. In her senior year at Coral Gables High School,
she won the Amidon Award as the outstanding music student.

Following high school, she attended Florida State University where, once again, she advanced to concertmistress
of the University Symphony and first trumpet in the Symphonic Band. During her years at FSU she also played a
great deal of chamber music (including solo violin recitals),
performed as a violin soloist with the orchestra, and heard
performances of her chamber music and works for the Symphonic Band, the FSU Symphony, and the Tallahassee Symphony. As an undergraduate, she received three prizes from
the Florida Composers League--for a sonatina for trumpet
and piano, a string quartet, and an orchestral work.

After receiving her master's degree from FSU in
composition, with a minor in humanities, she moved to New
York City where she studied violin with Sally Thomas and
Ivan Galamian. Here she had considerable professional ex-
perience as a violinist. She was a member of the American
Symphony Orchestra under Leopold Stokowski for seven years.
Zwilich describes the audition that was required for member-
ship in the orchestra:

> Stokowski had compiled his own set of audition books
> for each instrument of the orchestra. He included
> a number of "thorny" orchestral excerpts to test
> the technical capabilities of the auditioner as well
> as the sensitivity to style and familiarity with the
> orchestral repertoire. He would also stop you in
> the middle of a phrase and ask what key you were
> in. Although it was not of the modern behind-the-
> screen variety, I thought "Stokey" gave a good au-
> dition.

During the years that Ellen Taaffe Zwilich played with
the American Symphony Orchestra, she recalled, "I always
felt that playing in an orchestra was an immeasurably valuable experience for me as a composer, primarily because
I don't believe you can learn music in a passive way. There
are so many things about music that a composer can only
learn by performing. Then, too, we had many excellent con-

Whitestone Photo/Heinz H. Weissenstein

ELLEN TAAFFE ZWILICH

ductors, so I had the opportunity to observe first-hand many
different perspectives on music." Besides Stokowski, the
long list of distinguished conductors under whom she played
included Ernest Ansermet, Karl Böhm, Eugen Jochum, Paul
Kletzki, Aram Khachaturian, Igor Markevitch, Yehudi Menuhin, André Previn, and Gunther Schuller.

While she was playing in the American Symphony Orchestra, she decided to study composition further. She ap-

plied to the Juilliard School because they had an outstanding
and diversified composition department. During her time at
Juilliard the composition faculty included Roger Sessions,
Elliott Carter, Milton Babbitt, Otto Luening, David Diamond,
and Vincent Persichetti. "All of my teachers were important
to me, but especially Roger Sessions with whom I studied
the longest, and Elliott Carter, with whom I worked for a
short but significant period of time." Her experience at
Juilliard and her philosophy is:

> Going to Juilliard represented a full commitment
> to do what I wanted to do most of all--to write
> and to grow as a composer. There is so much
> to learn! Happily, composition is something that
> can never be completely mastered (consider the
> fact that Mahler, with all his experience as a com-
> poser and conductor, was constantly revising!).
>   My central concern in composition at that time
> was finding my own voice. I think I write because
> of an inner need to express and develop something
> very personal, and the people I studied with en-
> couraged me to move in my own directions.

Although the history of women's music has documented
many cases over the past decades of outright refusal and rejection of women applying to departments of composition for
admission, Zwilich was accepted into the doctoral program
in composition at Juilliard. She said, "Although there are
still individuals whose prejudice against women artists is
deeply rooted, I think that the general outlook and opportunities for women have improved greatly in the past ten years
or so. (I might also point out that Roger Sessions taught
Miriam Gideon and Vivian Fine at a time when some people
scoffed at the idea of a woman composer.)" Zwilich received the Rogers and Hammerstein Award Scholarship as
well as annual honorary scholarships from Juilliard. She
also received the Marion Freschl Prize three times and the
Elizabeth Sprague Coolidge Chamber Music Prize from Juilliard.

Each composer develops a unique synthesis of her
own experience, and performing is central to the way Zwilich
thinks about music. "I always have a strong image of my
music as it will sound in performance. I believe a composer
should be very well-informed and skilled in numerous composition techniques, but the primary focus should be on how
something sounds and works in performance. For me, music
is a very intense form of human communication and the live

performance is at the center of the composer, performer,
and listener's experience." Whatever her theories may be,
the listener is immediately aware of the incredible beauty
found in her music.

"My String Quartet (1974) is the result of my deep
feelings for the quartet literature, probably the most magnificent body of music there is. There are also certain
attitudes I find in quartet literature that motivated me, for
example, the concept of four equal partners engaged in a
virtuosic dialogue. I love the feeling one gets from the great
quartets of a transfer of electricity from one player to another."

Her String Quartet was selected for performance in
the International Society for Contemporary Music "World
Music Days" in 1976. It was premièred in Boston by the
New York String Quartet. The ISCM "World Music Days"
was founded in 1922 and represents thirty-two member countries in Europe, the Americas, and the Far East. The
festival has been held yearly since that time except for the
years of World War II. Wherever held in a particular year,
the festival week of concerts offers the opportunity to hear
music reflective of present day trends that has been selected
by an international jury. It is an honor to be selected, for
only a small percentage of the compositions submitted are
accepted. It was a double honor for Zwilich, since she was
the only woman composer presented in the 1976 series, a
series which programmed music from some twenty-eight
countries.

For the first time in the history of the ISCM, the
performances were held in the United States. The enormous
cost of presenting the festival was supported by the Bicentennial Fund, with grants from the Fromm Music Foundation,
long respected for its support of contemporary music, and
the National Endowment for the Arts. Credit for making
the festival a reality belongs to many people, but special
mention goes to Hubert Howe Jr., president of the United
States section of ISCM, conductor Gunther Schuller of the
New England Conservatory of Music, and Nancy Barry. National Public Radio broadcast the entire series and taped it
for re-broadcast at later dates.

The enormity of reviewing throughout the week some
ten to twelve concerts is not an easy task. The concerts
included between fifty and sixty pieces, many of them premières. One must wonder, and occasionally doubt, the musi-

cal stamina of several of the critics whose anxiety over
coping with the responsibility was obvious in the reading of
their reviews.

Perhaps it was too much to expect music critics to
listen to the entire festival, but in what other manner could
a judgment be reached on which compositions would have
lasting value and continue to be performed?   How pleased
composer Zwilich must have been when numerous critics
singled out her work as one of the highlights of the entire
festival.

Ellen Taaffe Zwilich's String Quartet received plaudits
from many music critics, including Allen Hughes and Donal
Henahan of The New York Times.   The following excerpt of
a review by Leighton Kerner on November 15, 1976, is from
the Village Voice:

> WORLD MUSIC DAYS: UP FROM THE WASTE-
> BASKET
>
> An international law should be passed requiring all
> festivals of contemporary music to hang large signs
> proclaiming to performers and audiences:
>
> "Better Far To Have Living Music By Dead Com-
> posers Than Dead Music By Living Composers."
>
> The idea struck me halfway through the third
> concert of the 13 that constituted the International
> Society of Contemporary Music's 1976 World Music
> Days, held in Boston October 24 through October
> 30....   And all three works sounded like composi-
> tion exercises found in a wastebasket in a Viennese
> classroom recently unlocked for the first time in
> forty years.
> Half the music in the ISCM festival's first two
> concerts, given the previous day, had seemed
> similarly suggestive of dust and mice.   And as
> the afternoon and evening concerts passed into the
> archives, and as other musicians, from Boston,
> New York, and points west, took the stage of the
> New England Conservatory's venerable Jordan Hall,
> that Viennese wastebasket seemed bottomless.
> But "damn it" is easily said: even the dullest
> of the week's concerts has at least one item to
> wake the mind and entertain the ear, and--one rip-
> off from Hamlet deserves another--there's the rub.

Some of those doldrum cures were actually descendants, to varying degree, of that very Second Viennese School of Schoenberg where our bottomless wastebasket was found.

Other good music had a decidedly mainstream feeling, as if composed not in the Schoenberg tradition but in one of the many respectful reactions that have flowered on both sides of the Atlantic. Such were a String Quartet by Ellen Zwilich and Echoes and Anticipation, a chamber concerto for oboe by Ezra Laderman. Both New York composers had found fresh things to say in musical styles much nearer than far-out. The quartet grew naturally from a violin solo, yet the increase in conversational activity never distorted the smooth shape of the entire work.

From the Boston Evening Globe for November 1, 1976, here is a partial review by Richard Dyer:

A MUDDLED FINALE TO MUSIC DAYS

Much happier memories were left by the afternoon concert, which featured the Collage Contemporary Ensemble and the New York String Quartet ... Wolf won the largest personal ovation of the festival.

Almost as much applause went to Ellen Taaffe Zwilich for her String Quartet--and to the New York String Quartet that played it so well. Her piece is original structually, full of imaginative sonorities and contrasts of sonority, worked out in a most craftsmanlike way, gracefully written for the instruments. It has the striking qualities of the new, and the solidity of something that has been there all along. It was, in short, music. (Reprinted courtesy of The Boston Globe.)

The Patriot Ledger (Quincy, Mass.) November 4, 1976, a review by David Noble stated in part:

SPECIAL MOMENTS FROM THE WORLD MUSIC DAYS

Thirteen concerts performed within the same week, encompassing 66 pieces of contemporary music by composers from 28 countries--this is still a formidable mass of experience to evaluate, even as

one looks back at it from the distance of half a
week.

Saturday afternoon was another American day,
with players from the Boston group Collage doing
lovely things with music by Donald Sur, Jacob
Druckman, and Ezra Laderman.

The most memorable event of that afternoon,
however, was the String Quartet by Ellen Taaffe
Zwilich, a student of Elliott Carter, played by the
New York String Quartet. Zwilich emerged in this
piece as very much her own composer, one of the
brave ones in the emerging area of transition shock
--or perhaps I should say direct motion. (Reprinted
by permission of The Patriot Ledger.)

The String Quartet, published by Margun Music, Inc., was
subsequently performed in New York in Alice Tully Hall, in
the League of Composers/ISCM series in Carnegie Recital
Hall, and in the 1977 Aspen Music Festival in Aspen, Colorado. Zwilich received the Elizabeth Sprague Coolidge Chamber Music Prize for this quartet in 1974. It was recently
recorded for Cambridge Records No. CRS 2834 by the New
York String Quartet, under a grant from the Martha Baird
Rockefeller Fund for Music. The following program notes
were written by the composer to be used when programming
the String Quartet (I: Maestoso, II: Allegro moderato e
vigoroso, III: Lento e tranquillo, and IV: Rapsodico):

String Quartet (1974) is in four movements, of
which the first serves as a prologue and the fourth
as an epilogue to the piece as a whole. The two
inner movements explore contrasting facets of string
playing; the second movement is dominated by material of a marked and vigorous character; the
third movement is predominantly lyrical.

All the basic materials of the piece (including
thematic fragments to be developed in the second
and third movements) are introduced in the first
movement. The quartet opens with an extended
statement for violin I alone. In the course of the
work each player has an individual response to the
initial material; the work comes to a close after
a rhapsodic variation for the cello in the fourth
movement.

The formal structure of all four movements
might best be described as a fluid process of evolution of the musical materials. Further, the four
individual movements are parts of a larger design,

forming, in essence, a single movement. The
work is also motivated by the drama inherent in
a conversation among four equals.

Composer Zwilich's orchestral talents were revealed
in her piece for full orchestra, titled Symposium, written in
1972-1973. Dedicated to Pierre Boulez, Symposium received
its world première under his baton in 1975. Boulez presented it with the Juilliard Orchestra in Alice Tully Hall in
one of two Special Concerts of New Music.

According to the composer the première was

an exciting and wonderful performance. Boulez
was in marvelous form and I couldn't ask for more
understanding or enthusiam than his performance
demonstrated. Also, Boulez feels it is important
for the composer to engage in some kind of encounter with the audience so that listeners can better
relate to new music. He decided that, since Symposium is such a virtuoso piece, we should "rehearse" parts of it in front of the audience before
the performance, exchanging ideas with each other
and the musicians. I think he is correct in trying
to bring the audience closer to the composer and
the music.

One would readily agree with Boulez and Zwilich that
there is indeed a void between the contemporary composer
and the audience that needs and deserves attention and action.
Boulez has been an advocate of better communication between
audience and new music throughout his entire career. He
joins other contemporary musical leaders at a propitious
time in American music, for we now enjoy a two-way street
with the flow of musical influence between the United States
and Europe. It is important to foster a better communication through analytical program notes, lectures with composers, conductors, and musicians discussing unfamiliar
pieces that will continue to promote independence.

Following the premiere of Symposium, it was subsequently designated an official United States entry for the
International Society for Contemporary Music "World Music
Days" in Paris. It was also performed in 1978 in Carnegie
Hall by the American Symphony Orchestra under the direction
of Kazuyoshi Akiyama; the concert was recorded for broadcast over the Voice of America. Symposium is available on
rental from Theodore Presser Company. The following are

excerpts from reviews of the première and the Carnegie Hall performance:

Andrew Porter, in the February 10, 1975, New Yorker, wrote: "Paul Alan Levi's Symphonic Movement and Ellen Taaffe Zwilich's Symposium are both coherent, soundly planned structures that hold the attention."

Another appeared in the Westsider on February 6, 1975, by William Zakariasen (partial):

THE BAD NEW DAYS

Pierre Boulez conducted three considerably shorter new works at the Juilliard Orchestra concert Friday night. Most of the time was spent in having the composers speak of their compositions to the audience while Boulez conducted examples of it. This worked best with the Symposium for orchestra by Ellen Taaffe Zwilich (wife of a veteran violinist with the Met Opera Orchestra), where she sensibly, and at times humorously, showed the extreme difficulty of her writing by having parts of the orchestra rehearse certain spots several times. This made more sense than the metaphysical explanations given by the other composers, and her work to boot was the best on the program. Symposium is quite Mahlerian--the sort of thing that composer might have written had he lived longer--it's steady, superbly-orchestrated crescendo of intensity marred by an unsatisfying inconclusive ending. Unlike Feldman, Mrs. Zwilich seems to underestimate her talents. (Reprinted by permission from The Westsider.)

In a review by Andrew Derhen in High Fidelity/Musical America (September 1978) we read:

AMERICAN SYMPHONY (AKIYAMA)

The title Symposium for orchestra hardly suggests a rip-roaring musical entertainment. As one might suspect, this recent composition by Ellen Taaffe Zwilich which was performed by the American Symphony Orchestra under Kazuyoshi Akiyama at Carnegie Hall on May 21 has an academic flavor to it. Mrs. Zwilich, a Floridian who studied at Juilliard, obviously has absorbed the intricacies of textbook

atonality as well as the work of such cerebral
figures as Roger Sessions and Elliot Carter, both
of whom have been her mentors. If her piece
suffers from lack of individual profile, it nevertheless does realize the intention implied in its title
of giving each player "something of particular interest to contribute," and there is sufficient variety
of tempo, texture, and dynamics to hold interest
through its twelve-minute length. (Excerpted from
High Fidelity/Musical America by permission.
All rights reserved.)

The Daily News, Tuesday, May 23 1978 carried a
review by Bill Zakariasen (partial):

Though Kazuyoshi Akiyama will be guest conductor
of the American Symphony Orchestra next season,
Sunday's concert was his last appearance as music
director (Sergiu Commissiona takes over in July
as director in every way but name). The orchestra
played better than sometimes in the past, and the
program was spiced with a couple of novelties.
    Ellen Taaffe Zwilich's Symposium for Orchestra
is a strong, well-organized study in sonority, and
it was good to hear it again, even if in its 1975
world première Pierre Boulez and the Juilliard
Orchestra gave it more tension. (Copyright © 1978
New York News, Inc. Reprinted by permission.)

Composer Zwilich wrote the following notes on the
sonorous twelve-minute work. "The piece is a one movement work for virtuoso orchestra, in which, as the title suggests, each player is viewed as having something of particular interest to contribute. The 'topic' under discussion is
presented in an opening statement, and the remainder of the
piece is given to various (sometimes character variations,
sometimes more abstract permutations) elaboration, and commentary on the subjects at hand."

Tragedies leave one sensitive to the beauties of the
world. When two people have shared an extensive and rewarding artistic life, as well as the mundane concerns for
daily living, it was an unfathomable experience when death
silently and swiftly shattered this unique marriage. The
passing in 1979 of her husband, Joseph Zwilich, brilliant
Hungarian-American violin virtuoso, brought to a close a
beautiful and inspiring relationship for Ellen Taaffe Zwilich
and saddened hundreds of music lovers and admirers.

A glimpse into the artistic career of Joseph and Ellen Taaffe Zwilich can be traced through her piece, Sonata in Three Movements for Violin and Piano written in 1973. She recounted,

> It was written for my husband who first performed the work on a tour of European capitals in 1973. Writing for the violin has a special meaning for me, and this work grew out of my feelings for Joseph, as well as my special fondness for the violin; it was my own instrument. I wanted to explore, in modern terms, the wonderfully dramatic and expressive powers of the violin. The work is cast in three movements of which the first is the most complex, with contrast between lyrical and marked thematic material and contrast between relatively free recitative-like material (culminating in a cadenza for violin) and the otherwise strict tempi. The second movement is slow, lyrical; the third is short, fast, and rhythmically propulsive.

Fortunately the piece was recorded by Joseph and pianist James Gemmell when it was premièred in New York. It is available from Cambridge Records No. CRS-2834, and published by Theodore Presser Company. In 1975 Sonata in Three Movements received a gold medal in the twenty-sixth Annual Composition Competition, "G. B. Viotti," in Vercelli, Italy.

From scores of reviews written in Germany, Belgium, Italy, and Australia, the following two, from Holland and England, have been selected:

> Yesterday evening a violin recital was given by the American violinist Joseph Zwilich, assisted at the piano by Michael Isador. The program was opened by the Sonata in D Major by Antonio Vivaldi. A work, which was interpreted by Joseph Zwilich in an extremely fine way.
> This also was the case in Sonata No. 3 in D minor by Johannes Brahms, a clean and clear performance by the violinist. After the intermission the two artists continued the program with the Sonata in Three Movements, a very contemporary work by Ellen Taaffe Zwilich. This composition in three movements was composed from very complicated figurations, extremely difficult for the

violinist. Also here, Joseph Zwilich proved his ability by a virtuoso realization in cooperation with Michael Isador. Nigun by Ernst Bloch, Melody by Gluck-Kreisler were the popular notes the program offered, followed by a Hungarian Dance by Kreisler. Here Zwilich showed his Hungarian origin, by a very temperamental interpretation of this sparkling work.

Finally we heard Copland's Hoe Down, with which the concert ended. (Reprinted by permission from Dagblad Voor West-Friesland, April 26, 1973.)

VIOLINIST SHOWS HIS SKILL

Recital by Joseph Zwilich--Reld School of Music

The Hungarian-born American violinist made his Edinburgh debut last night following his 1972 European engagements.

Like all well-established players of class he must be judged in the reaches beyond technique and on that score he demonstrated in first-half Vivaldi (Sonata in D) and Brahms (Sonata in D minor) that he possesses a vivid and colourful outlook backed by power and delicacy.

He also has an attractive and talented wife, who was present as he gave the first performance-- faithful and skills at that--of her Sonata (1973), written one might say, with his special leanings very much in mind.

And that, together with Nigun by Bloch and a trio of party pieces completed this most pleasant recital that received much benefit from the unfailingly musical accompaniments of Michael Isador. (Reprinted by permission of the Associated Newspapers Group, Ltd.)

Sonata in Three Movements was chosen for inclusion on the 1980 competition list for string players in the Kennedy Center-Rockefeller International Competition. This competition is intended to stimulate a greater interest in recital music written by American composers since 1900; each year it features a competition for pianists, singers, or string players. It is an honor to have one's music chosen and listed in the repertoire, for it assures performances and brings the literature to the attention of performers, teachers, and students.

In 1979 Boston Musica Viva, conducted by Richard
Pittman, commissioned Zwilich to write a chamber piece
for them.   The group has long championed the cause of contemporary music and has premièred many important twentieth-
century works.   Zwilich was writing Chamber Symphony for
this group when her husband died.   She said, "I had written
quite a bit of the work before Joe's death, but when I was
finally able to write again, I felt so totally different that I
couldn't write the same piece I planned.   Though I did use
some of the basic material, it evolved in a very different
way."

The composer's program notes are as follows:

Scored for flute doubling piccolo, clarinet doubling
bass clarinet, violin, viola, cello and piano, the
work is cast in a single movement which evolves
from the initial material.   Perhaps the most significant formal process in the piece is the development of long lines from shorter ideas.   The character transformation that occurs in the course of
thematic and motivic evolution is also of formal
importance.   In Chamber Symphony the 'orchestration' also contributes to the shape and meaning of
the work.   I sought both to exploit the solo capabilities of each instrument and to contrast that with
the use of doublings and other devices to achieve
an almost orchestral sound.
   For me, however, the ultimate meaning of this
Chamber Symphony is in connection with the fact
that it was written not long after the sudden death
of my husband, violinist Joseph Zwilich.

There are a number of feelings that can't be fully
orchestrated since they are psychological, but they can be
implied and thus shared with the listener.   Although Zwilich's
Chamber Symphony is singly a beautiful and stimulating piece
of music, it can perhaps be even more readily identified, in
a subconscious manner, by those whose lives have been
voided through death.   It vividly describes the struggle of
the survivor, the dreams and aspirations that are crushed in
a wave of grief, followed by the personal effort and strength
needed to pursue one's identity.

Richard Buell, for The Boston Globe, reviewed the
première on December 3, 1979:

MUSICA VIVA'S STRANGE MIXTURE

There was a strong feeling of polarization to this
program by the Boston Musica Viva, containing as
it did a pair of works (by Seymour Shifrin and
Pierre Boulez) whose strategies of discourse could
hardly fail to summon up resistance in the listener,
pitted against one (by Ellen Taaffe Zwilich) that
made a direct appeal to near-traditional notions of
coherence, sentiment and instrumental beauty.   It
all added up to a strange sort of sandwich, did
this concert.

The audience response to the Zwilich Chamber
Symphony (1979) was unusually warm, spontaneous
and prolonged by the new-music concert standards,
and the reason was right there in the music. Long-
lined and predominantly elegiac in tone, here was
a piece that convinced you at once that it was directly imagined for the instruments (flute, clarinet,
violin, viola, cello and piano) that were to be playing it.   It made sonorous good sense not only with
its chamber-musical byplay and its orchestral resonance but with its daring, un-modish use of big,
open unisons and such effect-laden markings as
"cantabile" and "molto tranquillo."   It wouldn't be
either easy or helpful here to try to peg the piece
--a reckless or unkind person might say "feminist
Shostakovich"; certainly it was odd to hear, in
conductor Richard Pittman's introductory remarks
that he did not wish to imply that the Chamber Symphony was tonal music, its A major-minor beginning and end notwithstanding.   Away with such ob-
fuscation--Ellen Zwilich's Chamber Symphony demands to be heard in performance, speaking for
itself.   Manifestly, it is music that can take care
of itself.

Though the Musica Viva's performance of the
Zwilich was quite sound and sturdy enough, it was
also one to make you suspect that these players
can be a bit wary and awkward with music whose
emotional content lies close to the surface or has
a strong, insistent pulse (this being particularly
true of their Copland).   Therefore, presumably
their extra measure of devotion to the microscopic
particularities of Boulez's Le Marteau sans Maître
and to Seymour Shifrin's The Nick of Time, a work
that struck these ears as labored, dour and uninter-
esting.   Adelle-Nicholson was the buxom-sounding

and reasonably fleet mezzo in the former; the latter
came off brushed, balanced and orderly.   But truth
to tell, one would have had to come to this concert
already caring, and caring deeply, for these two
pieces to matter very much as anything other than
intricately patterned sonic stimuli.   But for the
Ellen Zwilich première--much thanks.   (Reprinted
by courtesy of The Boston Globe.)

In the Boston Herald American, December 3, 1979,
Ellen Pfeifer wrote:

ZWILICH'S NEW SYMPHONY RICH IN MUSICAL
IDEALS

In its Friday night performance, the Boston Musica
Viva continued its admirable practice of performing
both established 20th-century classics and promoting
the creation of new works.   The concert at the
Longy School in Cambridge featured the premier of
Ellen Taaffe Zwilich's Chamber Symphony and Pierre
Boulez' Le Marteau sans Maître.
    Commissioned by Musica Viva and conductor
Richard Pittman, Zwilich's very beautiful work
was written during a period of mourning for her
husband, who died last summer.   And it is tinged
with the sadness of that time.
    Scored for violin, viola, cello, flute, clarinet
and piano, the Chamber Symphony evolves from
A-major/minor harmonies.   And the atmosphere
throughout is decidely romantic, with long, long
melodic lines, intense emotional warmth, delicately
beautiful combinations of instrumental colors, even
some almost 19th-century roulades for the piano.
    This is not to suggest that the writing is mind-
lessly'or cynically retrospective.   Rather this
thoroughly contemporary work shows that there
are still rich possibilities in the traditional musical ideals of expressivity, direct communication
and thorough craftsmanship.   (Reprinted by permission from the Boston Herald American.)

Besides Boston, the Chamber Symphony has been
heard in the following places: New York City, Cleveland,
Chicago, Pittsburgh, Florida, Yugoslavia, Hungary, Spain,
Germany, Portugal (at the Gulbenkian Festival), Bulgaria,
(on Sofia television), and London (for BBC broadcast).   Chamber Symphony is published by Theodore Presser Company and

recorded on Cambridge Records No. CRS-2834 by the Boston
Musica Viva with Richard Pittman, conductor, under a grant
from the Martha Baird Rockefeller Fund for Music.

Music by Ellen Taaffe Zwilich has been heard frequently on New York radio stations WQXR, WNYC, and WNCN;
on WCLV in Cleveland; and WGBH and WCRB in Boston.   In
a radio series called Speaking of Music, produced by the
American Music Center for distribution by National Public
Radio, Zwilich was chosen to be one of the three composers
featured on the broadcast, "The Young American Composer."

Zwilich's Clarino Quartet, written in 1977, was premièred in March 1979 in St. Paul by the Minnesota Orchestra's trumpet section.   In addition, the piece was chosen
for performance in the 1979 Festival of Contemporary Music
at Tanglewood, Lenox, Massachusetts.   This was indeed an
honor for Zwilich, since this festival is internationally acclaimed and recognized.   In 1981 the Clarino Quartet was
performed in Paris by the Pierre Thibaud Ensemble.   The
Minnesota première was reviewed for High Fidelity/Musical
America in July 1979:

MINN. BRASS: ZWILICH PREMIERE

The renaissance of interest in Baroque music has
led to renewed enthusiasm for the clarino style of
high trumpet playing that died out toward the end
of the eighteenth century, and a few contemporary
composers have begun to include clarino parts in
their music.   Among them is Ellen Taaffe Zwilich,
whose engaging Clarino Quartet for B-flat piccolo,
D, C, and B-flat trumpets was given its première
March 4 at Hamline University, St. Paul, by members of the Minnesota Orchestra trumpet section.
    The quartet is cast in three compact movements:
the first Maestoso/allegro vivo, brisk and bitingly
disonant; the second Largo, contrastingly placid;
and third, Veloce, highly syncopated and full of
phrase fragments tossed so quickly among the players that the overall effect is of vivid musical pointillism.   The quartet's formidable difficulties include a piccolo trumpet part which lies mainly in
the clarino register.   At one point the clarino player is asked to produce a blistering high F-sharp,
and four measures of high F, enough to discourage
all but the most secure virtuosos.   Zwilich, a
Florida native who now lives in New York, gives

substantial, important roles to the other three instruments, allowing each timbre opportunity for
display.   There's a constant variety of tone, con-
sequently--reminiscent of fine string quartet writing.
     The able performers, appearing as guest artists
on a program of the Minnesota Brass Quintet, were
Charles Schlueter, Clement Volpe, Ronald Hassel-
mann, and Merrimon Hipps, Jr. Schlueter, principal trumpeter of the Minnesota Orchestra, played
the clarino part on a valved instrument of his own
design.   (Reprinted by permission from High Fidelity/
Musical America.   All rights reserved.)

Composer Zwilich is equally at home writing for voice.
She said, "I'm someone who loves to read poetry, but only
rarely do I find a text that I feel strongly attracted to and
at the same time have the impulse to add another dimension
to it."   Einsame Nacht, poems by Herman Hesse, and music
by Ellen Taaffe Zwilich, was composed in 1971.   The following program notes were written by the composer:

     Einsame Nacht (1971) is a song-cycle for baritone
     and piano on six poems from Herman Hesse's Die
     Gedichte.   Einsame Nacht roughly translated "Lone-
     some Night," is the title of a poem I originally in-
     tended to include in the cycle and later discarded;
     however, the title (and, indeed the poem itself)
     seemed to provide a focus for the set of poems I
     finally used.
          The poems of this cycle, like much of Hesse's
     poetry, are concerned with existential loneliness
     (elsewhere Hesse has written: "Leben ist Einsam-
     sein," roughly "To live is to be lonely").   Yet,
     while themes of homesickness, alienation, and loss
     are explored, there is a wonderful life-affirming
     sensuousness and immediacy in the poetry.   The
     images are almost palpable and there is sheer joy
     in the words themselves.   One experiences, with
     Hesse, a recognition of the isolation of the human
     condition together with a profound yearning for con-
     nection.

Below are excerpts from a review written by Raymond
Ericson for The New York Times on March 15, 1979:

MUSIC: 2ND WOMEN'S FESTIVAL BEGINS

The Women's Interart Center is sponsoring a four-

program Second Festival of Women's Music at
Christ and St. Stephen's Church, 120 West 69th
Street, and the opening concert was on Tuesday
night. Its subject was vocal music, and it was
performed by Janet Steele, soprano, and Patrick
Mason, baritone with Michael Fardink as pianist.

As before, the festival has sought to establish
the continuity among women composers, and there
were examples of music by Hildegarde von Bingen
(12th century), Barbara Strozzi (17th century), Elis-
abeth Jacquet de la Guerre (late 17th and early 18th
centuries) and Josephine Lang (19th century). Today's composers were represented by Gloria Wilson
Swisher, Ellen Taaffe Zwilich, Victoria Bond and
Peggy Glanville-Hicks.

There weren't any dull moments in the program,
and there was a goodly amount of stimulating material. What was interesting was the fact that the
two most satisfactory works--to this listener's
ears, at least--were very much in strong traditions
of the past. These were a set of eight German
songs by Lang and Einsame Nacht, a cycle based
on poems of Hermann Hesse by Miss Zwilich.

Miss Zwilich's cycle of six songs looks back to
the 20th-century Viennese school of Berg, Schoenberg and Webern, suitable, certainly, to the Hesse
texts. The composer works very smoothly within
the style, and it would have been hard to fault the
placement of a note in such concentrated music.
The cycle was written in 1971, and whether the
composer is developing a more individual style remains to be seen. But here her craftsmanship and
expressive power are first rate. (Copyright © 1979
by The New York Times Company. Reprinted by
permission.)

In the early 1970's a Swiss colleague of Zwilich's
gave her a book of Georg Tvakl's writing which immediately
captivated her, especially Trompeten, which she set for soprano and piano in 1974. Soprano Clamma Dale premièred
the work, in an English translation by the composer, in 1977
at Alice Tully Hall under the auspices of a Naumburg Award.
On a commission from the Hungarian soprano, Terézia Csajbók, Zwilich wrote Emlékezet on poems by Sándor Petöfi.
The work was recorded on Magyar Radio in Budapest, Hungary
by Miss Csajbók in 1979.

In 1980 Ellen Taaffe Zwilich received a Norlin Foundation
Fellowship from the MacDowell Colony in Peterborough, New
Hampshire, where she spent the summer composing and
joining evening impromptu instrumental ensembles by playing
violin. All awards are important, but one of the most coveted
and prestigious honors to be awarded is a John Simon Guggenheim Memorial Foundation Fellowship which Zwilich received
in 1980-1981 to assist her in artistic creation. During her
term as a Guggenheim Fellow, she began a major orchestral
work that was premièred on May 5, 1982, by the American Composers Orchestra under the direction of Gunther
Schuller. She also wrote Passages, a twenty-two minute
work (for soprano, flute/alto flute/piccolo, clarinet/bass
clarinet, violin, viola, cello, piano, and percussion), based
on poems by A. R. Ammons. Passages was premièred on
January 29, 1982, by Boston Musica Viva under the direction
of Richard Pittman. Her fellowship also permitted her to
travel throughout Europe, enabling her to attend performances
of her work in Budapest, Paris, Lisbon, West Berlin, Sofia,
and London; and, in the United States, in Cleveland and Chicago.

Zwilich has always enjoyed being involved in the preparation for performance of her music and attends as many
rehearsals as possible. It is important to get the feedback
from the musicians as well as the conductor. For the sake
of clarity, she will make changes in the score. She always
knows beforehand just how the music will sound.

In May 1981, her alma mater, Florida State University, chose her as the third recipient of the Ernst von Doh-
nanyi Citation, an award made in memory of the distinguished
composer who served on the FSU faculty from 1949 until
his death in 1960. In addition to receiving the citation,
Zwilich was a featured guest composer at the Festival of
New Music. Former colleagues and friends had the opportunity to hear her works, including the Sonata in Three Movements and the Chamber Symphony, works described by one
music critic as concise gestures and dynamic counterpoint
... dazzling chamber music.

Based on her respected reputation, Ellen Taaffe Zwilich
is emerging as one of America's gifted twentieth-century
composers. Her compositions are stimulating to the performer and the listener. That she is talented is easily recognized, but in addition she has the determination that it
takes to be a great artist. Certainly in music one must deal
with the intangible and imponderable, as well as possessing

the skills of the craft. One must admire her talent, capacity, and strength, for she is a determined composer. That takes a special breed. She noted, "Writing music is like living and breathing, I can't imagine life without it."

Discography

String Quartet, New York String Quartet, Cambridge Records, Inc., Number CRS-2834.
Sonata in Three Movements, Joseph Zwilich violin, James Gemmell piano, Cambridge Records, Inc., Number CRS-2834.
Chamber Symphony, Boston Musica Viva, Richard Pittman conductor, Cambridge Records, Number CRS-2834.

Address

Cambridge Records, Inc., 125 Irving Street, Framingham, MA 01701.

Selected List of Compositions

1979- Chamber Symphony, Theodore Presser Co.
80
1977   Clarino Quartet, piccolo Bb trumpet, D trumpet, C trumpet, and Bb trumpet, alternate version for four clarinets; Theodore Presser Co.
1973- Sonata in Three Movements, violin and piano; Theodore Presser Co.
74
1973   String Quartet, Margun Music Inc.
1972- Symposium, for orchestra; Theodore Presser Co.
73

Addresses

Margun Music, Inc., 167 Dudley Road, Newton Centre, MA 02159.

Theodore Presser Co., Bryn Mawr, PA 19010.

American Academy and Institute of
Arts and Letters 80, 136, 143,
173
American Composers Alliance 79,
132, 133, 151, 152
American Israel Cultural Founda-
tion 28
American Society of Composers,
Authors and Publishers 80,
169, 181, 182, 253, 254, 293,
317
American Symphony Orchestra
30, 51, 52
Anderson, Beth 1-24, 180
   Beauty Is Revolution 14, 15,
     16
   Cabrillo Music Festival 4, 6,
     19
   Compositions, list 20-22
     "Happening" 3
     "Hegemony HodgePodge"
      10
     "I Can't Stand It" 9
     "Joan" 4, 6-8
     "Peachy-Keen-O" 2, 3
     "Poem To Pauline" 10
     "Queen Christina" 4-6
     "Skate Suite" 12
     "The Eighth Ancestor" 18,
      19
   Ear Magazine 4, 8, 14-16
   Festival of Disappearing Arts
    13
   Franklin Furnace 10, 11
   Grants 19
   Kitchen 16
   National Endowment For The
    Arts 8, 19
   Poetry Is Music 8, 9
   Sound Texts 8, 9
   Source Magazine 3
   Recordings 22
   Reports From The Front 16-18
   Reviews 4-11, 13, 14
   Teachers: Ashley, Robert 4;
    Austin, Larry 4; Cage, John
    3; Chance, John B. 4;

    Lipscomb, Helen 1, 4; Riley,
    Terry 4; Rubin, Nate 4;
    Wright, Kenneth 4
Arlen, Walter (Los Angeles Times)
309, 310
Associated Press 293, 294
Atlas, Dalia 25-38
   American Symphony Orchestra
    30
   Awards 23, 33, 37
   Bernstein, Leonard 28, 29, 37
   Competitions (Conducting): Dimi-
    tri Mitropoulos 25, 27, 28;
    Guido Cantelli 25, 27; Royal
    Philharmonic 25, 27; Villa-
    Lobos International Competition
    25, 33
   Conductor
    A. B. C. Orchestras, Australia
     33
    Bournemouth Symphony Or-
     chestra 34, 35
    B. B. C. Symphony Orchestra
     33
    Halle Orchestra 33
    Houston Symphony Orchestra
     32, 33
    Israel Philharmonic Orchestra
     33, 36
    Israel Radio Orchestra 36, 37
    Massachusetts Institute of
     Technology Orchestra 30,
      31
    Rio de Janeiro Orchestra 33
    São Paulo Symphony Orchestra
     33
    Tasmanian Symphony Orchestra
     34
   Ormandy, Eugene 23, 37, 38,
    40
   Reviews 27, 30-38
   Tanglewood 29
   Technion University 29, 30
   Teachers: Celibidache, Sergio
    26; Ferrara, Franco 25,
    26; Swarowsky, Hans 26,
    27

Bacewicz, Grazyna 49, 64, 224
Baltimore Sun 13-14
Bauer, Marion 79, 119, 286-288
Belt, Byron (Long Island Press, Newhouse Newspapers, The Jersey Journal) 91, 92, 167, 168, 175, 176, 178, 267
Bennington College 80, 87, 108
Berkshire Music Center (see also Tanglewood) 29, 41, 65, 158, 356
Bernheimer, Martin (Los Angeles Times) 317
Bernstein, Leonard 28, 29, 37
Blum, Jerome L. (New York Times, New York Herald Tribune) 82
Bond, Victoria (see also Volume I) 6, 111, 175, 176, 299, 358
Boston Musica Viva, Richard Pittman, Conductor 353, 354, 355, 359
Boulanger, Lili 49, 110
Boulanger, Nadia 53, 143, 206, 311
Bowles, Paul (New York Herald Tribune) 124
Brico, Antonia (see also Volume I) 106, 110, 312
Broadcast Music, Inc. 144, 253, 254
Buell, Richard (The Boston Globe) 353, 354, 355

Cabrillo Music Festival 4, 6, 19
Cage, John 3, 169, 183, 184
Caldwell, Sarah 39-57
    American National Opera Company 45, 46
    Boston Opera Group 42, 43
    Boston University Opera Workshop 41
    Caldwell, Sarah 65
    Celebration of Women Composers Concert 48-50
    Central Opera Company of Peking 51, 57
    Goldovsky, Boris 40, 41
    Macbeth 57
    Metropolitan Opera 42, 52, 53
    New England Conservatory 40
    New York City Opera 52, 53
    Opera Company of Boston 43, 46
    Opera News 50
    Operas

        "Be Glad Then America" 53, 54
        "Don Carlos" 44
        "Don Pasquale" 55-57
        "Falstaff" 45, 46
        "Intolerance" 44
        "La Finta Giardiniera" 40
        "La Traviata" 52, 53, 57
        "Les Troyens" 44, 47
        "Lulu" 46
        "Mathis der Maler" 41
        "Moses and Aron" 43, 44, 45
        "Riders To The Sea" 41
        "Tosca" 43, 45, 46
        "The Rake's Progress" 41
        "Voyage To The Moon" 42
        "War and Peace" 43
    Orchestras
        American Symphony Orchestra 51, 52
        Indianapolis Symphony Orchestra 52
        Milwaukee Symphony Orchestra 51
        New York Philharmonic Orchestra 48-50
        New Orleans Symphony Orchestra 51
        Philadelphia Orchestra 51
        Pittsburgh Symphony Orchestra 51, 55
        San Antonio Orchestra 51
    Pension Fund Concert 48
    Recording, "Don Pasquale" 55-57
    Reviews 44-58
    Tanglewood 41
    Teachers: Burgin, Richard 40; Flourel, George 40; Koussevitzky, Serge 41
Canby, Edward Tatnall (Audio) 323, 324
Carnegie Music Hall 163, 196, 198, 200, 201, 267, 286, 292, 325, 348
Celebration of Women Composers Concert 48-50, 64, 65
Cogan, Robert 65, 67, 68
Cohn, Arthur (American Record Guide) 128
Copland, Aaron 1, 78, 158, 267, 281, 286, 288, 289, 390
Cowell, Henry 82, 83, 167, 168, 174-177, 202, 254
Craddock, Peter (London Strad) 226
Craig, Mary (Courier) 290
Cramer, Edward C. (New York Times) 253, 254
Crawford, Ruth (Seeger) (see also

Volume I) 48, 49, 64, 71, 73,
169, 183, 281, 288
Creston, Paul (Dobbs Ferry
Register) 201-203, 211
Croan, Robert (Pittsburgh Post-
Gazette) 246
Cunningham, Carl (Houston Post)
32, 266

Dagblad Voor West-Friesland 352
Dallapiccola, Luigi 81
Daniels, Mabel 84, 109, 293-295
Davies, Dennis Russell 6, 35
Davis, Peter G. (New York Times)
333
Diemer, Emma Lou (see also
Volume I) 224, 233, 294
Donahue, Michael (Memphis Press-
Scimitar) 327
Downes, Edward (New York Times)
132
Dyer, Richard (Boston Globe) 55,
56, 346

Ear Magazine 4, 14-16
Eckert, Thor Jr. (The Christian
Science Monitor) 30, 31
Elwell, Herbert (Plain Dealer)
148, 149
Ericson, Raymond (New York
Times) 135, 217-219, 329,
330
Escot, Pozzi 58-70
    Awards 59, 60, 62, 65, 67
    Belgrade Radio and Television
    65
    Celebration of Women Composers
    48, 49, 50, 64, 65
    Compositions, list 75
        "A Trilogy" 62
        "A Christhos" 62, 63
        "Differences" 63
        "Lamentus" 60, 62, 63, 64
        "Little Symphony" 59
        "Sands" 64, 65
        "Visione" 62
    Discography 69
    Notation 61
    Reviews 62-65
    Sonus 67, 68
    Thomson, Virgil 61
    Teachers: Bergsma, William 59;
        Jarnach, Philipp 59, 60, 61;
        Persichetti, Vincent 59
    (Aufbau) 173, 174

Evening News 352
Evett, Robert (The New Republic)
149, 150
Express and Echo 35, 36

Fine, Vivian 71-91, 183, 184, 294
    American Academy/National In-
    stitute of Arts and Letters
    80, 81
    American Composers Alliance
    78, 79
    American Society of Composers,
    Authors and Publishers 80
    American Composers Alliance
    Bulletin 76, 77
    Awards: ASCAP 80; Dollard
    Award 80; Ford Foundation
    Award in Humanities 80;
    Guggenheim Fellowship 80;
    National Endowment for the
    Arts 80, 87; Rothschild Foun-
    dation 80, 81; Wooley Foun-
    dation 80; Wykeham Rise
    Commission 80; Yaddo Award
    80
    Bennington College 80, 87
    Broadcast Music Inc. 79
    Composers Forum 82
    Compositions, list 89-91
        "A Guide to the Life Expect-
        ancy of a Rose" 81, 82
        "Alcestis" 83, 108
        "Comfort To a Youth That
        Had Lost His Love" 78
        "Concerto For Piano, Strings
        and Percussion 85
        "Meeting For Equal Rights"
        85-87
        "Missa Brevis" 84, 85
        "Opus 51" 78
        "String Quartet" 82
        "The Race of Life" 77, 78
        "The Women in The Garden"
        87, 88
        "They Too Are Exiles" 78
        "Tragic Exodus" 78
        "Two Neruda Poems" 85
    Cowell, Henry 82, 83
    Dance Perspectives 73-75
    Discography 91
    Graham, Martha 81-83
    Guggenheim Fellowship 80
    Humphrey, Doris 73, 75-77
    Imperial Philharmonic Orchestra
    83, 84
    International Society For Contem-
    porary Music 73, 79, 80

Juilliard School of Music 80
Pan American Association of
    Composers 79
Port Costa Players 87
Reviews 76, 77, 82, 84-89
Riegger, Wallingford 78, 81
Teachers: Crawford, Ruth
    (Seeger) 71-73; Lavoie-Herz,
    Djane 71; Sessions, Roger
    73, 75; Szell, George 73;
    Whiteside, Abby 71
Weidman, Charles 73, 78
Finn, Robert (The Plain Dealer)
    227
Frank, Peter (Fanfare) 250
Fulbright Fellowship 143, 243,
    247, 265

Galt, Martha C. (Music Clubs
    Magazine) 310, 311
Gardner, Kay 92-117
    Blue Hill Chamber Ensemble
        112
    Compositions, list 115-117
        "Atlantis Rising" 104, 105
        "Beautiful Friend" 101
        "Changing" 101, 113, 114
        "Crystal Bells" 104
        "Inner Mood I" 101
        "Inner Mood II" 101
        "Ladies Voices" 111, 112
        "Lunamuse" 100, 101, 103
        "Mooncircles" 98-101, 103,
            105
        "Moon Flow" 101
        "Prayer to Aphrodite" 100,
            101
        "The Rising Sun" 112
        "Wise Women" 101
    Conducting 92, 106-109, 114
    Discography 117
    Emerging 104
    Healing Music 101-104
    Hilderley, Jeriann 98
    Lavender Jane Loves Women
        96, 97
    New England Women's Symphony
        106-111
    Norfolk Chamber Consort 95
    Paid My Dues 102-104
    Reviews 101, 104-112
    Separatist 97, 98
    Southwest Chamber Opera 111,
        112
    Stony Brook 95, 96
    Teachers: Baron, Samuel 95,
        96; Brico, Antonia 106;

Green, Elizabeth 93
Women's Music Festival 97,
    106
Wise, Laurel 98
Gideon, Miriam 118-141, 183, 294
    American Academy and Institute
        of Arts and Letters 136
    American Composers Alliance
        124, 125
    American Composers Orchestra
        135
    American Music Festival 122
    Ariel Quintet 127
    Awards 129, 130
    Commissions 123, 127, 130,
        135, 136
    Compositions, list 137, 138,
        139, 140, 141
        "Adon Olam" 127
        "Condemned Playground" 128
        "Dances For Two Pianos" 122
        "Fortunato" 128
        "Galgenlieder" 129
        "How Goodly are Thy Tents"
            127
        "Lyric Piece For Orchestra"
            122, 123
        "Mixco" 128
        "Nocturnes" 135, 136
        "Rhymes From The Hill" 126,
            129
        "Sacred Service" 130-132
        "Shirat Miriam L'Shabbat"
            130, 133, 134
        "Songs of Youth and Madness"
            135
        "Spirit Above the Dust" 136
        "Symphonia Brevis" 128
        "The Adorable Mouse" 126,
            127
        "The Hound of Heaven" 126,
            129
        "The Seasons of Time" 129
        "Three Biblical Masks" 127
        "To Music" 128
    DeMain, John (conductor) 135,
        136
    Discography 139-141
    Distinguished Alumni at Boston
        University 135
    Dixon, James (conductor) 135
    Imperial Orchestra of Tokyo 122
    Jewish Theological Seminary 121
    London Symphony Orchestra 122
    Monod, Jacques (conductor) 128
    Most Recorded Woman Composer
        125-129
    National Endowment For The
        Arts 135

New England Women's Sym-
   phony 123
National Federation of Music
   Clubs, National Award 129
Reverse discrimination 125
Reviews 122, 123, 124, 126-
   136
Strickland, William (conductor)
   122
St. Paul Chamber Orchestra
   135
Teachers: Bauer, Marion 119;
   Fox, Felix 119; Haubiel,
   Charles 119; Pillois, Jac-
   ques 119; Saminsky,
   Lazare 119; Sessions,
   Roger 120, 121
Weisgall, Hugo (conductor) 122
Weisser, Albert 130-134, 137
Zurich Radio Orchestra 128
Glaglia, Gisela (Frankfurter All-
   gemeine Zeitung) 180
Glanville-Hicks, Peggy 142-162
   American Academy of Arts and
      Letters Grant 143
   American Composers Alliance
      151, 152
   Article, P. G. H. 151, 152
   Athens Music Festival 152,
      153
   Berkshire Music Festival 158
   Boult, Sir Adrain (conductor) 143
   Boston Symphony Orchestra 158
   Butler, John 150, 151
   CBC 144
   Composers Forum 158
   Compositions, list 159-162
      "A Season in Hell" 154
      "Choral Suite" 143, 144
      "Concertino da Camera"
         144, 145
      "Concerto for Piano and
         Wind Octet" 159
      "Letters from Morocco" 145,
         146
      "Nausicaa" 152, 153
      "Rapunzel" 159
      "Saul and The Witch of Endor"
         154
      "Sappho" 154
      "Sonata for Harp" 145
      "The Masque of the Wild Man"
         150, 151
      "The Transposed Heads" 146-
         150
      "The Wind Remains" 159
      "Thomsoniana" 155
      "Tragic Celebration" 154
   Ford Foundation Grant 143, 153

Fulbright Fellowship 143, 152
Guggenheim Fellowship 143
International Society for Contem-
   porary Music 143-145, 158
Juilliard Review 155-158
Louisville Opera Company 142,
   146
Les Trois Arts 145
Music critic 154, 155
Music in Our Times Series 142
Octavia Scholarship 143
Reviews 146, 148-150, 154
Rockefeller Grant 143
Royal College of Music 143
San Francisco Opera House 153
Spoleto Festival 150
Stokowski, Leopold (conductor)
   146
Tanglewood 158
Teachers: Benjamin, Arthur
   143; Boulanger, Nadia 143;
   Hart, Fritz 143; Lambert,
   Constant 143; Sargent, Sir
   Malcom 143; Williams, Vaug-
   han 143
The New York Times 146-148
Unesco 158
Zabaleta, Nicanor 145
Gradenwitz, Peter (Frankfurter All-
   gemeine Zeitung) 153
Graham, Martha 81-83
Greene, Patterson (Los Angeles
   Examiner) 315
Guggenheim Fellowships 80, 81,
   143, 359

Hays, Doris 163-190 (see also
   Volume I)
   American Society of Composers,
      Authors and Publishers 169,
      182
   Banks Haley Art Gallery 172
   Bavarian Ministry Fellowship
      166
   Bonn Music Festival 180
   Cadek, Harold 165, 166
   Cage, John 183
   Carnegie Music Hall 163
   Chattanooga Symphony Orchestra
      182
   Compositions, list 187-190
      "Adoration of the Clash" 178,
         179
      "Sensevents" 172, 173
      "Southern Voices" 181, 182
      "Sunday Nights" 163, 177, 178
      "Tunings" 179, 180

"Uni Suite" 173
"Wildflowers" 178
Cowell, Henry 167, 168, 174-
    176
Crawford, Ruth (Seeger) 169,
    183
Creative Arts Project 184
Crescent Quartet 180
Discography 190
Electronic Music Plus 181
Expressions 185, 186
Georgia Council on the Arts 171
Holland 170
International Competition for
    Interpreters of New Music
    143, 170
International League of Women
    Composers 182
Karp, Richard 173, 174
Lincoln Out-Of-Doors Art Festi-
    val 172
Manhattan String Quartet 179
McClellan Foundation 166
Meet The Women Composer
    185, 186   .
Messiaen, Oliver 170
Munich Hochschule Für Musik
    166
National Endowment for the
    Arts Grant 173, 181
New Amsterdam Symphony 176
Omaha Symphony Orchestra U. S.
    Première 175
Silver Burdett Company 170,
    171
Reviews 167, 168, 173-176,
    178-180
Rockefeller Foundation 183,
    184
Teachers: Badura-Skoda, Paul
    166; Cadek, Harold 165, 166,
    168; Plettner, Arthur 173;
    Somer, Hilde 168, 169;
    Wuhrer, Friedrich 166
Women's Music Radio Series
    185, 186
Harrison, Jay S. (New York Herald
    Tribune) 290
Harvy, John (St. Paul Pioneer Press)
    135
Henahan, Donal (New York Times)
    48-50, 84, 85
Herman, Robert (Gazette Journal)
    136
Hertelendy, Paul (Oakland Tribune,
    San Jose Mercury News) 234-236
High Fidelity/Musical America 54,
    247, 248, 349, 350, 356, 357
Hochschule für Musik 59, 166

Howe, Mary 84, 294, 322
Hubert, Karl (The Mercury) 34,
    35
Humphrey, Doris (American Com-
    posers Alliance Bulletin) 76,
    77

Il Populo 150, 151
Imperial Philharmonic Orchestra
    83, 294
International Society for Contem-
    porary Music 18, 73, 83, 143,
    144, 158, 224, 240, 344-347
Israel Philharmonic Orchestra 33,
    36, 37

Jarrell, Frank P. (The News and
    Carrier) 179, 180
Jennings, Don (Composers Record-
    ing) 83
Jerusalem Post 37
Johnson, Tom 9
Johnstone, Anne (Evening Times)
    36
Jolas, Betsy (see also Volume I)
    80, 183
Jones, Nancy (Live) 10, 11
Jones, Robert T. (Opera News) 50
Juilliard School of Music 59, 80,
    275, 276, 281-283, 322, 343

Kamien, Anita (The Great Neck
    Record) 330
Kapp, Paul (Stereo Review) 127
Klein, Howard (New York Times)
    216, 217
Kolb, Barbara (see also Volume I)
    81, 111, 183
Koussevitzky, Serge 41, 158

L. R. (New York Times) 201, 202
Lavender Jane Loves Women 96,
    97
Lawshe, Mark (Santa Cruz Sentinel)
    7, 8
Lhevine, Rosina 264, 322
Liverpool Daily Post 27
Los Angeles Examiner 316
Luening, Otto 244, 325, 328,
    343
Lutoslawski, Witold 233, 243

McCoy, W. U. (The Daily Okla-
    homan) 264, 265
MacDowell Colony 253, 325, 359
Martin, John (New York Times) 77,
    78
Meet The Composer 182, 185,
    299
Mehta, Zubin 26
Millay, Edna St. Vincent 268,
    308
Miller, Joy (Associated Press)
    293, 294
Miller, Philip L. (American
    Record Guide) 129, 130
Mills College 3, 307
Moore, David (American Record
    Guide) 331, 332
Ms. magazine 48, 64
Musgrave, Thea (see also Volume
    I) 49, 64, 111

National Endowment For The Arts
    8, 19, 80, 87, 173, 253, 295,
    318
National Federation of Music Clubs
    294-296, 325, 326
National Women's Music Festival
    97
New Alsacian 224
New England Conservatory 344
New England Women's Symphony
    107-111, 117
Newall, Robert (Bangor Daily News)
    112, 113
Newman, Bob (Grass Roots) 101
New York Herald Tribune 214-216
New York Philharmonic Orchestra
    28, 48-50, 64, 195, 212, 311
Noble, David (The Patriot Ledger)
    286, 346, 347
Nord, Paul (The Villager,
    The National Herald) 212-214

Oliveros, Pauline (see also Volume
    I) 6, 108, 109, 181
Ormandy, Eugene 23, 37, 38

Paid My Dues 102-104
Palmer, Robert (New York Times)
    9, 11, 12
Parmenter, Ross (New York Times)
    124, 125, 283, 285, 286
Perkins, Francis (New York Herald

Tribune) 216
Petrides, Frederique 191-237,
    275, 276, 278, 283
A Lady Conductor in Pepy's
    Time 204
An Unusual Subject By An Un-
    usual Woman 207
Carl Schurz Park Concert Series
    214-216
Carnegie Chamber Music Hall
    196, 197, 200, 201
Creston, Paul 200, 202, 203
Festival Symphony Orchestra
    215-218, 232, 233
Masters School-Dobbs Ferry 211
Musical Review 207-209
New York University 194
New York Philharmonic Orchestra
    195, 212, 214
Orchestrette Classique 194-200,
    201, 277, 278, 283
Orchestrette of New York 195,
    201, 202
Outline of A Prejudice 207-210
Petrides, Peter 203
Reviews 196-203, 211-214, 216-
    219
Rosenker, Michael 212
Royal Conservatory in Brussels
    193
Stokowski, Leopold 206
Teachers: Crickboom, Mathieu
    192; Mitropoulos, Dimitri
    193
Vienna's Surprise to Old New
    York 205
Washington Square Park Concerts
    212-214
Weingartner, Felix 193
West Side Orchestra Concerts
    216-219
White, Paul 198
WJZ National Broadcasting Com-
    pany 207
Women in Music 203-206
Pfeifer, Ellen (The Boston Herald
    American) 355
Pittman, Richard (conductor) 353-
    356
Playboy 168
Porter, Andrew (New Yorker) 176,
    177
Price, Theodore (High Fidelity/
    Musical America) 175
Ptaszynska, Marta 221-239
    American Percussive Arts So-
    ciety 229
    Avant-Garde Works 224, 226,
    227

Beck, John, letter 229
Boulanger, Nadia, recommenda-
  tion 222, 223
Brooklyn Ensemble 230
California State Hayward Per-
  cussion Ensemble 234, 235
Circle of Young Composers
  224, 225
Colorful World of Percussion
  233, 234
Compositions, list 254, 255
  "A Concerto For Percus-
    sion" 233
  "Cadenza For Flute and Per-
    cussion" 231, 233
  "Constructions" 233
  "Classical Variations" 229
  "Epigrams" 231, 232
  "Fantasmagoria" 227, 232
  "Five Improvisions" 233
  "Hieraklitiana" 233
  "Interpretations" 233
  "Madrigal Chanticum Sonarum"
    225
  "Magic Spaces" 236
  "Mobile" 233
  "Momentum" 230
  "Preludes for Vibraphone and
    Piano" 224
  "Ritmi ed Antiritmi" 230
  "Siderals" 229, 230
  "Spectri Sonori" 226
  "Tale of the Nightingales"
    225, 232
  "Two Madrigals" 225
  "Variations for Solo Flute"
    225
Discography 239
Instituto Nacional de Bellas
  Artes 235, 236
International Society For Music
  Education, World Congress
  224
International Symposium of Per-
  cussionists Festival 224
Kosciuszko Foundation 223
Pozman Spring Festival 233
Ruch Muzyczny 225, 230, 233
Slonimsky, Nicolas, letter 229
Picasso, Pablo 228
Polish Composers Union 224,
  225
Reviews 224-227, 230-236
Teachers: Boulanger, Nadia
  222, 223; Duff, Cloyd 223;
  Erb, Donald 223; Paciorkie-
  wicz, Tadeusz 222; Rudzinski,
  Witold 222; Sledzinski, Stefan
  222; Weiner, Richard 223;

Zgodzinski, Jerzy 222
Virtuoso Solo Percussionist 221,
  224, 226, 227

Richter, Marga (see also Volume I)
  178, 180
Rockwell, John (New York Times)
  18, 51, 52
Roos, James (High Fidelity/Musical
  America) 297, 298
Rosenfield, John (Dallas Morning
  News) 280, 281, 282
Rowan, Diana Hewell (Sojourner)
  109, 110
Royal Philharmonic in Liverpool
  27
Ruch Muzyczny (Musical Move-
  ment) 225, 233

S. L. (New York Times) 123
Salzman, Eric (New York Times)
  18, 128
Saminsky, Lazare 120-123
Sargeant, Winthrop (The New Yorker)
  44, 46, 154
Saturna, Andrzej (Music Movement)
  230
Schonberg, Harold C. (New York
  Times) 52, 53, 253, 286, 287
Schonthal, Ruth 183
Seeger, Ruth Crawford see Craw-
  ford Ruth (Seeger)
Semegen, Daria 240-260
  Associate Director of the Elec-
    tronic Music Studio 246
  Awards 253
  Broadcast Music, Inc. Award 253
  Columbia-Princeton Music Center
    244
  Compositions, list 257, 258,
    259
    "Arc: Music for Dancers"
      249, 250
    "Electronic Music Composition
      No. I" 249
    "Electronic Music Composition
      No. II" 256
    "Jeux des Quatres" 245, 246
    "Music for Violin Solo" 248,
      249
    "Poème 1er Dans la Nuit"
      244
    "Quattro" 247
    "Three Pieces for Clarinet and
      Piano" 248, 249

Discography 259, 260
Letter to the Editor (New York
Times) 253, 254
International Electronic Music
Competition Prize 249
Leuning, Otto 244
Mimi Garrard Dance Theater
250
National Endowment For The
Arts 253
New York State University Re-
search Foundation Grant 256
Once More With Feeling 251-
253
Paving new roads 255
Polish Radio Station 243
Princeton Electronic Music
Center 244
Professor of Music 246
Reflections of her studies 241
Reviews 246-250, 254, 256
Southeastern Composers League
Chamber Music Competition
Prize 247
Teachers: Alder, Samuel 241;
Gauldin, Robert 241; Holden,
David 241; Lutoslawski,
Witold 243; Phillips, Bur-
rill 241; Ussachevsky, Vlad-
imir 244
Yale University Fellowship 244
World Music Collection 244
Sessions, Roger 71, 73, 75, 79,
81, 120, 254, 343
Shere, Charles (Oakland Tribune,
High Fidelity/Musical America)
87, 88, 89
Sherman, Robert (New York Times)
230, 267, 268, 296
Simons, Netty 96, 254
Singer, Samuel L. (Philadelphia
Inquirer) 38
Sloper, Michael (Albuquerque
Journal) 111, 112
Smeltzer, Susan 261-273
Akademie Für Musik 265
American Landmark Festival
268
Awards 263, 265, 266, 268
Bicentennial Celebration 267
Carnegie Recital Hall Debut 267
Congress on Arts and Communi-
cation 271
Compositions, list 272, 273
"An American Tribute for the
Royal Wedding" 272
"El Matador" 263
"Furious Wind" 262
"Jonathan Richard, My Bicen-
tennial Baby" 269
"The Bald Eagle March" 269,
270
"The Brotherhood March" 270
"Theme and Variation for Two
Pianos" 265
"Twelve Mood Pictures" 268
Copland, Aaron 266, 267
Distinguished Alumni Award 268
Florida Symphony Orchestra 269
Fulbright Fellowship 261, 265
Gateways 270
International Biographical Centre
271
Neue Hofburg Palace 265
Oklahoma City Orchestra 263-
265
Poems 270, 271
Ravel's G Major Concerto 269
Reviews 264, 266, 267
Sapulpa Historical Society 269,
270
Selected Orchestrations of Poetic
Expression 271
Sigma Alpha Iota 265
Sword of Honor 266
Teachers: Burg, Clarence 263;
Dichler, Joseph 265; Laughlin,
Robert 263; Scott, Ernestine
263; Steuber, Lillian 263,
264
Van Cliburn International Piano
Competition 266
Voice of America 266
Weidinger, Hildegard 265, 266
Smith, Julia 274-304
American Music Festival 284
American Women Composers
294
American Society of Composers,
Authors and Publishers 293
Associated Press 293, 294
Bain, Wilfred C. 278, 279, 284
Barlow, Howard (conductor) 278
Bostleman, Louis (conductor) 286
Books--written by Julia Smith
288, 289, 290, 291, 295, 304
CBC 278
Carnegie Hall Pop Concert 278,
286, 292
Cleveland Orchestra 291
Columbia Broadcasting Commis-
sion 281
Compositions, list 300-304
"American Dance Suite" 277,
291
"Characteristic Suite" 285
"Cockcrow" 290
"Concerto" 281, 282

"Cynthia Parker" 274, 279, 280, 284
"Daisy" 281, 297
"Episodic Suite" 281, 288
"Folkways Symphony" 285
"Hellenic Suite" 283
"Hin and Zuruck" 283
"Little Suite Based on American Folk-Tunes" 277
"Liza Jane" 281, 286
"Our Heritage" 291
"Sonatine in C" 285
"Stranger of Manzano" 283, 284, 286
"String Quartet" 288
"The Gooseherd and the Goblin" 284, 287, 291
"The Shepherdess and The Chimney Sweep" 292, 299
"Trio Sonata II, Flute, Cello and Piano" 287, 288
"Three Love Songs" 290
"Two Pieces For Viola and Piano" 290
"Two Romances for Violin and Piano" 275
"Variations Humoresque" 288
Copland, Aaron 281, 286, 288, 289, 290
Corona, Leonora 279
Dallas Symphony Orchestra 279, 281, 282, 291
Directory of American Women Composers 295
Discography 304
Fennell, Frederick (conductor) 286
Ford Foundation 298
Fort Worth Opera 292
Friedberg, Carl 275, 282, 291
Hartt College of Music 282-285
Honigman, Hinda 294, 295
Houston Symphony Orchestra 286
Juilliard Orchestra 281
Juilliard School of Music 274, 279, 280, 282, 283
Kruger, Richard 292
Lange, Hans (conductor) 285
Meet The Composer 299
Michna, Marienka 285
Montgomery, Merle 295, 296
National Association For American Composers 288
National Endowment for the Arts 295
National Federation of Music Clubs 293, 294

New Jersey Symphony Society 286
New York Composer's Forum 286, 287
New York's Town Hall 285, 287, 290
North Texas State School of Music 278, 284
North Texas State Teacher's College 274, 282, 284
Oklahoma City Symphony Orchestra 291
Orchestrette Classique 277, 278, 283
Opera Guild of Greater Miami 297, 298
Paramount Pictures 280
Paranov, Moshe (conductor) 284
Petrides, Frederique 275, 276, 278, 283
Puerto Rico 288
Reviews 278, 280-287, 289-294, 297, 298
Sherman, Robert 296
Somohano, Arthur (conductor) 288
Strickland, William (conductor) 294
Teachers: Anderson, Mary 274; Bauer, Marion 286, 287; Epstein Lonny 274; Friedberg, Carl 274, 275, 282; Goldmark, Rubin 275, 277; Jacobi, Frederick 275, 277; Thomson, Virgil 286; Schenkman, Edgar 275; Von Mickwitz, Harold 274, 275; Wagennar, Bernard 274, 281; Watson, Jack 286
The Music of Aaron Copland 286
Toledo Ohio Friends of Music Commission 285
Vashaw, Cecile 288, 291
Vielehr, Oscar 279, 289
Vought, Mrs. Frank 298
Women's International Year 299
Sommers, Scott (Performing Arts) 254, 255
Sonic Design: Practice and Problems 71
Steinberg, Michael (Boston Globe) 44, 45, 47
Strickland, William (conductor) 83, 122, 294, 310
Stokowski, Leopold (conductor) 28, 206, 341, 342

Talma, Louise (see also Volume I) 84, 183, 184, 294-296

Tanglewood (see also Berkshire
    Music Center) 29, 41, 65,
    158, 288, 356
Taubman, Harold (New York Times)
    196, 197, 199-201, 289
Technion Orchestra and Chorus 30,
    37
The New Records 256
The New York Sun 198, 199
Thomson, Virgil 61, 79, 286
Thuysen, E. Van Ben (Daily News)
    231, 232
Treanor, Jean Aline (Blade) 285
Trimble, Lester (Stereo Review,
    New York Herald Tribune) 126,
    128

Van de Vate, Nancy (see also
    Volume I) 117, 182
Varèse, Edgard 81, 229, 254
Variety 153

Ward, Charles (Houston Chronicle)
    32
Warren, Elinor Remick 305-321;
    293
    Assisting Artist 307
    Athens Orchestra 312
    Avery Fisher Hall 311
    Awards 317, 318
    Brico, Antonia (conductor) 312
    CBS 312
    Coates, Albert (conductor) 309
    Compositions, list 318-321
        "Abram in Egypt" 313-315,
            317
        "Awake! Put on Strength"
            313
        "Collection of Twelve Songs"
            318
        "Four Sonnets For Soprano
            and Quartette" 316
        "Good Morning America" 317,
            318
        "More Things Are Wrought By
            Prayer" 312
        "Requiem" 317
        "Singing Earth" 312
        "Sing to the Lord, All of the
            Earth" 316
        "Suite for Orchestra" 310,
            317
        "Symphony In One Movement"
            317
        "The Crystal Lake" 311

"The Harp Weaver 312, 315
"The Idylls of the King" 309
"The Legend of King Arthur"
    309, 310
"Theme for Carillon" 312
"Transcontinental" 310, 311
Concert tours 307
Discography 321
Dorothy Chandler Pavilion 312,
    317
Griffin, Wayne Z. 307, 308
Herodicus Atticus Coliseum 312
Hollywood Bowl Board 312
Honolulu Orchestra 318
Israel Music Festival 313
Kostelanetz, Andre (conductor)
    311
London Symphony Orchestra 313
Los Angeles International Music
    Festival 313, 315
Los Angeles Philharmonic Or-
    chestra 310, 311, 317
Los Angeles Master Chorale
    309, 310, 312
Mac Millan, Sir Ernest 311
Metropolitan Opera Singers 307
Millay, Edna St. Vincent, con-
    versation 315, 316
Mills College 307
Minnesota Symphony Orchestra
    311
Mormon Tabernacle Choir 312
Musart String Quartet 316
National Endowment for the Arts
    318
New York Philharmonic Orches-
    tra 311
Occidental College Commission
    317
Ojai Festival 312
Oslo Philharmonic Orchestra 310
Parades, Andreas (conductor) 312
Roger Wagner Chorale 312, 313,
    315, 317
Reviews 309, 310, 315-317
Samuel, Gerhard 317
Strickland, William (conductor)
    310
Suder, Louis Commission 313
Teachers: Beruman, Ernesto
    307; Boulanger, Nadia 308;
    Cocke, Kathryn 305; Dicker-
    son, Clarence 307; La Forge,
    Frank 307
Toronto Symphony Orchestra 311
Wagner, Roger (conductor) 312,
    313, 317
Wallenstein, Alfred (conductor)
    310

Woman of the Year 318
Weber, Henriette (New York Eve-
  ning Journal) 197, 198
Webster, Daniel (High Fidelity/
  Musical America) 53-55
Weisser, Albert (Congress Bi-
  Weekly, Journal of Synagogue
  Music) 130-134
Whitlock, E. Clyde (Fort Worth
  Star-Telegram) 282, 292
Williams, Ken (Evening Echo) 33,
  34
Wilson, Susan (Boston Globe) 104,
  105
World Theatre 150

Yaddo 80

Zaimont, Judith Lang 322-339
  American Music Center 330
  Artist's Diploma, Master in
    Piano 325
  BMI Prize 326
  Carnegie Hall 325
  Compositions, list 336-338
    "A Calendar Set" 331-333
    "Chansons Nobles et Senti-
      mentales" 331, 333
    "Concerto For Piano and
      Orchestra" 326
    "Devilry" 334
    "Four Songs for Mezzo-
      Soprano and Piano" 326
    "Greyed Sonnets" 328
    "Nocturne" 331-333
    "Portrait of a City" 326
    "Sacred Service" 326, 329,
      330
    "Songs of Innocence" 327
    "The Chase" 331
    "The Magic World: Ritual
      Music For Three" 334
  Concert for Two Pianos 323-
    325
  Debussy Fellowship of the Al-
    liance Française 326
  Discography 338, 339
  European countries 322
  Great Neck Choral Society 330
  Gregg Smith Singers 327
  Hear America First 328
  Ives, Charles Scholarship 325
  Juilliard School of Music 322
  Juilliard Preparatory School 322
  Kosloff, Doris Lang 323

  Kwartin, Paul (conductor) 329
  Lang, Judith and Doris 323
  MacDowell Fellowship 325
  Miller, Mitch 323, 324
  National Federation of Music
    Clubs 325, 326
  New Music Festival IV 327
  Peabody Conservatory 326
  Performer with sister 323
  Poulenc, Francis--First Ameri-
    can Recordings 323, 324
  Recording by Zaimont 329, 331,
    332
  Reviews 323, 327-333
  Smith, Gregg (conductor) 327
  Steigerwalt, Gary 333
  Teachers: Beeson, Jack 325;
    Lhevinne, Rosina 322; Leun-
    ing, Otto 325, 328; Jolivet,
    Andre 326; Thompson, Leland
    322; Weisgall, Hugo 325
  Tonality Revived 328
  Washington, D. C. 325
  Welk, Lawrence, Show 323
  Woodrow Wilson Fellow 325
Zwilich, Ellen Taaffe 340-360
  Alice Tully Hall 348, 358
  American Composers Orchestra
    359
  American Symphony Orchestra
    341-343, 350
  Annual Composition Competition:
    G. B. Viotti 351
  BBC London 355
  Boston Musica Viva 353-355
  Boulez, Pierre 348, 354
  Budapest, Hungary 358
  Carnegie Recital Hall 349
  Compositions, list 360
    "Chamber Symphony" 353-
      355, 359
    "Clarino Quartet" 341, 356
    "Einsame Nacht' 357, 358
    "Emlékezet" 358
    "Passages" 359
    "Sonata in Three Movements
      for Violin and Piano" 351,
      359
    "String Quartet" 344, 345,
      346, 347
    "Symposium" 348, 349, 350
    "Trompeten" 358
  Dale, Clamma 358
  Discography 360
  Festival of Women's Music 358
  Guggenheim Fellow 359
  Hesse, Herman 357
  Honored Alumnus 359
  International Society For Con-

temporary Music 344, 348
Juilliard School of Music 343
Kazuyoshi, Akiyama 348
Kennedy Center-Rockefeller
International Competition
352
MacDowell Colony 359
Marion Freschl Prize 343
Martha Baird Rockefeller Fund
347, 356
Minnesota Orchestra Trumpet
Section 356
Naumburg Award 358
New York String Quartet 344
Pierre Thibaud Ensemble 356
Pittman, Richard (conductor)
356, 359
Rodgers and Hammerstein
Award Scholarship 343
Reviews 345-347, 349, 350,
352-358
Schuller, Gunther (conductor)
344, 359
Tanglewood 356
Teachers: Carter, Elliot 343;
Galamian, Ivan 341; Murphy,
Bower 340; Sessions, Roger
343; Thomas, Sally 341
Voice of America 348
Zwilich, Joseph 350, 352
Zakariasen, William (Westsider,
The Daily News) 349, 350